No Race, No Country

DEBORAH MUTNICK

No Race, No Country
The Politics and Poetics of Richard Wright

The University of North Carolina Press *Chapel Hill*

© 2025 The University of North Carolina Press
All rights reserved
Set in Arno Pro by Westchester Publishing Services
Manufactured in the United States of America

Library of Congress Cataloging-in-Publication Data
Names: Mutnick, Deborah, author.
Title: No race, no country : the politics and poetics of Richard Wright / Deborah Mutnick.
Description: Chapel Hill : The University of North Carolina Press, [2025] | Includes bibliographical references and index.
Identifiers: LCCN 2024045119 | ISBN 9781469685489 (cloth) | ISBN 9781469685496 (paperback) | ISBN 9781469685502 (epub) | ISBN 9781469687612 (pdf)
Subjects: LCSH: Wright, Richard, 1908–1960—Political and social views. | Wright, Richard, 1908–1960—Criticism and interpretation. | African American communists. | African American radicals. | BISAC: SOCIAL SCIENCE / Ethnic Studies / American / African American & Black Studies | HISTORY / Modern / 20th Century / Cold War
Classification: LCC PS3545.R815 Z777 2025 | DDC 813/.52—dc23/eng/20241031
LC record available at https://lccn.loc.gov/2024045119

Cover art: *New York, New York. Richard Wright, Negro Poet, In His Study*, by Gordon Parks, 1943. Library of Congress Prints and Photographs Division.

This book will be made open access within three years of publication thanks to Path to Open, a program developed in partnership between JSTOR, the American Council of Learned Societies (ACLS), University of Michigan Press, and The University of North Carolina Press to bring about equitable access and impact for the entire scholarly community, including authors, researchers, libraries, and university presses around the world. Learn more at https://about.jstor.org/path-to-open/

For product safety concerns under the European Union's General Product Safety Regulation (EU GPSR), please contact gpsr@mare-nostrum.co.uk or write to The University of North Carolina Press and Mare Nostrum Group B.V., Mauritskade 21D, 1091 GC Amsterdam, The Netherlands.

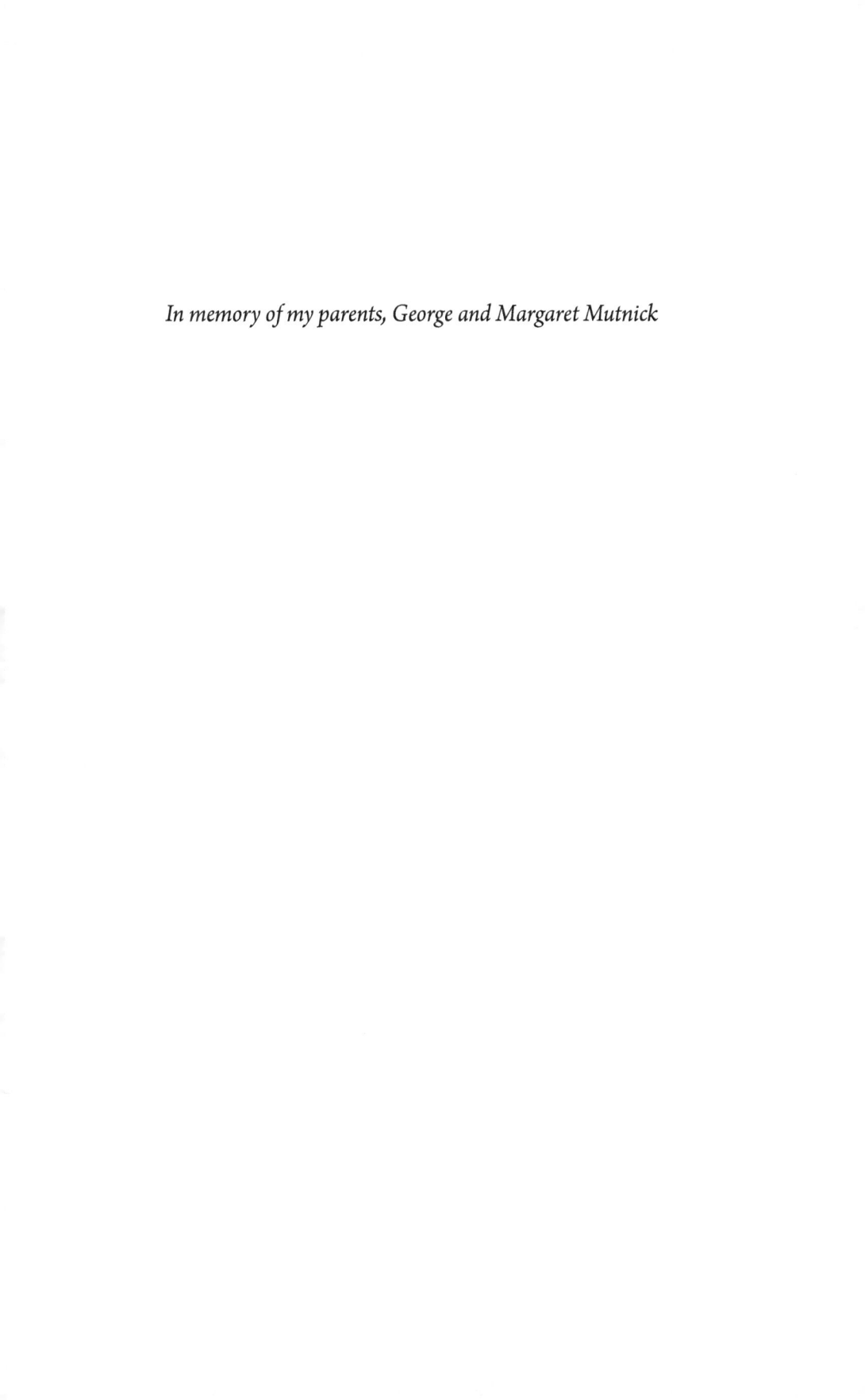

In memory of my parents, George and Margaret Mutnick

Contents

List of Illustrations ix

Introduction 1

CHAPTER ONE
More Bitter Truths of a Native Son 15

CHAPTER TWO
A Consuming Curiosity: Reading, Writing, and Traversing the World 47

CHAPTER THREE
On Becoming a Marxist 79

CHAPTER FOUR
Rediscovering America as a Black Federal Writer 111

CHAPTER FIVE
Seeing Deeper: Writing with Marxist Lenses 143

CHAPTER SIX
Ecologies of Empire: Worlds Being Born, Worlds Dying 176

CHAPTER SEVEN
Yearning for What Never Was 210

Acknowledgments 247

Notes 251

Bibliography 273

Index 285

Illustrations

Richard Wright reading to his daughter Julia Wright 57
Richard Wright with Dorothy and George Padmore 177
Richard Wright with Leopold Senghor and others at the
    First International Congress of Negro Writers and Artists 195
Richard Wright at the Café Tournon 233

No Race, No Country

Introduction

Born in 1908 to a sharecropper and a schoolteacher outside Natchez, Mississippi, Richard Wright came of age in the Jim Crow South during a period of radical political and cultural awakening. He arrived in Chicago in the winter of 1927 as part of the Great Migration of Black southerners to the urban North and was drawn into a milieu of left-wing writers, artists, and intellectuals after the 1929 stock market crash. To these encounters he brought his personal knowledge of growing up Black in the segregated South and his desire to write. By 1940, schooled by the Communist Party USA (CPUSA), the New Deal Federal Writers' Project (FWP), and the University of Chicago's Sociology Department, he became the preeminent African American author of his time. He lived for a decade in New York City, chose exile in Paris, and wrote, traveled, and published books about his visits to the Gold Coast, Spain, and Bandung. Yet, despite significant new Wright scholarship, his reputation has fluctuated since the 1940s, mired in anticommunist ideology and critiques, often echoing James Baldwin's famous attack on the "protest novel." As Irving Howe declared in 1963, Wright told "a truth so bitter" that his contemporaries "paid him the tribute of trying to forget it."[1] My aim in *No Race, No Country: The Politics and Poetics of Richard Wright* is to remember that "truth" and illuminate how his life and work speak to our own era of systemic crisis marked by the specter of fascism, racial terror, unchecked capitalist accumulation, and ecological devastation.

My first exposure to Wright came as a teenager when I read *Native Son* and *Black Boy* at the recommendation of my mother, a high school English teacher and, later in life, a reference librarian. She and my father, a lawyer, were radicalized in the late 1930s at the University of Michigan, where they joined the Young Communist League and went on to remain committed leftists for the rest of their lives. Wright's books were never assigned to me in high school or college. Like many who read books by Wright, it was only those two titles that I associated with him, and it was only in teaching *Black Boy* as part of a first-year writing class that I reread them as an adult. By then, having taught college writing and literature courses for more than a decade, I returned to *Black Boy* with a new appreciation for his coming-of-age and political awakening stories, which resonated with what I imagined my parents had experienced as young Communists in Ann Arbor, a few hundred miles northeast from Chicago. I was deeply influenced by them and had questions about their youth, the Party, the Popular Front, World War II, and the Cold War that I could no longer ask, and that Wright's life story seemed to address. The deeper I dove into his extensive bibliography and the virtual mountain of biographical and critical responses to his writing, the more impressed I was by his literary brilliance and political insight, and the better I understood why he had not been assigned or even discussed in any of the literature courses I took and why so many of my students had never heard of him.

Despite a renaissance in Wright scholarship and a recent wave of praise for Wright after the first-time publication in 2021 of the complete version of *The Man Who Lived Underground*, he remains a controversial figure who deserves a wider readership and whose legacy has yet to be fully understood. How, then, to account for the vagaries of his literary reputation? What was the impact of Cold War ideology and covert operations on his career? What new insights can be gleaned about his education, his involvement in the FWP, his political evolution and commitments, his attitude toward women, his role in anticolonial movements, and what I am calling his proto-ecological consciousness? The ebbs and flows of his reception reflect the tide of twentieth-century migrations, revolutions, economic depression, fascism, imperialist war, Cold War politics, the US civil rights movement, and anticolonial struggles abroad. In 1949, in "Everybody's Protest Novel," his protégé James Baldwin declared that Wright's great antihero, Bigger Thomas, in *Native Son* had continued "that monstrous legend it was written to destroy." Twelve years later, Baldwin would express remorse in "Alas, Poor Richard" for having used the earlier essay as a "springboard" for his career, admitting that it had formed "a kind of . . . a road-block in my road, the sphinx, really, whose riddles I had to answer before I could become myself."[2] But it is the 1949 essay that reverberates in the public imagination.

In 2015, for example, the *New York Times Book Review* published essays by Ayana Mathis and Pankaj Mishra asking if Baldwin was right to denounce *Native Son* as a "protest novel." Their answer was a decisive yes: his attack on Wright was justified and held sway. For Mathis, *Native Son* is "limited by a circumscribed vision that fails to extend much beyond the novel's moment in 1940." Mishra cites an exchange between two other literary rivals, Turgenev and Dostoevsky, rehearsing a well-worn critique of Wright that he needed "a telescope to see America" and suffered from "alienation from his subject." He argues that Baldwin "unmasked treacherous clichés in ostensibly noble programs of protest and emancipation," insisting that "such failure was latent in the causes and manifestoes built on abstract notions about human freedom and fulfillment—those elusive things, which could not be 'legislated' or 'charted.'" Mathis calls Bigger Thomas "a rapist and a murderer motivated only by fear, hate, and a slew of animal impulses. He is the black ape gone berserk that reigned supreme in the white racial imagination." She concludes, "Certainly the racism that made Bigger Thomas still exists, but, thank God, Bigger Thomas himself does not—he never did."[3]

Such cavalier dismissals of Wright's work—*Native Son*, in particular, often is seen as the symbolic sum of his achievements—say less about its literary merit than about the deep chill of Cold War anticommunism and the advent of New Criticism, which proposed to seal off literary texts from their sociohistorical contexts, silencing voices like his and thereby altering the course of radical politics and literature in the 1950s and beyond. Though Mathis and Mishra are obviously not the only gauge of Wright's reception today, their *New York Times* essays reflect the persistence of popular attacks on Wright. In 2012, after praising Zora Neale Hurston, Ta-Nehisi Coates wrote in *The Atlantic*, "I found Wright to be pretty much the opposite—didactic, cranky and insecure. I never believed Bigger to be an actual person. In fact, I thought Wright actually ended up doing the work of the racists he sought to denounce, by committing the common lefty mistake of portraying a people under siege as devoid of humanity."[4] In 2019, after the release of the third, rather diluted film version of *Native Son*, Hannah Giorgis commented that Wright's novel is "grisly and heavy-handed." Monica Castillo's review noted that "the source material has not aged gracefully." Writing in the *New Yorker*, Troy Patterson likewise derided the novel as "a crucial text of the black experience, but asterisks append to its classic status. On the surface of the prose, the paragraphs drag. The book, which has the texture of an existential penny dreadful, could be cut in half just by excising its many repetitions, which do little other than establish a heavy mood."[5]

Along with the political chill of McCarthyism in the 1950s, New Criticism, a cultural counterpart to Cold War politics, elevated form over content through its reification of "close reading," discouraged literary study that drew on historical or other extratextual elements, dominated the teaching of literature until the 1970s, and often continues to exert an invisible force in high school and college classrooms. According to Terry Eagleton, the New Critical emphasis on formalist interpretations of literature and figures of speech "proved deeply attractive to sceptical liberal intellectuals disoriented by the clashing dogmas of the Cold War."[6] The "Cold War poetics" of New Criticism, observes Mark Walhout, "popularized the skills of language analysis necessary for the successful conduct of geopolitics in the Cold War and for the restoration of American spiritual superiority in the nuclear age"—skills employed by what William J. Maxwell calls J. Edgar Hoover's ghostreaders.[7] As the impact of New Criticism faded, postmodern theory replaced it as an even more persuasive, interdisciplinary approach to knowledge, encouraging generations of students to reject Enlightenment values, universal truths, and grand narratives. Marked by relativism and extreme skepticism, postmodernism theorizes reality as socially constructed, fluid, and characterized by multiplicity. Hostile to the social realism associated with Wright and the interwar literary left, the theory presumes "a crudely totalizing—indeed, 'totalitarian'— equation of 'Stalinism' with Leninism with 'orthodox' Marxism with positivism."[8] Like New Criticism, this vilification of Marxism has had a lasting impact on academic and political left-wing orientations and discourses.

In contrast, Wright argues in "Blueprint for Negro Writing" that "a Marxist analysis of society . . . creates a picture which, when placed before the eyes of the writer, should unify his personality, organize his emotions, buttress him with a tense and obdurate will to change the world."[9] He was confounded by Baldwin's and other attacks on *Native Son* as a "protest novel" with more sociological than literary merit. They not only missed the point of a socially relevant literature that intervened in real-world struggles for justice and freedom but also retreated to the view of art for art's sake, rejecting social realist writing that sought "to change the world." Also discounted by critics was the influence of modernist and experimental literary techniques on his writing, which enabled him to fuse politically conscious "protest" with new aesthetic forms and aspects of his own experience to "create a meaningful picture of the world today."[10] Thus, whereas Baldwin has become an avatar of struggles for racial justice in the 2020s, Wright's reputation continues to fluctuate amid prevailing mid-twentieth-century judgments, including Baldwin's youthful denunciation of his "protest novels" and stereotypical Black characters.

In addition to New Criticism's repudiation of politically engaged writing in exchange for "pure art," and Baldwin's assertion that "to speak of a 'new' society" is romantic, meaningless, and "impossible to conceive," many reviews of Wright's work, during his lifetime and for decades to follow, contain conscious and unconscious racist biases toward him and his writing that confirm Hazel Rowley's assertion that he was always a "'signifier' for race."[11] Insofar as class snobbery intertwines with racial codes, it was as much bourgeois disdain for his working-class roots as it was racist ideology that prejudiced critics against both his explosive subject matter and the quality of his prose, lacing verdicts on his style with class-based stereotypes and the racial politics of poetics. James T. Farrell, for example, declared in 1938 that Wright is "addicted to certain mannerisms" in *Uncle Tom's Children* and "gets lost in complicated or swift moving narrative"; Henry Seidel Canby, quoted on the jacket of the first edition of *Native Son* in 1940, damned the book with faint praise as "certainly the finest novel as yet written by an American Negro"; after declaring the novel to be the most powerful fiction to appear since *The Grapes of Wrath*, Clifton Fadiman noted that it "has numerous defects as a work of art, but it is only in retrospect that they emerge"; and in 1992, Louis Menand proclaimed that Wright's "novels tend to be prolix and didactic, and his style is often dogged."[12]

Fadiman also insisted that "Mr. Wright is too explicit. He says many things over and over again. His characterizations of upper-class whites are paper-thin and confess unfamiliarity. . . . He is not a finished writer." Such appraisals fail to appreciate Wright's literary prowess or see that his genius in *Native Son* was to produce a double-voiced narrative in which Bigger Thomas's limited point of view intertwines with the author's critical grasp of class and racial dynamics. Mr. Dalton, for example, is a millionaire who smugly lets it be known that he supports the National Association for the Advancement of Colored People (NAACP) when he hires Bigger to be the family chauffeur. Later, more than a third of the way into the novel, Wright reveals through Bigger's eyes that Dalton is also a slumlord "far away, high up, distant, like a god" who owns the South Side Real Estate Company that collects rent for the Thomas family's one-room, rat-infested kitchenette. He supplements Bigger's point of view by giving details about Dalton's property both in the city's "Black Belt" and in white Chicago, explaining that Bigger could not cross the line dividing them and that it was only "in a sullen way [that] Bigger was conscious of this."[13] Ironically, Fadiman sets out to praise the novel but portrays Wright as uneducated and adrift, only to dismiss these "facts" as irrelevant to his evaluation: "That he received the most rudimentary schooling, that for most of his life he has been an aimless itinerant worker are interesting facts but of no great moment in judging his book." Ultimately, it is Dreiser he lauds, claiming that *An American Tragedy* is the "greater, more monumental, more controlled, more knowledgeable" of the two books.[14]

In 1958, Nick Aaron Ford called Wright's last novel published in his lifetime, *The Long Dream*, "a colossal disappointment."[15] Even Irving Howe, who meant to defend Wright, presumed that *Native Son* "has grave faults that anyone can see. The language is often coarse, flat in rhythm, syntactically overburdened, heavy with journalistic slag." He further declared that the "inescapable truth . . . and terror . . . which Wright alone dared to confront" was "that violence is central to the life of the American Negro, defining and crippling him with a harshness few other Americans need suffer." Describing Bigger's panicked response after killing Mary Dalton as a "hunger for violence," he conflated Wright with his character and excused him from failing to transcend it: "That he did not fully succeed seems obvious; one may doubt that any Negro writer could."[16] Such reviews indicate an enduring pattern of subjective, patronizing, racial and class bias, an obligatory jab at the first best-selling Black American writer.

Another misperception about Wright in relation to his writing is that he was an autodidact. While he was clearly self-taught to an extent, the legendary story of his ascent from an impoverished childhood in the Jim Crow South with only erratic schooling to world-renowned author has mystified other aspects of his education that suggest a more complex, rounded portrait of his intellectual and social development. His two best-known books, *Black Boy* and *Native Son*, can be read as educational narratives in the tradition of the bildungsroman, the one relating the formative stages of his own intellectual development, and the other, Bigger's awakening to "this eternal reaching for something that was not there."[17] A more socially situated account of his educational experience, including his own deep interest in the role of education in liberating human potential, illuminates his journey from the Deep South to the urban North to Paris and beyond. His geographical mobility put him in life-altering historical contexts that included the Great Migration of Black southerners to northern cities, the interwar radical literary and political milieus in Chicago and New York, and the postwar Paris communities that provided refuge for Black expatriates from American racism.

He resided by happenstance but also by the logic of his life and times in three world cities vital to political and literary history, especially with respect to African American literature and art, thrusting him together with some of the most influential writers, artists, and thinkers of the period. As he observed repeatedly, most boldly in his narrative of the Great Migration, *12 Million Black Voices*, it was his own traversal of stages of history from the feudal conditions of the Jim Crow South to the industrializing urban North that anchored his reflections about the nature of struggles for freedom in his writing.[18] Once he freed himself from the chains of the South, his education was thoroughly socialized, defined by his avid participation and leadership in literary and political circles sponsored by the CPUSA, the FWP, the Sociology Department at the University of Chicago, and other supportive milieus.[19] Neither timeless nor universal, most of these "literacy sponsors"[20] were themselves part of a vibrant radical mobilization responsive to a revolutionary zeitgeist and the most severe economic crisis America had hitherto experienced, intensified by threats of fascism and impending war.

Like misperceptions of Wright's education, his involvement in the Communist Party from 1932 to 1944 has been distorted by racial and Cold War ideologies and the conflation of communism with Stalinism, Trotskyism, and other "red" tendencies that biased readings of his work. His life in the Party and its influence on his intellectual and literary growth has been perceived negatively, bolstered by the suppression of histories of left-wing struggle. While he chafed under CPUSA discipline and felt frustrated by sudden shifts in Soviet policy, the Party's formative impact on him was clouded by his final break from it in 1944 and by Cold War representations of American communists—particularly Black communists—as dupes of dogmatic, authoritarian ideology, slavishly dependent on the Soviets absent any indigenous homegrown radicalism. His dialectical approach to place and history, nationalism and internationalism, politics and poetics, central to his literary legacy, strongly reflects the influence of Marxist thought on his writing and is more or less indiscernible in bourgeois readings of his work. At the same time, contrary to standard views of him as only or merely a social realist writer, he complexly and deliberately blended naturalism with modernist, surrealist, and pulp detective styles to fuse a new, radical set of literary, psychoanalytic, and political principles most clearly set forth in "Blueprint for Negro Writing."

THAT WRIGHT'S PLACE in the pantheon of major twentieth-century writers is at once assured and precarious can be explained by a "politics of poetics," as Barbara Foley reminds us, which understands the degree to which "the poetics we adopt in analyzing and evaluating literary works are saturated in ideological assumptions."[21] It means reassessing his Marxist perspective and confronting not only anticommunist, liberal, and racist critiques of his work but also essentialist, nationalistic views of race that periodically resurface from earlier formulations in Garveyite, Nation of Islam, negritude, and single-issue radical movements that silo structures of oppression. Wright's inquiries into three key aspects of the logic of capitalist development are the focus of this book: (1) the dialectic of race and class in relation to chattel slavery, colonialism, Jim Crow racism, and the perpetuation of neocolonial dependency; (2) the triple oppression of Black women, particularly evident in his unpublished novel "Black Hope" and sociological research on 1930s "slave markets" in New York City; and (3) the environmental impact of social inequality and imperial conquest on African Americans and colonized peoples. Wright sought to fuse these political economic investigations into literary art through a historical materialist, antiracist, dialectical method drawn from the "materials and experiences" of his own life.[22]

From today's vantage point, clarified by a succession of US social movements—especially America's quintessential, foundational struggles for Black freedom, Black power, and Black lives—Wright's work speaks prophetically about twenty-first-century realities and challenges. Since his premature death in 1960, the world has undergone a sea change from the one he knew, and yet, despite economic development and civil and human rights victories, the prospects for a more just, egalitarian, survivable future have barely improved, and in many respects have diminished, both for the dispossessed of the world, who have suffered for millennia, and now for humanity en masse, confronted with the climate crisis. We will never know what Wright might have written about the fall of the Soviet Union in 1991, the end of the Cold War, the globalization of capital, the rise of China, the great acceleration of climate change, or the persistence of the problems at the heart of his life's work —racial, class, gender, and neocolonial oppression. But we can imagine that he would have been saddened by the intensification of global inequalities following the economic crisis in the 1970s and the neoliberal capitalist era that followed, of privatization, deregulation, financialization, austerity, outsourcing, and persistent imperialist rivalries that assume new forms in response to multiple systemic crises.

Wright would have also understood and exposed the relationship between capitalism and environmental depredation as the mutually reinforcing exploitation of workers and nature, designed to extract profits from labor and natural resources from the earth. In his own time, he was well aware of the devastating consequences of the Great Mississippi Flood in 1927 and he would have followed reports of the ecological disaster of the Dust Bowl in the 1930s. The same Faustian forces that caused such severe flooding forced Black men to shore up the levees at gunpoint; they also built Chicago into a world city that rendered South Side slums unfit for human habitation and caused severe drought and raging dust storms, unnatural consequences of emerging agricultural methods that stripped the Great Plains of vegetation and destroyed sod in order to grow wheat for profit.[23]

Still, the most brilliant insights of Wright's legacy speak to Black liberation as necessary for the liberation of us all. His response to police and vigilante murders of Black people in his lifetime echoes in the global Black Lives Matter movement, especially the summer of 2020 protests following the police murder of George Floyd, and in the tributes paid to him by his daughter

Julia Wright, his grandson Malcolm Wright, and his great-grandson Maxime Desirat. Recalling her father's focus on the theme of lynching "from the poem 'Between the World and Me' to *Black Boy*, from *Uncle Tom's Children* to *The Long Dream*," Julia Wright recalls his "*sense of dread . . .* when confronted with the photo of Emmett Till in *JET* magazine." Malcolm Wright pays tribute to the grandfather he never met, declaring, "We've been taught by the giants that raised us up, that we must do more than just survive as individuals." Maxime Desirat says of his great-grandfather and his books, "He is one of the first African American authors to have lifted the veil on the living conditions of black people in the United States. His books offer a historical perspective on today's Black Lives Matter movement. His writings contain the literary and historical soil enabling an understanding of the roots of the claims being made so articulately these past few weeks."[24] The release in its entirety in 2021 of *The Man Who Lived Underground*—a surrealistic novel finished in 1942 about a Black man arrested and tortured by police for a crime he did not commit—further illuminates Wright's lifelong preoccupation with policing and racial terror as produced by the same social forces and relations that manufacture the glittering commodities in the nightmarish underground world into which his protagonist Fred Daniels descends.

In his most creatively fertile period in the late 1930s and early 1940s, with his newly wedded second wife Ellen Poplar, Wright visited Chicago to work on *12 Million Black Voices*, drawing heavily on the ethnographic research he had done as a federal writer in the 1930s with Horace Cayton and others, funded by the Works Progress Administration (WPA) and the Julius Rosenwald Foundation. The sociologist Robert Park happened to be in the city at the time, after having left the University of Chicago to teach at Fisk, and he met the Wrights at the Good Shepherd Community Settlement House, where they were staying with Cayton and his wife. The elderly Park insisted on getting up in Wright's "honor," then stared at him and asked, "How in hell did you happen?"[25] *No Race, No Country* is an extended answer to that question.

THE CHAPTERS THAT FOLLOW draw out themes of Wright's education, geographical roots and routes, literary influences and legacy, and contribution to struggles for freedom and equality. His genius as a writer was to fuse experience with a Marxist sociology of race, class, and, less consistently, gender in fast-paced stories blending naturalist, modernist, pulp, and surreal genres. In nonfiction works, including his travel books, he drew on ethnographic and journalistic skills learned as a federal writer in the FWP and as a reporter for *New Masses* and the *Daily Worker*. Informing almost all his writing is history that he understood shaped his world: the rise of chattel slavery, colonialism, capitalism, and their aftermaths, including the depredation of nature and its dire consequences for humanity. A blend of biographical, literary, and historical analysis, the book is divided into seven chapters that reassess his life and work, seeking to recover what has been ignored, erased, distorted, or suppressed at a time when his insights are more relevant than ever to twenty-first-century audiences.

Chapter 1, "More Bitter Truths of a Native Son," examines *Native Son*, Wright's most acclaimed novel, in relation to *The Man Who Lived Underground*. Although Wright's "truth," as Howe called it, can be traced throughout his writing, it was *Native Son* that catapulted him to international fame in 1940 and *The Man Who Lived Underground* that reintroduced him, however evanescently, some eighty years later to a new generation of readers. This chapter situates Wright's shocking portrayal of the consequences of racism in *Native Son* in the context of Bigger Thomas's lumpen class roots and the descent in *The Man Who Lived Underground* of his doppelganger Fred Daniels—a married, steadfast, soon-to-be father—into a surreal underground nightmare after being falsely accused of murder and savagely beaten by police.

Though typically viewed as an autodidact, Wright benefited from an extraordinary extracurricular education in a succession of community, literary, and political circles throughout his life. Chapter 2, "A Consuming Curiosity: Reading, Writing, and Traversing the World," traces his education from his erratic schooling, supplemented by his mother Ella's instruction, to the cultural and political worlds he encountered in Chicago and New York and the last thirteen years of his life as an expatriate living in Paris and extensively traveling.[26] Through delineating the "hidden transcript" of his education in relation to the history of African Americans secretly "writing in the spaces left," as Frederick Douglass put it, this chapter examines the relationship between his intellectual quest and the geography of his life and work, from Natchez, Mississippi, to Chicago to New York to Paris to his world travels.[27]

Wright's relationship to Marxism has been subject to a great deal of debate, with more recent scholarship contesting Cold War critiques of his writing and interpretations of his break from the CPUSA.[28] Chapter 3, "On Becoming a Marxist," traces his political evolution, from his early lessons in Jim Crow to his participation in the John Reed Club (JRC), which he joined in 1933 and where he met "men and women whom I would know for decades to come and who were to form the first sustained relationships in my life," to his break from the Party in 1944, and finally to his role in anticolonial struggles and the founding conference in Bandung of twenty-nine non-Western

African and Asian nations.[29] I also examine his perspective on gender and Black nationalism in relation to Marxist thought and refute the belief that his "roll in the hay with the existentialism of Sartre" replaced his Marxist outlook and derailed him after he moved to Paris.[30]

Chapter 4, "Rediscovering America as a Black Federal Writer," delves into Wright's acceptance into the Illinois branch of the FWP, known as the Illinois Writers' Project (IWP), in 1935 in the midst of that city's Black Renaissance, and his transfer to the New York Project in 1937. I first examine the impact of radical writers associated with the John Reed Clubs and the CPUSA on the FWP and its reciprocal influence on their careers. Second, I take up Wright's unsigned, relatively unstudied writing for the IWP and the New York Project along with his photodocumentary collaboration with Edwin Rosskam on *12 Million Black Voices* and his ethnographic approach to *Native Son*, *Black Boy*, and his travel books. As much as he benefited from the FWP, he contested its romantic vision of unity and cultural pluralism by uncovering a more historically divided, conflicted nation whose future depended, as he put it in *12 Million Black Voices*, on a recognition that "if we black folks perish, America will perish."[31]

Chapter 5, "Seeing Deeper: Writing with Marxist Lenses," turns to critical interpretations of Wright's work that demonstrate his transnational revolutionary thought and appreciation for the "poetic Marx" from his early poetry to his nonfiction travel books written in the 1950s. Linked to specific Marxist concepts, the chapter focuses on his early militant poems, his first novel (posthumously published as *Lawd Today!*), his short story collection *Uncle Tom's Children*, *12 Million Black Voices*, and *The Outsider*. I then go on to reassess his perspective on gender oppression and his treatment of female characters in "Bright and Morning Star" and his unpublished manuscript "Black Hope," in particular, in answer to his feminist critics.

Chapter 6, "Ecologies of Empire: Worlds Being Born, Worlds Dying," rereads Wright from an ecocritical/ecosocialist vantage point in relation to his travel books as well as some of his earlier works, his involvement in anticolonial movements, and his critique of empire. Recent Wright scholarship has begun to take up his ecological consciousness, but it remains outside the frame of most research and criticism of his writing. Considering African American literature from this perspective uncovers its "referential dimension" in response to a "nature" that not only is a subject of human consciousness but necessarily embodies and reflects it.[32] It is in this light that Gregory Rutledge proposes that "it would be profitable to approach [Wright] as a writer attuned to ecological rhythms who connects the Great Migration, the homesteader migration to the Great Plains, and the Dust Bowl."[33]

Chapter 7, "Yearning for What Never Was," focuses on Wright's late writing—*The Long Dream*, the unpublished manuscript "Island of Hallucination," the story "Man of All Work" in *Eight Men*, and his haiku—as illustrating the continuous, evolving, expanding course of his life and work. Rather than causing him to abandon his roots and lose touch with his supposedly natural subject matter, life abroad gave him a wider-angle lens through which to see America in relation to the rest of the world, which was fraught with Cold War espionage and burgeoning anticolonial movements. Rather than trading in Marxism for existentialism, he read and critiqued existential philosophy, rejecting its nihilistic, relativistic tendencies and integrating what was useful to him into a historical materialist worldview and his intuitive sense of the crisis of modernity from growing up Black in America.

Wright continued to break conventions in his writing in the last decade of his life, fusing experience with new modernist techniques and a political outlook that lacked the certainty of earlier work but reflected his need for new forms to express his perceptions of rapidly unfolding global realities. As an African American expatriate on the Left Bank, he was able to some extent to escape American racism and Cold War politics, though eventually he discovered that France was not the safe haven he had once thought and he remained under surveillance until his death in 1960. His life and work speak to twenty-first-century crises of racial terror more than one hundred years after his birth in 1908, profound global inequalities, ecological catastrophe, and histories of radical movements. Commenting on *Native Son* in 1967, Frantz Fanon observed, "In the end, Bigger Thomas acts. To put an end to his tension, he acts, he answers the world's anticipation."[34] Profoundly and enduringly, Richard Wright did, too.

IN THE LAST EIGHTEEN MONTHS of his life, Wright composed thousands of haiku. In 1960, he submitted 817 of them for consideration to William Targ at World Publishing Company. Targ declined the manuscript, titled "This Other World: Projections in the Haiku Manner," which was finally published in 1998 as *Haiku: The Last Poems of an American Icon: Richard Wright*. Suffering from chronic illness, financial problems, personal losses, and anxieties about Cold War espionage, Wright found in haiku a form that he could write from his sickbed and that reunited him spiritually with the natural world of his boyhood, a world Julia Wright remembers he once disliked because it "reminded him of the physical hunger he had experienced as a poor black child in one of the world's most fertile landscapes." His appreciation of nature can be traced throughout his writing, from lyrical passages in *Black Boy* to descriptions of natural beauty and cruelty in *Uncle Tom's Children* to his travel books on the Gold Coast, Spain, and Bandung to his late haiku. As Julia Wright notes, "A form of poetry which links seasons of the soul with nature's cycle of moods enabled him to reach out to the black boy part of himself still stranded in a South that continued to live in his dreams."[35] Taken from Haiku 308, the title of the last chapter of *No Race, No Country* is "Yearning for What Never Was," which seems to me to encapsulate Wright's "unfinished quest" for a world that did not yet exist.[36]

> A sleepless spring night:
> Yearning for what I never had,
> And for what never was.[37]

I imagine the speaker of this poem lying awake at night as winter gives way to the tension and desire of new life. Sleepless, filled with regret, he yearns not for what he lacked but for what he never had, what never existed yet is already possible through his evocation of it—not food or books or education or even love but rather a future that has yet to unfold. It is that Richard Wright—tender, fierce, loving, sensitive, awake, visionary—who inspires this reconsideration of his life and work.

CHAPTER ONE

More Bitter Truths of a Native Son

For the rest of his life, Wright continued telling the "bitter truth" that Howe had praised in *Native Son*, in works that were often disparaged, forgotten, or altogether suppressed. The groundbreaking, unthinkable plot of *Native Son* had upset a cross-section of readers, from the Black bourgeoisie to white conservatives to fellow Communists to protégés like James Baldwin who found it violent, hateful, misogynistic, crude, and one-dimensional. Middle-class Black readers recoiled from what they saw as a racist stereotype in his portrayal of Bigger Thomas's violent murders of his employer's daughter, the white heiress Mary Dalton, and his Black, working-class girlfriend Bessie Mears. CPUSA reviewers objected to his representation of the Black working class, the absence of Black Communist characters, and the intra-Party naming of the character Mary Dalton after Mary Licht, a Communist whose revolutionary name was Mary Dalton—an allusion Wright knew would irk Party leaders like Harry Haywood, who had treated him insensitively as an aspiring, talented young writer. Still other critics decried the novel for vilifying white people despite Wright's explanation in "How 'Bigger' Was Born" that he had deliberately depicted the ravages of racism to avoid the mistake he made in *Uncle Tom's Children*, a book "even bankers' daughters could read and weep over and feel good about."[1]

After the publication of *Native Son*, which had unsettled but also greatly impressed readers, the publisher rejected a sequel to it begun in 1939 and a short novel that seized Wright's imagination in 1941 at a critical juncture of his political and personal life. That novel is *The Man Who Lived Underground* (*TMWLU*). In late 1941, after visiting Wright at 11 Revere Place in Brooklyn, the poet and novelist Arna Bontemps told Langston Hughes that Dick had "knocked out a new novel ... written at white heat."[2] Despite Wright's excitement about the book, Harper and Brothers declined to publish it. More than eighty years later, it was published in 2021 for the first time in its entirety by Library of America, and it sharply resonated for readers in the aftermath of the previous summer's worldwide protest—massive, multiracial, youth-led uprisings—triggered by George Floyd's murder in Minneapolis during a global pandemic and yet another wave of police violence against Black men and women. Why did it take so long for the full novel to see the light of day?

A manuscript reviewer, Kerker Quinn, found the first part of the book "unbearable." The scenes of police torture and murder of an innocent Black man were too raw.[3]

The Production and Reception of *The Man Who Lived Underground*

TMWLU's reception in 2021 marked a reversal of opinion by many critics who had accused Wright of misogyny, violence, dogmatism, crude prose, and one-dimensional portraits of Black—and white—characters. Imani Perry, for example, admits in her review of the novel that she had already begun reassessing her disavowal of Bigger Thomas as "a protagonist stripped of any redeeming qualities, so distorted by the conditions of racism that he became an avatar more than a character, and an unsettling representation of Blackness." She repents: "Perhaps we have too readily judged Wright's bearing of witness to be reductively stark and fatalistic. What he observed is still happening, despite all those generations of unyielding hope."[4] Why did it take so long for Wright's critics to understand that the racial terror he persisted in writing about had hardly begun to be resolved in his lifetime? That the zenith of the civil rights movement in the mid-1960s with the passage of the Civil Rights Act in 1964 and the Voting Rights Act in 1965 had failed to achieve systemic change for poor and working-class African Americans and instead caused a racist backlash that ushered in the New Jim Crow?

The publication of *Underground* in 2021 enabled readers once again to experience "the shock of [Wright's] uncanny recognitions," as Jerry Ward put it in 2008.[5] Appearing truer in some decades than others, Wright's vision has yet to be fully understood, and who he was, what he stood for, what he achieved, and what he left to us is far from settled.[6] Concerned not only with life stories—his own and others'—and not only with social history, he theorized their fusion in order "to make articulate the experiences of men." In "Blueprint for Negro Writing," his first penetrating manifesto, he declared that Black writers must find the materials and experiences in their lives that give meaning to their world and integrate their own personalities to become strong enough to change it. This Marxist dialectic suffused his writing from the mid-1930s to his death in 1960.[7]

As he cultivated creative, intellectual, and political discipline, he was grappling with seismic shifts in his life as young writer, newly arrived in wintry Chicago in December 1927. The trauma of growing up Black in the Jim Crow South reverberates in the last two lines of Part One of the restored edition of

Black Boy published in 1991: "This was the culture from which I sprang. This was the terror from which I fled." Gone was the hope expressed in the first edition in 1945 that jettisoned Part Two's story of the Depression, the John Reed Club, the CPUSA, the FWP, and his everyday life of family, work, friends, and, at times, joblessness. The abridged version required a new, hastily written ending for a manuscript that he had told his editor, Paul Reynolds, was complete and would stand or fall as written.[8] No longer in print, the revised ending expressed a dialectic of space and time, past and the present, unfolding into a future that he was self-consciously formulating: "I was taking a part of the South to transplant in alien soil, to see if it could grow differently, if it could drink of new and cool rains, bend in strange winds, respond to the warmth of other suns, and, perhaps, to bloom."[9]

The opening lines of Part Two, excised from the abridged version that appeared in *The Atlantic* in 1944 as "I Tried to Be a Communist," belie that hope in the shock of his encounter with the gray, cold, modern, fast-growing, segregated midwestern city of Chicago: "My first glimpse of the flat black stretches of Chicago depressed and dismayed me, mocked all my fantasies." The city is "unreal," with "mythical houses . . . built of slabs of black coal wreathed in palls of grey smoke" whose "foundations were sinking slowly into the dank prairie." And the promise of warmth has evaporated in "flashes of steam . . . gleaming translucently in the winter sun." Despite its fast-growing size, the city "was somehow dangerously fragile." The South Side of the city, with its crowded, rat-infested, one-room kitchenettes "seemed makeshift, temporary." He depicts an "abiding sense of insecurity" in the people he met, their "stricken, frightened black faces trying vainly to cope with a civilization that they did not understand." For his part, he recalls, "I felt lonely. I had fled one insecurity and embraced another."[10] It is the fragility and tenuousness of his world and his place in it that resonate in *Underground* and the accompanying, previously unpublished essay "Memories of My Grandmother."

After he joined the John Reed Club in 1933, Wright began to publish poems in *Left Front* and other left-wing journals, including *International Literature*, a Soviet literary journal, which expanded his readership beyond the United States, a benefit enjoyed by young, unknown writers associated with the CPUSA. But it was only with the 1936 publication in the FWP anthology *Caravan* of "Big Boy Leaves Home," the lead story in *Uncle Tom's Children*, that he started to draw critical attention at home. A series of essays and stories followed, including "The Ethics of Living Jim Crow" and "Blueprint for Negro Writing," and he won first prize for "Fire and Cloud," one of 500 submissions in a *Story Magazine* contest for FWP employees. A year later he published the entire story collection with Harper and Brothers to critical acclaim, and the following year, in 1939, he received a $2,500 Guggenheim Fellowship. This string of successes culminated with the publication of his record-breaking novel *Native Son* in 1940. Yet, along with global acclaim came disappointments, including rejections of two novels he worked on during those years, "Cesspool," begun in 1930, repeatedly rejected and only posthumously published by a small press as *Lawd Today!* in 1963, and his second novel "Tarbaby's Dawn," rejected in 1937 and published as a short story, "The Man Who Was Almost a Man," in *Eight Men* in 1961.

There was thus an undercurrent of unease for Wright in a time of feverish excitement. Although early novels like *Lawd Today!* have been condescendingly viewed as his literary apprenticeship and the opening scenes of *The Man Who Lived Underground* were deemed "unbearable" for mid-twentieth-century readers by Quinn, their posthumous publication and subsequent re-evaluations raise questions about such pronouncements. To what extent did bias against modernist techniques in *Lawd Today!* influence publishers? What racist assumptions or inability to confront the savagery of racist attacks might account for repeated rejections of both novels? And what impact did such rejections of his writing have on Wright's career, intensifying anxiety from childhood traumas, economic insecurity, racial discrimination, and the pressures of sectarian, internal political discord? These existential fissures and the epochal leaps in his life simultaneously produced and enacted the archetypal story he told many times of Black southerners migrating North, from agrarian feudal to urban industrial stages of history in one generation. As Abdul R. JanMohamed argues, Wright epitomizes "the subject who is formed from infancy on, by the imminent and ubiquitous threat of death"—someone who bore witness as a child to lynching and other forms of racial violence and lived in extreme states of fear for himself, his family, and his people.[11]

The surreal, nightmarish allegory of the unabridged version of *TMWLU* illuminates the psychological and emotional toll of these life stresses. Writing the novel was exhilarating, freeing. In "Memories of My Grandmother," Wright describes this state of being as "a deeper feeling of imaginative freedom" that allowed him to write "in a way that flowed more naturally from [his] own personal background, reading, experiences, and feelings." He goes on to explain, reiterating the point with his oft-used signifier, "I mean," as if directing the reader to the essence of the matter: "What I mean is this... here, in this book, there is only one... far-reaching, complex, ruling idea-feeling hovering in the background, like the rhythmic beat of the bass in a jazz song." The musical reference evokes his interest in jazz and, as the essay makes clear, the book's "idea-feeling" of his grandmother's religion—both of which influenced the rhythms, cadences, and tenor of his writing. The ruling idea is the inner structure of his grandmother's religious disposition, further enunciated as his attempt to "strip the daily mask [of religion] from the many parallel experiences and show me that at bottom they were all one and the same." But the liberation he felt in writing *TMWLU* was also in some sense momentary relief from the spiraling pressures of government surveillance, public attacks from the left and the right, intra-Party politics, and agonizing rejections amid high praise for his writing. Added to these tensions was the strain of Jim Crow in the urban North, which was even more enervating precisely because it was not the promised land of other, warmer suns.[12]

In addition to repeated rejections of *TMWLU*, drafted in a burst of "sheer inspiration," Wright suffered setbacks on another novel begun after completing *Native Son* in June 1939. He had announced plans for this book, successively titled "Little Sister," "Slave Market," and finally, "Black Hope," in the closing paragraphs of "How 'Bigger' Was Born," having described writing *Native Son* as "an exciting, enthralling, and even a romantic experience." Aided by morning walks from the house of his friends Jane and Herbert Newton to the highest point in Fort Greene Park in Brooklyn, he would sit on a bench close to the Prison Ship Martyrs Monument, scrawling Bigger's story on yellow legal pads, and then return to the Newton home to read what he had written to Jane, an apt, sympathetic critic. At the end of the essay on Bigger, he promised that his next book would address "the status of women in modern American society," echoing the CPUSA's line on the "woman question." The idea for "Black Hope," he notes, "goes back to my childhood just as Bigger went, for . . . I was storing away impressions of many other things that made me think and wonder."[13] His oblique reference to the status of women, among other indications throughout his life and work, suggests that feminist critics may be mistaking his condemnation of misogyny and machismo for their enactment. He wrote two disjunctive drafts of "Black Hope" and continued to work on it for nearly a decade after having put it aside to write *The Man Who Lived Underground* in six feverish months.

This period for Wright was defined by interracial milieus of artists, writers, and leftists that he joined in Chicago amid depressing rejections, triumphs of acceptance, and a crystallizing consciousness, an acuity like "that of an x-ray enabling [him] to see deeper into the lives of men."[14] It suggests not only the thrill he got from writing and the evolution of his thinking about the dialectics of class, race, and gender, but also the depth of his dread in response to threats to his very existence and the precarity of the left-wing communities in

Chicago. Throughout most of the 1930s, he relied on left magazines like the *Anvil* and *Partisan Review* to publish his poems while he coped with rejections of his earliest novels. In Part Two of *Black Boy*, he conveys his anguish over the Party's dissolution of the John Reed Clubs in 1935, a decision that "stunned" him. Recalling a real or imagined confrontation with CPUSA leaders, he writes: "Why? I asked. Because the clubs do not serve the new People's Front policy, I was told. That can be remedied; the clubs can be made healthy and broad.... I asked what was to become of the young writers whom the Communist party had implored to join the clubs and were now ineligible for the new group, and there was no answer. This thing is cold! I exclaimed to myself."[15]

In 1935, he was still one of those young writers; by 1940, he had become a literary sensation, confidently anticipating his next book project: "Some experience will ignite somewhere deep inside me the smoldering embers of new fires and I'll be off again to write yet another novel. It is good to live when one feels that such as that will happen to one. Life becomes sufficient unto life; the rewards of living are found in living." The good life for him was contingent on the next novel, which must be written, read, and published. He did not know whether *Native Son* "is a good book or a bad book" or if what he was presently working on, the early drafts of "Black Hope," was good or bad, and he said, however dubiously, that he didn't really care: "The mere writing of it will be more fun and a deeper satisfaction than any praise or blame from anybody."[16] He worked on "Black Hope" intermittently between mid-1939 and 1947, the year he and his family permanently moved to Paris. It was only then that he abandoned the novel after having produced multiple, spidery, conflicting plot lines that he failed to resolve. Set primarily in Brooklyn, New York, the story in its various permutations involves Black female domestic workers and "slave markets" where Black women queued up in the 1930s to sell their labor as maids or prostitutes; it also turns on racial passing, class antagonisms, the threat of fascism, and union organizing. Whether it was discouraging feedback from his editor Paul Reynolds, who found the 900-page manuscript he read in early 1940 unwieldy, or other personal or political obstacles that derailed the publication of "Black Hope," Wright was again dealing with rejection. Nor was he ever free from the racial terror of the Jim Crow South and the constant threat of death that pervaded his life to form the "underlying teleological structure of his work."[17]

In addition to racial trauma, he felt increasingly conflicted about the CPUSA, which had supported his literary career in some respects but impeded it in others. Already frustrated by the Party's heavy-handed efforts to exert control over his writing, he disagreed with its retreat from militant struggle for racial justice and other concessions to build a united front against fascism, including unconditional support for the Roosevelt administration during the war. Even as he continued to publish and to win literary awards, including a Guggenheim Fellowship, securing him a permanent place in American literature, he suffered setbacks from rejections of four novels, including *TMWLU*, and the disorientation of his break with the Communist Party. He also experienced several life-altering events: he married and divorced modern dance teacher Dhima Rose Meadman, then married Ellen Poplar, who had their first child a year later in 1942. He wrote *12 Million Black Voices* and *Black Boy*, each begun and published in little more than a year, in 1941 and 1945, respectively. In the midst of rapid personal change and global upheaval, he also faced escalating government surveillance and repression. Although both books received generally favorable reviews, *12 Million Black Voices* provoked an FBI inquiry into whether it violated sedition laws, and US senator Theodore Bilbo, a Mississippi Democrat, denounced *Black Boy* as obscene. It was in this highly productive but unsettled period of his life that he drafted *TMWLU*, which can be read as a sequel to *Native Son* if Fred Daniels is seen as subject to the same racist system of capitalism—what Cedric Robinson called "racial capitalism"—as Bigger Thomas.[18]

Although *Underground* has generally been seen as a retreat from Wright's depiction of racial oppression and rebellion in *Native Son* to universal themes and allegorical surrealism, it arguably deepens modernist, philosophical, and political economic tendencies present in the earlier novel.[19] Rather than substituting religion or culture for the historical materialist worldview he cultivated in the CPUSA, he takes them as his subjects in a story that is at once an allegory of African American survival strategies and a cautionary tale of the deadly consequences of abstraction from the racial trauma that shaped his grandmother's religiosity and the secular "Negro" blues. Just as Fred Daniels descends underground to escape the unbearable police torture that ultimately results in his death, those who divorce themselves from reality to survive pain are unable to change the conditions that threaten to destroy them. The opposite of Bigger Thomas, grimly portrayed as a guilty Black man sentenced to death for committing gruesome murders of innocent women, Fred Daniels is an innocent Black man tortured and ultimately murdered by corrupt, white police officers.

Ironically, Daniels's story is by far more prevalent; he is not the mythical stereotype of the Black male rapist but the historical victim of white supremacist, state violence. Harper and Brothers rejected the book after two discouraging reviews that suggested not only that *TMWLU*'s graphic content was "unbearable" but also that it would be harder to sell than *Native Son*. In what follows, I consider the novels and accompanying essays as inverse appearances of Wright's effort to grasp and express the same reality. Rather than signifying a rupture in his literary and political career, they reflect a stylistic and political continuum. They represent his investigation of the inner processes of outer manifestations of an oppressive society that destroys both Bigger Thomas and Fred Daniels—one guilty, the other falsely accused of heinous crimes, one suffering from urban anomie and loss of traditional religious and cultural moorings in a rapidly modernizing world, the other traumatized by police violence that precipitates a break from reality similar to that experienced by Wright's deeply religious grandmother, Margaret Wilson.

The same pattern unfolds in the enigmas of Granny Wilson's religion, Bigger Thomas's declaration that "what I killed for, I *am*!," and Fred Daniels's eventual proclamation of his own guilt for a crime he did not commit. In each case, it is the abstraction of ideology from experience that alleviates the victim's suffering but reinforces its cause: it characterizes Bigger's grandiose dreams and Daniels's underground journey, setting the stage for a psychological break that Wright compares to schizophrenia and describes as the "kinship of insanity and religion." Fascinated by his Seventh-day Adventist grandmother's power, he struggles to understand her religious disposition and her cruel, irrational behavior, which included burning his books and otherwise tormenting him so severely that he ran away at the age of fifteen. Her brittle, religious convictions, he explains, arose from a desperate need to create her own reality as a Black woman excluded from the "daily, meaningful world in which the majority of people lived." She needed to drive out that world when it intruded "with all of the savage vehemence of one who felt that life itself was endangered."[20] This same need impels Daniels to flee underground to liberate himself from the shackles of a system that threatens to destroy him.

White-Black Conflicts and the Deepening Gloam of Fred Daniels's Life

In the opening pages of *TMWLU*, Wright establishes that Daniels works for Mr. and Mrs. Wooten and belongs to the White Rock Baptist Church. He wears a ragged cap and works six days straight in sweltering heat to earn enough money to pay for rent and food for the week. Pausing in "the deepening gloom" of twilight to count his earnings in crisp green bills, he imagines going to church on Sunday and returning to work on Monday, renewed by a day's respite. A sea breeze dries his shirt, wet with the sweat. Puncturing this deftly drawn scene of dusk falling, natural light replaced by blazing streetlamps, is the appearance of "the white face of a policeman peering over the steering wheel of a car," which sets the rest of the plot in motion in the same tripartite structure of *Native Son* and *The Long Dream*. Part One describes Daniels's violent interrogation by Officers Lawson, Johnson, and Murphy, who hoist him upside down on a chain strapped to a steel hook, beat him with a blackjack, kick him, sock him between the eyes, and leave him sprawled unconscious on the floor. Throughout this ordeal, he insists he is innocent and that the Wootens and his church pastor, Reverend Davis, can vouch for him. When he wakes, bloody, groggy, practically wordless, weeping, he is forced to sign a confession.[21]

The next morning, the police take him to the scene of the crime, grilling him despite his pleas of innocence, and then drive to his apartment after one of them recalls they promised to let him see his wife if he signed the confession and another coolly remarks that nobody can say they mistreated him if they let him see his "old lady." Murphy takes him upstairs to find Rachel, heavily pregnant, hysterically crying, struggling to comprehend what happened. After a brief, tender scene between the couple, Murphy rises to leave just as Rachel goes into labor, screaming in distress. The police drive the couple to the hospital, where Daniels, left unguarded when Murphy goes to the men's room, escapes by jumping out a window. He lands on his back in a dark courtyard, hitting his head and briefly losing consciousness. Vision impaired when he wakens, dazed, a constellation of color and light gradually vanishes so he "*could see clearly now.*"[22] After briefly taking refuge in a dark apartment vestibule, he runs across a rain-flooded street to a half-opened manhole through which he descends to an alternate reality. That he can "see clearly" after escaping his captors signals a rift in his life after his arrest that echoes the first lines of the novel in which he enters twilight's "deepening gloam." It is this new clarity of vision that Wright turns on its head in Part Two as the narrative unfolds underground and Daniels sets out on a nightmarish, hallucinatory journey from daylight and the aboveground world's whiteness to the pitch-black tunnel that surreally mirrors pieces of his life in Part One.

The parallels between his life aboveground and underground, however, are lost in the abridged versions of the novel published between 1942 and 1961, which omit mention of all the events leading up to his descent through the manhole. Two short excerpts first appeared in the journal *Accent* in 1942, edited by Kerker Quinn, a faculty member at the University of Illinois who also served along with Wright's agent, Paul Reynolds, as a reviewer of the manuscript that Harper and Brothers declined to publish. Two years later, Wright shortened the novel by more than half, cutting the aboveground scenes of police violence, for Edwin Seaver's *Cross-Section: An Anthology of New American Writing*. It was then reprinted in a 1945 anthology of short stories edited by Bennett Cerf, and finally appeared in Wright's short story collection *Eight Men*, which he was completing at the time of his death in 1960 and which was published posthumously in 1961. It was the depiction of police violence in Part One of the 2021 publication of the entire novel, not surprisingly, that most powerfully struck reviewers fresh from an epidemic of extrajudicial murders of Black people in 2020, culminating in the savage asphyxiation of George Floyd by Minneapolis police officer Derek Chauvin.

The story in *Eight Men* begins with Daniels crouching in the corner of the vestibule on a rainy night, sirens blaring, telling himself that he has to hide: "They're looking for me all over." There is no liminal space, no shudder of recognition when the white faces in the squad car appear. Instead, we see Daniels as he discovers the open manhole and lowers himself into the "watery darkness" below. Relying on ambience and innuendo to establish the narrative rather than the "unbearable" details in Part One, Wright omits any reference to Daniels's job, his religiosity, his interrogation and torture by the police, his wife's pregnancy, or his desperate, childlike terror. This excision of the plot isolated key elements of the narrative, abstracting them from the grueling scenes of police brutality in Part One: all that can be discerned from the symbol-heavy, streamlined short story is that Daniels needs to hide on a rainy night filled with the sound of sirens. Readers of the abridged version are thus left to imagine what triggers his disappearance into the manhole, severed from any instigating events or meaningful symbols except the trope of the sirens and his fear, a stylistic default that many critics applauded for honing in on the existential theme and resulting in "an appreciable lack of the immediate, the ephemeral, and the well-worn white-black conflicts."[23]

Until the 2021 publication of the novel, it would have been impossible to assess such claims without reading the full manuscript in Wright's papers. No connection could be made between the expurgated aboveground trauma and Daniels's revelatory tour of the city's sewer system, where he discovers a church, a corpse, a funeral home, a movie theater, a meat market, a radio shop, an insurance company, a safe with green bills, a typewriter, and other strange phenomena, including floating dead babies and a nude woman, all of which appear as fragments of his aboveground life. Along with Wright's shocking, all-too-familiar story of police violence, which contributed to Harper and Brothers' refusal to publish the novel, Part One is a study of the metaphor of whiteness, aboveground light, and the darkness below. As Toni Morrison brilliantly concluded many years later in her study of American literature, "Images of blackness can be evil and protective, rebellious and forgiving, fearful and desirable—of the self-contradictory features of the self. Whiteness, alone, is mute, meaningless, unfathomable, pointless, frozen, veiled, curtained, dreaded, senseless, implacable."[24]

In *TMWLU*, the grammatical subject of the opening sentence, "The big white door," is completed by the words, "closed after him," marking a metaphorical point of no return for a Black man, falsely accused of murder and tortured by police, who escapes underground to an alternate, arguably Afrofuturist universe, only to return to his inevitable death. After the first few paragraphs—two of which are one-line dialogues of Daniels talking to himself—he sees "the white face of a policeman" and "two more white faces" in the backseat of the police car and as he panics he reassures himself that all he needs to do is let them know that he belongs to the White Rock Baptist Church. At the precinct he is asked to confess to the crime he did not commit by signing a "white sheet of paper covered with blurred lines of black," a "white blur" with "print running in hazy black waves across the wavering white," a "white splotch of paper," and a "smear of white" that "fascinated him with a deep and terrible finality."[25] After signing the confession at four in the morning, stupefied, "he held the pen over the island of white, poised, as though willing and ready to write on and on." When the officers jerked the chair from under him because he was unable to sit upright, he fell on the floor, where he "drifted into a faraway land of blinding sunshine, filled with huge white-hot rocks." White paper tied to the glowing rocks, a black fountain pen in his right hand, "he went and signed his name to each page of white paper, signed his name carefully and slowly, whispering 'Yes, sir . . . Yes, sir. . . .'" The next day when the officers take him back to the crime scene, he sees "Mrs. Wooten's big white house." At the hospital there are "white-coated attendants" and "two black women dressed in white." The nurse telling him that Rachel is in labor is a "white blur"; he notices the "stony whiteness of the tile," and when he escapes, leaping ten feet to the courtyard and briefly knocking himself out, "a sheet of white flicked past his eyes."[26]

In his account of *TMWLU*, Michel Fabre asserts that "the hero is an outsider whose color is no longer important," quoting a letter from Wright to Paul Reynolds on December 13, 1941, in which he remarks, "It is the first time I've really tried to step beyond the straight black-white stuff."[27] Reviewing the complete novel in 2021, Douglas Field denounces the opening passages as "heavy-handed," lacking in subtlety and nuance.[28] Although such depreciations of Wright's literary merits are less prevalent today, they persist, often missing clues that contradict his remark to Reynolds that the novel goes beyond race. Given this seemingly forthright statement of intention, Fabre's assertion that color was no longer important to the writer is understandable, but it is not borne out by *Underground*'s themes. Nor does it reflect the complexity of Wright's political, personal, and artistic evolution, a point that Field's dismissal of the metaphor of whiteness entirely misses, including the paradox of moving beyond race for a Black Communist convinced of the historic role of class struggle in a nation rife with racial conflict. Even if Wright was stepping beyond the "straight black-white stuff," it did not mean he was leaving behind the "Negro problem" or the "Negro question" about which he briefly comments in "Memories of My Grandmother." Situating racial oppression in the essay on his grandmother toward the end of a long list of the many themes of the novel, he describes it as "suggested in a rather muted way," observing almost casually, "After all, Fred Daniels is a Negro, and Negroes in America are accused and branded and treated as though they are guilty of something." Belying this emotional coolness, he then dryly states the plain truth that such treatment has "made a lot of Negroes write a lot of impassioned books saying: 'Look, here, I ain't done nothing. Give me a break, for Christ's sake.'" Ironically, he concludes, "So much for that theme."[29]

His comments about the "problem of the Negro" occur in the last third of the essay, after he moves from a general discussion of religion in relation to his grandmother and "Negro blues songs" to explanations of those experiences, to concrete descriptions of "the actual process of the writing" of *TMWLU*. He perceives his grandmother's fetishized religious world and its secular counterpart in blues songs as forms of "abstract living." By "abstraction" he says he means "simply any way of life that does not derive its meaning from the context of experience." This interanimation of experience, theory, and art, enabled by the dialectical materialist method he learned as a young Communist, suffuses his work from the mid-1930s to the end of his life. That worldview shaped what he meant by getting beyond the "straight black-white stuff" and how he treated racial identity in *TMWLU* and other works. His fusion of theory and experience reflects both his understanding of the historical production of race and racism and his profound sympathy with the suffering and aspirations of the disinherited and the wretched of the earth, especially people of color—those most oppressed, fighting to claim their full humanity.[30]

Reeling from the police murders of Black Americans in 2020, most of the reviewers of *TMWLU* focused on its previously unpublished episodes of police torture and murder of an innocent Black man. Wright knew firsthand the terror of perennial racial violence in the United States and the trauma it caused. That he cared deeply about the victims of racial violence and injustice can be seen not only in his writing but also in his involvement in political cases like that of the Scottsboro Boys and criminal cases in which Black men were convicted of rape and murder, including those of Robert Nixon, the prototype for Bigger Thomas, and Clinton Brewer, imprisoned for nineteen years at the New Jersey State Prison at Trenton for stabbing his teenage wife to death.[31] For contemporary audiences horrified by the murders in 2020 of George Floyd, Breonna Taylor, Ahmaud Arbery, and countless others, *TMWLU* is like a message in a bottle washing ashore to remind us that Richard Wright was one of America's most prescient twentieth-century writers.[32]

But in the late 1950s, critics scoffed at his blunt portrayal of racial violence in Mississippi in *The Long Dream*, published in 1958. They accused him of losing touch with the changing realities of America during what Bayard Rustin called the "classical phase" of the civil rights movement from *Brown v. Board of Education* in 1954 to the passage of the Voting Rights Act in 1965. As Nick Aaron Ford acerbically put it: "Probably the most disconcerting fact about the book . . . is that Wright is fighting a battle that has already been conceded. Although there are still instances of denial to the Negro of the most elemental rights of freedom . . . the targets now are equality of job opportunity, the right to vote in the deep South, integrated housing, and integrated schools."[33] The previous year, an angry white mob protected by local police had blocked nine Black high school students from entering Little Rock Central High School. Five years later, in 1963, four little Black girls died in the Sixteenth Street Baptist Church bombing in Birmingham, Alabama, and Medgar Evers was assassinated in Wright's home ground of Jackson, Mississippi; the next year, civil rights workers James Chaney, Andrew Goodman, and Michael Schwerner were killed, followed by the murders of Malcolm X, Martin Luther King Jr., and legions of lesser-known victims of racial terror. In 1967, racial uprisings in over 160 cities in the United States led the Kerner Commission, appointed by President Lyndon Baines Johnson, to famously conclude, "Our nation is moving toward two societies, one black, one white—separate and unequal." Despite the clear evidence that racism continued to divide America, the color-blind perspective of Wright's critics prevailed, and the election of the United States' first Black president, Barack Obama, in 2008 was widely hailed as ushering in a postracial era. Two years later, Michelle Alexander published *The New Jim Crow: Mass Incarceration in the Age of Colorblindness*.

Alexander tells a story about seeing a flyer in Washington, DC, with the slogan "The Drug War Is the New Jim Crow." At the time, she thought to herself, "Yeah, the criminal justice system is racist in many ways, but it really doesn't help to make such an absurd comparison. People will just think you're crazy."[34]

Convinced otherwise, her influential book on the New Jim Crow threads the needle of systemic racism from the loophole in the Thirteenth Amendment allowing penal slavery to Jim Crow segregation to the war on drugs fought through heavily militarized police and mass incarceration of Black Americans in the late twentieth century. By the end of Obama's first term in office, after the murder of Trayvon Martin, and certainly by 2016 and the election of Donald Trump, the scourge of racial hatred was out in the open again, with blatantly racist attacks on voting rights, critical race theory, Black history, and "wokeness." By 2021, the postracial moment having totally collapsed, the time was ripe to publish *TMWLU*, including scenes of police violence that clarify the connection between Fred Daniels's false arrest and torture and the surreal nightmare that follows; but the nearly universal praise for the novel has yet to recover the full range and power of Wright's prophetic voice.

Political and Literary Yearnings: A Tense and Obdurate Will to Change the World

Several reviewers comment on Wright's references in "Memories of My Grandmother" to his growing dissatisfaction with the CPUSA.[35] His frustration reached a breaking point over the Party's U-turn on US participation in World War II after Hitler invaded the Soviet Union on June 22, 1941. A month later, he began the new novel. In the accompanying essay, he observes that to be "accused without cause" was perhaps the most important of the novel's themes. He had been unjustly accused twice in his life, he wrote, once by an unnamed "minority political party"—an "agonizing, devastating, blasting, and brutal" experience—and once as a child, for allegedly stealing biscuits. Denounced as an "intellectual," a "smuggler of reaction," a "petty bourgeois degenerate," and a "Trotskyite," he recalls having been "pitched headlong through the air" to the curb by comrades at a May Day parade. Despite his perpetual hunger as a child, when he was accused of stealing, he left his uncle's dinner table "stoically and tr[ied] to forget about it."[36] Implicitly, however, what it meant to be accused without cause was to have been born Black in the early twentieth-century Jim Crow South. Drafting *TMWLU* enabled him to express the bewildering pain of these accusations. He was ultimately defending himself not against the charge of stealing biscuits or disloyalty to the Party per se, but against the experience of "being pushed out from that warm circle of trust that exists in all families if they are families at all"—a bittersweet reflection on his relationship with his family, the Party, and the world into which he was born.[37]

Most recent Wright scholars agree that he remained a Marxist after publicly breaking with the CPUSA in 1944. What sort of Marxist and how that worldview played out in his life and work are subject to debate, especially given his renunciation of Communism as a "spectacle of horror" in "I Tried to Be a Communist." Despite bitter conflicts with the CPUSA prior to 1941—the year the Soviets entered the war and the Party reversed its antiwar position—he remained a Communist until 1942, quietly resigning while continuing to participate for at least two more years in Party functions. Whatever his political commitments were at the time, the abridged versions of *TMWLU* are typically seen as a symbolic departure from politics and race, dealing with more universal themes of fear and guilt. When he published *The Outsider* in 1953, his first, long-awaited novel after *Native Son*, one reviewer concluded in *Jet* magazine that he had come to believe that "the reds are now the villains."[38] However, read in light of Wright's coded use of oblique, double-voiced narratives, neither novel is apolitical or clearly anticommunist but rather indicative of his need to insulate himself against Cold War attacks and editors and publishers who controlled and censored his writing in response to market demands and "the racial and economic politics of their days." That is, insofar as he relied on a 1950s literary establishment under pressure from the CIA and other government agencies to silence radical intellectuals by not publishing them, he paid financially and politically for his refusal to shut up about American racism and anticolonial struggles for self-determination.[39]

What explains his migration from Natchez to Memphis to Chicago to New York City to Paris and beyond? To begin: the trauma of growing up in the Jim Crow South; his disposition to read and write, soak up knowledge, and fight to be free of the racial and class constraints of his childhood; his transformational political education as a member of the John Reed Club and the CPUSA; his intellectual discipline; his long, difficult break with the Party over political disagreements and personal hurt; his unquenchable curiosity; his will to transmute the surface forms of experience into expressions of their essential relations; his dedication to anticolonial and antiracist struggles; and the consequent government surveillance and repression that brought him to financial ruin and possibly premature death, nearly persuading him to abandon his career as a writer.[40] These cumulative, epoch-leaping experiences shaped his literary legacy even as the unpredictable paths he took confounded readers. Criticisms of style and erudition were often veiled attacks on substance: his prose was deemed turgid, repetitive, and heavy-handed; and after he left the United States, his writing suffered from living abroad and his supposedly "ill-digested" foray into existentialist philosophy.[41] As Troy Patterson put it as recently as 2019, commenting on *Native Son*, "the book... has the texture of an existential penny dreadful."[42]

The 2021 publication of *TMWLU* challenged some of these judgments, but the flurry of publicity over the book did little to resolve the riddles of his life and work. Along with market-driven demands and racial and class politics, he was dealing with critics who viewed his aesthetic experiments as deviations from naturalist writing rather than a deliberate use of diverse literary forms that advanced his aims as a writer. This embrace of modernism was not a new phenomenon for him; his experimentation in *TMWLU* with modernist themes and techniques had emerged more than a decade earlier in 1930 in his first novel, *Lawd Today!*, originally titled "Cesspool." As James Smethurst puts it, Wright can be seen as "writing after modernism"—that is, under its influence, an inheritor of the "modern protagonist... who has fallen out of society, has no roots, and is a sort of luftmensch."[43] A Black southern migrant thrust into the tumult of the industrializing urban North, he experienced its dynamic, modern possibilities and deprivations firsthand as he began to read modernist literature even as he struggled to qualify for a permanent position in the Chicago Post Office by gaining enough weight to compensate for years of intense hunger, only to be laid off after the stock market crash and then reassigned in the summer of 1930.

It was upon his return to the mail room that he began drafting "Cesspool" in an interracial milieu of postal workers who were also students and aspiring writers, including Abraham Aaron, whose spirited, militant talk on the job he recalls in *Black Boy*: the 2 million unemployed "don't count"—"They're always out of work"; "Read Karl Marx and get the answer, boys"; "There'll be a revolution if this keeps up"; "Hell, naw. Americans are too dumb to make a revolution."[44] Modernist themes of alienation, isolation, escape from an unbearable history, rootlessness, the weight of the past, religious rituals, and oppressive family ties—as well as literary techniques of stream of consciousness, use of newspaper items and radio announcements, and limited third-person point of view—can be traced to this first novel, "Cesspool," in which he chronicles a Joycean day in the life of disgruntled postal worker Jake Jackson. Some critics applauded the novel when it was published posthumously in 1963 as *Lawd Today!*, while Nick Aaron Ford, among others, dismissed it as "an apprentice novel," and "dull, unimaginative... with a multitude of hackneyed experiences."[45] That Wright was reading modernist literature by Central and Eastern European writers like Franz Kafka and Nikolai Gogol and European and American writers like James Joyce and Gertrude Stein can be seen in his library collection, his diary entries about his reading, and his reflections on their influence on him, especially Stein's.[46]

In "Memories of My Grandmother," it is Stein's story "Melanctha" that he says linked his grandmother's life to his own by "rousing sleeping memories and bridging gulfs between peaks of forgetfulness." In reading the story of this "Negro girl," as he describes her, written by a bohemian, dope-smoking, white expatriate in Paris, he recalls that he "began to hear the English language for the first time ... as Negroes spoke it: simple, melodious, tolling, rolling, rough infectious, subjective, laughing, cutting," familiar words suddenly made strange to him, defamiliarized, that signified "the winding psychological patterns that lay back of them!" Stein, too, was trying "to coordinate the composition of the language with the process of consciousness, which ... was to her a close reflex of the total living personality." This fusing of language and consciousness to render the "total living personality" reflects Wright's dialectical theory of composition in "Blueprint for Negro Writing" in which fusing and articulating "the experiences of men [sic]" depends on the writer's "potential cunning to steal into the inmost recesses of the human heart" and "create the myths and symbols that inspire a faith in life."[47]

His decision to embark on *TMWLU* and set aside the projected sequel to *Native Son* against his editors' wishes occurred at a complex political and personal conjuncture for him. As conflict broke out across Europe in 1939, before the Germans invaded Russia, the Comintern adamantly opposed US involvement in a war that the world Communist movement believed was not in the interests of the proletariat. For Wright, an antiwar position was fundamental to defending the rights of Black Americans, who continued to be severely oppressed by Jim Crow laws in the South and de facto segregation in the North. Even more odious to Wright and other Black activists, the US military remained segregated. He was thus shocked when the CPUSA reversed its antiwar position and subordinated other programs to the war effort after Hitler invaded the Soviet Union on June 22, 1941. Just two weeks earlier, at the Fourth American Congress of Writers meeting, Wright had given a powerful, anti-imperialist speech, published in *New Masses* as "Not My People's War," against US participation in the expanding European war. In May, he had been one of forty signatories to an appeal by the League of American Writers (LAW) opposing US intervention. The CPUSA's sudden about-face in June further shook his confidence in the Party, even though he compliantly softened criticism of the Roosevelt administration and signed a petition, "Communication to All American Writers," drafted by then LAW president Dashiell

Hammett, in support of US entry into the war after the Japanese bombed Pearl Harbor on December 7, 1941.

Undiminished by the widening gulf between him and the Party, Wright's critique of imperialism remained a cornerstone of his worldview and his commitment to colonial and postcolonial struggles. "There is ample evidence at hand," he declared, "that the current war is nakedly and inescapably an imperialist war, directed against the Negro people and working people and colonial people everywhere in this world."[48] Despite the CPUSA's failure to address issues of racial discrimination and violence during the war, he stuck with the Party until 1942. Clearly, he was discouraged by its retreat from anti-imperialist demands for peace and international worker solidarity, which literally turned overnight into populist, patriotic, albeit antifascist calls for war. But whatever its shortcomings, the Party had been a lodestar for him and many others in navigating a complex, modern world in crisis. As he was drafting *TMWLU*, he was thus anticipating the loss not only of an organized, militant, interracial organization but also of close comrades, a vibrant left-wing cultural and activist milieu, and a political home that had supported his literary career and embraced him as a fellow human being for more than a decade.

Certain antinomies are bound to circulate about an iconic figure like Wright: he rejected Communism in 1942 and embraced existentialism; he pursued an analysis of racism and colonialism that minimized class; he was a social realist whose experiments in existentialist, modernist forms failed; his writing declined in exile because he lost touch with his roots. The critical response to *TMWLU* in 2021 tended to emphasize political themes of police brutality or existential ones of betrayal and universal guilt. As a prominent Black American Communist writer trying to make sense of unprecedented events, it could not have been easy for Wright to come to terms with his own conscience, his political commitments, and his needs and desires. He had benefited from the Party's interracial camaraderie and support for his literary career and political education despite higher-ups' insensitivity to his needs as a writer. He was confronting a maelstrom of global conflict, the spread of fascism, and the Party's patriotic call for unity across ideological lines. He beheld the contradictions of a second world war in the wake of the first major socialist revolution that to him and tens of millions of people worldwide represented profound hope for a more egalitarian, classless future. LAW secretary Frank Folsom describes a phone call he received minutes after news broke of the German invasion. "What do we do now?" the caller asked. Folsom remembers: "It was Richard Wright calling. Few people were thrown more off balance than he by the abrupt and violent change on the world scene.... I don't recall how I responded to Dick's disturbed inquiry. I was taken as much by surprise as he was."[49]

It was this "violent change on the world scene" that set the stage a month later, in July, for Wright to begin writing *TMWLU*. Inspired by multiple, contradictory forces in his life, including his imminent official but still quiet break from the CPUSA, drafting the novel was for him fraught, liberating, and necessary to preserve his sense of integrity. As he wrote Fred Daniels's story, he faced a potent mix of psychological, ideological, and material conflicts: his feelings of betrayal by the CPUSA—which had fought for Black people's rights and freedoms and given him conceptual tools to theorize racial oppression—for unjustly accusing him of counterrevolutionary tendencies and for subordinating antiracist campaigns to the war effort; his determination to tell the story, omitted from excerpted versions of the novel, of racial terror that had shaped his own existence and destroyed countless other Black people, even as he aimed to "get beyond the straight black-white stuff"; his fascination with his grandmother's religious convictions, which he flatly rejected but which haunted him; the deep hurt he felt as a Party member when his comrades turned against him; his ambitions as a writer to concretize experience in words, fused like jazz or the blues, "freely juxtaposing totally unrelated images and symbols and then tying them into some overall concept, mood, feeling." The goal, he had declared in "Blueprint," was to create "a picture which, when placed before the eyes of the writer, should unify his personality, organize his emotions, buttress him with a tense and obdurate will to change the world."[50]

In his review of *TMWLU*, Colin Asher describes the novel as "a meditation on isolation, survival, and the ability of faith to make sense of the world's chaos and predations." He further remarks, "I like to think that [Wright] was drawn to the riddle of his grandmother's religiosity as his faith in the Communist Party was faltering."[51] Joseph Ramsey argues that Wright's description in "Memories of My Grandmother" of being falsely accused as a "member of a minority political party" exemplifies "cancel culture," a phrase that took hold in the early 2020s to describe a form of public shaming.[52] These assessments of the novel are not wrong: Wright struggled to make sense of the "world's chaos and predations"; his interest in his grandmother's religiosity coincided with his escalating conflicts with the Party; and his comrades' false accusations resemble contemporary public shaming and ostracism. But the complexity of Wright's position and the fullness of his vision are rife with contradictions. He would soon break from the CPUSA but remain a Marxist whose subsequent views on the Party are ambiguous; he had always, even before his radicalization, been primed to go beyond "the straight black-white stuff" but never ceased to experience, document, and protest racism; and even as he turned to surrealist, modernist imagery and techniques, defying critics who pegged him as mainly this or that, a naturalist, a Black writer, or a communist, he set out to tell the all-too-real story of an innocent Black man, falsely accused of a crime he did not commit, who was killed to cover up police brutality and misconduct. For that, he paid the price of rejection of the full manuscript.

The Typewriter as Oracle: Beyond the Rim of His Life

As Wright makes clear in "How 'Bigger' Was Born," Bigger's monstrousness was meant to awaken readers to the deracinating effects of centuries of racial oppression, aggravated by the migration of millions of Black southerners who flooded into the vortex of an industrializing, modernizing, alienating, northern, urban society, replete with de facto racist policies and practices they had hoped to escape. Further destabilizing their lives was the tumult of a global depression with skyrocketing unemployment rates and long breadlines that hit Black Americans particularly hard. Fred Daniels is the flip side of the world's Biggers, Black and white, American, German, and Russian, estranged from religion and folk traditions that had sustained previous generations and deeply resentful of mainstream culture that surrounded yet disenfranchised them. Until his savage arrest, Daniels was an ordinary, young, Black, churchgoing man with a pregnant wife, content with his life and glad for his paycheck. Afterward, accused of a crime he did not commit and traumatized by police brutality, he flees underground to discover a parallel universe that mocks the aboveground realities of glittering wealth and inexplicable suffering, side by side, in the same space and time, subjected to the same forces of exploitation, commodification, and false hopes and dreams that destroy Bigger. Parallels between the two books abound.

Native Son was inspired by the 1924 murder cases of Richard Loeb and Nathan Leopold, two young Jewish men sentenced to life imprisonment for murdering a fourteen-year-old boy, and the 1938 case of Robert Nixon, a young Black man described as "slow-witted" who was arrested, convicted, and sentenced to death for the rape and murder of a white fireman's wife and four additional murders to which he confessed during a protracted, brutal interrogation. Wright modeled *The Man Who Lived Underground* on a story in *True Detective* about a thirty-three-year-old white, unemployed, former sewer worker named Herbert Wright who tunneled through Los Angeles at the height of the Depression and stole $11,000 from a safe, along with typewriters, linen, food, and other items.

In the opening pages of *Native Son*, Bigger kills a large rat in his mother's apartment that terrifies his sister Vera; at the beginning of Fred Daniels's sewer odyssey, he kills a "huge rat, wet and coated with slime, blinking beady eyes and showing tiny fangs."[53]

When the Chicago police discover Mary Dalton's burnt remains in the furnace, Bigger runs upstairs to the chauffeur's bedroom inherited from his predecessor, leaps headlong from the window into the "icy air," and lands dazed in a pile of snow below (220–21); when Daniels eludes the police at the hospital where his wife Rachel is giving birth, he jumps from a window and lands, briefly losing consciousness, on the pavement. Later, he finds himself in a furnace room, where he unrepentantly steals sandwiches and tobacco from an old man with "gaunt cheekbones" and a "white face lined with coal dust," shoveling coal in the dark because he had done it for so long, he had no need for light (76).

Bigger flees from a massive police manhunt across tenement rooftops in the South Side of Chicago; Daniels escapes from police down a manhole to the dark, muddy waters of a cavernous underground sewer in an unnamed city that is probably New York. Like Bigger, a fugitive from the law who must hide in abandoned buildings, Daniels is out of sight, privy to scenes of life in the buildings he accesses from the sewer that mirror and mock the aboveground reality from which he fled.

Hiding from police on the rooftop, seeing without being seen, Bigger Thomas observes a family through a window with no shades: "three naked black children looking across the room to the other bed on which lay a man and woman, both naked and black in the sunlight" (247). Similarly hidden from sight, Daniels observes a service at the "colored folks' church." He chokes back a laugh and recalls praying with brothers and sisters aboveground, feeling what they felt, "but here in the underground, distantly sundered from them, he saw a defenseless nakedness in their lives that made him disown them" (63). It is the seeing without being seen and the distance from the churchgoers that gives him a "terrifying knowledge" that they should "assume a heroic attitude" even though he had not. When he hears them sing, he feels a throbbing pain "in his calves and a deeper pain . . . induced by the naked sight of the groveling spectacle of those black people whose hearts were hungry for tenderness, whose lives were full of fear and loneliness, whose hands were reaching outward into a cold, vast darkness for something that was not there, something that could never be there" (63). In other words, the conditions of life revealed to Bigger and Daniels in their heightened states of awareness as fugitives are intolerable but also, for them, ineffable and inexorable. Playing on the familiarity of sites of human suffering in both characters' prior lives, Wright creates a sense of *presque vu*, the almost seen, near epiphanies of the meaning of the scenes from new vantage points.

Caught in "the rhythms of his life: indifference and violence ... like water ebbing and flowing from the tug of a far-away invisible force," Bigger and his friend Jack duck into a dark movie theater in the middle of the day to see *Trader Horn* (29). They masturbate furtively, giggling, and watch a newsreel of Mary Dalton, the daughter of Bigger's prospective employer, on vacation in Florida with a "well-known radical" (32). Underground, Daniels breaks through another basement wall to find himself in a theater with a neon red E-X-I-T sign, a stretch of human faces, shadows high on a screen of silver. Like the churchgoers, "these people were laughing at their lives, at the animated shadows of themselves." He imagines trying to reach them but concludes, "It could not be done. He could not awaken them" (74–75).

Just after he declares that the thought of his wife Rachel is repugnant because it crowds "more important things from his mind," Daniels sees a "little nude brown baby snagged by debris and half-submerged in water." The "thing was dead, cold, nothing, the same kind of nothingness he had felt while looking through the slit at the men and women singing in the church." The dead baby's fists are "doubled, as though in vain protest." He remarks, "Some woman's thrown her baby away" (65). The baby is his enemy; like the police, it makes him feel guilty. Similarly, in *Native Son*, Bessie Mears turns into Bigger's enemy, her vulnerability and fear so threatening that he coldly murders her.

Daniels discovers an undertaker's office and sees the nude, waxy body of a Black man, one of several corpses he confronts that signify his own mortality and the vulnerability of Black bodies to premature death by racial violence, poverty, and crime; he washes his hands in water that looked like a spout of blood. A "rich red lather blossomed in his cupped fingers, like a scarlet sponge" (68–72). In flight from the police, Bigger sees the Black Belt of Chicago more clearly: Black people are kept "bottled up here like wild animals" and realtors rent to Black people only in racially designated areas, while most businesses are owned by Jews, Italians, and Greeks; the only Black-owned businesses are some funeral parlors because "white undertakers refused to bother with dead black bodies" (249).

Daniels seems to sleep and dream: he walks over swirling currents of sewer water and sees another nude woman holding another nude baby, or perhaps they are the same—a holy mother and child. The woman drowns and he takes the baby. The baby floats, so he dives into the water to rescue the woman, and when he surfaces, the baby, too, is agonizingly gone.

He enters another basement room and climbs through a window to a passageway, where he hears the sound of typing and sees a tiny disc of stainless steel—a combination lock—and an "eerie white hand, seemingly detached from its arm" (81). The door opens to reveal wads of green bills and rows of coins. He tries to learn the combination. He steals a radio.

He digs another hole and enters a meat market. A butcher is selling meat, cutting it with a bloody cleaver. He leaves, and Daniels steals the cleaver. He returns to the room with the safe; a blue-eyed white girl sees him and screams. Her male colleagues ridicule her and say she's hysterical and "She ought to get married" (86).[54] He waits for someone to open the safe. "It was not the money that lured him, but the fact that he could get it with impunity, without risking reprisal" (87). Just as he's about to give up, the hand reappears and opens the lock. He writes down the combination and sees a watchman stealing money. The business is HILLMAN AND SWANSON. REAL ESTATE & INSURANCE. The firm, he recalls, "collected hundreds of thousands of dollars in rent from poor colored folks" (90).

As Bigger searches for an abandoned building where Bessie and he can hide, he sees a sign: THIS PROPERTY IS MANAGED BY THE SOUTH SIDE REAL ESTATE COMPANY. He knows the company is owned by Mr. Dalton and realizes it is he to whom his mother pays eight dollars a week in rent for their "rat-infested room." Wright notes that "Bigger could not live in a building across the 'line'" dividing white and Black Chicago: "Even though Mr. Dalton gave millions of dollars for Negro education, he would rent houses to Negroes only in this prescribed area, this corner of the city tumbling down from rot." These ideas are latent in Bigger, unvoiced or only partly and desperately voiced, perhaps altogether inarticulable: "In a sullen way Bigger was conscious of this" (174). Wright uses the same double-voiced narrative in *TMWLU*, a technique that allows him not only to comment on the story but also, more consequentially, to create characters whose capacity to change the conditions that oppress them is limited by their partial, liminal knowledge of the historical and material forces that produce them.

Wright speaks for both protagonists, bringing to light the crushing social limitations they face as oppressed minorities "who are surrounded with daily items of civilization to which they cannot react frontally" (173). Standing on the street with his friend Gus as a plane flies overhead, Bigger dimly perceives his own doomed life in terms of "being black and they being white." Gus says,

"Aw, for Chrissake! There ain't nothing you can do about it.... You black and they make the laws." Bigger replies, "Why they make us live in one corner of the city? Why don't they let us fly planes and run ships?" (16–20). In relating how he came to write *TMWLU*, Wright likewise tells us that his grandmother "had more of her share of handicaps to keep the daily, meaningful world in which the majority of people lived from her; and knowing that such a world was not for her, she gave it up" (174).

Eventually, Daniels opens the safe and fingers the crisp green bills he finds inside, "as though expecting [them] suddenly to reveal secret qualities" (90). He spies a typewriter: "Never in his life had he used one of them. It was a queer instrument, something *beyond the rim of his life*" (91; emphasis added). He pecks his name: *freddaniels*. He takes the typewriter and reflects that the radio, cleaver, money, and typewriter were all "on the same level of value.... They were the toys of the men who lived in the dead world of sunshine and rain he had left, the world that had condemned him." The queer typewriter *beyond the rim of his life* alludes to his circumscribed existence. To make use of the typewriter other than pecking out his name or a simple sentence is beyond him; at the same time, the typewriter signifies Wright's authorial presence and capacities beyond the rim. By relegating the stolen items to the same level of value, Daniels calls into question the entire edifice of the society he fled—"the dead world of sunshine and rain . . . the world that condemned him"—and divorces himself from any possibility of changing it. He recalls the church members, the theatergoers, the dead baby, the nude man. "He saw these things hovering before his eyes and he felt that some dim meaning tied them together, that some magical relationship made them kin" (92). His certitude mirrors Granny Wilson's religious convictions, a fetishization of random, meaningless abstractions that magically ward off evil even as they block engagement with the conditions that force her retreat from reality.

Daniels hooks up electricity in his lair in the sewer and reflects on the nature of money. Then he inserts paper into the typewriter and types: *itwasalonghotday*. He learns how to make capital letters and spaces and retypes the sentence correctly. In a mocking, childish gesture, he parodies someone conducting business: "Yes I'll have the contracts ready tomorrow" (95). Bigger is the more literate of the two, based on the ransom note he writes to throw the police off his track and profit from Mary Dalton's unexplained disappearance. In light of Wright's Marxist interpretation of stages of history, to which he often alluded, particularly in *12 Million Black Voices*, we know that he understood Black southern migration as a movement through time as well as space, transforming the children of sharecroppers into alienated, uprooted urbanites who rejected their parents' mores, including religion, and were catapulted into modernity. Although both live in northern cities, Bigger is more modern and street-smart than Daniels. Not only does he know to disguise his handwriting by wearing gloves and writing with his left hand, he also is able to think rhetorically, consider whether to use first-person singular or plural pronouns, and plot how best to convince Mr. Dalton his daughter is still alive.

Yet it is not the story of the heinous criminal Bigger but that of innocent Fred Daniels, a working-class Black man falsely accused and brutalized by police, that troubled Wright's agent Paul Reynolds and other early readers of the manuscript. Finished typing—a symbol of muteness—Daniels glues green bills to the wall, triumphing "over the world aboveground ... free!" (95). He explores another basement, discovers rings and diamonds, and dreams he is standing in a room "watching over his own black, nude waxen body lying stiff upon a white table" (99). He sees the sleeping night watchman and gazes "like an *invisible man* hovering in space upon the life that lived aboveground in the darkness of the sun" (103; emphasis added), a reference that predates Ellison's novel by the same name by more than a decade. Taking the guard's gun and cartridge belt, Daniels thinks, "What a fool! A man with a gun risking his precious life each night—the only life he will ever have on this earth—to protect sparkling bits of stone that looked for all the world like glass" (104).

Although he perceives the irrationality of this fetishized form of value, Daniels cannot explain why the guard is a fool. Similarly, Bigger Thomas senses how Mary Dalton and Jan Erlone objectify his racial identity, making him acutely conscious of his skin color. He intuits they must "get something out of this." Even if they did not despise his black skin, they made him feel despised "by just standing there *looking* at him" (emphasis added). "He felt he had no physical existence at all right then: he was something he hated, the badge of shame which he knew was attached to a black skin. It was a No Man's Land, the ground that separated the white world from the black that he stood upon. He felt naked, transparent. He felt that this white man, having helped to put him down, having helped to deform him, held him up now to look at him and be amused" (67).[55]

And because of that, he felt toward them "a dumb, cold, and inarticulate hate" (67). In both novels, Wright's commitment was to rewriting African American history and revealing the vulnerability and liberatory promise of that combative space. It was precisely his own working-class background, offset though it was by his mother's petit bourgeois roots, that attracted him to the literary left—in particular, the CPUSA—even as it forged his critique of the Party and his resolve to skewer the Black bourgeoisie and defend the rights, interests, and potentialities of the international Black working class.

When Daniels wakes, he hears the church hymns and feels "a fast and old conviction seeking to rise again." It frightens him because he feels that if he succumbed to "this nameless feeling that was trying to capture him... he would never be free again." Then a strange new knowledge comes to him: "In some unutterable fashion, he was *all* people and they were *he*" (106). He experiences a dialectical "obliteration of self" and knowledge of "the inexpressible value and importance of himself." Like Bigger, he doesn't "think these things; he feels them through images." The songs "batter the cliffs of his consciousness." He knows not what he will do or say—the words are unutterable—only that he will very soon return aboveground: "He could not question what he felt, for *he* was *it* and *it* was *he*" (107).

Fetishizing the assorted objects he collects—a metal box of rings, a glass jar of diamonds, a bloody meat cleaver, a radio, green bills plastered on the walls, and glittering coins—he "felt that the true identity of these forces would slowly reveal themselves, not only to him but also to others" (109). Along with merging and reifying abstract economic forms of value with symbols of butchery and mass communication—inanimate objects whose "true identity" would reveal the "secret" of their collective guilt—Daniels fantasizes escaping from the artificial, disciplined, industrial capitalist constraints of time. As time no longer exists for him, he wants to get rid of the watches that are "measuring time, making men tense and taut with the sense of passing hours, telling tales of death, *crowning time the king of consciousness*" (109; emphasis added).

Turning on the radio, listening to the news, he looks down at the diamonds like a sky full of stars until the floor turns into its opposite, and his perspective shifts so that he is looking from above in the air at the city lights and the land and the sea below, enmeshed in war "as men fought, as cities were razed, as armies marched or planes scattered bombs." Horrified, witnessing "the reasonlessness of human life made him understand that no compassion of which the human heart was capable could ever respond adequately to that awful sight." He despairs that nothing short of a god could behold such a "hopeless spectacle" and comprehend its meaninglessness because "men were overwhelmed with shame and guilt when they looked down upon the irremediable frailty of their lives" (112–13).

After pushing through the manhole and climbing to the street above, he discovers NICK'S FRUITS, where he devours bananas, pears, and oranges, and sees a newspaper headline: HUNT BLACK WHO COMMITTED DOUBLE

MURDER. Then he sleeps, waking to contemplate his bounty by the light of a match, the objects trembling, brooding, winking, mocking, as if alive. These objects—the bloody cleaver, the gun barrel, the green bills, the ticking gold watches—are again "crowning time the king of consciousness" and "defining the limits of living." He hears the church choir and sees a Black girl sing, "Glad, glad, glad, oh, so glad / I got Jesus in my soul." It is here, at the climax of his quixotic journey, that he discovers the secret: "Guilt! That was it! Insight became sight and he knew that they thought that they were guilty of something they had not done and they had to die." He thinks: "Their search for a happiness they could never find made them feel that they had committed a great wrong which they could not remember or understand" (119–20).

Like a Dickensian visit to ghosts past, present, and future, Daniels reenters the rooms adjacent to his underground refuge and observes first Lawson, then Murphy, then Johnson interrogating innocent men accused of crimes that Daniels believes he committed. Overwhelmed by the moral ambiguity of his situation, he alternates between adhering to his newfound abstract realization that all people are and always have been guilty and questioning his complicity in the police abusing men he knows to be innocent. He considers returning the money but thinks better of it because the man being questioned, though not guilty of stealing it, is nonetheless guilty and has "always been guilty." When Lawson leaves the room, the man—who is "tall, lean, young, with a straight-forward, clean-shaven face"—shoots himself in the head, and Lawson finds him in a "widening pool of blood" (122–23).

Daniels then sees Murphy grilling the night watchman and he wants to scream, "He's innocent! I'm innocent! We're all innocent!" Again, he concludes that though the watchman is "innocent, he was guilty, though blameless, he was accused . . . [and] must live a life of shame." Finally, he goes up the rickety steps to the room where he took the radio, identifies the racial differences between white and Black voices, and hears Johnson interrogating a Black boy for stealing the radio, followed by thudding sounds that he assumes are blows to the boy, whom Johnson calls a "black bastard" and who cries out, "I ain't took no radio. I got my own radio at home." Daniels wants to rescue the boy and tell him to confess because both he and Johnson are guilty, but he can only silently cry, "Why do you want to beat this innocent boy?" (127–29).

In the untitled Part Three of *TMWLU*—titled "Fate" in *Native Son*—Daniels surfaces aboveground, blinded by sunlight, filthy, mud-caked, clothes in tatters, and is mistaken for a sewer worker. Determined to turn himself in, he goes to the police precinct but cannot explain what he wants, eliciting ridicule from officers who treat him like a crazy person. After he remembers his employers' name, Wooten, and the name of the murdered couple, Peabody, an officer connects him to Lawson's beat and escorts him upstairs to the room where he was tortured and where Lawson, Murphy, and Johnson are now playing cards. They, too, believe Daniels is "batty" when he tells them he went underground and offers to sign more papers confessing his guilt.

Daniels babbles incoherently about the underground and the three officers' questioning innocent men just as they questioned him, insisting paradoxically on his own and everyone's guilt until Lawson declares, "That lunatic will queer everything." He reminds the other officers that first they told the press that Daniels confessed and escaped; then, when they caught the "Wop" (the "Eyetalian"), they told the papers that they "steered them wrong to catch the real guy, see?" (146–47). Marshaling his partners and Daniels into the police car, Lawson tells Daniels to show them where he has been as they continue to ridicule him, calling him batty, loony, a clown, a coon, nuts, off his nut, crazy.

Lawson operates outside yet under cover of the law. Like many of Wright's characters, the play on words in his name is significant: he is the "son of law" who re-presents Max's soliloquy in *Native Son* on the difference between law and justice, injustice and oppression.[56] It is precisely the law that Max questions in his brief to the court, arguing that what is at stake in Bigger's trial is not "injustice" but "an accomplished fact of life . . . oppression, an attempt to throttle or stamp out a new form of life," built on centuries of enslavement and held captive as a separate nation within the United States, "stunted, stripped . . . devoid of political, social, economic, and property rights" (391, 397). Lawson enacts this "accomplished fact of life," both reflecting the actual legal system and operating outside the law in his savage abuse of Daniels. When Daniels starts to sing the same song overheard in the church—*Glad, glad, glad, oh, so glad / I got Jesus in my soul*—the officers cuff him, ridiculing his mental state. Lawson wonders if he has delusions of grandeur and Murphy comments that "colored boys sure go off their nuts easy," to which Johnson replies, having absorbed the psychoanalytical-political zeitgeist of his day, "It's because they live in a white man's world" (154).

In the dramatic scene in which Daniels's final moments unfold on a rainy night very much like the one during which he fled underground, he stands at the entrance to the manhole, struggling to pull off the heavy cover, dark waters swirling below, eager to retrace his journey and share his discovery of universal guilt, childishly expecting the officers to follow him. Meanwhile, air raid sirens start blaring, silver planes whirl in beams of light, people shout and scream on wet streets, running, weeping, half-dressed, pulling on overcoats. These menacing aboveground signs of war mirror the underground world to which he will momentarily return, each environment dominated by random, fragmented symbols of the forces that paradoxically modernize and barbarize human existence. Amid streaks of light across the night sky, wailing sirens, tall buildings, and sounds of distant explosions, he sees his cache of diamonds, his radio, and the $100 bills pasted on the wall; he hears the ticking golden watches. But the "truth" he has grasped is useless against the powerful agents of war embodied in the air raid sirens, the warplanes, and relatedly, the state-supported, if tacit, warrant for police to kill with impunity. As the planes fly overheard, Lawson decrees Daniels's death, explaining as he shoots and kills him, "You've got to shoot his kind. They would wreck things" (159).

Could a Negro Ever Live Halfway Like a Human Being in This Country?

In a 1970 letter to literary critic Stanley Edgar Hyman, Ralph Ellison adamantly denied that Wright had influenced *Invisible Man*, declaring, "As for my narrator, he comes out of Dostoevsky's *Notes from Underground*, not Wright's 'Man Who Lived Underground.'" Ellison went on to dismiss the character Fred Daniels as "incapable of simple thought much less of philosophical articulation," further distancing himself from his one-time mentor and echoing his 1963 critique in "The World and the Jug" that "Wright as writer was less interesting than the enigma he personified . . . that he could be so wonderful an example of human possibility but could not for ideological reasons depict a Negro as intelligent as creative or as dedicated as himself."[57] Yet, in 1942, after reading excerpts of the novel in *Accent*, Ellison had written to congratulate Kerker Quinn on publishing an important new work that treated Black religious experience. And in "Richard Wright's Blues," published in 1945, he commended his mentor for "convert[ing] the American Negro impulse toward self-annihilation and 'going-under-ground' into a will to confront the world, to evaluate his experience honestly and throw his findings unashamedly into the guilty conscience of America."[58] Clearly, Ellison had by then read at least the shortened version of *The Man Who Lived Underground*, so to deny Wright's influence on *Invisible Man* in 1970 was, at best, a lapse of memory.[59]

Celebrating Wright's achievement in *Black Boy* in 1945, Ellison calls him "an important writer, perhaps the most articulate Negro American. . . . Imagine Bigger Thomas projecting his own life in lucid prose, guided, say, by the insights of Marx and Freud, and you have an idea of this autobiography." It was Wright's extraordinary capacity to project such insights through characters with limited awareness, Ellison argues, that enabled him to reveal both their full humanity and the degree to which "the Southern community renders fulfillment of human destiny impossible."[60] Yet, by 1953, during the Cold War, Ellison would chastise Irving Howe for casting him and Baldwin as villains, "'black boys' masquerading as false, self-deceived 'native sons.'" He went on to describe Bigger as "near sub-human" and "nonconscious" and to conclude that "Wright could imagine Bigger but Bigger could not possibly imagine Wright. Wright saw to that."[61] That Bigger Thomas and Fred Daniels could imagine, dream, and begin to understand their circumstances but not yet be able to speak or act to change them is precisely the dilemma that most troubled Wright and that he spent his life interrogating.

The decision by Library of America to publish *TMWLU* and the overwhelmingly positive response to it cast new light on the critical reception of Wright's work. In the broadest sense, the publication of the novel and accompanying essay raises questions about Wright's relationship to the publishing industry, the decades-long suppression of his story of a Black male victim of police violence, and assumptions about race and class that distorted the critical reception of his writing. Though mainly laudatory and, in some cases, contrite for having previously condemned Wright as crude or hateful, numerous reviews of *TMWLU* continued to replay themes that have undermined his reputation since *Uncle Tom's Children* appeared in 1937, many echoing Baldwin's and Ellison's attacks on their literary mentor. Other posthumously published and late work like *Lawd Today!* as well as his first expatriate novel, *The Outsider*, received mixed to negative reviews that improved over time as critics reconsidered his relationship to the Communist Party and Marxism, his stylistic strengths and weaknesses, and his theoretical perspicacity. These reconsiderations raise questions about both the fate of rejected, unpublished works such as "Black Hope" and "Island of Hallucination" and the psychological and financial toll of bad reviews and the sting of rejection on the arc of his career.

In this respect, writing *TMWLU* was for Wright a liberation as much from the constraints of the publishing industry as from the CPUSA. The book signals Wright's growing disaffection with the Party, but it also turns out to be very much about police brutality. It is fundamentally a book about racial and class oppression and state violence that reveals the historically specific political economic forces that create those conditions. It is a book that interrogates how religion and the blues shield the oppressed from the daily psychological harm of the oppressor and being falsely accused of a crime—murder, political betrayal, stealing biscuits off the dinner table, being born Black—and it is a book that blends genres, resists categorization, and refuses to conform to the expectations of publishers, readers, and reviewers. It is a book, finally, in which Wright pursues his investigation of the complex interaction of form and content, appearance and reality, to discover the inner processes that often appear in inverted form and that suppress and destroy or liberate human potential.

The novel resonates with JanMohamed's thesis that throughout his life, Wright was working through the trauma of his childhood and the collective memories of Black Americans, particularly poor and working-class southerners and the millions who migrated North, documenting the relentless, debilitating terror inflicted by state and extremist violence, most personally on his family and him despite his entry into the echelons of literary fame. Even in New York City, Wright experienced virulent racial hostility that left him with no place to stay on a trip to Manhattan for the American Writers' Congress in 1935, prompting him to ask, "Could a Negro ever live halfway like a human being in this goddamn country?"[62] He was five months into drafting *TMWLU* when his good friend and fellow Communist Herbert Newton was arrested and severely beaten by police for leading a protest against the firing of 15,000 WPA workers; Newton reported being punched, kicked, and struck on the back of the head. Police jumped on his back and broke several ribs, probably contributing to his early death of a heart attack a few years later at age forty-four. Wright denounced the New York City Police Department in a story about the incident by Beth McHenry in the *Daily Worker*. In 1945, the New York department store Bergdorf Goodman refused to let three-year-old Julia Wright use its restroom.[63]

Responses to Wright have been refracted through the prisms of his political affiliations and consciousness; his racial and class background; and his resistance to categorization as a social realist, naturalist, modernist, surrealist, existentialist, or Black writer. His Jim Crow, southern, sharecropper, working- and middle-class roots uniquely positioned him to embrace and critique the Communist Party and to apply Marxist theory to the Black diaspora in world contexts. The traumas of his childhood and youth made him "skeptical of everything while seeking everything, tolerant of all and yet critical."[64] He broke new ground in American literature, tearing away the veil of the racial subjugation of "decorous [Negro] ambassadors who went a-begging to white America" to reveal the oppression of Black Americans as systemic and brutal. His own complicated, harrowing life history taught him to stand up for himself and for those whose suffering won his sympathy, but it also subjected him to the vicissitudes of market demands and Cold War sabotage that threatened to destroy his commercial success and financial stability. When he pursued literary and political directions other than those the market and ideological forces dictated, he was punished; the rejections and scathing criticism persisted, accompanied by anxiety exacerbated by serious financial difficulties and constant US surveillance from 1945 to the end of his life.

At the time he was drafting *Underground*, Ellen was pregnant with Julia. Perhaps Fred Daniels's pregnant wife Rachel reflected Wright's anxiety about America's future and having a baby, which ultimately led him to leave the United States in hopes of escaping Cold War McCarthyism and protecting Julia from American racism. Interpretations of *TMWLU* have almost all missed the throughline of the novel in its entirety—it is not a retreat to religion or existentialism but rather another brilliant study of the psychology of oppression of people whose consciousness is limited by their defensive reactions to the conditions that keep them oppressed.

CHAPTER TWO

A Consuming Curiosity
Reading, Writing, and Traversing the World

Richard Wright wanted not only to reflect the world in his writing but also to change it. His main weapon was the word, a lesson he may have intuited as a child but learned explicitly at age nineteen from the iconoclastic writer H. L. Mencken. Wright used the word to interrogate complex realities of a fast-changing world and to awaken readers to the underlying historical and material forces, including the collective agency of human beings, that continually transformed it. He assured his one-time protégé James Baldwin that he was proud to write protest novels; he could not understand how writers could do otherwise. As he put it to Baldwin at the Brasserie Lipp in Paris in 1949 after reading "Everybody's Protest Novel" in *Zero* magazine, "What do you mean, *protest*? *All* literature is protest. You can't name a single novel that isn't protest."[1] What explains Wright's rise from a famously bleak childhood with only a ninth-grade education to become an internationally renowned author? Situating his life in the historical context of African American literacy education and addressing parts of his autobiographical writing that have been hidden in plain sight suggest that his experience growing up as a Black child in the Deep South predisposed him to a lifelong search for knowledge and expression; in this respect, he was exceptional but not anomalous.

In a 1945 interview after the publication of *Black Boy*, he told Charles J. Rolo, "Some people see a ballgame and they want to play ball; some see water and they want to swim; when I saw print, I wanted to write." Rolo describes Wright's achievement as a "miracle" akin to "Beethoven's genius" or Rimbaud's "poetic gift," and he concludes, "The autobiography fails in one crucial respect: it does not explain Richard Wright."[2] His bewilderment echoes the sociologist Robert Park's blunt question to the young author, "How in hell did you happen?"[3] Such pronouncements, combined with Wright's own well-crafted, multivocal, not always factually accurate self-narrative, have forged a view of him as a born genius and autodidact whose widespread acclaim is a mystery if not a miracle. They reflect not only homage to Wright but also pervasive, if unwitting, racist assumptions that surface like monsters from the deep, often in otherwise glowing appraisals that comment on his stylistic incompetence or mistake the character he portrays for his authorial voice, damning him with faint praise as a Black writer rivaling some white writer, Theodore Dreiser or John Steinbeck, but less eloquent and more violent. Simply the insistence on seeing his rise to fame as an inexplicable "miracle" suggests that it was unimaginable for a Black man, born and raised in the Jim Crow South, to become an accomplished writer. Such damning praise also stems from myths and misconceptions about literacy education that have consequences for those most vulnerable to stereotypes and whose sites of learning are furthest from mainstream education that has marginalized them.

Asked by Rolo why he turned out differently than Bigger, Wright answered, "Well, for one thing, I kept out of jail; I never got caught. And when I had enough money to start north, I never stole again."[4] This deceptively simple answer sums up the ideology of the "New Jim Crow" of mass incarceration, rooted, as Michelle Alexander observes, in slavery, penal labor, and racial apartheid. Unlike his creator, Bigger Thomas got caught, albeit for heinous crimes that his lawyer Boris Max puts into the same historical context as Alexander does. However broken by systemic racism Bigger may be, he is far from the backward "ape" depicted by the fictional public and press and the real-life reviewers and critics of *Native Son*.[5] After his arrest for the murders of Mary Dalton and Bessie Mears, he proves he is literate enough to throw the police off his trail and forge a ransom note to the Daltons, and conscious enough, according to Wright's friend, the Marxist historian and critic C. L. R. James, to "attain the highest stage of his development" in grasping the lesson of class solidarity across racial lines. Ultimately facing death by execution for an accidental murder that forced him to fight for his own survival against "the whole powerful white world," he takes responsibility for his crimes, famously asserting to his lawyer Boris Max that "what I killed for, I am," and thereby committing a "revolutionary act" of survival, challenging that world and, for a time, outwitting the police.[6]

Without in any way diminishing the depth, breadth, and brilliance of Wright's achievements, this chapter looks more closely at the formal education he received as a child, the contradictory influence of his racial and mixed class background, and the impact of informal learning on his work and life, especially but not only during his twenties and the decade he spent in Chicago. Reading against the narrative of Wright's literary genius as a miracle, I situate his childhood literacy development first in the political economy of education and sponsors of literacy amid shifting national priorities; second, in the history of African American literacy traditions, from slavery through Reconstruction to Jim Crow and beyond, that resisted oppression and circumvented laws that forbade or restricted literacy learning in Black communities;

and third, in sociocultural and liberatory theories of literacy and cognitive development that recast Wright's autodidacticism in light of some effective, if limited, classroom instruction and abundant informal education.[7]

"A Sense of the World No Education Could Alter"

To put a finer point on the oft-repeated question about Wright's intellectual and literary attainments, how did a Black southerner with an erratic ninth-grade education come to write a best-selling novel in the early twentieth century and forge a cutting analysis of capitalism and slavery, class exploitation and racial oppression? He owed a debt to his mother, in particular, and to the deep-rooted aspirations, efforts, and wisdom of African American communities who were excluded from educational and job opportunities and willing to break antiliteracy laws to become educated.[8] He also benefited from teachers and classmates in the segregated schools he irregularly attended from age six to seventeen, as well as the dynamic cauldron of political and literary activity that became his "university" in Chicago.[9]

His formal education was repeatedly interrupted by personal tragedy and frequent moves to the homes of relatives or to cheap rentals in polluted, segregated neighborhoods. When he was old enough, he left school more than once to make money to support his family. By age twelve he had yet to complete a solid year of school, but he found some stability in Jackson, where he spent two years at Jim Hill Public School from 1921 to 1923, and another two at Smith Robertson Junior High from 1923 to 1925. The highest level he completed was the ninth grade (essentially a repeat of eighth grade), ten years after he first entered school at the Howard Institute at age six, later than usual because he had no respectable clothes to wear. When he graduated in 1925 as his junior high school's valedictorian, he was nearly seventeen. As a six-year-old, paralyzed with fear, he was unable to speak in the classroom even though he understood everything being said. On the playground that first day, he eagerly learned every four-letter word the older boys knew, memorizing a schoolyard rhyme "replete with filth" about sex. Later that day, with a piece of soap, he scribbled all the obscenities he had mastered on store windows, only to be dragged back to the stores by his mother Ella, who made him scrub the words off the windows until he sobbed, "blind with anger," resolving to keep such words to himself from then on.[10] Ten years later he would not be silenced by his "bought" principal, whose canned speech he refused to read.

In the two tumultuous years after his uncle Silas Hoskins was lynched in Elaine, Arkansas, he moved twice and had no formal schooling. Back in West

Helena, where his mother Ella returned to escape Granny Wilson's strict religious rule over her Jackson household, he reentered school. As in his first classroom experience, he was overcome by anxiety, unable to perform the simple task of writing his name and address on the blackboard in front of his classmates. Their laughter embarrassed and enraged him; he wondered why he was made to feel so stupid in front of a crowd when he knew how to read and write, probably "better than any of them," and "could talk fluently and expressively" elsewhere. School was dismissed early the day World War I ended to a cacophony of bells and whistles, and he walked through packed streets, fearful of the white crowd but relieved to discover the same glad excitement among Black people in his own neighborhood. He saw his first plane, which he thought was a bird, and a stranger lifted him onto his shoulders and said, "Boy, remember this. . . . You're seeing man fly"—an extracurricular lesson of the sort that characterized his early education and reverberates in the scene in *Native Son* on Chicago's South Side in which Bigger and his friend Gus contemplate a skywriting plane far above them and Bigger resentfully and wistfully observes, "I could fly a plane if I had a chance," to which Gus retorts, "If you wasn't black and if you had some money."[11]

After his mother suffered a stroke, he went to live with his Uncle Clark and briefly attended school in Greenwood, Mississippi, where his primary recollection was of proving himself on his first day in a physical scuffle at recess with other boys. Having learned to defend himself, to assert his prowess as a fighter, he succeeded in driving off the classmates who taunted him and befriending the others. He had "won his right to the school grounds," only to learn that he had been sleeping in the bed of the dead son of his uncle's landlord, who lived next door—a boy his age. This information kept him awake, disturbing him so deeply that he started to get failing grades and begged his uncle to let him return to Jackson and his bedridden mother. He had not yet completed a full year of school, his uncle protested, but he ultimately agreed to let him go home. There, instead of returning to school, he played alone, read books, idly bounced a ball against a fence, and accompanied his mother and Uncle Edward on a sad trip to a nearby town for an operation that left Ella an invalid for ten years, never to recover fully from her stroke.

At the end of chapter 3 of *Black Boy*, Wright expresses the essence of what he had learned up to that point in his life at age twelve without one full year of formal schooling. Speaking as the adult writer rather than the pubescent boy, he describes an education far beyond what any school would have taught him—a manifestation of everything that was to follow.[12] It was his mother's suffering, he tells us, that "set the emotional tone of my life . . . [and] determined my attitude to situations and circumstances I had yet to face." He had acquired "a sense of the world" that was his, one that "no education could alter," enabling him to express in a "clearer tongue" his passage from early childhood's cryptic world to the sharper meanings of experience he began to grasp in early adolescence. Already he was forming an analysis of social relations, of the meaning of human suffering, and of his position as skeptical yet open, critical yet tolerant, "strangely tender and cruel, violent and peaceful." Already he had resolved to seek answers, "to drive coldly to the heart of every question and lay it open to the core of suffering I knew I would find there." His mother's suffering had kindled his sympathy for others and focused his quest for knowledge on the nature of human existence and struggles to be free of fear, hunger, poverty, and racial terror. These existential and political questions would put him "on the side of men in rebellion" who envisioned an egalitarian society based on the satisfaction of human need, the alleviation of suffering, and the abolition of profit, even as they aroused in him "a sense of wonder and awe in the face of the drama of human feeling that is hidden by the external drama of life."[13]

Back in Jackson with his invalid mother, he briefly attended a Seventh-day Adventist school under his Aunt Addie's supervision. Having just completed her own Seventh-day Adventist studies to become the school's only teacher, Ella's youngest sibling, Addie, was both zealous in her religious mission and insecure about her authority, especially with her young, skeptical nephew in the classroom. Though he fought to attend public school, Wright had no real choice in the matter, given his position as a minor dependent on his extended family for support. Already a cause of concern to his deeply religious grandmother because of his apparent lack of faith in God, to have done otherwise would have cast him as a "horrible infidel" and a "hardhearted ingrate." At school, the conflict between him and Addie climaxed when she beat him with a tree switch on his hand and the back of his legs for a minor infraction he did not commit. He resolved never to be beaten by her again, especially because the beating had been unfair, unlike others that he vaguely felt he had deserved. When she tried to lash him again in Granny Wilson's kitchen, he grabbed a knife and they fell wrestling on the floor. This bold act of resistance was yet another sign of his sense of justice, independence of thought, and determination to be free of religious and other constraints his family tried to impose on him.[14]

In "Memories of My Grandmother," his essay about writing *The Man Who Lived Underground* (*TMWLU*), he probes the mystery of Granny Wilson's religious beliefs, which profoundly shaped his childhood despite his precocious skepticism. What baffles and perturbs him is the psychological structure of her beliefs, or, as he put it, not her "interpretation of religion" but her "interpretation of life" as a religious person. In particular, he was puzzled by the contradiction between her abstract love for humanity and her disdain for people and adherence to a set of otherworldly ideas that had no connection to the material conditions of life that preoccupied him, most palpably the gnawing physical hunger that plagued him throughout most of his childhood. He observes that he had never been swayed by religion because his "sensibilities were too much claimed by the concrete externals of the world," an insightful observation encapsulated in his memory in *Black Boy* of the gospel of "the moon turning to blood" and "water changing into wine" inside Granny's Seventh-day Adventist Church and his epiphany as he exited into the "bright sunshine and felt the throbbing life of the people in the streets" that "none of [the sermon] was true and nothing would happen."[15]

Wright's surreal dramatization of his grandmother's religiosity in *TMWLU* may have coincided with his retreat from Communism but it did not diminish his secular, scientific, Marxist outlook on life. On the contrary, it was precisely her incapacity to act—her retreat from a real world too harsh to abide, too terrifying to tolerate, to a religious sphere that welcomed her—that suggested to him how mediums as different as religion and the blues structure personalities, shielding Black Americans like his grandmother from the harsh material and psychological realities of racism. He goes on to compare her religious beliefs to schizophrenia, noting that she was a sane woman who fulfilled all her worldly responsibilities yet "did all of these things without ever really understanding the world in which she lived. . . . She did not know the relationship of one thing in her environment to another . . . in an objective sense." Religion, the blues, and schizophrenia all function to constitute alternative worlds based on imagined or real bits of reality. Wright looked to these phenomena not as substitutes for a dialectical materialist worldview but as psychological reactions to oppressive forces that needed to be recognized and understood to enable conscious, organized struggles for liberation from them.[16]

Repeatedly, Wright describes standing outside a group, a discourse, or an ideology to be able to hear and understand or evaluate it. For example, in explaining his grandmother's belief in an invisible God who controlled their everyday lives, he writes, "It is but natural that I should have become excited over the question of how it would feel to stand outside of life and look at life." While he portrays Granny Wilson and Fred Daniels in similar terms—*outside* yet *within* life in their respective domains of religion and a hallucinatory underground—it is Wright's double consciousness that enables him to see deeper into their lives. The double-voiced narratives in *Native Son*, *TMWLU*, and other works by him reveal the interior life of ostracized characters whose struggles for what he calls *"freedom of action"* redeem them even though they are killed. Daniels's "dubious knowledge" of universal guilt and Bigger's realization that he didn't mean to commit murder (not once but twice) are liberating insights that reveal their social paralysis. Says Bigger: "I was trying to do something else. But it seems like I never could. I was always wanting something and I was feeling that nobody would let me have it." Famously, he concludes, "What I killed for, I am." Aside from dying for their actions or denying reality, neither of these characters nor Granny Wilson can change their circumstances, and it is this failure that Wright passionately seeks to understand.[17]

Although his schooling nurtured him intellectually and socially, reinforcing his belief in himself, it was never sufficient. In "Memories," he recalls how reading Gertrude Stein's story "Melanctha" about a Negro girl "opened wide to me the language of my entire race." The story was "written in such a manner that I could actually stand outside the English language and hear it." The English he learned in school, he reflects, was that of England, based on correct grammar rather than the intonations and rhythms of people he knew. Such an education, he explains, "is death to a man seeking to determine the nature of his experiences, for he is taught to shun the very things—words used by his closest friends!—that may open the door to the vast world of feeling existing about him." By the fall of 1921, having convinced his grandmother to let him attend public school, he entered the fifth grade at Jim Hill, two years behind his peers, and was promoted to the sixth grade two weeks later, winning praise from his generally disapproving family. School was an escape from the morally punishing, deprived conditions of his grandmother's house. As he put it, his "life depended not so much upon learning as upon getting into another world of people."[18]

His main concern that year was getting a job, like his classmates, so he could satisfy his incessant hunger and afford decent clothes, but his grandmother forbade him to work on Saturdays, the Seventh-day Adventist sabbath. When he convinced her otherwise, he inadvertently sold a newspaper with a pulp fiction magazine filled with Ku Klux Klan doctrine. After Essie Lee Ward's father pointed out the offensive content, he quit, but it was months before he found another job. Meanwhile, he wrote, "I burned at my studies. At the beginning of the school term I read my civics and English and geography volumes through and only referred to them when in class." He solved math problems before school and read detective stories in class, dreaming, and "weaving fantasies about cities I had never seen and about people I had never met." The jobs he eventually got contributed to his extramural education: he accompanied an insurance agent to delta plantations to sell insurance to illiterate sharecropper families; and he worked for white, blatantly racist families who quickly taught him "the reality—a Negro's reality—of the white world."[19]

Years passed, dominated by his need for wage-paying jobs but also enriched by friendships, some of them lifelong, with Dick Jordan, Joe Brown, Perry Booker, D. C. Blackburn, Lewis Anderson, Sarah McNearner, and Essie Lee Ward. At Smith Robertson Junior High School, he completed ninth grade and assumed a supervisorial role, "an honor," he wrote, "that helped me emotionally and made me hope faintly."[20] After he insisted on delivering his own commencement speech as class valedictorian, defying the principal and his uncle Tom, he briefly attended Lanier High School, dropping out to help support his family, and then enrolled for a few weeks in Hyde Park Public School in Chicago. That was the extent of his formal education.

By the time he arrived in Chicago in 1927 at age nineteen, eager to learn, he was a passionate reader, devouring books recommended by his favorite author H. L. Mencken, and a novice writer with college-level skills. He had become literate despite his erratic schooling, supplemented by significant informal support from his mother, in particular, and a powerful desire to write in order to reconstitute the beauty, mystery, and violence he perceived at age eight in tales like "Bluebeard and His Seven Wives." In Chicago, still untutored but ready to learn, he would soar to international acclaim by the time he was thirty-two. One can only speculate what path he might have taken in another place at another time, but after the crash in 1929, it would have been hard to avoid the vibrant mix of working-class, left-wing, avant-garde, and Black cultural and political groups that welcomed him. It was the confluence of these intersecting 1930s literary, cultural, and political milieus, responsive to the tumultuous times in which he lived, that fed his hunger not just for knowledge but for answers to the riddles of life that perplexed him. The John Reed Club, the CPUSA, and the South Side Writers Group enabled a crucial continuation of his political and literary education. At the same time, his early schooling, family, and wider southern Black community set him on this path to achievements that tend to have been ascribed solely to his autodidactic genius.

Hidden Transcripts of Black Lives in the Jim Crow South

Eluding many readers and critics are the interstices of Black life as experienced by children like Wright in the early twentieth-century Deep South—the negative spaces, or "spaces left," as Frederick Douglass referred to the empty pages of his young master's copybook. It is the dynamism of Black cultural history evident in the pages of *Black Boy*, for example, that made it possible for him to trick a librarian into lending him books on a card borrowed from a sympathetic Irish Catholic optical worker. Wright played on the librarian's racist expectations to convince her that he was requesting books not for himself but for his coworker. Just as the record of Black-led slave revolts and freedom struggles contests myths of the passivity, docility, and inferiority of enslaved people, understudied archives and published autobiographies reveal African Americans' eager pursuit of literacy in the most dangerous circumstances. Douglass's narration of the instructional spaces that he sought out in the nineteenth century to survive enslavement and escape captivity is one of the best-known accounts of learning to read, and it resonates in Wright's mid-twentieth-century memoir. Both men spoke for themselves and for the collective experience of Black people.

In chapters 6 and 7 of *Narrative of the Life of Frederick Douglass, an American Slave*, Douglass recalls learning to read from his mistress until her husband Hugh Auld forbade her to teach him. He then decoded the alphabet with the help of poor white urchins, often hungrier than he, who taught him in exchange for bread in a poignant act of cross-racial class solidarity. An astute observer of human nature, he describes the transformation wrought in Mrs. Auld, whose "tender heart became stone" after Mr. Auld convinced her "that education and slavery were incompatible with each other," distorting her personality and turning her crueler than he. She understood that "there would be no keeping" an enslaved person who knew how to read, a truth that revealed the path to freedom to Douglass and strengthened his resolve to become literate. By teaching him the alphabet, he wrote, "she had given me the inch, and no precaution could prevent me from taking the ell." He taught himself the letters *L*, *S*, *F*, and *A* by associating them with the signage for larboard, starboard, forward, and aft, at the Durgin and Bailey's shipyard. Once he knew those letters, he challenged boys to see if they could write better than he, as he learned to write with a lump of chalk on any surface that he could find and practiced copying words from Webster's *Spelling Book* in the "spaces left" in young Auld's copybooks. To escape, he would need to write his own pass—a survival tactic Wright echoes in his story of intellectual survival, forging notes to borrow library books on his Irish Catholic coworker's card.

Douglass was one of Wright's maternal grandfather Richard Wilson's heroes; the other was Lincoln.[21] Whether or not his grandfather's predilections influenced Wright, he echoed the themes of literacy and freedom in the narrative Douglass had published exactly a century before *Black Boy*. Some fifty years after the Civil War, in the segregated South where laws like those inscribed in the 1890 Mississippi Constitution disenfranchised Black Americans, it was mainly Wright's mother Ella who taught him to read at his insistence at age six. He would look at books dropped on the sidewalk by older children playing on their way home from school and question them about the "baffling print." Encouraged by Ella, he would "pick [his] way" through the pages, arousing such a "consuming curiosity" and asking so many questions that she refused to answer them all. One cold day with no heat in the house, she took his brother to work, bidding Richard to stay in bed until the coal man arrived. After lighting the furnace, the man asked Richard how much change he owed him, discovered his ignorance of basic arithmetic, and taught him to count to 100. Astonished that evening when he proudly recited his numbers, Ella set about teaching Richard to read, telling him stories, reading newspapers with him, and generally "guiding me and spelling out the words." His curiosity also led to his dawning consciousness of race relations, driven by the contradiction between his grandmother's white skin and Jim Crow South racial codes. This incongruity confused him, provoking questions he would ask for the rest of his life.[22]

From the child's curiosity about the uncracked code of the written word to "picking" through a story to fluently reading, learning to read and write are not givens. Unlike oral language, which most children acquire naturally, alphabetic literacy is never automatic and rarely, if ever, entirely self-taught. Even in enslavement, Douglass had the temporary support of Mrs. Auld, the kindness of the "hungry little urchins" who became his teachers, and the spaces left in young Auld's copybook; his material circumstances, as he notes, were better than those of many of the poor white children with whom he traded bread, pocketed from the Aulds' house, for "the bread of knowledge." Literacy requires at the very least access to print—books, newspapers, signs—along with a "reading public," as Samuel Taylor Coleridge termed nineteenth-century England's expanding readership, and support from a parent, teacher, or more advanced peer. Formal schooling can support or undermine learning, depending on degrees of inequality, curricular priorities, and conscious or unconscious teacher biases, goals, and expectations for different classes of students. Informal learning, on the other hand, is ubiquitous, infinite in its potential, and fundamental to literacy acquisition of all kinds.

Apart from the accounts of widely read, authors like Douglass, Olaudah Equiano, and Harriet Ann Jacobs, relatively few slave narratives or other stories of the millions of enslaved Africans in the United States were recorded or published. The vast majority of literacy narratives, oral or written, are unknown or unread; some have yet to be added to the invaluable archives of oral

Richard Wright reading to his daughter Julia. The Langston Hughes Collection, Beinecke Rare Book and Manuscript Library, Yale University. Courtesy of the Estate of Richard Wright. Reprinted by permission of John Hawkins and Associates, Inc.

history interviews of the last generation of formerly enslaved people done in the 1920s and '30s by faculty and students at Southern University and Fisk University and by WPA federal writers. For better-known authors like Douglass—who had to prove their authenticity to dubious, white readers—the process by which they became literate depended on stolen lessons and informal contact with teachers and more literate peers. These "hidden transcripts" of history, as Heather Andrea Williams calls them, reveal how Black communities exerted their collective will to become educated. Such secrecy meant that recovering voices of history from below for a writer like Toni Morrison required her to imagine the interior lives of people whose situations were so precarious that they could not speak or write freely in their own times, who calculated their words, as Douglass did, to reach the widest readership and avoid alienating potential white allies with fuller accounts of the violent abuse and terror to which they were routinely subjected.[23]

Evidence of Wright's educational experience is hidden in plain sight in *Black Boy* and elsewhere. As William A. Proefriedt observes in an uncharacteristically balanced assessment of *Black Boy*, "On the one hand, ... Wright rejected his childhood; but on the other, he celebrated it." Even though he reported many events in his life as "cruel and terrifying," they were "transformed by him into educational experiences, experiences that helped to form the inquiring and sympathetic attitude toward the world he describes."[24] Education was highly prized by African Americans, including Wright's maternal grandparents according to Constance Webb, and he was an apt learner in and out of brick-and-mortar schools, mostly in the classrooms of everyday life, from many different homes and neighborhoods to the bluffs of Natchez overlooking the Mississippi River. Like other Black children growing up in the South, his experience was defined not only by white terror and its debilitating impact on them but also by the solidarity and social cohesiveness of Black communities.

Born into a period of quickly shifting global economic forces, Wright benefited from African American literacy practices passed down generationally in a dominant white culture that prohibited or restricted education for Black children, de jure or de facto, intensifying patterns of pervasive racism in the urban North as well as the South. In addition to having more stringent restrictions on African American education, most schools in the South, Black and white, lacked rigor and were poorly attended not only by Black children with hardscrabble lives like Wright's but also by working-class white children whose parents doubted the value of education. Such skepticism reflected socioeconomic conditions in the early stages of a massive shift from rural to urban life and a rapid expansion of industry that drove millions of Black and white southerners, including Wright and his family, to move north in the Great Migration from 1910 to 1975, and millions more Southern and Eastern Europeans to migrate to US cities. Although reading and writing would become increasingly important to employment opportunities, the majority of jobs in Wright's lifetime required little if any literacy knowledge. In contrast to today's national obsession with illiteracy in an information economy with a perpetual literacy crisis, northern schools in the early to mid-twentieth century were more concerned with Americanizing and assimilating migrant populations, using dominant traditionalist approaches that stressed American values of individual freedom, self-reliance, and hard work, along with basic skills and rote memorization.

As technological and industrial advancements accelerated, new economies of production required more advanced forms of literacy to meet labor demands through what Deborah Brandt calls "literacy sponsorship," by which she means "any agents, local or distant, concrete or abstract, who enable, support, teach, model, as well as recruit, regulate, suppress, or withhold literacy—and gain advantage by it in some way."[25] From slavery to the Civil War to Reconstruction to Jim Crow to the eventual failure of school desegregation after *Brown v. Board of Education* to persistent "savage inequalities" in education, Black Americans learned to sponsor their own literacy development.[26] They did so through secret codes; clandestine meetings; their own schools, including Freedom Schools; an unquenchable desire for education; and an enduring belief in the promise of democracy in a country that has yet to contend with its legacy and perpetuation of crimes against humanity with African Americans at the epicenter. That was the world into which Richard Wright was born and came of age.

Critical Literacies: Political Economies of Education
and the Struggle for Black Freedom

Viewing Wright's experience in the multilayered social context of the early twentieth-century Deep South illuminates aspects of his autobiography that have often been overlooked. The wider Black communities in which he lived in Mississippi, Tennessee, and Arkansas were shaped by the oppressive, violent conditions of southern life. But they also contained more welcoming alternative sites, embedded in everyday mutual support for generations of Black southerners through mostly informal networks of friends, families, churches, political organizations, and schools. Despite the racial politics of

American public education, severely limiting Black children's access to school in the 1910s and beyond, Wright benefited intellectually and socially from the relatively few years he spent in classrooms and was prepared to excel academically by everything he had learned outside school for the first twelve years of his life. This perspective pushes against the dominant view of him as a miraculous autodidact with a devastatingly bleak childhood to suggest a more varied experience. He had obviously managed to thrive on informal education that positioned him, having yet to complete one full year of school by age twelve, to skip grades within weeks of entering a new school as a fifth grader. In spite of many personal hardships, including his father's desertion, Granny Wilson's religious strictures, atomizing family tensions, near-deadly whippings, and his mother's protracted illness, he drew sustenance from the everyday world of his family, the wider community, and his mother Ella, who tutored him as a small child. Also vital to the development of his personality was the world of nature, which spoke to him, especially as a child and late in his life when he was ill and turned to writing haiku.

He had a natural brightness, aptitude, and inquisitiveness that sparked his curiosity, infused him with a desire to read, write, and learn, and prepared him to take what he could from the classroom, but that is not to say he was unique. His proclivity and potential as a writer, which secured him an enduring place in the annals of American—and world—literature, was realized through a process of socialization that he underwent like everyone else coming of age. Nor was it his intent to set himself apart from those for whom he spoke, as he explained in an interview in *PM* magazine: "I wanted to give, lend my tongue to the voiceless Negro boys. . . . That was one of my motives."[27] His exceptionality was thus enabled by the wider Black community in "hidden transcripts" in *Black Boy* that eluded that book's readers just as, in another era, they had eluded white slaveholders. To reveal the hidden-in-plain-sight text of the autobiography reevaluates his reputation as an autodidact—an inexplicable genius—in light of theories of human development that proceed from social to individual being, rather than the opposite. In addition to the political economic conditions that shape education in specific places and times, this dialectic of social and individual growth helps explain the inexplicable Richard Wright. It recasts the narrative of his childhood as pitilessly harsh in the context of the southern Black culture that produced him and classmates like Dick Jordan, Joe Brown, and Essie Lee Ward who also migrated to Chicago.

It was Essie's father, unnamed in *Black Boy*, who questioned Richard about the newspaper he was delivering to make a little money and read a pullout magazine featuring pulp fiction. The episode illustrates the social cohesiveness and high level of education, political consciousness, and caring of Black adults looking out for their own and other children in Jackson, Mississippi, in the early twentieth century. Mr. Ward, a family friend acting out of "racial pride," according to Wright, patiently led Richard to his own discovery of the racist content of the Klan-sponsored paper. Having delighted in the paper's "cheap pulp stories," the boy had never glanced at its other content until Mr. Ward asked him if he saw the cartoon of a Black man "with a greasy, sweaty face, thick lips, flat nose, golden teeth" sitting with his feet on a desk below a portrait of Abraham Lincoln depicted as a gangster. "Well, just look at that. Take your time and tell me what you think," he said, letting him puzzle over the image and draw his own conclusions. Even after Richard understood that the paper was preaching "Ku Klux Klan doctrines," Mr. Ward refrained from telling him what to do.

Rather, he acknowledged why it was important to him to sell the paper: "Listen, son. . . . You're a black boy and you're trying to make a few pennies," leaving it up to Richard to decide how to respond. The lesson proceeds with Mr. Ward reading aloud an article that argued lynching is "a solution for the problem of the Negro." Horrified, a chastened Richard promised "never again" to sell the paper and gave Essie's father back his dime, which he kindly returned, counseling, "Keep the dime, son. . . . But for God's sake, find something else to sell."[28] Mr. Ward's Socratic questions formed one of the "hidden transcripts" of Wright's boyhood education across several Black southern communities that punitively and lovingly nurtured the young to survive in the carceral state of Jim Crow. A quick learner, Richard needed a "teacher" to raise his awareness of the racist content of the newspaper, which he found in Mr. Ward, a community member and family friend. Eventually, Wright would abstract the general concept of the global oppressed and "the possibility of uniting scattered but kindred peoples into a whole" from the particular case of the Jim Crow South to "see deeper into the lives of men," as he put it, in their historically specific forms. His ability to do so sprang from his collective educational experience in the southern Black communities of his childhood and the interracial literary and political milieus of his adulthood that enabled him to generalize his early experience.[29]

Reading the World: The Unity of the Ordinary with the Extraordinary

A highly stylized bildungsroman, *Black Boy* reflects Wright's literary and political consciousness of himself as character and narrator, hero and author, everyman and rising literary star. Like Douglass in *Narrative of the Life of Frederick Douglass* and Joyce in *Portrait of the Artist as a Young Man*, Wright sought to speak for a people through a coming-of-age story situated in exigent historical contexts. How well he succeeded depended on his reader. Lewis Gannett wrote in the *New York Herald Tribune*, "It is an unforgettable book, and one which leaves you at the end questioning and wondering, as good books do." He concluded that it "may be one of the great American autobiographies." In a scathing critique in the *Tribune's Weekly Book Review*, W. E. B. Du Bois warned the reader "to regard it as creative writing rather than simply a record of life" and echoed harsh comments by white and Black critics alike who rejected Wright's representation of the deracinating effects of racism as a "misjudgment of black folk and the difficult repulsive characters among them that he is thrown with." On the other hand, asserting that Wright essentially had one story to tell, his friend, the sociologist Horace Cayton, observed that "in *Black Boy* he has retold it with even greater insight—with sharper tools he has dug out a deeper meaning." He also addressed the complaint about the book's "hatred and bitterness," incisively expressing Wright's central literary and political goal: to deliver "a sudden and violent rent in the veil behind which the Negro is living."[30]

Wright's tightly controlled, creatively written autobiography was meant to personalize the fictional stories he told in *Uncle Tom's Children* and *Native Son* in order to drive home the "bitter truth" of the dehumanization of Black Americans in an era when submission to the white power structure was expected, and mere existence—a suspicious laugh or the wrong way of looking at a white man or woman—was not tolerated, often provoking brutal, if not fatal, consequences. The central contradiction at the heart of the autobiography is between Wright's portrayal of his childhood and youth in light of the author he became and his representation of a collective Black experience—the "voiceless Negro boys"—of the Jim Crow South. As he told the *New Yorker* after the book appeared in 1944, "One of the things that made me write is that I realize that I'm a very average Negro.... Maybe that's what makes me extraordinary." It is this unity of the ordinary with the extraordinary that illuminates not only Wright's own life but also the truth he came to tell: the achievements, potential, and lost potential of millions of Black Americans forged by such circumstances.[31]

In *Black Boy*, he recalls a young schoolteacher, Ella, a boarder at his grandmother's house in Jackson, whose books intrigued him and who was "so remote and dreamy and silent... that I was as much afraid of her as I was attracted to her." Despite knowing that Granny Wilson disapproved, he begged Ella to tell him what was in the book she was reading. Reluctantly, fearing his grandmother's wrath, she beckoned him closer to whisper the story of Bluebeard, a man who "had duped and married his seven wives ... loved and slain them ... [and] hanged them up by their hair in a dark closet." Wright recalls that he "ceased to see the porch, the sunshine, her face, everything." Her words "fell upon new ears" and "as she spoke, reality changed, the look of things altered, and the world became peopled with magical presences.... The sensations the story aroused in me were never to leave me." He is transported to another world that will call to him for the rest of his life. That his trance is broken by Granny Wilson's outburst—Ella is an "evil gal," the books are "Devil stuff," and Richard will "burn in hell"—only quickened his desire for the "sharp, frightening, breathtaking, almost painful excitement" the folktale had awakened. He yearned to know the end of the story whose violent plot and secret murders so deeply fascinated him.[32]

At a certain point, it struck him that neither of his two major works of fiction—*Uncle Tom's Children* or *Native Son*—had pushed readers to confront the realities of Jim Crow as he had hoped. *Uncle Tom's Children* drew tears of pity from white liberals like Eleanor Roosevelt and *Native Son* failed to shock readers into recognition of the devastating effects of racial oppression. He was too far ahead of his times to win sympathy for a young, angry, urban-dwelling, alienated Black character like Bigger Thomas whose acts of violence challenged the very foundations of a social order at once righteous and profoundly hypocritical in its moral sense of itself. Instead, in his efforts to tear away the veil of racial codes and proprieties that governed Jim Crow America—to tell the truth about the demeaning, brutal racial relations that permeated everyday life—Wright unsettled middle-class Black audiences as much as or more than their white counterparts. When his friend Horace Cayton persuaded him to accept an invitation to speak at Fisk University in 1943 despite his disdain for the Black bourgeoisie, his speech was met by silence. He realized he was "saying things that Negroes were not supposed to say publicly, things that whites had forbidden."[33]

It was his reception that evening at Fisk that inspired him to start the autobiography that had been only a glimmer of an idea until then. He thought, "Although they might be able to ignore Bigger as a monster of fiction, they would have a difficult time rejecting the experiences of his creator." The story he would tell in *Black Boy* about his education was thus a literary record of growing up Black in the Jim Crow South that hinged on his own experience and the collective life he represented rather than his uniqueness, as many of his interlocutors insisted. Through his extensive study of Wright's life and work, Michel Fabre understood that he was "asserting the value of every human being and using his own life as the most convenient source of truth with which to reclaim the dignity of every black man." But even Fabre, perhaps influenced by Wright's detractors, white and Black, expressed doubts about the literary value of his work, referring to it as "never wholly successful." Nor does Fabre question the label "autodidact" that came to define Wright's intellectual and creative prowess as simultaneously exceptional and coarse, unrefined, never wholly equal to his white counterparts'. Even well-meaning contemporaries like Rolo revealed their insidious racial biases in marveling too much at what they saw as his inexplicable achievements.[34] Such reactions fail to grasp the dialectical process by which Black southerners created new subjectivities and forms of social reproduction, including education and art, to withstand the ruthless conditions of the Jim Crow South.

Neither Wright's ordinary childish curiosity nor his impulsive, often destructive behavior, nor still the social world into which he was born, were unique to him; rather, his childhood was in many respects typical in its hardships and trauma, caused by family members as well as the wider society, and in the richness of African American cultural beliefs and practices. Although his maternal grandparents were uneducated, they were proud that eight of their nine children survived and, to varying extents, thrived. Constance Webb writes, "All were educated. And to the Wilsons book learning was almost more important than food." Richard's mother Ella, their fourth child and second eldest daughter, born in 1883, became a schoolteacher who taught spelling, arithmetic, and geography in a one-room country school for four months a year, based on an agrarian calendar for growing and harvesting cotton. Webb describes her as "outwardly tractable" with "an unyielding determination to think her own thoughts and to act upon them."[35]

Given Webb's close friendship with Wright from 1944 to his death, her access to his files, including two diaries, hours of conversation with him in New York, Long Island, and Paris, and her evocative descriptions of his family, especially Ella, are telling: "Instead of sitting beside her mother in the evening or entering into long religious discussions, Ella often stood on the porch and leaned against the wall of the house. Usually she just stared up at the sky or into the dark night and watched the kerosene points which flickered from lamps in distant houses. At times she closed her eyes and seemed to be listening to the most ordinary sounds—crickets, or the wind in the grass, or the tree tap-tapping against the house. Mooning, her mother called it, but nothing she said made a difference or changed Ella." Even more instructive is Webb's observation that Ella "ignored racism as if it did not exist. All men and nature were part of a whole, she felt, and there should not be so much friction in the world." Nor, despite their class and educational differences, did Ella feel superior to Nathaniel Wright, Richard's father, whom she met at age twenty-four and fell in love with at a Methodist church social. They married a month later in defiance of her parents, who disapproved of him because he was an illiterate sharecropper, declaring, "He's not our kind."

Webb also describes Richard's father more warmly as a handsome young man "with high cheekbones inherited from his Indian forebears and a face kept from starkness, softened, by his African heritage." These portraits of Wright's grandparents and parents reveal a different side of them than he depicts in his autobiography from the perspective of a grandson and son, especially as he recalls the violence and harshness of his early childhood years. In Webb's biography, based on her conversations with him, we see his maternal grandparents as eager for their children to become literate and enjoy a life of the mind, and his parents as youthful lovers, lacking class pretensions, his mother filled with inexpressible longing for a life beyond Granny Wilson's religious constrictions, his father beaten down by the impoverished conditions into which he was born. The value that his family placed on education and his mother's experience as a teacher until financial stress forced her to work as a cook for white employers underscore the tenor of the social world into which he was born, infused by the aspirations and achievements of two generations. Such hopes and dreams, particularly with respect to education, were common in southern Black communities, especially in cities like Jackson and Memphis.[36]

To reiterate Wright's paradoxical, incisive explanation of what made him extraordinary: it was his recognition of his ordinariness. One of the most vivid examples of preliteracy learning in *Black Boy* appears in the opening pages of the book, immediately after a bored, rebellious, four-year-old Richard set fire to his grandmother's white curtains, ignoring his younger brother Leon's protests, hid under the porch of the burning house until his father spied him, and then suffered in bed, besieged by nightmares, after his frantic, furious mother whipped him with a tree limb to the point of unconsciousness. For the young Richard, the event and its aftermath were terrifying; it must have been as bad or worse for everyone who feared he had died in the fire. But Webb's note that the Hoskins, his cousins, who lived a few blocks away in Jackson, "thought it was something of a joke" since no one was injured, suggests that the event was perceived differently by adults. Webb describes them as being amused by Richard's antics: "That child! What will he do next?" At the same time, foreshadowing his literary future, his dreams were full of "huge wobbly white bags, like the full udders of cows," which he feared would burst and douse him with "some horrible liquid." His Freudian nightmares were steeped with the terrifying knowledge that his mother had come close to killing him. And yet, he then turns to a poetic invocation of the natural world by the "yellow, dreaming waters of the Mississippi River from the verdant bluffs of Natchez," which spoke to him in boyhood "with a cryptic tongue."[37]

This Whitmanesque homage to nature does two things: it contrasts sharply with the delirium from his whipping and his resentment—he was "angry, fretful, and impatient"—at being cooped up and told to keep quiet in his grandmother's house because she was ill; and it conjures a boyhood filled with infinite possibility, with "tantalizing melancholy," "aching glory," "cosmic cruelty," and "quiet terror." Absorbing the world around him, he notices garden paths, wild geese flying south, the smell of burning hickory, sparrows in the "red dust of country roads," a crawfish tortured in a rusty can, green leaves rustling like rain, a blue-skinned snake asleep in the sun. The narrative voice fuses with the child's perception. That this lyrical interlude comes early in the book, describing sun-strewn paths and dreamy waters overlaid by foreboding signs of bleakness, torture, secrecy, panic, death without dying, and terror, attests both to the beauty he perceived in his surroundings and to the conditions of life that necessitated what the Brazilian literacy educator Paulo Freire calls "reading the world" as a way of knowing, a means of survival. That the interlude directly follows the trauma of the fire and his mother's violent, near-lethal punishment signals the immediacy and ambiguity of the existential threats he endured, resonating with the epigraph to Part One, "Southern Night," from Job: "His strength shall be hunger-bitten, / And destruction shall be ready at his side" (18:12). Of course, it is the poet Wright whose language conveys these sharply etched memories, but it is the young boy who attentively listens to the world's cryptic tongue.[38]

Another early childhood lesson in the accretion of Wright's formative experiences takes place in Memphis, where his family of four moved that same year into a one-story tenement with one bedroom and a kitchen. What stays constant in his young life are the stultifying constraints of silence and suppression of youthful energy imposed first by his grandmother's illness and then by his father's authoritarian rule and work schedule as a night porter at a Beale Street drugstore. Sternly warned to be quiet during the day to let his father sleep, Richard had to submit or risk punishment. He had come by then to see his father as an ominous force in the cramped tenement: the "lawgiver... quite fat [with a] bloated stomach... always a stranger to me, always somehow alien and remote." When a stray kitten insistently meowed even after Richard and his brother fed it, their father yelled at the cat and then shouted, "Kill that damn thing." Though Richard knew not to take his father's words literally, he saw an opportunity for revenge and resolved to kill the kitten. His younger brother Leon, who had warned Richard against setting fire to their grandmother's curtains, now admonished him not to kill the cat. Undeterred, Richard tied a rope around its neck and hung it from a tree. "You did bad," his brother moralized, running to tell their mother.[39]

Horrified to see the cat dangling from the tree limb, Ella Wright took Richard to his father's bedside. When Richard said he only did what he was told, his father, disgusted but disarmed, told him to get out of his sight. Wright concludes: "I had my first triumph over my father. I had made him believe that I had taken his words literally." Such literacy lessons are rhetorical rather than alphabetic, part of a natural process by which children acquire not only language but also a way of being-in-the-world, an attitude, a capacity to discern, to puzzle, to question, to talk back, to interpret signs whose meanings are often the inverse of how they appear. Richard's insight enabled him to take his father's figurative expression literally to resist and defy him. It was his mother who taught him to regret his actions, by insisting that he owed a debt he could not repay to the innocent cat. She forced him to confront the "moral horror involved in taking a life" and rejected his excuse that he did as his father told him, whacking him across the mouth and exclaiming, "You stop that lying! You knew what he meant." Later, she ordered him out into the dark night to untie the stiff dead kitten, dig a grave, and bury it, after which she made him pray with her, asking God to spare his life although he had not spared the kitten's and "not to snatch the breath of life" from him as he slept. Terrified, he ran into the dark, "crying, shaking with dread."[40]

Racial and Class Consciousness: Speaking with a Clearer Tongue

These dramatic scenes of Wright's childhood depict the harsh conditions of his early life, defined by racial terror and poverty, family fractures, and the fraught relationship of Black Americans to the white-ruled South. But they also evoke, if only implicitly, the "richness of southern black culture," a quality of life that bell hooks comments on in relation to what it was like to live in segregated southern Black communities as she was growing up in the 1950s. Reflecting on that environment, having lived and worked in predominantly white communities and colleges as an adult, she remarks, "Black southern folk experience was the foundation of the life around me when I was a child:

that experience no longer exists in many places where it was once all of life that we knew."[41] Without sentimentalizing an often unhappy existence, one that Wright described as bleak and barren but also as "breathlessly anxious fun" with an "aura of limitless freedom," his experience resonates with the fierce love and communal values of the Black South that hooks recalls, evinced by his mother's sometimes violent lessons, her siblings' responsiveness to her sons' and her needs after she fell ill, and neighbors like Mr. Ward who looked after other peoples' children as well as their own. This rich southern Black life also enveloped Wright as a child, encompassing the full range of the human experience, good and bad. Dehumanized by the dominant white culture, impoverished by racial oppression, that life, including scenes of education routinely elided in readings of *Black Boy*, was forged by untold or underacknowledged Black struggles for freedom and equality that spanned American history, driving the nation toward the ideals on which it claimed to have been founded.

The literacy narrative embedded in Wright's autobiography echoes and attests to the importance that generations of African Americans conditioned by slavery, Jim Crow, and the long civil rights movement placed on learning to read and write, seeking education wherever they could find it. They did so primarily and atypically, not in response to economic imperatives of the state or solely for their own financial gain but rather to participate in civil society. Such education was delivered clandestinely, in the antebellum South, where learning to read often met with severe punishment; in churches tolerated as places of worship that also served as community schools; in African Free Schools before and after the Civil War; in segregated public schools during Jim Crow; and in Freedom Schools during and after the 1960s civil rights movement. Even in the best circumstances, literacy development relies on informal learning as much as or more than on formal education. That informal learning includes talking, singing, storytelling, and reading aloud, assisted by adults and older children. A social tool gradually internalized as inner speech or thought, language is key to two of the early childhood dramas that establish a foundation for the life story Wright tells, retells, writes, and rewrites at various junctures before and after drafting *Black Boy*. Double-voiced in its individual and collective portraits of Black boyhood in the Deep South, his autobiography also depicts the social world that shaped him and his generation.

While much has been said about the consequences of his wanton destruction of property (his grandmother's curtains) and life (the noisy kitten), and the near-fatal corporal and moral punishment he suffered as a result, far less attention has been paid to their sociocultural meaning and educational impact. Each event speaks to the violence and complex expressions of love in African American family relations in the white-ruled South, culminating in Wright's awakening to the mysteries of the natural world after recovering from his mother's beating for setting fire to the curtains and an Oedipal victory over his father by twisting his words to his own advantage, offset by his mother's morality lesson. This mix of curiosity and resistance, self-assertion and self-abnegation, love and rage, sympathy and sternness, discipline and abuse in Wright's recollections of childhood has been lost on readers who only perceive its negative valence, insensible to the survival lessons that were essential to educating Black children.

Readers from his biographer Michel Fabre to his friend Ralph Ellison have dwelled on how ferociously Ella Wright punished Richard, whom she nearly beat to death more than once. In "The Ethics of Living Jim Crow," he tells a story more fully than in *Black Boy* of a cinder fight between two gangs, one white and the other Black, during which one of the white boys hurled a broken milk bottle at him that left a gash behind his ear in need of three stitches. A neighbor saw the fight and took him to a doctor, after which, mulling over what happened, he waited outdoors for his mother to get home from her job as a cook for white people, certain she would comfort him. Instead, she slapped him and yelled, "How come yuh didn't hide? . . . How come yuh awways fightin'?" According to Wright, she then "grabbed a barrel stave, dragged me home, stripped me naked, and beat me till I had a fever of one hundred and two. She would smack my rump with the stave, and, while the skin was still smarting, impart to me gems of Jim Crow wisdom."[42]

This wisdom was—and continues to be in the New Jim Crow era—a reality Black parents face that white and other more privileged groups are spared. For a Black mother, to beat a son senseless was to teach the lessons of Jim Crow in order to keep him alive. The scenes of punishment in Wright's autobiographical writing thus reveal deep maternal love as well as brutal physical and psychological punishment, the latter having often eclipsed the former in the child's memory. A year or so after he set the house on fire, Ella more purposely taught him the value of a living creature when she made him bury the cat in the dark of night. In each instance, Richard's curiosity, rebelliousness, and energy tested adults whose actions and enigmas angered, perplexed, and fascinated him. His invocation of the language of nightmares, his homage to nature's beauty and terror, enact the verbal potential of a child voiced by the adult poet he would become, expressing the spontaneous consciousness of what must have been mainly a felt sense in childhood. It is the mother-child relationship, in particular, that infuses such drama with tenderness, love, and the pedagogical intent of protecting the young from the terrors of Jim Crow. Wright's dedication of *Native Son* to his mother reminds us of his gratitude for her impact on his literary imagination: "To My Mother who, when I was a child at her knee, taught me to revere the fanciful and the imaginative."

His prose style has been called course, flat, "syntactically overburdened," prolix, didactic, and dogged, among other pejoratives.[43] Yet, his early and late poems and the poetic quality of so much of his writing—fiction and nonfiction—belie such critiques; consider, for example, the lyrical passages woven into his narrative of early childhood. The first passage follows the episode of the fire, taking us to the hauntingly fierce beauty of the Mississippi delta. Twice more the poet's voice appears at a point of crisis in a sort of adult ventriloquy of the child's felt but not yet fully verbal appreciation of the world, as if only poetic language could give shape and meaning to the early revelations of preliterate life. The second outpouring of free verse follows Richard's obscene response to Granny as she sat watching his brother and him bathe in separate tubs, flinging sudsy water at one another and disregarding her reprimands to stop their foolishness. Thoroughly annoyed, she called Richard to her. He walked naked, soaking wet, across the floor to her chair, where she washed his ears and face, then told him to bend over, and began to scrub his anus. "When you get through, kiss back there," he said to her dreamily, not really knowing what the words meant, whereupon Granny froze in horror and whipped him with the wet towel. He ran naked out of the room, chased by his mother, who was equally horrified to hear what he had said, through the kitchen and outside the house into the backyard, where he stubbed his toes and screamed. Finally, he hid under the bed as his grandfather threatened to get his gun and he begged, "Please don't shoot me."[44]

Ultimately, his behavior resulted in another maternal beating and also the eviction of the young schoolteacher Ella, whose wicked stories Granny blamed for Richard's moral depravity despite his protestations that he didn't know where he learned the words whose meaning he had yet to understand (possibly, he thought, at a saloon where customers had amused themselves by getting the six-year-old boy drunk on whiskey). After relating this incident, Wright bursts into free verse marked by repetition of "There was" at the beginning of each long line except the first and the last. The first line recalls the "cryptic" world the younger Richard perceived, announcing that the "days and hours" had begun to speak with a "clearer tongue." Like the first litany of experiences, each with a "sharper meaning of its own," this poetic incantation is a paean to nature—fireflies, sweet magnolias, tall green grass, "a boll of cotton whose cup had spilt over," a bumblebee, the taste of persimmons, wild hickory nuts, blackberries, and "stolen, unripe peaches." It also deepens and softens our appraisal of his relationship with his grandparents—he goes fishing and visits a sawmill with his grandfather and is amused by the "baffled stares" of townspeople at his grandmother, "an old white woman," with her two Black grandchildren in tow. The final line, which breaks the pattern, describes "long, slow drowsy days and nights of drizzling rain . . . ," ending in an ellipsis that suggests this tribute to the child's still unvocalized response to the mysteries of existence is far from done; he has yet to fuse thought and language into the written word.[45]

The last poetic interlude, also in chapter 2, signals Wright's emergence from spontaneous fantasies into a consciousness of race, the wider world, and his first inkling of the possibility of acting on that world. After his battle with Granny Wilson, connoting the end of early childhood, his brother, mother, and he traveled to Elaine, Arkansas, to stay with his aunt Maggie and uncle Silas Hoskins, who owned a saloon profitable enough to make it desirable to white men who threatened to lynch him and eventually did. Hoskins's murder forced Wright and his family to flee the next morning, foregoing any funeral arrangements or even a period of mourning as they sought to escape "that white-hot face of terror that we knew loomed somewhere above us," an experience, notably, "*as close as white terror had ever come*" to Wright (emphasis added). When he asked Ella why they had not "fought back," out of fear, she slapped him silent. A year later, over several days starting on September 30, 1919, more than 100 African Americans attempting to unionize and negotiate better wages and working conditions were killed by a white mob in what became known as the Elaine massacre. But well before these terrifying events, which scarred Wright for life and which almost certainly influenced the story "Bright and Morning Star" included in the second edition of *Uncle Tom's Children*, he describes his own dawning consciousness about race after having learned to count from the coal man and begun to read the Sunday newspaper with his mother's guidance.

He recalls that it was then, at age six, that he was wondering about the "relations between whites and blacks," and he notes that "what I learned frightened me." Although surrounded by white people, he had not been conscious of Black-white relations, he speculates, because there were so many white-looking people in his family, including his grandmother, "who was white as any 'white' person" but "had never looked 'white'" to him. When news circulated that a white man severely beat a Black boy, he interpreted the event as normal, assuming that the man was the father of the boy and therefore had a paternal right to punish him. But when he asked his mother about it, she corrected his use of the word "whipping" to describe what happened: the man *beat* the boy, Ella firmly told Richard; he did not *whip* him. When Richard asked why, she told him he was too young to understand, whereupon he declared that he would never let anyone beat him. "Then stop running wild in the streets," she snapped.[46]

At the Jackson train station, with his newfound "sense of the two races" engendering "a sharp concreteness" in his appreciation of the reality of his social world, Richard noticed the segregated "white" and "black" ticket lines and asked Ella if he could go "peep" at the white people. Her admonition to stop "talking foolishness" triggered a stream of questions about the "two sets of people who lived side by side and never touched, except in violence." In one of many dialogues with Ella that captures her gift for repartee, her words full of impatience, protectiveness, humor, and love, he asked about his grandmother, whose whiteness further complicated for him the peculiar nature of race relations. The conundrum of her appearance and her conflicting racial identity—she looked white but was not—pushed him to seek explanations wherever he could find them for the discrepancy between exterior forms and interior meanings. Was she born white? Did white people think she was white? If she looked white, why was she living with them? Did she become colored when she married his grandfather? How could she be Black if she was white? In the course of this conversation, Ella "grudgingly" told Richard that his grandmother was Irish, Scotch, and French, into "which Negro blood had somewhere and somehow been infused," and that his father had red, white, and Black in him, to which Richard replied, "Indian, white, and Negro?" This disjuncture between skin color and ethnicity in which white-looking people like Granny Wilson were seen as "Black" opened Wright to a new, critical, higher level of consciousness of the world into which he was born.[47]

Resettled with Aunt Maggie—Richard's favorite aunt, "another mother" to him—in West Helena, Arkansas, after a brief stay with his grandmother, the matriarchal home to which his brother, mother, and he repeatedly returned, Richard bore witness to his aunt's second panicked departure to escape white violence. This time, police were more justifiably in pursuit of his new "uncle," Professor Matthews, as Maggie called the mysterious man who secretly visited her at night. He had knocked a woman unconscious as he was robbing her and then set fire to her house to conceal his crime. That night, Richard awoke to the sound of Maggie sobbing as she and her boyfriend hastily prepared to flee town despite Ella's objections, leaving Richard once again to grapple with the fear of racial violence and his mother's grim, severe response to it. Sternly, she warned him never to mention what happened, because if white people thought he knew, they would kill him. When he timidly asked if

Maggie's boyfriend had killed somebody, his mother snapped, "If anybody heard you say that, you'll die."[48]

Shortly after Aunt Maggie's departure, a final burst of poetry in *Black Boy* resounds with superstition, religion, folktales, fairytales, and childhood in a litany of "if-then" declarations that begins, "Up or down the wet or dusty streets, indoors or out, the days and nights began to spell out magic possibilities." These sayings range from the familiar ("If I walked under a leaning ladder, I would certainly have bad luck") to the arcane ("If I wore a bit of asafetida in a little bag tied about my neck, I would never catch a disease"). It is the pages that follow, however, that demand attention in relation to Wright's education in and out of school, for it is here that he traces his own process of becoming, from the heady assertion that "anything seemed possible, likely, feasible, because I wanted everything to be possible" to the acknowledgement that "he had no power to make things happen outside of me in the objective world," and further that it was because his "environment was bare and bleak" that he "endowed it with unlimited potentialities, redeemed it for the sake of my own hungry and cloudy yearning."[49]

By age nine or ten, Wright had permanently internalized a "dread of white people" as World War I was subsiding and the intensifying racial tensions and conflicts throughout the South were affecting him far more directly than had the distant war. The incessant threat of "invisible whites" and stories of white violence against Black people filled him with "awe, wonder, and fear," leading, as was always the case, to endless questions. A story that would form the basis for the character Aunt Sue in "Bright and Morning Star" nearly twenty years later recounts the heroism of a Black woman who tricked a white mob who had lynched her husband into allowing her to attend his burial, during which she unwrapped a gun from a folded sheet and killed four men. Whether the story was factually true or not, Wright declares it was "emotionally true" and he would "emulate the black woman," observing that her courage had given "form and meaning to confused defensive feelings that had long been sleeping in me." The pivotal moment in this series of reflections illuminates his struggle to grasp the meaning of his existence beyond "spontaneous fantasies," which compensated for the helplessness he felt under constant threat of violence. Thus, he affirms, even as he clung to them, that his "imaginings . . . had no objective value whatsoever" because the fantasies lived only in his head. Though these imaginings formed a "moral bulwark" protecting his "emotional integrity" and would become a condition of his existence, he intimates the possibility that, even if knowledge could not save him from a white mob, it would transcend "spontaneous fantasies" and have objective value. Here is the internationally renowned writer and Marxist analyzing his childhood, echoing the teachings of Vladimir Lenin on the transformation of spontaneous to conscious working-class activity as workers came to understand that only planned, collective action could advance their struggle not only to win better working conditions but also to abolish the system that exploited them.[50]

The Valedictorian: Richard Wright Goes to School

Smith Robertson Junior High School closed in 1971 during the court-ordered desegregation of Jackson public schools. When it first opened in 1894, it was the West Jackson Colored School, known as the "Mother School," the only public elementary school for Black children. In 1903, it was renamed Smith Robertson in honor of the city's first Black alderman. Born into slavery in Alabama in 1847, Robertson had bought his freedom and moved to Jackson, where he worked as a barber and became involved in local politics. The school was rebuilt in brick after the wood-framed building burned down in 1909 and remodeled in art deco style in 1929, and after it closed in 1971, it was designated as a historical site on the National Register of Historical Places in 1977. That building still stands as the Smith Robertson Museum and Cultural Center, established in 1984 after a group led by the historians Jessie Bryant Mosley and Alferdteen Harrison petitioned the city to save it and preserve African American history with exhibits on the Great Migration, treasures of Africa, and the school's story. At the entrance to the museum, visitors encounter the word "Awkwaba," meaning "welcome" in Twi, a dialect of the Akan language in southern and central Ghana. It was at Smith Robertson that Wright completed his last two years of school from 1923 to 1925, graduating from the ninth grade at age seventeen as class valedictorian. His name is emblazoned on the bronze plaque outside the museum, attesting to local appreciation for the famous alumnus but also for the school that nurtured him, at least for a while, and generations of other Black children.

The history of Smith Robertson epitomizes the counternarrative about Wright that I've tried to convey in this chapter—a story of collective struggle and determination, of communities of color in the Jim Crow South who fought for freedom and equality, and who saw education and literacy as tools not only for economic survival but also for full participation in civil society. To make this claim is not to idealize African American history or to deny Wright's negation of "black life" as absent "real kindness" as well as tenderness, passion, hope, joy, traditions, memories, and human bonds, and his further observation of "how shallow was even our despair." I do not mean to minimize the "essential bleakness" and "cultural barrenness" he describes in two, oft-quoted paragraphs at the beginning of chapter 2 of *Black Boy* that echo his depiction of impoverished, alienated Black life in *Native Son* and that deeply offended many critics, especially the Black bourgeoisie.

There is much to say about these paragraphs: they are parenthetical. Why? Because they are born of his "habit of reflection." And what does he mean by "reflection"? Is he here alluding to dialectical materialism, the method he advocates in "Blueprint for Negro Writing"? Is this habit of reflection akin to the spectacles he imagines having put on in "How 'Bigger' Was Born," with power like "that of an x-ray enabling me to see deeper into the lives of men"? Four other parenthetical passages weave together the autobiography, three of them in Part Two, "The Horror and the Glory." Like the poetic interludes, the bracketed reflections interrupt and interact with the narrative. Here is Wright thinking aloud, in dialogue with himself and his reader, striving to grasp the interpenetration of opposites—black and white, barrenness and fullness, the natural and the cultural—wondering if the human qualities he so desperately seeks are "native with man" or "fostered, won, struggled, and suffered for, preserved in ritual from one generation to another." Following the list of negative qualities, he comments on the irony of popular perceptions of "Negroes" as emotionally strong when he saw instead "our negative confusions, our flights, our fears. Our frenzy under pressure." The problem Wright presents is that Black Americans had not been "allowed to catch the full spirit of Western civilization, that they lived somehow in it but not of it."[51]

The parenthetical commentaries that follow deepen the dialectical process by which his life story and the critical consciousness shaping it forge individual and communal realities. It is in these passages—which function like answers to the poetic interludes representing the child's spontaneous responses to the world—that Wright pulls away the veil to reveal the essential relations of structural racism that simultaneously oppressed and empowered Black Americans. For, as he notes in the penultimate parenthetical meditation,

> I would make it known that the real danger [to the ruling class] does not stem from those who try to grab their share of wealth through force, or from those who try to defend their property through violence, for both of these groups, by their affirmative acts, support the values of the system in which they live. The millions that I would fear are those who do not dream of the prizes that the nation holds forth, for it is in them, though they may not know it, that a revolution has taken place and is biding its time to translate itself into a new and strange way of life.[52]

Wright's critique of the crass materialism of Western life, which reduces everything to "making more and more articles for [people] to consume" is implicit in this passage about the danger to the ruling class: neither fighting for wealth nor defending property on the part of the masses of working and poor people would dismantle a system based on private property that inexorably produces more useless commodities and more inequality. Rather, it was those who rejected the hollow prizes of such a structurally unequal, commodified system who constituted a revolutionary force capable of ushering in a new society.[53]

The paragraph that follows in the fourth interjection moves from a class analysis to discussion of the "Negroes' relation to America" as "symbolically peculiar," creating an exigency for Black Americans, from whose "ultimate reactions to their trapped state a lesson can be learned about America's future." This perspective echoes the closing lines of the essay "Portrait of Harlem," which Wright coauthored with Claude McKay in 1938 for the WPA volume *New York Panorama*: "The question of what will ultimately happen to the Negro in New York is bound up with the question of what will happen to the Negro in America. It has been said that the Negro embodies the 'romance of American life'; if that is true, the romance is one whose glamor is overlaid with shadows of tragic premonition." The unambiguous message from white America to African Americans in *Black Boy* is that "their native land is not their own"; that when they act according to universal human impulses—by which I think he broadly means the yearning to be free and to thrive—white racists "retaliate with terror," ignoring "the consequences should the Negroes give up completely." To "give up" in this context was to cease demanding inclusion in an inherently unequal system; the alternative was to engage in or be coiled for revolutionary action. Wright decisively concludes, "An insurgent act is but a man's desperate answer to those who twist his environment so that he cannot fully share the spirit of his native land. Treason is a crime of the state." That is to say, it was the state, not those who revolted against it, that had created inequalities, permitted exploitation of labor, betrayed its own promises and people, and instigated revolutionary movements; moreover, Wright prophesied, the fate of America was bound up with the fate of its most oppressed population, working-class African Americans.[54]

The second, third, and fifth sets of parenthetical comments touch on, respectively, the complexity of race relations and the material conditions that shape individuals' destinies according to their racial classification; the psychology of racial oppression and the existential crisis it sets in motion; and the conflict between "the artist and the politician," who were "committed to the same vision" yet "locked in a struggle." The passage on the psychology of racial oppression follows two very different scenes of Black submission to white rule: a description of the Black elevator operator Shorty's painful self-degradation to get a quarter from a white man in return for letting him kick "his broad, fleshy ass," and an account of Wright's deep fear of white people enacted in his encounter with a sympathetic white northerner who saw how hungry he was and offered him a dollar. Eighteen years old, working in Memphis for an optical company, and always suspicious of any white person's intentions, Wright did his best to decline the offer and politely walk away, but he also had to abide by the Jim Crow code of not offending white people. These white men formed a "kind of superworld," he observes; the white Yankee "did not know how dangerous his words were."[55]

Explaining the chasm between white and Black worlds in the next set of comments, Wright alludes again to the story of Shorty, who taught him that "perhaps even a kick was better than uncertainty," and notes that, for himself, Wright chose "not to submit" and thus "embraced the daily horror of anxiety, of tension, of eternal disquiet." He calls the "area into which the Negro mind in America had been shunted" a "No Man's Land," a term for the disputed territory between opposing armies, which resonated with the experience, in particular, of Black soldiers returning from service in World War I. Also appearing in *Native Son* and "How 'Bigger' Was Born," for Wright the phrase defines a liminal space in which the Black proletariat is "hovering unwanted between two worlds—between powerful America and his own stunted place in life." To be in No Man's Land is to be trapped, in limbo, prompting Wright to wonder "if there had ever existed in all human history a more corroding and devastating attack upon the personalities of men than the idea of racial discrimination." He concludes that his own coming to consciousness of the effects of racism was in response not only to external events like lynchings, of which he was well aware, but also to "crossed-up feelings ... psychic pain ... [in which] Negro life was a sprawling land of unconscious suffering."[56]

The last set of parenthetical comments in the autobiography is in response to the CPUSA's decision to dissolve the John Reed Clubs, which deeply distressed Wright, for whom the club had provided vital support. Even as he criticized the Party's unilateral decision, he acknowledged that writers like him who were "at odds with our culture" had responded energetically and enthusiastically to the Party's assurance that "your rebellion is right.... We will support your vision with militant action." Among other reasons to join the Party, young radical writers had an international readership insofar as their writing was translated and published in multiple languages worldwide. As

Wright put it, "Who had ever, in all human history, offered to young writers an audience so vast?" Moreover, he and the other writers "wrote what we felt." They were "confronted with a picture of a revolutionary and changing world" and "our hope, our anger at oppression, our dreams of a new life ... spilled out without coercion, without the pleading of anyone."[57] Indicative of Wright's lifelong interrogation of class and racial conflict and his "dreams of a new life," these passages suggest the process by which he was working out the theoretical concepts and political economic conditions of class struggle in relation to the history of chattel slavery, the rise of capitalism, and the resurgence of white supremacy throughout the South after 1877. In this pursuit he joined Black radicals, including, among others, W. E. B. Du Bois, Cyril Briggs, Otto Huiswoud, Frantz Fanon, and Eric Williams, to whom he dedicated *Black Power*, who brought their own lived experience to bear on their analysis of global capitalism and the particular form it took in the Americas and the large swaths of the world that had been colonized. The dialectical relationship between class and race not only enabled a theoretical analysis of the dynamics of capitalism but also cast African Americans in the role of revolutionary leaders, possessed of what Du Bois famously termed "double consciousness" and Wright called "double vision," as class conflict deepened and took on a new, sharper character in the United States in the aftermath of the Russian Revolution.[58]

Wright's grasp of the historical material forces and relations of production of slavery and its virulently racist aftermath—which his generation suffered acutely in its close proximity to the Civil War, the failure of Reconstruction, and the rise of Jim Crow—was rooted in his racial and class consciousness as the son of a tenant farmer father and a declassed petit bourgeois schoolteacher mother whose disability after multiple strokes at a young age left him mainly to fend for himself. That literacy figures so prominently in his coming-of-age story is no accident; nor are his accounts of his own literacy education and the importance he attaches to becoming literate for others with less access to tools to explain the world he was so curious to understand. The representation of reality through symbols—text, numbers, and images—in what he perceived and what he created was a portal to unlocking the mysteries of the world he knew, the past that produced it, the imagined universe of tales like Charles Perrault's "Bluebeard," a vision of humanity's future, and a weapon that he came to share with left-wing socialists, communists, anarchists, unionists, and Pan-Africanists fighting as, with, and for the world's dispossessed.

CHAPTER THREE

On Becoming a Marxist

Wright's engagement with Marxism has been the subject of much debate. Some observers insist that his move to Paris in 1947—his "roll in the hay with the existentialism of Sartre," as Arna Bontemps put it—derailed his career, his radical vision, his African American roots, and his commitment to social realist literature. When his eagerly awaited, second novel *The Outsider* was published in 1953, thirteen years after *Native Son*, Lorraine Hansberry blasted his "new philosophy" as "the glorification of—nothingness," lamenting that he had "been away from home for a long time" and had forgotten "the beauty of strength in the eyes of the working people of the Southside." Wright, she declared, was himself "an outsider . . . outcast from his own people. He exalts brutality and nothingness; he negates the reality of our struggle for freedom and yet works energetically in behalf of our oppressors."[1] In 1944, conservative and liberal critics had welcomed his public break from the CPUSA, while his former comrades upbraided him for it. His close friend in Paris, the cartoonist Ollie Harrington, intimated that he remained more than a Marxist and that he "never failed to credit" his literary success "to his discovery of Marx, Engels, and Lenin."[2]

Celebrated and attacked from the left and the right after the appearance of his first collection of stories in 1938, Wright has variously been seen as a dupe of US Communism; a puppet of Moscow; a student of Marx and Lenin victimized by ham-fisted Party leaders who disrespected his literary ambitions; the most illustrious writer in the Party; and a traitor for leaving, choosing exile, and forsaking emancipatory struggles in the United States. He was, in other words, an enigma whose political perspective, especially after 1944, became increasingly hard to decipher. As Cedric Robinson notes, "Distinct and, in some instances, opposing political factions . . . concur[red] on the desirability of the suppression of his work and ideas."[3] The conflation of the CPUSA with Stalinism and Marxism, together with well-funded Western campaigns to destabilize the left internationally, further complicate evaluating the arc of his life and work in relation to Marxist thought and his creative process. That he adopted a Marxist worldview in the 1930s is clear. In 1938, he told the *Daily Worker*, "I owe my literary development to the Communist Party and its influence. . . . It gave me my first full-bodied vision of Negro life in America."

The key to whether and to what extent he remained a Marxist after he quietly broke with the CPUSA in 1942 is rooted in how he became a Communist.[4]

In a tantalizing reply to a question about his reading habits in a September 1960 interview, Wright listed his usual favorite novelists, including James T. Farrell, Nelson Algren, Dostoevsky, and Theodore Dreiser, and then told the French journalist Annie Brièrre, "And I should like to add that I am fond of Freud and Marx, not from a political angle but because they are poets."[5] His political evolution as a Marxist, from his arrival in Chicago in 1927 to his departure from the United States and move to Paris in 1947, involved his membership in the John Reed Club, which he joined in 1933, meeting "men and women whom I would know for decades to come and who were to form the first sustained relationships in my life"; his recruitment to the CPUSA in 1934; his move to New York City in 1937 to advance his career as a writer; and his final official break from the Party in 1944. The impact of those two decades on Wright—what led him to see Marx as a poet—is embedded in the political institutions and relations that shaped him and so many other members of the radical cultural front of the 1930s.[6]

Portrait of the Artist as a Young Communist

Early on, Wright sought to tear away the veil of "racial uplift" maintained in its various guises by the white liberal establishment and Black bourgeoisie, a "talented tenth," and stand in solidarity with the global masses of Black peasants and domestic and industrial workers whose conditions of life gave them a unique historical role to play. In 1937, when he published "Blueprint for Negro Writing," he was addressing early twentieth-century Black leaders, including, presumably, W. E. B. Du Bois, who coined the term "talented tenth"—a concept he later modified as he moved to the left—as well as the conservative accommodationist Booker T. Washington. Wright denounced them as voices "of the educated Negro pleading with white America for justice," whose best writing was "rarely . . . addressed to the Negro himself, his needs, his sufferings, his aspirations." Meanwhile, he envisaged a mass Black readership as part of a revolutionary vanguard. He shifted the debate from cultivating a "talented tenth" of vanguard intellectuals to a fervent call for writers to emulate militant Black workers. "That Negro workers, propelled by the harsh conditions of their lives," he declared, "have demonstrated this consciousness and mobility for economic and political action there can be no doubt."[7]

Such consciousness, he explained, could be seen in their support of the labor organizer Angelo Herndon, charged in Atlanta, Georgia, with insurrection for possession of Communist literature, and the Scottsboro Boys, falsely accused of rape in Alabama, as well as Black workers' efforts to unionize and mobilize antilynching campaigns—all of which were endorsed, supported, and often organized by the CPUSA. To the question of whether "creative writers had taken advantage of their unique minority position," Wright's answer was a decisive no; the rest of the essay can be read as an explanation of this failure and a challenge to Black writers to take up the tasks he outlined as necessary.[8] Nearly a decade after writing "Blueprint," he published Part One of *Black Boy*, amplifying yet also complicating this political challenge.

Despite a review of *Black Boy* by Du Bois calling it a "fictionalized biography," most readers assumed Wright's portrayal of his impoverished, violent childhood constituted the whole of his fabled life story. Although it was close enough to Wright's experience to be called an autobiography, Du Bois's point was well taken. Wright's first biographer, Constance Webb, observed that to represent the deep suffering of masses of Black southerners, he understood that *"his own family's essentially middle-class status would have to be underplayed; their attitudes had been essentially white middle-class attitudes"* (emphasis added). The "Richard" or "Dick" in the book had become, as intended, "a symbol of all the brutality and cruelty wreaked upon the black man by the Southern environment."[9] Neither as abjectly poor nor as educationally deprived as the protagonist of *Black Boy* is typically understood to be, he could identify with the feudal world of his father by dint of his class roots despite their estrangement, while escaping the worst effects of Jim Crow oppression through his closeness to his mother's more literate, petit bourgeois family. It was thus his personal history, together with the radical decade in which he came of age and his early political and literary affiliations in Chicago, that distinguished him from middle-class, highly educated Black radicals like Du Bois. This confluence of factors in turn provided educational opportunities he would likely not have had otherwise at the same time that it deepened his grasp of class struggle in relation to racial oppression, enabling him to recognize the revolutionary potential of the Black proletariat in solidarity with white workers.

In a series of letters from 1938 to 1945, he congratulated his childhood friend Joe C. Brown on having joined the Young Communist League (YCL), the youth group of the Party, declaring, "You are now in the main stream of mankind's history. You have taken your place along side of those who are changing this world. That, in my opinion, is the best thing a Negro can do in this day." A year later, on March 29, 1939, he told Joe he was happy to meet Mississippians at the National Convention of the Communist Party USA in

New York who were "actually joining the Communist Party and struggling for Negro freedom in the very midst of the blackbelt." His last reference to the CPUSA was in a letter dated April 29, 1940, in which he asks, "How is your class consciousness coming along? How close are you to the labor movement? You ought to get close, boy. Big things are coming along in this world." Allusions to Joe's involvement with the Party end after that date. In an introduction to a collection of the letters published in 1968 by Kent State University Libraries, where the letters are archived, Thomas Knipp frames them as documenting the "literary tragedy" of Wright's failure to write another great novel equal to the three works for which he is best known: *Uncle Tom's Children*, *Native Son*, and *Black Boy*. Knipp allows that Wright retained a Marxist orientation but asserts that "it ceased to be a shaping force in his life"; his late publications are "distinguished" and the fiction he produced during that period is "undervalued," but it is nevertheless "inescapable" that "the promise of this enormously talented man remained unfulfilled."[10]

Although his mostly sympathetic, if lukewarm, assessment of Wright's later literary works anticipates post–Cold War valorizations of the author's left-wing politics and his writing after he left the Party, Knipp's equivocations still echo the standard view that his great achievements were over and he had more or less abandoned Marxism, for better or worse, by the early 1940s. *The Outsider* was widely panned despite its modernist themes and sometimes brilliant interrogation of global contradictions of the postwar era. It was also interpreted as anticommunist, replete with grotesque representations of Communist officials and a rejection of class struggle. Yet, during that period, he helped establish the short-lived, "third way," left-wing group Rassemblement Démocratique Révolutionnaire, which was critical of both the Soviets and the Americans, and became involved in the Pan-African movement, counting among his associates C. L. R. James, George Padmore, Léopold Senghor, and Frantz Fanon, all of whom were discussing and debating theories of Marxism in relation to anti-imperialist and anticolonial struggles, particularly in Africa and the Caribbean. As Kevin Kelly Gaines observes, "However unfashionably idiosyncratic Wright may appear to us today, it is important to realize that he was not the lonely rebel he often made himself out to be. With fellow black radical intellectuals in exile, including George Padmore and C. L. R. James, Wright was engaged in theorizing the revolutionary aspirations of black and African peoples' struggles against Western oppression."[11]

According to Alan Wald, Wright remained "a small c-communist" after he broke from the Party, operating "as a 'free radical' within the delicate chemistry of the revolutionary anti-Stalinist tradition." Wald concludes that for Wright, "the Communist experience was . . . a wound that never healed."[12] In *Daemonic Genius*, Margaret Walker compares the CPUSA unfavorably to the FWP, declaring that the latter "had political and social significance in a period when communism and fascism were threatening American democracy" and calling Marxism an "intellectual fad."[13] Two of Wright's biographers omit "Marx" or "Marxism" from the books' indexes, ducking the question altogether.[14] Michel Fabre emphasizes Wright's political awakening described in a condensed passage that survived cuts to the *Atlantic* article in which he devours copies of the *New Masses* after his first visit to the John Reed Club. Fabre observes that Wright "came to see in Marxism an organized search for truth about the life of oppressed peoples, and this convinced him that the Communists were sincere."[15] It was precisely this "organized search for truth" through activism and the analytical lens of Marxism that survived his tense involvement in the CPUSA. That search, for Wright, was necessitated by his eagerness to explain and transform the social relations encapsulated in the last two lines of Part One of *Black Boy*: "This was the culture from which I sprang. This was the terror from which I fled."[16]

The Communist Party That Wright Joined: "United in Action, Thought, and Feeling"

The ambiguities and competing narratives of Wright's breaks from the Party, including his own contradictory accounts, complicate an assessment of his politics.[17] Key to reevaluating his allegiances, commitments, and perspective is the radical zeitgeist, rooted in utopian socialist communities in the early 1800s, that shaped his political consciousness in Chicago in the late 1920s. That history can be seen in newspaper columns by Marx and Engels in the *New York Daily Tribune* from 1852 to 1861, the advent of the Marxist-oriented Workingmen's Party in 1876, and a series of splits in the Socialist Labor Party and Socialist Party that gave rise to the Communist Party of America in 1919.[18] Rank-and-file Party members were involved in the 1920s in militant trade union activity amplified by the CPUSA-subsidized Trade Union Educational League. Under William Z. Foster's leadership, the Party also exerted increasing influence on organized labor through the creation of the International Labor Defense (ILD) in 1925. The ILD mobilized support for jailed striking workers, imprisoned radicals (notably, the Italian anarchists Nicola Sacco and Bartolomeo Vanzetti), and antilynching, anti-Klan, and civil rights campaigns. A decade later, in 1931, the ILD led the defense of the Scottsboro Boys—nine

Black teenagers, ages thirteen to twenty, falsely accused of raping two white women near Scottsboro, Alabama—and Angelo Herndon, a young Black Communist arrested and tried in Atlanta, George, in 1932 on charges of inciting insurrection. Both cases formed a crucial learning ground for Wright.[19]

In addition to the Party's Black-led legal defense campaigns and militant, antiracist labor organizing, its evolving analysis of the "Negro question" placed Black freedom struggles at the center of building a radical movement in the United States, a standpoint that drew young Black radicals like Wright into Communist circles. This understanding of a Black revolutionary vanguard had been advanced by Cyril Briggs, an African Caribbean radical who started the Pan-African paper *The Crusader* in Harlem in 1918 to "project a shared proletarian identity between Black and white workers as the counterweight to the dominant system."[20] Together with fellow Caribbean Marxist Richard B. Moore, Briggs formed the African Blood Brotherhood (ABB), an independent, anticapitalist, Black nationalist association allied with the CPUSA after both leaders were recruited in 1921, and participated in developing Party positions concerning Black oppression. Still earlier, the first Black member of the CPUSA, Surinamese-born Otto Huiswoud, had attended the US party's founding meeting in 1918. He was followed by other Black Marxists, many from the People's Educational Forum in Harlem, who contributed to the Party's efforts to reformulate the "Negro question" from its earlier "color-blind" phase in which racism was understood as secondary to class struggle to seeing Black liberation as central to revolutionary social transformation. When Wright joined the Party in 1934, he was standing on the shoulders of these Black Communist leaders.

At the Sixth World Congress of the Comintern in Moscow in 1928, a new generation of Black Communists had risen through the ranks. Harry Haywood (born Heywood Hall), a thirty-year-old Black Communist from Nebraska who followed his brother Otto Hall into the CPUSA, had spent four years in Moscow. Haywood would go on to become the Party leader in Chicago who antagonized the young Richard Wright by pressuring him to forgo his writing for routine organizing assignments. In Moscow, together with Charles Nasanov, Haywood had submitted the "Resolution on the Negro Question," theorizing a dual position that became known as the Black Belt thesis, recognizing Black Americans in the South as an oppressed nation and setting demands for full racial and economic equality in the urban North. Built on Bolshevik theories of anticolonial national liberation, the resolution was passionately debated with no initial support from Black Communists other than Haywood. The key question was whether focusing on Black nationalism would undermine mobilizing an international working-class movement. Ultimately, the resolution passed, bolstering the Party's commitment to combating white chauvinism and supporting Black nationalism as a genuinely progressive force, a decision that in turn engaged new layers of Black activists and elevated African Americans from a subsidiary to a central role in building a revolutionary mass movement.[21]

It was this phase of the Party's twists and turns during the interwar period that Wright entered after he moved to Chicago in 1927. He was drawn into the Party's orbit by its policies of self-determination for Black Americans and its affiliated cultural front groups, particularly the John Reed Club. Of great interest to him was Stalin's *The National and Colonial Question*, which he described as a "politically sensitive volume that revealed a new way of looking upon lost and beaten peoples . . . a method by which scores of backward peoples had been led to unity on a national scale" in contrast to how "Negroes were sneered at in America." He was also impressed by Stalin's writing about phonetics experts involved in literacy campaigns in undeveloped regions of Russia who had encouraged "these forgotten folk . . . to keep their old cultures, to see in their ancient customs meanings and satisfactions as deep as those contained in supposedly superior ways of living." The incident that provoked this reflection on Stalin in Part Two of *Black Boy* was a conversation with a Black Communist functionary who called Wright out of his home one night to question him about a series of profiles of Black Bolsheviks he had started to write. Leaving him aghast, his interrogator reminded him that the Soviet Union had expelled Trotsky for counterrevolutionary activity and "had to shoot a lot of intellectuals."[22]

Before and after he left the Party, he responded variously to the vicissitudes of its policies, especially with respect to the "Negro question," from initial skepticism about the Communists' sincerity to gratitude for the camaraderie, interracial unity, and cultural outlets the Party offered, to deepening mistrust of its bureaucratic tendencies and policy reversals. Though influenced by the Black Belt thesis in his Depression-era writing, he proclaimed it "an absurd theory" in 1957 in *White Man, Listen*. His frustrations were stoked by Third Period anti-intellectual sectarianism to which he had been personally subjected, the Party's less militant support for Black liberation after the Nazis invaded the Soviet Union in 1941, and its insensitivity to his creative needs as a writer. He found Harry Haywood—who arrived in Chicago in 1932 to expel David Poindexter from the Party—particularly obnoxious. Introducing him in *Black Boy* pseudonymously as Buddy Nealson, "the party's theoretician on the Negro Question," intent on eliminating "Negro Trotskyite elements," Wright unflatteringly describes him as "a short, black man with an ever-ready smile, thick lips, a furtive manner, and a greasy sweaty look."[23] Among his grievances was that Haywood forced the young writer to head a committee to protest the high cost of living, subordinate his writing to political organizing, and cease interviewing Black Communists like Poindexter, whose enthralling stories of his childhood in the South inspired Wright's story "Big Boy Leaves Home."

David Poindexter: The Best-Known Communist Speaker in Chicago

In addition to Haywood, Wright also had unpleasant dealings with Oliver Law (Ed Green in *Black Boy*) and John P. Davis (referred to only as "Smith"). He describes Law as "tall, taciturn, soldierly," sincere with a "long militant record in the Communist Party," and "organically capable of only the most elementary reactions"; Davis was "a short, yellow man who carried himself like Napoleon."[24] One day, Law barged in on Wright during an interview with Poindexter (Ross in *Black Boy*). "What's happening here?" Law demanded to know. An ILD representative defending Poindexter against assault charges, Law suspected Wright's motives based on Party rumors that he was a spy. Wright told him that he wanted to write a series of biographical profiles on Black Communists, starting with Poindexter, whose southern background and spirited militancy greatly interested him, and suggested he might like to interview Law, too. He soon learned that Poindexter had been accused of "'antileadership tendencies,' 'class collaborationist attitudes,' and 'ideological factionalism.'" Wright had been branded as "a smuggler of reaction," "a petty bourgeois degenerate," "a bastard intellectual," and an "incipient Trotskyite" with "seraphim tendencies."[25]

Sectarian attacks against rank-and-file Party members like Poindexter and Wright reflected fraught relations stemming from internal divisions in the Soviet Union that had led most consequentially for the international Communist movement to Leon Trotsky's expulsion from the Party in 1927. Wright understood Party discipline as "the highest injunction that a Communist could receive from his party." That the Soviet Union was under attack by its enemies was clear to him and other Party stalwarts and fellow travelers.[26] But his story of estrangement from the CPUSA resonates not only with the personal cost of inflexible disciplinary practices and policy reversals but also with the left's failures to overcome sectarianism and unify its forces. Haywood's interest in making him a "mass leader" and his crude attempts at discipline infuriated Wright. Having disrespected the unproven young writer, Haywood would later denounce the world-famous author for depicting lumpen characters like Bigger Thomas.[27] National Party leader and renowned ILD attorney William Patterson recalled that in Wright's case, Haywood "did not exhibit the slightest appreciation that he was dealing with a sensitive, immature creative genius with whom it was necessary to exercise great patience.... Name-calling resulted and Haywood used his political position to get a vote of censure against Wright, who thereupon resigned from the Party." Patterson also praised Poindexter as the "best known among the Communist speakers ... who had learned his oratory right there at the park" and had a "great natural ability as a speaker."[28]

According to Wright in *Black Boy*, Poindexter was charged with "wrongdoing" not by Haywood but by his own friends, a "crushing" experience under which Poindexter "wilted."[29] Claude Lightfoot, another Black Communist in Chicago, recalled the trial differently: it was Haywood who presented a long list of Poindexter's "deviations" from the Party line as the room buzzed with the sound of surprised, indignant Poindexter supporters. True to his reputation as a scrappy street fighter, he responded defiantly to the charges: "If my Party seeks to sever me from the revolutionary movement which I have served faithfully, so be it." This ironic pronouncement was followed by repeated "if ... so be it" clauses. In contrast, Wright portrays him as humiliated, in tears: "Comrades, ... I'm guilty of all the charges, all of them." Although the trial was in 1934, the year Wright joined the Party, and he remained active at least until 1942, his memory of Poindexter's show trial marks one of many endings of his romance with the CPUSA, illustrating both the ambiguity of his relationship to the Party and the indignity and pain inflicted by what he felt were unfounded, often ridiculous accusations that he speculated, only half in jest, might have led to his exile or execution in the USSR. As Rowley puts it, "As he saw it, he himself was on trial by proxy."[30] Appalled by the proceedings, he fled the room, "anxious to get out of the hall and into the streets and shake free from the gigantic tension that had hold of me."[31]

Speaking to "Listening Ears": From the Third Period to the Popular Front

Wright made no secret that he was a Communist from 1934 to 1942 as he rose to literary stardom, placing poems in left-wing magazines, winning literary prizes, and achieving unprecedented fame with the publication of *Native Son*. He joined the JRC in 1933 and the CPUSA a year later, toward the end of the Third Period, and remained outspoken as a Communist throughout the Popular Front period from 1935 to 1939 and beyond, until he broke from the Party quietly in 1942 and very publicly in 1944 in the *Atlantic* essay "I Tried to Be a Communist." But he chafed against unilateral Party dictates, especially to terminate the John Reed Club, quarreled with leaders, and resented their indifference to his needs as a writer. If the Third Period was defined by the belief that capitalism was in an acute phase of political economic crisis and revolution was imminent, the Popular Front ushered in a period of tacit endorsement of Roosevelt's New Deal, a retreat from militancy, and an alliance with liberal reformers against fascism. The political impact of this period was complicated by abrupt policy reversals in response to the Molotov-Ribbentrop Nonaggression (Hitler-Stalin) Pact in 1939, followed by the German invasion of the USSR on June 22, 1941. While some Communists left in disgust after the nonaggression pact was signed, Wright remained staunchly against the war until 1941. By that point, distressed by what he saw as diminished support for racial equality in order to build a united front against fascism, he was inching toward his final break with the Party.

In general, the Third Period is considered to have been destructive of mass organizing and recruitment efforts by the CPUSA. Such efforts were undermined by the Party's sectarian attacks on other left-wing tendencies for being "social fascists," much like similar attacks in Germany that divided the German left and contributed to the exponential growth of the Nazi Party. However, the Third Period also gave rise to highly effective campaigns to organize the urban unemployed, build trade unions, and adopt and energetically pursue the Party's positions on the struggle for Black liberation. As the first majority white organization to develop an antiracist, Black nationalist position in its everyday practice and revolutionary goals, the CPUSA organized Black and white labor, defended civil rights, vigorously opposed racism by educating white workers, and supported interracial class solidarity, insisting that, given their historical formation as an oppressed, national minority, African Americans had a vanguard role to play in a US revolutionary movement. Additionally, the Party sponsored organizations like the John Reed Club and workers' schools that promoted the study of revolutionary communism while providing an array of cultural and educational opportunities.

It was precisely these social milieus that so deeply appealed to Wright: the interracial cultural front in Chicago of trade unionists, intellectuals, writers, and artists who saw past the color line to fight against racism and for better pay and working conditions for all workers and believed that it was only through organizing the proletarian masses that the power to abolish wage slavery could be mobilized to usher in a new world. If abolishing capital was the dream—a goal that Wright would often appear to question in the new, postwar world order—his waking, sensory experience as a Communist was of collective struggle, incremental political gains, and camaraderie. Even if the dream was deferred and the waking experience short lived and riddled with contradictions, the wave of radicalization that swept Wright into worlds beyond what he could have imagined before migrating north in 1927 from Memphis resonated far beyond the 1930s, ebbing and flowing, indestructible no matter how repressive, brutal, and powerful the opposition would be. This sense of belonging to an international collective movement to change the world is the often overlooked "glory" in the title of Part Two of *Black Boy*, "The Horror and the Glory."

After the 1929 crash, Wright started meeting with friends ("white boys") from the post office in Abe Aaron's South Side hotel room to "argue the state of the world." Surprised to learn that many of them had joined the Communist Party, he recalls in *Black Boy* that he was encouraged repeatedly by one friend, Sol (Aaron's pseudonym), to attend a JRC meeting. It was Sol who "begged" him to attend the club meetings and told him, "They can help you to write." Dubious about the sincerity of Communists' interest in Black people and the capacity of white people generally to welcome a Black man into their group, Wright overcame his cynicism and resistance one Saturday night and arrived at the address on the Chicago Loop to find that only the editorial board of the club's magazine *Left Front*, which published his first poems, was meeting. He was grateful to discover a sense of comradely communion and hopefulness in back issues of *New Masses* that "the outcasts could become united in action, thought, and feeling.... It was being done in one-sixth of the earth already. The revolutionary words leaped from the printed page and struck me with tremendous force." A heady mix of radical politics and serious discussion of literature in an interracial milieu that accepted, respected, and valued him as a writer, a Black man, and a fellow human being, convinced him to join the JRC. After he stayed up all night to read *New Masses*, he felt he "could speak to listening ears" and find common cause with white people, who had, for most of his life, threatened his survival.[32]

Despite the Party's missteps during the Third Period, its record of militant, antiracist support for Black Americans and rank-and-file labor in the late 1920s and early 1930s not only defies some of the stereotypical characterizations associated with it but also shows that its "audacity and radical approach, sectarian as it might have been, gained numerous supporters."[33] Ultimately, the failure of Third Period policy, particularly in Germany, where Hitler rose to power in the vacuum created by a divided left, led to a "period of political experimentation" and a pragmatic return to a united front in the United States in which Trotskyists, social democrats, and Wobblies formed "red unions" and built highly effective democratic, rank-and-file industrial movements.[34] These activities not only helped create militant, bottom-up trade unions that understood the power of the strike but also eventually won the CPUSA seats at the table in union and government bureaucracies and put pressure on Roosevelt to implement the New Deal in 1933 in response to mass protests of the unemployed, and the Second New Deal in 1935 after a wave of strikes and intensive workplace organizing from 1934 to 1937. Yet, these seeming advances by a united front, together with the Party's swelling membership list, ultimately weakened the Communists' position, leaving them open to increasingly vicious Cold War attacks.

The Comintern announced the Popular Front strategy at the Seventh World Congress in July 1935, the same month the Federal Writers' Project (FWP) was established. On the one hand, the Popular Front expanded the Party's influence and introduced mainstream Americans to socialist ideas by creating a broad alliance of leftists and liberals in the fight against fascism. It boosted the number of Party members and sympathizers, "serv[ing] as a dynamic wedge of radicalism within the dominant New Deal liberalism."[35] The New Deal–funded FWP, for example, put unemployed Black and white writers, historians, librarians, and other more or less qualified individuals, including Wright, back to work as federal writers. Together with other WPA industrial and cultural programs, the FWP with its pluralistic, inclusive, nationalistic vision contributed to this broad antifascist, increasingly pro-America front. On the other hand, Popular Front strategy was "profoundly utopian," and the alliance with the Democratic Party demobilized militant labor and racial justice struggles that had characterized Third Period organizing.[36] The new policy also resulted in the termination of the more radical John Reed Club, which had recruited young, unknown writers like Wright, a decision he poignantly protested: "I asked what was to become of the young writers whom the Communist party had implored to join the clubs and who were ineligible for the new group, and there was no answer."[37]

Popular Fronts: The League of American Writers and the National Negro Congress

Stimulated by the Depression, CPUSA membership nearly quintupled from 18,000 at the beginning of the 1930s to a peak of 85,000 in 1942, just as Wright had resolved to leave. During that period, he was actively involved in Popular Front programs, including the League of American Writers (LAW), established in 1935 with a politically broader, more select group of well-known writers, and the broad-based, Black-led National Negro Congress (NNC), which first met in February 1936. Many non-Party members joined both groups, but it was understood that they were CPUSA-sponsored. Despite his objections to dissolving the JRC, Wright signed the LAW's call for the first American Writers' Congress in 1935 in New York City, which declared, "The capitalist system crumbles so rapidly before our eyes that . . . today hundreds of poets, novelists, dramatists, critics, short story writers and journalists recognize the necessity of personally helping to accelerate the destruction of capitalism and the establishment of a workers' government." Other signatories included Nelson Algren, Earl Browder, Kenneth Burke, Theodore Dreiser, Mike Gold, Langston Hughes, Tillie Lerner (Olsen), and Nathaniel West. According to Frank Folsom, who served as the League's national executive secretary from 1937 to 1942, "most of the best writers in the country" were among the League's 820 members.[38] Three congresses followed in 1937, 1939, and 1941, reflecting the League's rise and decline in response to CPUSA policy shifts from opposing the war as imperialist and antiworker after the Hitler-Stalin Pact to supporting it after Germany invaded the USSR on June 22, 1941.

The League was an extraordinary association of leading American writers who supported left-wing labor, civil rights, and antifascist campaigns, provided material aid to the Popular Front in Spain during the Spanish Civil War, and assisted European writers escaping fascism. It was also a retreat from the more radical, proletarian perspective of writers, many of whom, like Wright, were young and inexperienced and had joined the John Reed clubs. The League's antifascist campaigns and tempered revolutionary goals and rhetoric appealed to a broad base that rose to peak membership in 1937 and declined by 1939, losing some of its best-known authors who were disgusted by the Nazi-Soviet pact as well as the Party's obedience to Moscow's shifting priorities and superpatriotic rhetoric after the United States entered the war. The smaller 1941 congress, with fewer celebrity authors, was the last. For Wright, the breaking point came that year. In April, he gave a speech first at Columbia University and then on June 7 at the fourth congress to a crowd of 3,000 people. The speech, "Not My People's War," appeared in *New Masses* on June 17, five days before Hitler invaded the Soviet Union. Wright blasted the hypocrisy of Roosevelt's Four Freedoms and US military policy upholding the segregation of Black and white troops, which had "proven satisfactory over a period of years." The war, Wright declared, was "nakedly and inescapably an imperialist war, directed against the Negro people and working people and colonial people everywhere in this world."[39]

More deeply rooted and longer lasting than the LAW, especially in the South, the NNC grew out of the League of Struggle for Negro Rights. Openly affiliated with the Party, it sought to promote unity between Black and white workers in a Popular Front agenda opposed to fascism, war, and racial discrimination. As Wright reported in *New Masses* on February 25, 1936, the NNC held its first meeting in "zero-cold" Chicago weather on February 14 at the Eighth Regiment Armory. Anticipating his photodocumentary book *12 Million Black Voices* published five years later, Wright titled his article "Two Million Black Voices" and framed it with two headnotes. The first stated that it was an era of Jim Crow, lynching, and deteriorating conditions of life for Black Americans; the second historicized the meeting place as the armory that had housed a Black Illinois regiment "whose ranks were decimated in Flanders to make the world 'safe for a democracy' the Negro people have never known." The 763 delegates and thousands of attendees pouring in from all over the country formed "a vanguard of a huge rising people, a section of a world-wide army of toilers driving toward liberation." A. Philip Randolph, president of the NNC and the International Brotherhood of Sleeping Car Porters, criticized the New Deal as inadequate in its failure to "place human rights above property rights" and proposed a Negro Bill of Rights. He called on the NNC to abandon the Democratic and Republican Parties for a new, anticapitalistic, farmer-labor party that was needed to check the "rapid march of imperialism and the trustification of monopoly capitalism," and laid out the demand for a new bill of rights based on cross-racial working-class solidarity and "the fact that Black America is a victim of both class- and race-oppression." Wright summed up the speech as envisioning "the possibility and necessity of an alliance of the Negro with all the progressive and class-conscious elements in America and the entire world."[40]

In addition to reporting in *New Masses* on the convention, Wright organized a panel, "The Role of the Negro Artist and Writer in a Changing Social Order," with Langston Hughes, the sculptor Augusta Savage, and the poet and novelist Arna Bontemps, which the *Chicago Defender* called a highlight of the conference.[41] It was out of this session that the South Side Writers Group was born, led by Wright, with Frank Marshall Davis, Fenton Johnson, Ted Ward, Margaret Walker, Arna Bontemps, Marion Perkins, and others, all unpublished at the time except Davis and Wright. With an express mission of radicalizing Black writers and grappling with "problems such as nationalism in literary perspective" and "the relation of the Negro writers to politics and social movements," the group discussed literary theory, politics, and works in progress. Wright read "Blueprint for Negro Writing" and the stories "Down by the Riverside," "Long Black Song," and "Bright and Morning Star"; Walker read drafts of her historical novel, eventually published in 1966 to critical acclaim as *Jubilee*; and Davis shared his poem "I Am the American Negro," which Wright criticized for its "hopeless bitterness." According to Walker, Wright was the "exciting hot center" of the group. Davis described Wright as "an extrovert, warm and outgoing with an often ribald sense of humor." On hearing him read "Bright and Morning Star," Davis remarked, "When he finished, nobody spoke for several minutes. We were too much moved by his power. Then there was a flood of praise. Frankly I was overwhelmed. We realized this was a major talent, but none of us dreamed how great he would become."[42]

The NNC was proposed in May 1935 at a meeting of the Joint Committee on National Recovery, a short-lived group of Black organizations spearheaded by John P. Davis to push for equal treatment of African Americans under the New Deal. It was Davis who called Wright a fool for preferring to focus on his writing rather than serve as a youth delegate in Switzerland, an exchange about which Wright later declared, "A breath more of anger and I would have driven my fist into his face." His meeting with Davis, arranged by Haywood in a South Side hotel, precipitated his first attempt to leave the Party, which he erroneously recalls happening in 1936 after Poindexter's trial. He resolved to resign and to tell his comrades that he "still adhered to the ideological program of the party," but refused "to be bound any longer by the party's decisions." At the next unit meeting, he resigned, asking to retain membership in Communist-sponsored organizations and promising to comply with those programs. His words were met with "profound silence" and a motion by Haywood to table the discussion. The next night, he was visited by two Communists who told him that Haywood would expel him from the Party rather than let him resign and accused him of being a Trotskyist and urging others to leave with him. Infuriated, Wright nevertheless remained in the Party and spoke publicly as a militant Communist until 1942, even as he suffered from rank-and-file hostility, especially in Chicago.[43]

Wright's embittered portraits of Haywood and Davis reflect his struggle to participate in collective political work while retaining his individuality. Other, more experienced comrades recall him in memoirs and interviews, often in passing, as brilliant but immature—a sensitive artist who rebelled against Party discipline—and criticize Haywood and Davis for their insensitivity toward him.[44] Emanating from his battle to survive his fanatically religious family and the Jim Crow South, Wright's rebelliousness laid bare his conflict between a need for individual freedom and his belief in collective political action, putting him at odds with the revolutionary movements he saw as the future of humankind. More objectively, he recognized the CPUSA's weaknesses, failures, and escalating infiltration by government agents, and turned his attention to persistent contradictions between national liberation movements of people of color worldwide and an increasingly sectarian, fractured left in actually existing communist and socialist states and parties. And yet, despite any shortcomings he saw in Davis and Haywood, he also must have been acutely aware of their dynamic leadership as Black Communists, including Davis's role in founding and co-leading the NCC with A. Philip Randolph.

Sponsored by the CPUSA as part of its Popular Front Strategy, the NNC effectively brought together an independent, left-liberal coalition of forces intended to unite a broad cross-section of labor, civil rights, and religious groups from across the country without antagonizing established civil rights groups like the NAACP. Although the NNC would begin to fray by 1940 after the Hitler-Stalin Pact, it became the locus of a nationwide, Black-led, interracial mobilization that formed regional councils in more than seventy cities. It also gave rise to the Southern Negro Youth Congress (SNYC), founded in Richmond, Virginia, in 1937 by young people who had attended the Chicago convention, including James Jackson, Helen Gray, Esther Cooper, Edward Strong, and Sallye B. Davis, Angela Davis's mother. SNYC headquarters moved to Birmingham, Alabama, in 1939—where Angela Davis was born, raised, and politicized—and eventually organized chapters in ten southern states with 11,000 members. The NNC program mobilized community activists nationwide in campaigns against lynching, police brutality, and Jim Crow segregation and discriminatory practices, and fought for fair housing, education, employment, recreation, and civil rights under Roosevelt's New Deal, forming a crucial alliance with organized labor that brought thousands of Black workers into steel, maritime, coalmining, and other unions, and won endorsements from top officials of the Congress of Industrial Organizations (CIO).

"Communism Is Twentieth Century Americanism": Victories and Betrayals

The Popular Front muted class differences by curtailing militant rank-and-file, anti-imperialist, and antiracist activities in accommodations to union and government bureaucracies. After having disparaged President Roosevelt as a "proto-fascist," the Party quietly endorsed him and supported New Deal policies that it had previously attacked for undermining revolutionary struggle and discriminating against women and African Americans, especially in its housing and employment programs. Under the Second New Deal, Congress passed the National Labor Relations Act, the Social Security Act, and the Fair Labor Standards Act to ease mass suffering caused by the Depression. Responsive to militant demands for relief by organized labor and mass left movements, the New Deal reforms effectively quelled class conflict and social unrest while gaining the support of CIO leaders and defusing a combative workers' movement.[45] In addition to enforcing the wartime no-strike clause on radical trade unionists and supporting the internment of Japanese Americans, the Party adopted a patriotic stance upholding America's revolutionary tradition of 1776 and its promises of democracy, declaring in a 1936 pamphlet, "Communism is Twentieth Century Americanism."[46]

After the Hitler-Stalin Pact in 1939, there was a sharp drop in CPUSA membership, including the loss of intellectuals such as Sherwood Anderson, Claude McKay, and Granville Hicks. And yet, despite anti-Soviet and anti-Stalinist criticism of the Party, membership rose to a peak of 85,000 three years later in 1942 after Hitler attacked the Soviet Union and the Soviets entered the war in June 1941, followed by the United States in early 1942. The expanding theaters of war meant a rapid return to the Popular Front strategy along with support for the war effort and the expansion of an antifascist coalition of trade union, socialist, liberal, and government allies in tandem with the Black-led civil rights movement and cultural work in the arts, literature, and worker education. For many participants, this period represented the high point of the Communist movement, but Wright and some other Black leaders were dismayed by the Party's diminished commitment to antiracist struggle, including the Double V campaign to fight fascism abroad and Jim Crow at home. Black Americans were still discriminated against in the workplace and the military, barred even from donating blood until rising demand led to their blood being stored in separate containers—policies that persisted despite the crucial role played by African American surgeon and researcher Charles R. Drew in discovering that plasma could be used to create a blood bank. For Wright, the subordination of Black oppression to the united front was an unforgivable betrayal of the fight for Black freedom. Meanwhile, the FWP was under fierce attack by the House Un-American Activities Committee led by Congressman Martin Dies. In a 1939 hearing, Congressman Joe Starnes from Alabama had blasted Wright's essay, "The Ethics of Living Jim Crow," as "the most filthy thing I have ever seen."[47]

Wright's Political Evolution: The Making of a Black Bolshevik

Several years after Wright left Chicago, he returned to research 12 Million Black Voices, the photodocumentary project for which former Farm Security Administration (FSA) photographer Edwin Rosskam had invited him to write the text for the book that Viking Press then commissioned. From southern slavery and sharecropping to the Great Migration that transformed the urban North, Wright's poetic narrative of Black America drew on Marxist dialectical materialist concepts of history and class division. He relied on sociological research by John Gibbs St. Clair Drake and Horace R. Cayton Jr. begun in 1935 under the aegis of the WPA and published a decade later, with Wright's introduction, as *Black Metropolis: A Study of Negro Life in a Northern City*. In *12 Million Black Voices*, his analysis of the forces that devastated Black southern existence and drove Black migrants north combined sociological knowledge—empirical and dialectical—with his experience growing up in the South. His poignant description of his father in *Black Boy* evinces that dialectic, counterposing his father as "a black peasant who had gone to the city seeking life, but who had failed in the city; a black peasant whose life had been hopelessly snarled in the city, and who had at last fled the city," to his own fate in that same city, Memphis, "that had lifted me in its burning arms and borne me toward alien and undreamed of shores of knowing."[48]

In Chicago—his first stop along those "undreamed of shores of knowing"—his political education coalesced in the schools of the JRC, the CPUSA, and other groups that he eagerly, if often skeptically, embraced. It was these overlapping milieus that shaped his worldview and infused his writing. The list of writers in them included Horace Cayton, Abe Aaron, Margaret Walker, Arna Bontemps, Fenton Johnson, Frank Marshall Davis, Jack Conroy, Nelson Algren, and Kitty Chappelle, to name a few. Sites of political study, organizational efforts, and frontline activism intersected with cultural forums like the South Side Community Art Center, the South Side Writers Group, the FWP, and the University of Chicago, contributing to what Robert Bone called the Chicago Renaissance, "a flowering of Negro letters," of which he proclaimed Wright to be "the towering figure."[49] Increased attention has since been paid to the Chicago Black Renaissance and the generation of writers and artists from 1935 to the 1950 who rivaled and regenerated the dynamism of its better-known New York counterpart, the Harlem Renaissance or New Negro movement.[50] There were also the schools of Bughouse Square's soapbox speakers, the Chicago Post Office, and the streets of Chicago's South Side. The latter, in particular, taught Wright about Jim Crow in the urban industrial North and informed his evolving political economic analysis of the Great Migration and the transfiguration of Black life. To one degree or another, all these milieus had absorbed the radical zeitgeist of the 1930s.

Bearing in mind inconsistencies in his chronology of events in *Black Boy*, Wright presents himself as fairly knowledgeable about the history of the Russian Revolution and some Marxist-Leninist principles prior to joining the JRC and the CPUSA. In an encounter involving Black Communists in Washington Park in the summer of 1932, he engaged in a conversation with a Communist soapbox speaker who predicted that so-called bonus marchers in Washington, DC, if evicted from the city, would "rise up and make a revolution." In his retelling of the encounter, Wright was sufficiently versed in Marxist theory and current events to dispute the speaker's propagandistic claim, remarking that "even if the United States Army actually kills the bonus marchers, there'll be no revolution." The bonus marchers, Black and white veterans, had convened on the nation's capital, demanding that President Hoover honor the government's promise for wartime bonuses. Instead, as Wright predicted, federal troops drove them out of the Hooverville camps along the Potomac River, killing two veterans and an eleven-week-old baby who died of gas-related injuries. When he returned to ask the Party member about the prophesied revolution, the man murmured, "The prerequisite conditions did not exist."[51]

Presumably, his political education had begun before 1928 when he qualified for a summer job at the Chicago Post Office, where he met Abe Aaron, the University of Chicago student who introduced him to the JRC, and several other postal workers, including Sam Gaspar and Dan Burley, all of whom became part of a group that Jack Conroy referred to as "the Chicago Post Office school." By 1930, Wright had gravitated away from an interest in Marcus Garvey's Universal Negro Improvement Association toward the CPUSA-sponsored League of Struggle for Negro Rights, the successor to the American Negro Labor Congress, which was protesting evictions and mobilizing campaigns for jobs and support for the Scottsboro Boys. But until he joined the JRC in 1933, it was probably a combination of reading newspapers and talking politics with his post office friends that informed his grasp of current events, given that, by his own account, most of what he read was literary.[52] And he read dozens of books, consciously developing his distinctive style by studying how to write dialect, for example, the results of which can be seen in his underrated novel "Cesspool," published posthumously in 1963 as *Lawd Today!*

Drawing on his experience at the post office, where he learned the game of bridge from coworkers during breaks in a mostly segregated basement canteen, he depicted the protagonist Jake Jackson and his three fellow Black postal sorters as expert players. The four working-class friends sort mail in backbreaking shifts under the surveillance of white supervisors who time their performance and humiliate them. Wright weaves detailed diagrams of their bridge games into the novel's modernist texture, along with running radio commentary on Lincoln's birthday and extensive dialogue in dialect he had diligently practiced in order to learn his craft. Despite its mostly negative reception in 1963 as stylistically flawed and counterrevolutionary, *Lawd Today!* can be read in retrospect as having done precisely what Wright declared the times required after his first JRC meeting: "to tell the Communists how the common people felt" in order to bridge the communication gap he perceived between the Black Chicago masses and the Party.[53]

Well before 1933, when he started to read political works and study Marx and Lenin, he would have absorbed radical ideas from the "Bug Club," as Bughouse Square in Washington Park was also known, Black nationalist and Communist soapbox speakers, discussions in Aaron's room at the Troy Lane Hotel, and his own experience of evictions, unemployment, going on the dole, and joining with fellow tenants to organize his building. He was also likely to have been aware of CPUSA-sponsored educational opportunities, including the "district school" at Party headquarters, which became the Chicago Workers School in 1932, and the city's some eighty-five neighborhood workers' schools by the mid-1930s. Margaret Walker recalls that under his "influence and partial tutelage," she bought books on "lay-away," including Marx's *Capital* and Adam Smith's *The Wealth of Nations*. The first book he gave her, explaining how the JRC got its name, was John Reed's *One Hundred Days That Shook the World*. She also read Maxim Gorky's *Lower Depths* and *Mother* as well as *Soviet Power* by Hewlett Johnson, the so-called Red Archbishop of Canterbury.[54] After Wright was elected secretary of the JRC, he gave a lecture, "The Literature of the Negro: A Marxian Interpretation by a Negro Writer," at the Open Forum at 312 West State Street. He also started a Saturday lecture series for which Ernest Burgess gave a talk on art in Soviet Russia; Lawrence Martin, a Northwestern University professor, delivered a lecture titled "The Collapse of Liberalism"; and the University of Chicago historian Lewis Gottschalk lectured on the French Revolution. Other guests included the British labor politician John Strachey, anthropologist Melville Herskovits, and University of Chicago English professor Robert Morss Lovett.[55]

Already by the early 1930s, Wright was theorizing a revolutionary poetics capable of puncturing political economic and religious myths of twentieth-century US capitalism to reveal particular forms of exploitation that had emerged during Jim Crow. Marxism was an indispensable guide for the development of such a poetics, but class analysis for Wright was always in dialogue with America's racial history and the global legacy of Western colonialism. As he recounts in *Black Boy*, he stayed up all night to read issues of the *New Masses* after his first visit to the John Reed Club in 1933 and woke up to write "I Have Seen Black Hands," expressing the core principle in interracial, working-class solidarity that would guide him throughout his life, even when he chafed against it:

> I am black and I have seen black hands
> Raised in fists of revolt, side by side with the white fists of white workers,
> And some day—and it is only this which sustains me—
> Some day there shall be millions and millions of them,
> On some red day in a burst of fists on a new horizon![56]

The Marxist Threads of Wright's Sociology

According to Carla Cappetti, Wright's associations with the John Reed Club, the LAW, and the FWP provided a basis for his "appropriation of a theoretical framework from sociology." But it was theories of conflict between the individual and society developed by the Chicago school of urban sociology, she argues, that formed an interpretive lens for *Black Boy*, structuring the autobiography along the lines of Wright's alienation from the three primary groups in his life—his family, the South, and the CPUSA—and serving as his "testament to the 1930s dying movement" of US Communism. She further suggests that the "irreconcilable contradictions between the individual and the group" in Wright's work are the source of both his conflicts with the Party and his appropriation of ethnographic tools for literary purposes. However, she omits the fact of Communist sponsorship of the JRC and LAW and the impact of Communist writers on the Illinois Writers' Project; more importantly, the sociological theory she invokes hinges on a normative structural analysis that reifies rather than challenges oppressive social relations, ignoring Marxist concepts of class division and class struggle in tension with Black nationalism, a dialectic that formed the critical lens through which Wright saw the world.[57]

Wright's interest in sociology vis-à-vis politics and social realist literature might instead be best understood in relation to the discipline's debt to Marx, evident not only in the early twentieth-century work of left-wing sociologists like Du Bois and Oliver Cox but also in Chicago school disciples like Horace Cayton, who became frustrated by its limitations, particularly its assertion of the ineluctability of assimilation as a final stage of social interaction for outsider groups.[58] To acknowledge this disciplinary history is not to minimize the Chicago school's influence on left-wing and militant thinkers like Wright. Nor were the empirical interests of the school necessarily antithetical to sociological inquiry rooted in dialectical materialism, even as they reflect a narrower understanding of the world on the basis of empirical observations.[59] That is to say, the empirical sociology of the Chicago school produced a body of knowledge through fine-grained, qualitative studies of the social structures of 1930s urban racial and economic relations that may lack the critical insights of Marxism but are not incompatible with Marxist analysis of the historical processes of the slave trade, chattel slavery, colonialism, and their aftermaths through which those structures emerged.

After a decline of disciplinary interest in Marxism during the Cold War, some American sociologists turned or returned to a dialectical historical materialist approach to social inquiry responsive to 1960s political unrest and social movements to develop a subfield of Marxist sociology in contradistinction to what is sometimes called "bourgeois sociology." Together with Marxist threads already woven into the discipline, the infectious spirit of 1930s radical thought prefigured left-wing influence on 1960s sociology, touching millions of people, including scholars, many of whom never became Communists but participated in protests or knew someone in the Party. While the Chicago school founders Robert E. Park and Louis Wirth recognized the oppressive urban conditions that stirred the city's Communists to action, the critical lens they applied to study them reinforced the liberal status quo. Rather than locating the source of exploitation in the historically specific character of capitalist relations of production, Park—who had been trained by Booker T. Washington—and, to a lesser extent, Wirth looked to universal theories of assimilation and social disorganization to explain poverty, crime, and inequality through a universal process of contact, competition, conflict, accommodation, and assimilation.

It was this universalizing, normative framework for social relations that their students, Cayton and John Gibbs St. Clair Drake, initially applied to their studies of the South Side of Chicago. Begun in the 1930s as a WPA unit headed by Cayton at the same time Wright was working along similar lines as a federal writer under the direction of Arna Bontemps and Jack Conroy, Cayton and Drake's research was eventually published in 1945 as *Black Metropolis: A Study of Negro Life in a Northern City*, a renowned work on the sociology of urban life. After leaving Chicago, Wright became close friends with Cayton, who recalled first meeting the aspiring young writer in Louis Wirth's office at the University of Chicago: "One day there came a tapping on the door of [the] office. I opened the door and there was a short brown-skinned Negro, and I said, 'Hello. What do you want?' He looked like an undergraduate, so I was perhaps condescending in a polite fashion, and, of course, he was also colored. He said, 'My name is Richard Wright. Mrs. Wirth made an appointment for me to see Dr. Wirth.' That made me a little more respectful. I told him to come in. 'Mrs. Wirth said that her husband might help me. I want to be a writer.'" Cayton went on to describe his empirical research with Wirth, "studying the vast complex of human beings who make up the complex of Chicago," about which Wright drolly observed, "You've got all your facts pointed, pinned to the wall like a collector would pin butterflies."[60]

Together with Cappetti, Bill Mullen argues that Wright realigned his 1930s Marxist orientation to fit more closely with the Chicago school, thereby distancing himself from the Communist past he had renounced. Mullen also contends that Wright's celebrity overshadowed Black artists and writers who remained committed to radical politics during and after the Popular Front period, and he concludes that reclaiming the history of twentieth-century Black culture and radicalism thus "requires reading both against and around Wright's critical legacy."[61] Support for this view of Wright can be found in his introduction to *Black Metropolis*, in which he declares, "It was the scientific findings of men like the late Robert E. Park, Robert Redfield and Louis Wirth" from which he had mined "the meanings" of all of his major publications—*Uncle Tom's Children, Native Son*, and *12 Million Black Voices*. However, Wright also listed works by Black scholars like E. Franklin Frazier, briefly a student at the University of Chicago, whose anticapitalist class analysis allied him with the left, if not the CPUSA, as a "self-professed and unswerving atheist with a commitment, however vaguely and inconsistently expressed, to socialist ideas."[62] Insofar as both sociology and Marxism rely on the scientific method to investigate social realities, Wright's tribute to the Chicago school arguably confirms rather than severs their connection. In practical terms, Cayton and Drake acknowledged the CPUSA's highly effective campaigns, particularly in defense of the Scottsboro Boys, which "stirred the imagination of the Negro people," and the organization of neighborhood Unemployed Councils to demand relief and resist eviction.[63]

While the majority of working-class Black Chicagoans might not have been conversant with Marxist-Leninist ideology, they understood the Party was on their side in their struggle to stay in their homes. As Cayton and Drake observed, "When eviction notices arrived, it was not unusual for a mother to shout to the children, 'Run quick and find the Reds!'"[64] Although Cayton held some anticommunist views, both Drake and he engaged with radical Marxist themes, acting at least as sympathetic observers of Party activities and recognizing the value of that work in support of African American equality. Nor was he unfamiliar with the Party, given that his brother Revels Cayton was a Communist labor organizer who held many leadership positions in West Coast longshore and maritime unions and eventually became the executive secretary of the National Negro Congress in New York City. In his first story in *The Nation* in 1931, Horace Cayton recorded his stunned response to a bloody attack by the Chicago riot squad on the "black bugs" (Black Communists) who had led a march and nonviolent protest against the evictions of an old woman and a family in Chicago's Black Belt. "Then I realized," he writes, "that all these people had suddenly found themselves face to face with hard, cold reality."[65] It was just such intensifying struggles, often led by the CPUSA, that suffused Wright's world. Despite his professed indebtedness to the Chicago school, neither *Black Metropolis* nor his own writing could help but reflect the radical ethos of the times.

Wright and the Marxist Tradition

That Wright retained a Marxist worldview after his break with the CPUSA is now widely accepted, but what exactly that means is debatable. As Alan Wald suggests, "There is no bright line demarcating political orientations on the left, and Wright's trajectory is among the hardest to trace." Echoing Wright's self-portrait, critics since the 1950s have maintained that he joined the CPUSA because it was one of the few avenues open to aspiring young Black writers. Walter Rideout asserted in 1956 that "literature and briefly Communism had come as keys to the prison of [Wright's] color," affirming the Party's role in his escape from Jim Crow but suggesting that it was merely a phase in his life. Describing *The Outsiders* as "explicitly anti-Communist," he echoed a critical consensus about the novel that misses its nuanced political valences and conflates Marxism with actually existing Communist states and movements. Robert Bone also praised the Party for opening doors to Black writers—being willing "to accept Negroes on the basis of social equality"—even as he condemned its manipulation of them: "Many young writers, both white and colored, succumbed to the flattering publicity which the party was willing to bestow—for a political price." In 1992, Louis Menand commented that Wright's portrayal of Bigger's discovery of murder as a form of self-realization "turned in Marx for Nietzsche," and that *Black Boy* delineates the oppressiveness of racism, religion, and the "totalitarianism of the Communist Party." Ian Afflerbach argued in 2015 that Bigger Thomas's radical lawyer Boris Max's speech in *Native Son* reflects not Communist (or Marxist) rhetoric but what he calls "New Deal Naturalism."[66]

Wright affirmed the Party's role as an escape route for him in a 1955 letter to his editor Edward Aswell about his break from the Party in 1944: "As anyone with common sense could easily guess, I was a Communist because I was Negro. Indeed the Communist Party had been the only road out of the Black

Belt for me. . . . The Party had a deep functional meaning for my life." He also felt a sense of loss: "I no longer had a protective barrier, no defenses between me and a hostile racial environment that absorbed all of my time, emotions, and attention."[67] Moreover, the Party, at one time, had assured him and other young writers, "Your rebellion is right. Come with us and we will support your vision with militant action." In addition to this revolutionary vision and political direction, the CPUSA gave writers an international audience, translating their writing into multiple languages and expanding their readership and reputation: "Who had ever in all human history," asked Wright, "offered to young writers an audience so vast?"[68] Nor by his own account did he feel pressured early on to abide by any official Party line, observing on the contrary that "our hope, our anger at oppression, our dreams of a new life ... spilled without coercion, without the pleading of anyone."[69] Along with early poems published in *Left Front*, *Anvil*, and *Midland Left*, and other left magazines, several appeared in *International Literature*, the journal of the International Union of Revolutionary Writers. These included "A Red Slogan" and "Ah Feels It in Mah Bones," which is notable for his use of dialect, situating the speaker of the poem in multiple dimensions of body, space, and time and capturing the bewildering yet freeing impact of the acceleration of modern life:

The whole world just done changed—
Ah feels it in mah bones . . .

* * *

Ah'm's ready—mah sail's set for whatever wind's in the sky!
An' brother, there's something a-comin'—
Ah feels it in mah bones![70]

Another ambitious poem was "Transcontinental," modeled on E. E. Cummings's translation of Louis Aragon's militant call to arms "Red Front," which in turn had been inspired by the Soviet poet Vladimir Mayakovsky's 1918 poem "Left March." Here again, propelling the poem forward, the arrow of time is recast as automobiles that speed across America as the speaker wonders "who owns this wonderland" of "the cool green of golf courses," amid the "ceaseless hiss of passing cars," "tinkle of ice in tall glasses," and "clacks of croquet balls scudding over cropped lawns." Midway through the poem, itinerant hitchhikers commandeer a car, announcing, "America is ours," to a refrain of "UNITED FRONT—SSSTRIKE" as they "head for the highway of self-determination" with comrades "coasting on momentum of Revolution," and ending, "Soon Soon you shall fly all over the hillsides Crowing the new dawn / Coasting Indulging in Lenin's dream."[71]

One of the most continuously circulating critiques of the Party is that its position on the "Negro question" was duplicitous and manipulative, a view reinforced by negative depictions by bourgeois liberal Black historians and civil rights leaders and some Black Communist writers, including Wright. In *The Negro and the Communist Party*, Wilson Record maintained in 1951 that African Americans had more than any other group in the United States rejected Communist appeals, and those who succumbed were subject to loss of independence and imaginative freedom. Commenting on the Party's "self-determination program," Record observed that the Black Belt thesis "was construed by many Negroes to be an ideological red-winged Jim Crow." He cited an unsigned editorial in the NAACP's magazine, *The Crisis*, which stated that "in advancing this theory of separation, the Communists are hand in hand with the southern ruling class which they so delight to lambast."[72] Concurring with Record in a review of his book, NAACP president Walter White denounced not only the Soviet Union and Stalin but also the radical US left for undermining Black interests.[73] In 1975, Addison Gayle condemned the Party's Black Belt thesis for emphasizing "the image of the dehumanized Black, crippled [by capitalism] as a human being" rather than heroic images of the strength and resilience of previous generations of Black writers. Only a "white deus ex machina," he declared, could alleviate Black suffering peddled as "the metaphor for suffering humanity," or, as Wright had called it, "America's metaphor."[74]

Assailing the imposition of Communist and left literary values on Black cultural expression, Harold Cruse amplified denunciations of the CPUSA's propagandistic, opportunistic practices in his 1967 book *The Crisis of the Negro Intellectual*: "Uncharted paths existed for the Negro creative intellectuals to explore, if only they could avoid being blinded by Communist Party propaganda."[75] Like many former Party members, Cruse repudiated his past and lashed out at the Party along with Black intellectuals, liberals, and integrationists. A provocative intellectual history, his book catapulted him to intellectual stardom and helped spearhead Black studies programs. He praised Wright's nationalist perspective in "Blueprint for Negro Writing," but believed he had failed to overcome the contradiction between Black nationalism and interracial class struggle, or "integrationism," as he called it. He derided liberal and Communist efforts to end Jim Crow but ignored their very different political goals, the one to quell racial unrest and reconsolidate capitalist priorities in the name of democracy, the other to unite Black and white workers in common cause to contest capitalist exploitation and ultimately overthrow the system. The contradiction remained unresolved for Wright, who contended with it first as a devoted Communist and then, after leaving the Party, as a more or less "free radical" for the rest of his life. Cruse, meanwhile, revealed his own limitations in how he framed the problem, attacking the interracial left and mistaking class rule for competing national interests in an antisemitic attack against Jews in which he claimed that Wright had been "ideologically blinded by the smog of Jewish-Marxist nationalism."[76] Less tendentiously, Bone credited the CPUSA with "enjoining the Negro author to explore his own tradition," even as he added that by doing so, "the Party inadvertently advanced the legitimate development of Negro art." He went on to declare that once again, "the American Communist party has done the right thing for the wrong reasons."[77]

Reconsiderations of "literary communism" had already begun by 1956, at the height of the Cold War, with Rideout's study of the American novel. Despite proclaiming the "almost complete rejection" of Communism by African Americans, Rideout's relatively unbiased evaluation of 1930s proletarian literature paved the way for further studies. Five years later, Daniel Aaron recast Communist writers of the interwar period in relation to American literary traditions, leading to still more vital research by Alan Wald, Barbara Foley, James Smethurst, Mary Helen Washington, and John McClusky, among others. Aaron challenged the dominant Cold War narrative that writers associated with the CPUSA were controlled by Moscow, pointing to historical precedents in the United States for the 1930s American literary left. Successive generations of American writers, he argued, had attacked "the unkillable beliefs of the bourgeoisie" in works ranging from protest novels like *Uncle Tom's Cabin* to less proselytizing critiques like *The Adventures of Huckleberry Finn*.[78] Thus, American literary communism in the 1930s represented "one more turn in the cycle of revolt," neither a creation of the Comintern nor a pawn of Moscow nor yet a victim of what Irving Howe and Lewis Coser described as the CPUSA's "profoundly destructive and corrupting influence upon American radicalism."[79]

The Proletkult (proletarian culture) and its influence in and beyond the Soviet Union contributed to the belief that Moscow controlled American communist writers. Established in 1917 on the eve of the Russian Revolution, the Proletkult was a Soviet movement that the American Communist writer and editor Mike Gold described as "Russia's organized attempt to remove the economic barriers and social degradation that repressed that proletarian instinct during the centuries."[80] The Proletkult appealed to left-wing American writers like Gold, who seized the idea of proletarian culture as an endorsement of worker education and found resonance with the radical democracy expressed by American poets like Walt Whitman, "the heroic spiritual father of our generation," who "dwelt among the masses" and from them "drew his strength."[81] In a brief announcement in *New Masses* about the newly formed John Reed Clubs, Gold called for a new "worker writer" to write as an insider about working-class life and industrial labor, "not like a bourgeois intellectual observer." Presaging the mission that the Federal Writers' Project proclaimed five years later with its American Guide Series, Gold imagined a "national corps" of writers in 1930 who would report on "each part of industrial America," an entirely new phenomenon in the history of writing, he declared, that would make writers more than "an imitation of Zola...a great pioneer but...always a tourist." These worker writers would become "the tongue of the working class."[82]

Proletkult literary studios inspired the JRCs to sponsor mass literacy education even as Marxist critics like V. F. Calverton dismissed the idea of building proletarian culture in 1930s America as a case of "Proletarianitis."[83] Nevertheless, Gold's call for proletarian writers who worked in industry and knew it from the inside contributed to a radically transformative moment in American culture led by the CPUSA and, later, the FWP, in support of writing from below. Meridel Le Sueur, for example, a Communist and a federal writer, prepared a manual for the Minnesota WPA, *Worker Writers*, in which she counseled her students, "Words are made to speak to others, to communicate, and without them we cannot create a new society. They are the blueprints of a new society. They are YOURS."[84] Wright emerged from this convergence of revolutionary ideals and a belief that art and literature could help change the world. Despite his association with the Proletkult, Gold was neither doctrinaire nor oblivious to matters of form in writing.[85] Rather than restricting the production of literature, as critics of proletarian writing contended, left-wing support for working-class writers enabled them to write from inside industrial America with the aim of forging working-class subjectivity. As Foley concludes, the literary left "neither march[ed] in lockstep with Soviet directives" nor "sacrifice[d] literature to propaganda." She also cautions, "To call for a serious reconsideration and positive reassessment of 1930s literary radicalism is not to proclaim its legacy unambiguous."[86]

"To Tell, to March, to Fight": The Echoes of Wright's Words

After the second *Atlantic* installment chronicling Wright's public break from the CPUSA, the Church of St. John in New York City approvingly declared in a parish bulletin "that he is thoroughly disgusted with his experiences as a

Communist," misquoting him as having written: "Communism is certainly not a panacea for the American Negro.... Communism is selfish, intolerant, bigoted and insincere." Horace Cayton recalled that Wright was in "open warfare" with the Party after 1944 and "from then on devoted (and wasted) much of his creative energy in fighting the Communists." Meanwhile, Communists deplored his betrayal of revolutionary ideals. *New Masses* editor Sam Sillen reproached him for denouncing the Party and losing the clarity of the Marxist outlook he had expressed in "Blueprint for Negro Writing": "Instead of slashing away at defeatism, he embraces defeatism. Not 'vision' but blindness he now exalts." Further, he had "cut himself off from the life of the masses" in a twofold tragedy: "The people lose an artist, and the artist loses himself." Frank Marshall Davis remarked that while he understood Wright's "antagonism" toward the CPUSA, he saw his public departure as "an act of treason in the fight for our rights," abetting "the racists who were constantly trying to destroy cooperation between Reds and blacks," which thus "damaged our battle." James W. Ford, the Party's vice presidential candidate in 1932, 1936, and 1940, called "Wright's shameful manner of writing about Negroes... disgusting and damaging to their dignity." Even more damning, in his review of *American Hunger* in 1977, George Breitman concluded in the *International Socialist Review* that "there is not much to be learned politically from this book" because Wright had never grasped the difference between "revolutionary Leninism and counterrevolutionary Stalinism."[87]

A fuller examination of his work and life, however, in and out of the Party, tells a different story. He came to detest the Communists' stifling directives, especially efforts by Law and Haywood to censor his projected series of Black Bolshevik profiles and force him to organize cost-of-living protests rather than concentrate on "Cesspool," eventually published as *Lawd Today!* But the underlying drama of his interactions with the CPUSA bespoke larger historical currents and contradictions. The currents swept him and other young writers and activists into radical maelstroms catalyzed by the Russian Revolution, the crisis of capitalism, and a rising global revolutionary tide. The contradictions deepened between revolution and counterrevolution; an international Communist movement increasingly dominated by Soviet exigencies and a US party with local chapters far from Moscow; a democratic centralist organization and tens of thousands of rank-and-file members involved in local union, housing, legal, and other campaigns as well as the arts, education, and culture; and the demands of a disciplined revolutionary cadre and the desire for individual freedom, especially for someone like Wright, who so desperately craved time and solitude for his writing. These dynamic factors bore not only on his relationship to the Party but also on its achievements and failures.

His break from the CPUSA signified not an abandonment of emancipatory political goals but a declaration of an aesthetic vision and practice incompatible with dogmatic Party discipline. His commitment to those goals resonates in his recollection of listening "for an echo" of his own words, hurled into darkness. "And if an echo sounded," he writes, "*I would send other words to tell, to march, to fight, to create a sense of the hunger for life that gnaws in us all, to keep alive in our hearts a sense of the inexpressibly human*" (emphasis added).[88] Multiple versions of what can rightly be called a confession, edited, restored, and finally published together with Part One of *Black Boy*, have blurred his own record of his experience as a Communist. All but erased or derided as superficial propaganda from standard readings of it are his passionate expressions of excitedly discovering like-minded, welcoming people, Black and white, willing to fight for an egalitarian society, to stand up for the world's disinherited, for African Americans and their colonized brethren. Further blurring his political worldview is the publication history of what eventually became Part Two of *Black Boy*, from *The Atlantic* in 1944 to *The God That Failed* in 1949 to a standalone version of *American Hunger* in 1977 to Harper Perennial's 1991 release of the entire book as originally intended as *Black Boy (American Hunger)*. Given the deletion of passages about his early years in Chicago and the Party's virtues from the *Atlantic* article, it is not surprising that Wright's complicated departure from the CPUSA has so often been misread.

Unlike ex-Communists who pivoted sharply to the right, Wright never abandoned his search for a revolutionary course of action that could end the hunger and suffering he had witnessed as a child growing up in the South— one attuned to the "inexpressibly human" yet painfully taut with the contradiction between the racialized history of capitalism and the need for interracial class solidarity to contest capitalist rule. It was the nexus of these contradictory forces that necessitated, however elusively, the liberation of people of color from wage (and penal) slavery in order to abolish race as a measure of one's value. While the last lines of the restored version of *Black Boy* have typically been interpreted as signaling "other words" than those of Communists or Marxists, closer to the "inexpressibly human" for which he yearned, a rejection of mass struggle to overthrow capitalism, and a retreat to an individualistic humanism, they can also be read as an expression of his ongoing commitment, albeit tempered by a more pessimistic view of history, to an emancipatory politics fully capable of realizing human potential for all.

From rereading those last lines as a declaration to continue "to march" and "to fight," it follows that his subsequent engagements as an expatriate built on rather than negated the years he spent in Chicago and New York in his twenties and thirties—years that launched his literary career and indelibly shaped his political consciousness. These new engagements included his relationships with French Marxists, particularly Jean-Paul Sartre and Simone de Beauvoir, and the Black socialists C. L. R. James, George Padmore, and Léopold Senghor, among other Anglophone and Francophone Pan-Africanists, as well as his travels to the Gold Coast, Spain, and the Bandung conference of nonaligned nations in Indonesia. During the ultraleft Third Period from 1928 to 1934—which coincided with his arrival in Chicago—the Party had played a leading role, however imperfect, sectarian, and utopian, in defending labor, Black, and women's rights. It exuded a giddy conviction among rank-and-file members, fellow travelers, and peripheral cultural and labor organizations that revolutionary change was not only needed and possible but inevitable. Despite his exasperation with the Party and his restless philosophical uncertainties, his years in Chicago and New York prepared him for several of the most consequential political movements and events of the twentieth century.

More recent considerations of Wright's politics counteract depictions of him as naive, duped, equipped only with "the facile answers of Marxism."[89] He could not have assumed such a significant, if controversial, role in global anticolonial and Pan-African literary and political movements, or dealt with competing Marxist, Black radical, communist, anticommunist, and socialist theories and practices, without deep knowledge of history, culture, and Marxist concepts. Uneasy about the reception of *Black Boy* after learning Harper would only publish Part One, Wright had sent the critic Joseph Gollomb a clarification of his politics that Gollomb quoted in his review of *Black Boy*: "Something more is involved than politics or race. I am as collectivist and proletarian in my outlook as when I belonged to the Communist Party, and the Negroes are my people. But there is a need to think and feel honestly, and that comes first."[90] His restless, unembarrassed, contentious need for honesty, combined with his double, if not triple vision as a Black American expatriate, gave him insights into global realities as colonized peoples of color struggled for independence in an increasingly unstable world. Already under FBI surveillance, and reflecting on his agitated state of mind in his personal diary in February 1945, he noted the defining contradictions of his life: he was a "plantation Negro" in New York, a peasant who was a writer, a Black man married to a white woman, and "a Communist who can not stand being a member of the Communist groups." He still subscribed to

Communist principles but could no longer tolerate CPUSA bureaucracy. "God knows," he wrote, "I am a hot and bothered man."[91]

As an expatriate, he engaged in intense private and public dialogues about twentieth-century political economic tensions in a world bewilderingly reordered through processes of industrialization, urbanization, imperialism, and decolonization. As an internationally renowned writer and intellectual, he helped form or participated in new left-wing organizations, including Rassemblement Démocratique Révolutionnaire, a short-lived political project closely associated with Sartre; the Pan-African movement; *Présence Africaine*, the Pan-African quarterly journal founded in 1947 that sponsored the First Congress of Negro Artists and Writers, which Wright helped organize; and the Nonaligned Movement, which met formally for the first time in 1955 at the Bandung conference that Wright attended and reported on in *The Color Curtain*. He bore witness to intensifying global conflicts and shifting alliances as movements for self-determination threw off the yoke of colonialism in the midst of clashing, postwar forces: the expanding reach of capitalism, a revitalized neofascism in Spain, the chill of the Cold War, faltering experiments in communism, and a socialist world still waiting to be born. As Frank Marshall Davis put it, "Basically he was still a Marxist.... He had merely quit the organization and dumped his former comrades, not the ideology."[92]

As the fog of anticommunist ideology continues to lift, Wright's political and aesthetic quest has come into clearer focus. In response to a fast-changing postwar global order, he sought new alliances and new pathways to a more egalitarian world, free of racial oppression, inter-imperialist wars, and capitalist exploitation. If, as Bill Mullen maintains in relation to popular fronts and the Black Chicago Renaissance, Wright cast a long shadow on other radical Black authors, it must also be said that his own legacy has too often been misjudged. In his "unreading" of Wright's status as the "towering figure" in Depression-era Chicago, Mullen claims that he had a "'permanent' political change of heart" and adopted a sociological framework to mask his radical past as "his own politics became calculatingly evasive and anti-Communist."[93] Such reappraisals follow a litany of critiques of Richard Wright, many of which reflect the temper of the times and the critics as much as his actual life and work. Meanwhile, his flight from the Party and country of origin positioned him as an expatriate "at the moment of potentiality between the no longer and the not yet" to confront the antinomies of twentieth-century global capitalism that continue to haunt us today.[94]

CHAPTER FOUR

Rediscovering America as a Black Federal Writer

In addition to encouraging Wright's development as a writer, the Federal Writers' Project (FWP) put him, along with some 6,500 other unemployed writers, teachers, lawyers, and secretaries, on the government payroll so he and his family could eat and pay rent. Under the aegis of the New Deal's Federal One program, established in 1935 as part of the Works Progress Administration (WPA), the FWP sponsored documentary research, writing, and photography in public humanities projects unlike any other in their magnitude, before or since. The FWP helped launch Wright's career along with those of hundreds of other lesser-known writers, many African American, in ways that would "dramatically influence the growth of serious professional black writing."[1] Wright's experience is both representative of other left writers of the 1930s and unique in his dazzling rise to fame. Not yet twenty, he arrived in Chicago in 1927 "in search of spiritual enlightenment" and "the warmth of other suns."[2] Between 1934 and 1940, he wrote poems, *Uncle Tom's Children*, and *Native Son*, along with essays, FWP materials, and over 200 articles in the *Daily Worker*. By the time he left for New York City in 1937, he had forged a method, a style, and a radically new voice in the American literary scene. Known for its cultural "rediscovery" of America, the FWP set out to document stories of diverse Americans, in support of a more inclusive, pluralistic ethos and politics. Wright both contributed to that effort and critically recast it through the eyes of a young, radical, Black writer.

Like other periods of radical upheaval and change, the 1930s saw a confluence of political, economic, and cultural forces that swept masses of people into the maelstrom of history and catapulted them into a world remade by imperialist war—what Lenin called "the highest stage of capitalism"—along with the 1929 stock market crash, a global depression, and the rise of fascism. Other large-scale social change was already underway with accelerating industrial growth, the Great Migration of millions of Black southerners to the urban North, and revolutionary movements at home and abroad, most notably in Russia in 1917, bolstered by the Second International, the federation of labor and socialist parties that succeeded the International Workingmen's Association. The Harlem Renaissance had by then nurtured a generation of African American and

Caribbean American writers, actors, musicians, artists, and intellectuals who made New York City a Black cultural mecca. As that movement waned, Black writers and artists in Chicago created a new, more critical politics of Black culture that came to be known as the Black Chicago Renaissance. It was against this turbulent backdrop that Wright joined other Black migrants to make a home for himself and his family on Chicago's South Side.

Supported by the voracious reading habits described in his autobiography, his earliest writings showed promise, but it was the crucible of the next seven years in Chicago that transformed him as a writer. Given his precarity before and after the Wall Street crash, there were no guarantees that he would realize his potential. According to his biographer Michel Fabre, "Circumstances favored less than ever Wright's ambition to become a writer, nor were his literary talents likely to keep him fed."[3] Orchestrating his richly varied experiences in those formative years was his membership in groups that contributed to his literary success, from the CPUSA-sponsored John Reed Club (JRC) to the South Side Writers Group, which he organized in 1936 and which included, among other emerging Black writers, Frank Marshall Davis, Margaret Walker, and Horace Cayton. He also worked for the Illinois state office of the FWP, established in 1935, writing ethnographic reports that contributed not only to his development as a writer but also to the concrete, specific knowledge he gained through fieldwork and archival research that enabled him to reconsider local and global histories in a more critical, comprehensive light.[4]

Despite feeling ashamed at the height of the Depression about "making a public confession of my hunger," he sought assistance from the Bureau of Public Welfare.[5] His case worker was Mary Wirth, wife of the sociologist Louis Wirth, whom he met along with Horace Cayton, then Wirth's research assistant, several years later at the University of Chicago. It was Mary Wirth who got him a job as an orderly at the Michael Reese Hospital after the 1929 crash forced him to seek public relief.[6] Eventually, he became an aide at the South Side Boys' Club, a "deeply engrossing" job in which he sympathized with boys whose "talk of planes, women, guns, politics, and crime," "figures of speech," and "word-rhythms" infused his fiction.[7] In 1935, Wirth enrolled him in the Illinois Writers' Project, where he was assigned to research local history as he continued to labor over his own writing. By then, he had published "I Have Seen Black Hands" and several other poems, founded and coedited *Left Front*, and begun to share drafts of the novellas for *Uncle Tom's Children* with the South Side Writers Group. In 1938, he won the *Story* magazine award for the best FWP submission for "Fire and Cloud."

As his fellow federal writer, comrade, and friend Nelson Algren put it, "The writer whom the Illinois Writers' Project helped the most was Dick Wright."[8] Margaret Walker declared, "The explosion of his creative genius coincided with this cultural explosion of the WPA."[9] As much as the FWP nurtured his and other writers' careers and documented American life in the throes of world crises, it was a state-sponsored program obliged to maintain political neutrality whose very existence depended in many respects on radical ideas, methods, and protest from below. According to Jerre Mangione, the FWP editor of the state guides and a former JRC member, the Federal One projects might never have happened were it not for left-wing protests agitating for relief through the Unemployed Writers Association and the Writers Union.[10] Wright and other proletarian avant-garde writers, many of whom were also JRC members, infused the FWP with radical ideas and insights that pushed the egalitarian, democratic spirit of its publications to the left of center. Although the JRC was not officially affiliated with the CPUSA until 1932, and not all members were Communists, its radical left-wing spirit reverberated in the slogan "Art is a class weapon." This indirect influence intensified the contradiction between the FWP as a state-sponsored project and the militancy of so many of its writers, especially for its director, Henry Alsberg, who had to answer to the newly formed House Un-American Activities Committee (HUAC). Rather than "rediscover America," an announcement of the club's formation in a 1929 issue of *New Masses* declared that its purpose was "to bring closer all creative workers . . . to maintain contact with the American revolutionary labor movement" and to connect with similar groups abroad.[11]

At its peak in 1934, a year before the creation of the FWP, thirty JRC chapters with 1,200 members had been formed nationwide. Along with Wright, members included Mike Gold (one of eight *New Masses* editors who founded the clubs), John Dos Passos, Kenneth Rexroth, Meridel Le Sueur, Tillie Lerner (Olsen), and Langston Hughes. In his autobiography, Wright recalls that the JRC "was demanding that the government create jobs for unemployed artists; it planned and organized art exhibits; it raised funds for the publication of *Left Front*; and it sent scores of speakers to trade-union meetings."[12] Michael Denning likewise notes that once the WPA was established, "the alumni of the Reed clubs carried their proletarian aesthetics into the guidebooks and folklore collections of the Federal Writers' Project."[13] While the FWP advanced the careers of promising young authors like Wright and produced a trove of state guides, interviews, folklore, and life stories, as well as its highly significant collection of slave narratives, neither its extraordinary achievements nor those of its writers would have materialized without the radical alchemy of the interwar period.

The Federal Writers' Project Rediscovers America

Widespread discontent among unemployed workers, who made up nearly one-quarter of the nation's population by 1934, and militant pressure exerted by organized labor and left-wing parties forced the Roosevelt administration to enact a series of relief programs to alleviate the impact of the Depression, culminating in the establishment of the WPA in 1935. Primarily designed to put the unemployed to work on infrastructure projects constructing roads, bridges, schools, libraries, armories, and other public needs, the WPA had neglected the plight of cultural workers. Wright was among the artists and writers in Chicago and elsewhere, many of whom already belonged to the JRC, the CPUSA, or other left organizations, who helped mobilize street protests to push for support for literature and the arts. Their efforts led to the creation, under the aegis of the WPA, of Federal One, an afterthought about which director Henry Hopkins famously quipped, "Artists have to eat, too." In addition to the FWP, other programs in Federal One included art, music, and theater projects and a historical records survey.

A year after the FWP's establishment, it was clear that its coverage of African Americans was largely absent from publications, and where present, it was often distorted. In response to protests by Black leaders, Alsberg appointed Howard University professor and author Sterling Allen Brown as the Project's national editor of the Office of Negro Affairs, enabling him to set in motion a plan for seventeen publications on African American history. Ironically, despite efforts to distance the FWP from its radical influences, including the demand for Black representation, it fell prey to HUAC, led by Congressman Martin Dies, which launched a series of anticommunist attacks against writers, Wright among them, ultimately leading to the Project's demise. For Wright and thousands of other federal writers across the country, the FWP not only gave them a paycheck but also engaged them in methods of documentary writing that influenced their careers and imbued American culture with a new ethos of pluralism and bottom-up inclusion of the voices of women, workers, and immigrants across racial and ethnic lines. New and established tools of ethnography, oral history, and archival research emerged at the junction of anthropology, sociology, documentary film, muckraking journalism, and radical mobilizations of artists and writers who appropriated and applied them for their own purposes. These tools equipped Wright "to fuse and make articulate the experiences of men" and find in his own life "those materials and experiences."[14]

Under Alsberg's direction, the FWP established headquarters in every state that reported to the central office in Washington, DC, ensuring it could fulfill its main objective of putting unemployed Americans back to work (to be hired, one had to be unemployed), whether or not they were professional writers, by engaging them in research and production as well as writing. In addition to the American Guide Series of travel guides to all forty-eight states, the FWP produced the *American Life Series: Manuscripts of the Federal Writers' Project, 1936–1940* and *Born in Slavery: Slave Narratives from the Federal Writers' Project, 1936–1938*, together with several smaller collections of urban and rural folklore. Research conducted by federal writers, including Wright, contributed to subsequent publications such as Arna Bontemps and Jack Conroy's photodocumentary book, *They Seek a City*, republished in 1997 as *Anyplace but Here*; St. Clair Drake and Horace Cayton's *Black Metropolis: A Study of Negro Life in a Northern City*, with Wright's introduction; and *The Negro in Illinois: The WPA Papers*, a collection of essays, anecdotes, and "folksy tidbits" that "shows the significant contribution of Chicago's South Side to the African American experience," published for the first time in 2013.[15]

This archive of American history continues to be mined for content not hitherto brought to light, including Wright's unsigned ethnographic reports. In its mission of rediscovering America, the FWP sought "to introduce America to Americans" through an array of projects, including the state guides, or Baedekers, honoring ordinary people whose lives were upended and encouraging cross-country travel in automobiles, which had become more common even as the nation struggled to recover from the Depression. As a federal writer, Wright supported that mission but also challenged its romantic bid for inclusiveness in the face of the country's persistent, systemic inequalities, particularly for Black Americans. After he moved to New York City and lived there long enough to qualify for a job on the New York Writers' Project, he contributed to chapters in the *WPA Guide to New York City* and coauthored the chapter "Portrait of Harlem" in its companion book, *New York Panorama*, chronicling Black history in New York City and cautioning that the nation's future is inextricably entwined with that of the "Negro in America."[16] Such commentary set the guides apart from the pocket-sized Baedekers that ranked sites using a star system and advised travelers on tipping and other local practices. According to Daniel M. Fox's appraisal of the FWP guides, "the proposed and published volumes moved steadily beneath the surface of American life," from encyclopedic tour books to introductory essays, local histories, and folklore studies to case histories best represented by *These Are Our Lives*, a collection of thirty-seven life histories in a regional study of work in the South.[17]

Despite increased interest in the FWP today, its history, achievements, and literary and cultural legacies remain underappreciated. Outside of a relatively small number of scholars and fans, it remains little known despite the digitalization and greater availability of many FWP publications. After the 2008 financial crisis—and again, during the 2020–23 global pandemic—a flurry of journalists, writers, scholars and elected officials called for a new WPA to put Americans, including writers and artists, back to work. Even if that call had been heeded and material support was provided to individuals or groups, a twenty-first-century FWP would be unlikely to duplicate the explosion of public art and literature sparked by Federal One's collective ethos, national structure, and public mission. Moreover, if it projected the same pluralistic values of the 1930s FWP, it would almost certainly draw the ire of right-wing anticommunists banning books and courses on LGBTQ and Black history in the mid-2020s. Wright and other radical writers played a key role in the New Deal–era experiment in mass public projects, which located the production of culture not only in literary and artistic virtuosity (Wright's included), but also, and primarily, in the stories, dreams, aspirations, histories, and conditions of life of ordinary people—a "history from below" perspective that emerged at the intersection of the nascent fields of anthropology and folklore studies, the creation of Federal One, and the proletarian culture of the literary left.

The materials Wright produced as a federal writer show the relevance of his work on the Illinois Writers' Project (IWP) to his literary career, exemplifying both the FWP's achievements and the zeitgeist of the period. The IWP benefited from dynamic interactions of its members, including Wright, with the John Reed Club, the Sociology Department at the University of Chicago, and the South Side Writers Group. For Wright, like many of his contemporaries, these formative experiences altered the course of his development as a researcher, a writer, and, for him, a soon to be world-renowned author. Even though the phrase "history from below" had yet to emerge in the 1930s, the concept describes the historical materialist, dialectical viewpoint that suffused that era's labor, radical, and cultural movements. Each of the overlapping literary and political scenes that Wright discovered in Chicago to his astonishment and delight reflected the spirit of uncovering and recovering voices missing from historical narratives: the masses of people whose names may be recorded only in birth and death certificates, census reports, tax records, or property deeds (for many, not even those traces remain), whose life stories are omitted from the annals of history. It was the desire to recover those stories—echoing in struggles for freedom and inclusion of African Americans, women, immigrants, workers, and other marginalized groups—that drove the development of oral history in its modern form.

Fisk and Southern Universities in the late 1920s, followed by the FWP in the 1930s, began collecting oral histories two decades before Allan Nevins established the Oral History Research Office at Columbia University in 1948, widely credited as the first such program. These pioneering projects contested the "Great Man" theory of history in ways the Columbia program did not. Expressing a different set of values from Nevins's elitist approach to oral history, they were committed to giving a platform to voices from below, rooted in struggles of those relegated to the dustbins of history. In this light, Wright's research for the FWP in Chicago from 1935to 1937 and in New York City from 1938 to 1940 involved not only the acquisition of skills but also a profound revision of history as it had previously been told. This wider lens on Wright's contributions to the IWP archives, the *New York City WPA Guide*, and *New York Panorama* reveals a dynamic interplay between the JRC and the FWP, despite their differences, that helps explain the groundswell of interest in popular history and the fate of the "common people."[18] Some scholars have begun to pay attention to the FWP materials Wright produced in Chicago and New York; others have linked this documentary writing to subsequent books, especially *12 Million Black Voices*, *Native Son*, and *Black Power*.[19] Still others have highlighted the journalistic training he got as an editor in 1937 for the *Daily Worker*, for which he wrote more than 200 articles, and his associations with left-wing periodicals, including the *Left Front*, *New Masses*, and the short-lived *New Challenge*.[20]

Emerging in the fuller picture suggested by these insights into Wright's methods and style is the impact of his immersion in documentary writing in the 1930s on his literary pursuits from then on. Alternately linked to proletarian, social realist, naturalist, and modernist literary movements, Wright employed a variety of stylistic and rhetorical devices to achieve different aims, influenced as much by Gertrude Stein as by Theodore Dreiser. But it is how he envisioned his own future at the end of Part Two of *Black Boy* that aligns most compellingly with the ethos of bottom-up documentary art in his desire "to build a bridge of words between me and the world outside" and "hurl words into this darkness and wait for an echo"—a signal "to tell, to march, to fight, to create a sense of the hunger for life that gnaws in us all, to keep alive in our hearts a sense of the inexpressibly human."[21] In this sense, Wright fused artistic creation with the struggle for freedom from oppressive conditions that suffused his childhood and haunted the rest of his life. As he told Baldwin in Paris at the Brasserie Lip, he saw all literature as political. Assuming he meant that all literature reflects the human condition in the broadest sense of political life, he was using ethnographic and sociological tools and concepts along with literary techniques to fulfill the task he set for Black writers to "create a meaningful picture of the world today."[22]

The materials he produced for the IWP, in particular, demonstrate his capacity for "thick description" of the sort that according to Clifford Geertz defines the intellectual enterprise of ethnography, while his essay on Harlem in *New York Panorama*, against the grain of mainstream history, would have required deep research that probably included digging into archives at the Schomburg Center for Research in Black Culture, then called the New York Public Library Center for Negro Literature, History, and Prints. These unsigned pieces by Wright resonate with Farm Security Administration director Roy Stryker's definition of documentary as "an approach, not a technique; an affirmation, not a negation."[23] Tom Rankin interprets Stryker's aphoristic comment to mean "that in documenting 'our time and our surroundings,' documentary artists not only affirm through the act of witnessing but also affirm the valued role of engagement. Documentarians participate, intervene, and act in the communities, struggles, and stories that they record."[24] The complexity of the relationship between the documentarian and the subject takes on new and different meanings when researchers like Wright not only bear witness and engage with the subject but also tell their own stories. Questions of standpoint, subjectivity, and (mis)representation have often been raised about FWP materials. It was only in 1926 that the Scottish filmmaker John Grierson first invoked the term "documentary" to refer to new modes of research and genres across artistic and academic disciplines. Yet even as it became a dominant approach in New Deal arts and literature, producing works familiar to twenty-first-century publics, like Dorothea Lange's and Gordon Parks's photographs, Jacob Riis's *How the Other Half Lives*, and James Agee and Walker Evans's *Let Us Now Praise Famous Men*, the documentary form was beginning to be called into question by practitioners as well as critics and audiences.[25]

Wright incorporated documentary methods into his writing at the same time that he stood outside the practice, critically commented on it, and at times, fell prey to its seductions. How he negotiated these tensions troubles the FWP's romanticized rediscovery of a country he described as making him and other Black Americans feel "that the whole world was alien and hostile," a contradiction inherent in the government-backed project that helped launch his career.[26] Through the bifocal lens of his Marxist critique of capitalism and his experience as a Black American writer, he uncovered the racist history that had fueled America's rise to power in a "tragic premonition" of the class and racial divisions at the heart of its contradictory legacy. While the FWP helped catapult him to literary fame and spurred research that would unfold over his lifetime, it was no more able to confront the realities he lay bare than the state that had created it.

Wright's Bolshevik Biographies and Jim Crow Terror

An early instance of Wright's research skills can be found in his notes on interviews with David Poindexter (Ross in *Black Boy*) for "Biography of a Bolshevik," one of a series of biographical sketches of Black Communists that he envisioned but never completed.[27] The idea for the series came in response to his mother's horrified reaction to a "lurid Mayday cartoon" on the cover of a copy of the *Masses*, revealing the distance between the Party and the "disinherited" like her whose "ideal was Christ upon the Cross" and who loathed the magazine that persuaded him that "here at last in the realm of revolutionary expression was where Negro experience could find a home, a functioning value and role." Unable to explain the lurid cover or the Party's appeal, he reread the magazine and concluded that it "embodied what the *artists* thought would appeal to others, what they thought would gain recruits. They had a program, an ideal, but they had not yet found a language." He thus resolved to "put some of that meaning back" in words that would reach both the Communists who "had missed the meaning of the lives of the masses" and the "common people" who had yet to grasp the "self-sacrifice of Communists, who strove for unity among them."[28]

Although the FWP had not yet been created or even conceived, Wright was already enacting its mission of recording stories of diverse Americans through his project of developing biographical profiles of Black Communists, exemplifying the documentary experience he and his fellow radicals brought to the FWP. In his profile of Poindexter, he aimed to bridge the serious communication gap he saw between the Communist Party and the Black masses it sought to recruit. The collection of biographies of Black Communists he envisioned would be titled "Heroes, Red and Black," and would include stories that resonated closely with his own as a Black southerner who migrated north and became a Communist as the only solution that he had found to the problem of Jim Crow racism. Thus, his evolving ethos as a Black writer who embodied America's trauma of racial oppression and as a Communist in the radical cauldron of 1930s Chicago had already infused his literary imagination with a "documentary impulse" prior to his employment as a federal writer.[29] It was his earlier experience of meeting sympathetic comrades in the Chicago Post Office and the JRC, white and Black, that enabled him to see the possibility of radical struggle and racial solidarity and imagine such a project as the biographical profiles. As a young, emerging writer, he was discovering both the constraints of party discipline and an alternative to feeling "like an animal in a jungle" in an "alien and hostile" world that he survived by "denying what I saw with my eyes, disputing what I felt with my body" in order "to keep my identity intact."[30]

Thwarted in his planned biographies by Party bureaucrats who suspected him of being a "bastard intellectual" and an "incipient Trotskyist," Wright and the archives lost a crucial chapter of Black activism in the 1930s. Under indictment for a disorderly conduct charge, Poindexter, known as "Dex," had been arrested with other Black comrades at a 1932 protest against a city crackdown on radical speech in Ellis Park, a smaller, alternative site for the historic Washington Square Park soapbox platform. Prior to joining the CPUSA, Wright was harshly critical of Black Communist speakers at Washington Square, disdainful of their naivety and superficial mimicry of revolutionary figures like Lenin.[31] But it was these same men, or men like them, that he later befriended and whose stories he sought to tell, suggesting that his perspective had changed through direct contact with them in the Party. He portrays Poindexter as a southern-born Black man, "typical of the effective, street agitator" who "reflected the crude hopes and frustrations of the peasant in the city ... a bundle of the weaknesses and virtues of a man struggling blindly between two societies, of a man living on the margin of a culture."[32] He was fascinated by Poindexter's stories of his boyhood in the Deep South and his rugged life as a stevedore on the Mississippi River, which included witnessing a lynch mob kill a friend at the age of thirteen. When Wright's activities aroused Party leaders' suspicions that he was an informer, he told them that Poindexter's stories had inspired a story, "Big Boy Leaves Home," that he had already sold.

First published in 1936 in the anthology *The New Caravan* and later included in *Uncle Tom's Children*, "Big Boy" tells the story, largely in dialogue in Black dialect, of four boys who innocently skip school, playing a version of the dozens based on a popular song with the refrain "*Yo mama don wear no drawers.*" They walk idly through the woods to a pasture and lie on the grass, knees bent, "faces square to the sun." Big Boy hangs back as the other boys debate whether to go swimming and head for a creek, and then he roughly persuades them to continue wandering through the woods until they come to a swimming hole on "ol man" Harvey's property. Despite seeing a "no trespassing" sign and knowing that Harvey has shot at Black swimmers, Big Boy convinces them to go swimming and leads the way. After stripping naked, they push each other into the water, only to see a white woman at the tree where they left their clothes. As if the sun had gone under a cloud, the mood of the story darkens as they confront the woman and her companion, who has a rifle and is dressed in an army uniform. The man, who they later find out is Harvey's son Jim, kills two of the boys before Big Boy grabs the gun and shoots and kills him. Big Boy runs home, and his family frantically confers with community elders, who arrange for him to hide in a kiln overnight and wait until morning for a truck driver who will take him north. Big Boy hides, fights off a large snake and a dog, and bears witness to a terrifying white mob that lynches the other surviving boy, his friend Bobo.[33]

Wright had thus by 1934 evinced a commitment to literature that would "fuse and make articulate the experiences of men," a disciplined approach to literary technique and field research, sharply aware of his subject position as a Black Communist writer.[34] It would lead him to renounce the sentimentality of readers that *Uncle Tom's Children* had evoked, vowing if he wrote another book that "no one would weep over it; that it would be so hard and deep that they would have to face it without the consolation of tears."[35] By the time his social worker Mary Wirth assigned him to work on the IWP, he had published enough poems in left-wing periodicals that he was allowed to devote some of his time to his own writing as he carried out assignments for the Illinois state guide and the *Negro in Illinois*. This recognition of his potential enabled him to complete all four novellas in the first edition of *Uncle Tom's Children*, including "Fire and Cloud," selected out of 600 entries to win first prize ($500) in *Story Magazine* in 1937. That same year, he moved to New York City to pursue his career as a writer and wrote the brilliant story "Bright and Morning Star," which appeared in *New Masses* and was included, along with "The Ethics of Living Jim Crow: An Autobiographical Sketch"—first published in *American Stuff: WPA Writers' Anthology*—in the second edition of *Uncle Tom's Children* in 1940.[36] It was this essay that drew the ire of Dies's House Un-American Activities Committee, presaging the State Department, FBI, and CIA harassment Wright would suffer for the rest of his life.

One of the men he had naively thought of interviewing, Oliver Law (Ed Green in *Black Boy*), died at age thirty-four fighting fascism in Spain, where he was the first Black commander of a predominantly white unit of the Abraham Lincoln Brigade. According to Wright's account in *Black Boy*, Law barged in on one of his meetings with Poindexter to interrogate them. When Wright explained his purpose and suggested that he might like to interview him next, Law retorted, "I'm not interested." Little is known about Oliver

Law today, attesting to the documentary force that motivated Wright and other 1930s artists and writers to tell history from below. That widely felt impulse, though rooted in the politics of proletarian struggle, reflected a desire across the spectrum of interwar liberal and left ideologies to democratize the nation by retrieving the life stories of those otherwise "hidden from history."[37] But the documentary gaze that mediated these stories differed across that spectrum, so while race, ethnicity, gender, and class all shaped the power relations of the observer and the observed, it was often, decisively, ideology that determined how one perceived the other and vice versa.

Liberal and some more radical documentarians might reflect a combination of class snobbery, uncritical belief in a free market system, and/or unconscious racist attitudes—particularly among white culture workers, but also the Black bourgeoisie who wanted to "uplift" the race rather than focus on the traumatic impact of hundreds of years of slavery and servitude.[38] In contrast, Wright's experience as a politically conscious Black American with working-class roots facilitated the shift in his point of view, which was further defined by his dialectical grasp of the history of capitalism. Though Wright came to understand why the biographical profiles project had aroused Party leaders' suspicions that he was an informer, he was less interested in Poindexter's politics than in his story's typification of "certain traits of the Negro migrant." In seeing Poindexter as a "peasant in the city," straddling two worlds while "living on the margin of a culture," Wright was already applying a Marxist interpretation of history, to be more fully developed in *12 Million Black Voices*, with Black migrants dominated by the Lords of the Land in the feudal South having to contend with the Bosses of the Buildings in the urban North and its specific forms of racial degradation, shattering their dreams of freedom.[39]

The main focus of most accounts of Wright's experience as a federal writer, including his own, has been on the fact of his employment, the financial relief it afforded him and his family, the prize-winning literary publications he produced between 1935 and 1939, and the HUAC attacks on the Project that took aim in particular at his essay "The Ethics of Living Jim Crow." In part because the guides are more accessible than unpublished or recently recovered physical archives—many of which are still scattered, and in some cases, lost—more emphasis has been placed on Wright's unsigned "Portrait of Harlem," coauthored with Claude McKay, in *New York Panorama* than on the materials he produced for the IWP. There have also been more close, critical readings of *Black Voices*, one of several documentary works, including Bontemps and Conroy's *They Seek a City* and Drake and Cayton's *Black Metropolis*, that emerged after the FWP's demise in 1939. Much less has been written about

Wright's ethnographic studies of Chicago.[40] Yet these works not only have literary, sociological, and historical merit in and of themselves but also anticipate his breakthrough literary success and integral place in American and world literature.

Geographies of South Side Chicago: "If You Wasn't Black . . . You Could Fly a Plane"

It was the same cold, dark streets of Chicago that had greeted him in 1927 that Wright started researching in November 1935, along with forty other field workers, for the Illinois state guide under the direction of the geography professor Nathan Morris. In 1933, he had lost his job at the post office and reluctantly gone on relief, working successively as an orderly at a medical institute, a street sweeper, and a counselor at the South Side Boys' Club. Along with his studies in literature and Marxism, pursued independently and in the JRC, he was deeply interested in anthropology and sociology. Eager to study these disciplines more systematically, he approached Louis Wirth, who gave him a reading list for an intermediate sociology student and was impressed by his deep absorption of the material. Cayton, Wirth's graduate assistant, recalls Wright walking into the professor's office to introduce himself and boldly announcing, "My name is Richard Wright. Mrs. Wirth said that her husband might help me. I want to be a writer."[41] The knowledge and skills he acquired through his various studies prepared him to delve into IWP research to tell America's story. Twice a week, he reported to an office on Wells Street to turn in his work and pick up a new assignment, spending most of his time at local libraries, especially the Newberry Library, which held a trove of archives. His earliest writing for the IWP on file, dated December 11, 1935, is titled "Ethnographic Aspects of Chicago's Black Belt." The last dated piece is March 1937; in May, he moved to New York City to pursue his literary career.

In a great service to those interested in IWP materials, accessible until recently only in physical archival collections, Brian Dolinar edited previously unpublished, scattered material in *The Negro in Illinois: The WPA Papers* (2015) as well as a collection of Wright's ethnographic reports and bibliographies in *Southern Quarterly* in 2009.[42] In a file on the Chicago Urban League, dated January 8, 1936, Wright lists the sources available to the public that informed his reports: letters, accounts of investigations, surveys, and bulletins (96). Under "Material on Race Relations and 1919 Race Riot," he adds statements of the governor, records of conferences, questionnaires, memoranda on housing, census data, surveys "relating to the Negro in industry, labor, and housing," copies of the Urban League's publication *Interracial Messenger*, "correspondence between the mayor and governor relating to the calling of troops to suppress the riots," and more (97). Such lists reveal the research methods with which Wright and other federal writers challenged the period's standard treatments of American history dominated by the "Lost Cause" school's redemption of the Confederacy, representing slaveholders as kind and protective of their human property and the enslaved as docile, happy, and inferior to white people.

The primary research done by Wright and other FWP employees in library or municipal archives and on the streets of Chicago contested such biased histories. Yet the state guides as a whole were uneven in their representations of American life, reflecting diverse ideological perspectives of more radical, racially integrated northern and urban offices and their typically whiter, more conservative southern and rural counterparts. On the one hand, the scale and achievements of the FWP guides and other projects remain unmatched; they reflect emerging sociological and anthropological methods together with left-wing perspectives and the work of a handful of historians like W. E. B. Du Bois, Charles and Mary Beard, and C. Vann Woodward. On the other hand, the FWP's state-sponsored nature and the relative autonomy of state offices resulted in serious gaps and stereotypes in representations of local histories. State guides tended to omit Black, Hispanic, and Indigenous history, for example, and to suffer from historical inaccuracies and cultural insensitivity. One way to understand the Project's shortcomings is in relation to the Popular Front. Just as the Popular Front sought to unite Americans across racial and class lines to fight fascism, the FWP aimed to rediscover a pluralistic, inclusive America. The country, however, was then, as now, deeply divided, racist, and unequal, a contradiction that neither words nor slogans could overcome and that diluted the FWP's democratic values, weakened the left, defanged the labor movement, and to an extent put civil rights, to Wright's dismay, on the back burner.

Wright's unsigned contributions to the Writers' Projects in Chicago and New York City from 1935 to 1939 are skillfully researched and written, reflecting the dialectical method that defined even his least overtly political writing, such as the haiku he wrote toward the end of his life. In the IWP report filed in December 1935, he notes that 10 percent of the national Black population already lived above the Mason-Dixon Line by the turn of the century, including those who had escaped the South via the underground railway before the Civil War. That number increased by 148.5 percent in a single decade between 1910 and 1920, driven by the twin search for "opportunity and justice" (92).

The sharp rise in the southern migrant population, he explains, occurred as immigration from enemy nations ceased during World War I and decreased from other countries even as northern industry in the United States expanded. Black-owned southern newspapers printed "glowing appeals to their exploited race" to travel north at a time when industries faced increasingly militant trade union demands and "welcomed cheap southern Negro labor," a conflict of interest that pitted white and Black workers against one another, and a topic Wright would pursue in "Death on the City Pavement," the third chapter of 12 Million Black Voices. He delineates the precise blocks occupied by Black migrants in Chicago "between 22nd and 39th streets, and Wentworth Ave." As the population pushed beyond that area from 1917 to 1921, white reaction to "the coming hordes of Negroes" led to years of racial violence instigated by white Chicagoans that included arson, stoning, "armed clashes" and fifty-eight bombings (92).

Specifying the affected streets and avenues, he notes that the expanding Black population reached as far as the lake and had begun "filtering into the Hyde Park and Englewood areas" (93). Based on the 1900 census, he reports that two-thirds of Black men in northern cities were employed in industry, a marked shift from previous labor statistics showing that the vast majority of Black Americans had domestic or agricultural jobs. This influx of Black industrial workers reflected companies' heightened demand for labor, especially amid strikes by trade unions that despite their expanding class consciousness still excluded Black members. Although Wright acknowledges union officials' fear that management was importing Black workers from the Deep South to drive down wages, he states there was no evidence to corroborate that belief. Most troubling was the increase in racial violence against Black newcomers, from a series of more or less minor incidents starting in February 1917 to a major riot on July 27, 1919, at a local beach. Triggered by a brawl that led to the drowning of a young Black boy, the fight erupted into "mob violence" that lasted for three days, culminating in the deaths of "23 Negroes and 15 whites" and injuries to 537 people. State militias were called in to quell the riot, which finally dissipated on August 6. The riot reflected "pent up energies" caused by "housing and labor troubles"; however, by 1935, Wright observes, a "decline of migration has tempered the anxiety of the whites" (95).

This portrait of Chicago's painful racial transformation continues with Wright's report on the Chicago Urban League, filed on January 8, 1936. He describes the League's efforts to help the newly arrived Black migrants adjust to city life, crediting and relying on the League's data to comment on a variety of issues from race relations to school delinquency to health and observing that the organization's primary objective was to foster "interracial cooperation" (98). An addendum to that report, dated January 13, analyzes the impact of the racial turbulence following World War I, especially the riot in 1919, on the emergence of a Black middle class that "depended for its existence upon the residentially segregated laborer," and on a deeply disillusioned Black migrant working class. This disillusionment was further accentuated by the 1920–21 depression and contributed to the rise of Marcus Garvey's movement, which "fostered a vicious anti-white feeling to its utmost," attracting more than 5,000 members at its height (98). Noting both the internal class divisions among Black Chicagoans and a brief period in 1931 and 1932 in which radical groups successfully organized labor and eviction protests, Wright ends by noting that despite greater social stability by the mid-1930s, the city's future was unpredictable given persistent social problems such as inadequate housing. Among those listed at the end of the report as contacts who could provide data and information about Black history was Vivian Harsh, the first Black librarian in the Chicago Library system, who worked closely with Wright and other Black writers and activists in Bronzeville, a historic neighborhood at the center of Black culture on the South Side. She created the Special Negro Collection, later renamed the Vivian G. Harsh Research Collection of Afro-American History and Literature and housed at the Woodson Regional Library.

Subsequent reports filed by Wright in 1936 and 1937 build on the historical and sociological data he discovered through this wealth of library, archival, and public records research. In tours of Chicago neighborhoods, he observed everyday life and the built city, mapping playgrounds, schools, restaurants, hotels, stores, and clubs, and stopping to collect information about local establishments, sometimes to no avail despite repeated trips (101). He describes the features of the White City Amusement Park at 6300 South Parkway between Hyde Park and Englewood, giving the geographical boundaries of the four-square-block area and information about public transportation and parking facilities—all in keeping with the American Guide Series' emphasis on tourism and rediscovery of the nation. In this report, he lists main attractions including a skating rink, a bowling alley, and a sprawling outdoor dance floor that could hold up to 5,000 people, a list that is clearly intended as a guide for Chicago tourists. In a March 1937 report on hotels with detailed information about location, quality, pricing, and phone numbers, he highlights the impact of Jim Crow in the urban North by specifying which accommodations cater to the "white trade" and which to the "Negro trade." In contrast to this assortment of racially categorized information aimed at tourists or newcomers interested in where to stay and what to do in Chicago, he strikes a very different tone in a March 3, 1937, report titled "A Survey of the Amusement Facilities of District #35" in which he announces that "State Street, from 2600 to 3600 South, is almost solidly lumpenproletariat" (103).

Like in many low-income Black neighborhoods today, "beer taverns" predominated in this South Side community, along with "dingy cafes" and less conspicuously "lumpen" businesses like drugstores and movie theaters. The area as a whole, however, was in a state of decay, with abandoned, empty storefronts, condemned buildings, and "for rent" and "for sale" signs in the windows. As in many segregated Black neighborhoods, the majority of businesses were owned by Greek, Jewish, and Italian proprietors. Regardless of the owners' ethnic identities, Wright had nothing good to say about these establishments, denigrating poolrooms as even worse than other facilities, sinking "in general character even lower than the tavern and restaurant" (105). They were "bare and full of cobwebs ... littered with cigar and cigarette butts" with "bad plumbing" and "sagging billiard tables ... rickety chairs.... Stale air. One or two rusty spittoons.... That is all" (105–6). His terse, bleak description of their interiors prefigures his description of Bigger Thomas's impoverished world in *Native Son*, in which Bigger and his friend Gus enter a desolate poolroom in the novel's opening pages that is "empty, save for a fat, black man who held a half-smoked, unlit cigar in his mouth and leaned on the front counter. To the rear burned a single green-shaded bulb."[43]

Other streets in the same vicinity were less commercial, a "sharp contrast" to State Street: Wright describes Wabash Avenue as a mix of small businesses, churches, barbershops, hotels, and private homes; after similar descriptions of other streets, he provides additional racial demarcations, observing that the best medium-priced restaurant on Indiana Avenue, Sam's Buffet, "caters mostly to white trade," while the Trianon mostly served Black customers (107). It is this racial divide that Rosemary Hathaway remarks on in her essay on Wright's ethnographic writing, noting the "rigidly patrolled boundaries between black and white Chicago, emphasizing ... dangerous 'contact zones'" that Bigger Thomas must learn to negotiate to survive the ambiguity of the city's shifting racial lines.[44] For, as Wright makes clear, the steady stream of Black migrants that poured into the city were shaping and reshaping the borders of Chicago's Black Belt in ways that simultaneously hardened racial divisions and created invisible, circuitous, tacitly understood geographical and cultural constraints for Black and white Chicagoans: "It is not until we reach Cottage Grove Avenue that taverns and poolrooms again become prevalent. And it is well to remember that this street is the so-called 'dividing line' between the white and black neighborhoods. Naturally, some of the places are understood to be for white and others for Negro" (107). Familiarity with these racial codes was needed to navigate South Side streets whose boundaries only Chicago residents would recognize in the absence of signage—knowledge more essential to the safety of Black Chicagoans than their white counterparts, given the latter's violent response to what they saw as an invasion of their city by "hordes of Negroes." Wright's report thus addresses both the middle-class, mainly white tourist and the working-class Black Chicagoan. The tourist would learn where to stay and what to do according to the still-rigid racial divisions that accounted for the depredation of segregated, poor Black neighborhoods and the disproportionate impact of the Depression on them. The Black Chicagoan, who very well knew where it was or was not safe to go, would read between the lines to discern a more critical history of the South Side than would have been readily available elsewhere at that time.

Wright's other IWP writing continues in a similar vein, evincing his extensive knowledge of the city, its cultural attractions, and its economic and racial divisions and inequalities, as well as its impact on his ethnographic, research, and literary skills and knowledge of his decade-long literary apprenticeship in Chicago. He refers to the Grand Terrace Diner and Dance Cafe at 3955 South Parkway, home to the Earl Hines NBC orchestra; the Savoy Ballroom, where Louis Armstrong used to play; and the adjacent Savoy Outdoor Boxing Arena, where Joe Louis trained. Dance clubs, hotels, cafés, and parking accommodations all resonate with the touristic aims of the FWP to encourage travel to boost the economy and "introduce America to Americans" in spite of the unrest in urban America, in particular, which was shuddering from the economic blows of the Depression and the massive demographic remaking of northern cities. As Jerrold Hirsch argues, the FWP's romantic nationalist mission was not only to "rediscover America" but also to redefine who an American was in such a way as to encompass the plethora of groups who called it home, and thereby "to provide grounds for unity" (17).[45] However, the America that Wright maps out in his studies of urban life, like much of the other material in the state guides by fellow radical and Black writers, presents a more layered, complex, disturbing vision of the nation than would be included in a typical travel book or than was likely intended by FWP administrators.

In both his IWP reports and *Native Son*, Wright refers to movie theaters and popular films of the era. In "Amusements in Districts 38 and 40," he describes the Regal Theatre at 4723 South Parkway as "the largest and finest of the movie palaces to be found in the Black Belt area" (109). Named as well in

Native Son, the Regal is the theater in which Bigger and his friend Jack watch *Trader Horn*, a 1931 film about a safari, shot on location in Africa. In one scene in the theater, expurgated from the novel until the Library of America restored edition in 1991, Bigger and Jack masturbate in their seats, taunting each other and making explicitly vulgar comments about a woman who passes by them: "If she comes back, I'll throw it in her."[46] In contrast to the movie screen full of "pictures of naked black men and women whirling in wild dances," Bigger is preoccupied with his impending interview with Henry Dalton for a job as a chauffeur for which his relief worker recommended him, causing him to muse as he watches the film that "rich white people were not so hard on Negroes; it was the poor whites who hated Negroes" (33). In the same report that contains the reference to the Regal Theatre, Wright mentions *Imitation of Life*, a 1934 film about racial passing based on a novel by Fannie Hurst, directed by John M. Stahl, and starring Claudette Colbert and Louise Beavers, which was viewed at the time as a breakthrough treatment of racial prejudice and selected for preservation by the US National Film Registry. Such details reflect Wright's intense interest in popular culture and his disciplined efforts to fuse plot and theme, experience and ideas, space and time, in the creation of complex, multilayered fictional worlds, using references like this one pointedly and deliberately in nonfiction without explicating his intent. Here, the film's emphasis on racial tensions and identity acts as a vector signifying the complex portrait of Chicago that Wright aimed to create.

His first ethnographic report on record for the IWP includes his name and address, 3743 Indiana Avenue. In *Native Son*, we learn during Mr. Dalton's interview with Bigger that he and his family reside at 3721 Indiana Avenue.[47] Wright and his family moved repeatedly in their search for more adequate housing that they could afford. When his mother and brother joined him in Chicago, all three slept in the same tiny room he rented from his Aunt Maggie. After a series of rentals—one described as "a tiny, dingy two-room den in whose kitchen a wall bed fitted snugly into a corner near the stove" and which was "alive with vermin"—his family moved to somewhat larger quarters on Indiana Avenue where he had a room of his own, but it was so small, with one door and no windows, that Margaret Walker remarked in a 1971 reminiscence about her relationship with him, "Imagine my shock when I later realized it was a closet."[48] His closely observed personal experience suffused his depictions of life on the South Side for Black migrants like him and his family: "The kitchenette, with its filth and foul air, with its one toilet for thirty or more tenants, kills our black babies so fast that in many cities twice as many of them die as white babies."[49] Along with the street scenes, clubs, and a series of menial jobs that thrust him into the racialized, class-divided world of Depression-era Chicago, his relief work assignment at the South Side Boys' Club—the only other WPA job he found "deeply engrossing"—exemplifies his already developed ethnographic approach to grasping the essence of social relations.[50]

Ranging from eight to twenty-five years old, the boys at the club were "a wild and homeless lot, culturally lost, spiritually disinherited, candidates for the clinics, morgues, prisons, reformatories, and the electric chair of the state's death house." Not much older than some of them, Wright listened closely to their "talk of planes, women, guns, politics, and crime," interested not only in the themes and topics that preoccupied them but also in how they spoke: "Their figures of speech were as forceful and colorful as any ever used by English-speaking people." Already honing his craft as a writer and practicing the observational skills he acquired through his ethnographic studies of the city, Wright emphasized that he kept "pen and pencil in my pocket to jot down their word-rhythms and reactions."[51] Both the spatial mapping of the city he performed as a federal writer and his notes on the South Side boys' interactions, verbal and otherwise, enabled him to demarcate Bigger's racially and economically circumscribed world and to interweave the inner life of the protagonist with the author's sharp consciousness, which he compares to a "pair of spectacles whose power was that of an x-ray enabling me to see deeper into the lives of men."[52]

The boys' talk of planes at the club reappears in the poignant, shrewdly depicted scene early in *Native Son*, establishing the conditions that delimit such boys' futures, of Bigger and Gus leaning against a red brick building in the morning sunlight, smoking cigarettes, and idly talking. When they spot a plane in the sky spelling the words "USE SPEED GASOLINE," Gus says, "Them white boys sure can fly," to which Bigger longingly answers, "They get a chance to do everything." In banter much like what Wright reported hearing at the boys' club, Bigger maintains, "I *could* fly a plane if I had a chance," only to be reined in by Gus's wisecrack: "If you wasn't black and if you had some money and if they'd let you go to that aviation school, you *could* fly a plane."[53]

The Politics of Culture: Shadows of Tragic Premonition

After turning down an offer of a permanent position at the Chicago Post Office to pursue his writing career, Wright arrived in New York City in mid-1937. Unable to join the Writers' Project there until he had established six months of residence in the state, he took a job at the *Daily Worker* from June to

December of that year, writing more than 200 articles. Eligible by then to return to the FWP, he happily joined the New York Writers' Project, which allowed him to devote more time to his own projects, chiefly, *Native Son*. He drafted the novel while living with his friends Jane and Herbert Newton in Brooklyn at 175 Carlton Avenue and other nearby locations, often writing on a yellow legal pad in the shadow of the Prison Ship Martyrs Monument in Fort Greene Park. From Christmas 1937 through May 1939, on salary again with the FWP, he was assigned to contribute to the chapter on Negro, Spanish, and Italian Harlem in the *WPA Guide to New York City* and to complete a chapter begun by Claude McKay, "Portrait of Harlem," for a companion book titled *New York Panorama*. Like the materials he produced for the Illinois Writers' Project, Wright's unsigned portrait of Harlem synthesizes archival and historical research with his own on-the-ground walking tours and explorations of the second major northern city he would make his temporary home. Although Alain Locke found fault with "Portrait of Harlem" for its "superficial flippancy and hectic propagandistic exposé," the FWP director Henry Alsberg praised Wright for his "vivid writing."[54]

Nearly a century later, the essay attests to Wright's disciplined approach to writing and research and his stylistic dexterity across genres. The syntax, diction, and attention to geographical, historical, and sociological detail and accuracy evident in the IWP reports all point to Wright's primary role in composing the portrait of Harlem. In making no mention of McKay's coauthorship, Michel Fabre perhaps overstates Wright's work on the chapter as "virtually unaided."[55] Neither Wright's biographers nor very many critics have reviewed the chapter in depth. In his book on Communists in Harlem during the Depression, Mark Naison notes that Wright's chapter in the *WPA Guide to New York City* vividly describes "the social and religious customs of Harlem's population, their patterns of entertainment, and their growing militancy in the face of discriminatory practices," devoting "far more space to Harlem's nightlife than he did to leftist causes."[56] However, a closer examination of the two essays, especially "Portrait of Harlem," reveals a radical rereading of Black history. Wright likely would have consulted existing studies by Black scholars such as W. E. B. Du Bois, James Weldon Johnson, and Walter White, but the prevailing schools of history in the 1930s asserted the Lost Cause defense of the Confederacy, reinforced by de jure and de facto Jim Crow. Based on primary, secondary, and field research, "Portrait of Harlem" recast slavery and Jim Crow in the North, proclaiming not only Black aspirations and achievements but also deep-rooted Black resistance to white supremacy. The essay thus arguably foretold the New York Historical Society's

2005 exhibit on slavery in New York, hailed as "an unprecedented two-year exploration of this *largely unknown* chapter of the city's story" (emphasis added) by nearly seventy years.[57]

Even now, in the mid-2020s, this history is neither widely taught nor understood, and it is banned in an increasing number of conservative states that prohibit teaching "divisive topics." Wright's account of New York slavery is exceptional; it might well be used to introduce today's readers to the facts, including that the first eleven Africans arrived in New Amsterdam in 1626 in "the capacity of slaves."[58] Under Dutch rule, a mixture of indentured servitude and slavery enabled enslaved Black people to gain freedom and live less socially constricted lives. The British conquered the Dutch in 1664, ushering in a period of harsher, more restrictive codes in service of a more "profitable, flourishing and oppressive institution" that had swelled to 2,170 slaves by 1694 and, by 1709, supported open slave markets (133).[59] Nearly a third of the chapter recounts this history, documenting the first religious schools for Black children starting in 1704, the advent of secular education through African Free Schools in 1787, and Black resistance to slavery, including the 1741 insurrectionary plot mounted across racial lines by enslaved Black people and white indentured servants, leading to the imprisonment of 154 Black people, thirteen burned at the stake, and seventy-one deported to the West Indies; the arrest of twenty white people; and the execution of a Catholic priest. Wright follows the historical narrative from Black participation in American and British military forces during the Revolution to the 1799 Act for the Gradual Abolition of Slavery to the complete abolition of slavery in New York in 1827 to interracial antislavery protests, emphasizing the leading role of Black New Yorkers in struggles for the abolition of slavery and for human rights for all people of color.

As he did in his ethnographic essays for the IWP, Wright gives a rounded picture of Black life in Harlem that encompasses the ebb and flow of economic, social, and cultural activities from the antebellum and postbellum periods into the first three decades of the twentieth century. Similarly, he grounds descriptions of 1930s Harlem in historical contexts from the draft riots in 1863 to major race riots in 1900 and 1935. The 1900 riot ensued after a Black man killed a white man with whom he had quarreled. Immediately afterward, Black New Yorkers were beaten throughout the city, in many cases by police; the following year, Wright notes, more than 100 Black people were lynched across the United States. The 1935 riot reflected escalating racial tensions as Black Harlemites boycotted white-owned businesses that refused to hire Black employees. Intensified by some antisemitic agitation, tensions erupted when a Puerto Rican Black boy was caught stealing and false rumors spread that a white storeowner had murdered him. Wright reports that the riot resulted in "an orgy of window-smashing and store-looting" (142); according to *Daily News* headlines, some 4,000 people were involved, and one was killed.

The *New York Times* reported that over 100 people, white and Black, were injured, some critically; 121 were arrested; and over 200 shopwindows were smashed. In keeping with the FWP's liberal politics of neutrality, Wright makes no mention of CPUSA involvement in the riot, but the *Times* story focuses on the Party's role in stirring up, if not instigating, the unrest, distributing flyers condemning police brutality and copies of the *Daily Worker* with an editorial titled "Negro and White Workers Unite against Race Riot Provocation." According to the *Times*, three of the four "ringleaders" were white, and all of them were represented by a female lawyer from the International Labor Defense, the CPUSA-sponsored legal advocacy group. However, fellow traveler Adam Clayton Powell Jr., an early supporter of the CPUSA and the Popular Front, attributed the violence to racial discrimination and economic oppression: "Continued exploitation of the Negro is at the bottom of all this trouble . . . exploitation as regards wages, jobs, and working conditions."[60] His analysis was echoed by a commission appointed by Mayor Fiorello La Guardia, Wright notes, which found that "the outbreak had its fundamental causes in the terrible economic and social conditions prevailing in Harlem at the time." Wright goes on to credit various New Deal programs with alleviating the combined impact of the Depression and racial discrimination enough to lessen "the dangerous tension that pervaded Harlem in the dark winters of 1934 and 1935" (142).[61]

He praises Du Bois's seminal work, *The Souls of Black Folk*, for marking a "turning point in the history of Negro thought" and subtly approves of his refutation of Booker T. Washington's accommodationist philosophy (137). Yet, in keeping with his own proletarian outlook and sharp critique of the Black bourgeoisie, including Du Bois's conception of a "talented tenth," Wright emphasized that even as the Black middle class was expanding in Harlem in the early twentieth century, "the larger part of New York's Negro population, numbering some 60,000 in 1901, was excluded from trade unions, and Negro workers had to compete for jobs with newly-arrived immigrants at unequal odds" (138). In relating the impact of tens of thousands of Black southern migrants on Harlem demographics, he tells the story of the Black realtor Philip A. Payton's role in combatting the "social and economic war" waged by the white-owned Hudson Realty Company in response to the "invasion" of Black tenants, a story that echoed his IWP reports on Chicago's similar history. Despite some victories against such exclusionary tactics, Wright notes that educational facilities remained "woefully inadequate" and that restaurants, cafés, and bars still discriminated against Black residents, while some rooming-house windows in Harlem displayed "the familiar southern sign: 'For Whites Only'" (149).

Wright emphasizes Harlem's culture and nightlife—roughly a quarter of the essay deals with the neighborhood's literary renaissance, visual artists, theater, music schools, musicians, popular dances, movie actors, first film production company, famous athletes and sports, and newspapers—which reflects both the primary aim of the American Guide Series to stimulate the travel industry, promoting the discovery of the country's vastly diverse cultural experiences, and Wright's own deep, abiding interest in literary, performing, visual, and popular arts. In keeping with his view that all literature is protest, his interest and engagement in Black culture assumes a radical politics of its own. He was a connoisseur of jazz, photography, theater, film, and literature, and he tried with varying degrees of success to pursue all of these avenues of creative expression. He was also a big sports fan, especially of boxing, and wrote significant articles about Joe Louis for both *New Masses* and the *Daily Worker*. He even wrote lyrics for a song titled "King Joe," to music composed and performed by Count Basie and His Orchestra and sung by Paul Robeson in 1941 after Louis's victory over Max Baer in 1935.

Among the Harlem writers to whom he pays tribute are Alain Locke, Walter White, Eric Walrond, Jean Toomer, Claude McKay, Countee Cullen, Langston Hughes, Nella Larsen, Zora Neale Hurston, Arna Bontemps, and W. E. B. Du Bois. He describes the legendary Harlem Renaissance as a movement in which "for the first time the American Negro depicted his own life with a wide and varied range of talent and feeling" (142). Similarly, he lists Harlem painters, sculptors, and cartoonists, including Augusta Savage and Romare Bearden, noting that many were employed by the Federal Art Project, which sponsored the production of murals on the Harlem Municipal Hospital, aided in the creation of fifteen neighborhood art centers, and "discovered an immense amount of latent artistic talent among the Negro children of Harlem" (142). Notable Black playwrights, whose plays were rarely featured at the time on the American stage, even in Harlem, included Willis Richardson, Wallace Thurman, and Langston Hughes. The Federal Theatre Project provided homes for these Black authors, actors, and theatrical productions. Nationally known Black musicians such as Paul Robeson and Marian Anderson had ties to Harlem, while others were employed by the Federal Music Project. Wright refers as well to familiar names in Black Harlem culture like the tap dancer Bill "Bojangles" Robinson and the singer Josephine

Baker, even though she was a Harlemite only "by adoption" (146). Calling Duke Ellington's and Fletcher Henderson's jazz orchestras "the greatest of Negro bands," Wright declares in the vernacular of his times, "Whether it was jazz as it was 'jazzed' by Cab Calloway in the 1920's or swing as it was 'swung' by Jimmie Lunceford in the 1930's, the white popular jazz and swing orchestras took most of their cues from Harlem orchestras and their Negro leaders" (146).

Perhaps Wright's most literary evocation is his description of Harlem's new dance steps: "Just who initiated the 'truck' is not known. . . . It is interesting to note that there are many kinds of 'trucking'—the 'picket's truck,' the politician's truck,' the 'Park Avenue truck,' the 'Mae West truck,' and the 'Hitler truck.' Among other contemporary Harlem dances is the 'shimsham,' a time-step featuring the 'break' with a momentary pause; and the 'razzle dazzle,' which involves a rhythmic clapping of hands and a rolling of hips" (145–46). Wright's prose here exudes the playful exuberance of Harlem nightlife and his deep knowledge of its ethos, a knowledge expressed in street-smart idioms that demonstrate his interest in popular culture and honors the Black masses—ordinary, working-class, club patrons constituting the "who" in his observation that "Just who initiated the 'truck' is not known." He goes on to describe the Lindy Hop in equally colorful detail and to point out that the steps "can be seen in Harlem's dance halls, at house parties, on beaches in the streets in the summer to the tune of WPA Music Project bands" (145). These references to the WPA in 1930s Harlem would have been encouraged by the New York Writers' Project office but they also indicate the genuine relief the arts and literature programs afforded Harlemites.

Toward the end of the essay, Wright describes three Black-led political and social organizations: the National Association for the Advancement of Colored People (NAACP) founded by Du Bois in 1909; the National Urban League organized in 1911 to assist southern migrants pouring into cities; and the National Negro Congress, the CPUSA-sponsored group started in 1935 during the Popular Front era that aimed to unite religious, political, and labor organizations. From there, he lists fraternal societies such as the New York African Society for Mutual Relief in the nineteenth century; the Young Men's and Women's Christian Associations, which functioned, he notes, much like their white counterparts elsewhere; and unions active in Harlem, including A. Philip Randolph's Brotherhood of Sleeping Car Porters. He then quotes Du Bois at length in his eloquent description of the NAACP as an organization that aimed to become "so effective and so powerful that when discrimination and injustice touched one Negro, it would touch 12,000,000 . . . an organization that would work ceaselessly to make Americans know that the so-called 'Negro problem' is simply one phase of the vaster problem of democracy in America, and that those who wish freedom and justice for their country must wish it for every black citizen" (149).

Not surprisingly, he maintains that the strongest Black organizations in Harlem in the mid-1930s were unions: "Since the depression and the inception of the Committee for Industrial Organization, there is hardly a trade or profession in Harlem that is not organized. Barbers, clerks, laundry workers, newspapermen, bartenders, teachers and domestic workers have all formed unions for mutual protection" (150). Although he neither mentions the CPUSA nor dwells on left-wing politics, the tenor and thrust of the essay suggest a deeply political, engaged perspective, rooted in the concrete material conditions of life and driving his search for the "inexpressibly human," the last two words of his autobiography.[62] His emphasis on Harlem culture is critical to that endeavor, reflective of his view of Black folklore as the culture of "the Negro masses, unwritten and unrecognized" in contrast to that of "the sons and daughters of a rising Negro bourgeoisie, parasitic and mannered."[63] His analysis of the politics of culture, which permeates the body of his work, has yet to be fully appreciated. In "Portrait of Harlem," one sees his range of focus, from antebellum New York to the economies of the Great Migration and the Jim Crow North to the cultural mecca it created in Harlem to the prophetic question of "what will ultimately happen to the Negro in New York." His answer to that question casts doubt on the romantic nationalism at the heart of the FWP's mission: "It has been said that the Negro embodies the 'romance' of 'American life'; if that is true, the romance is one whose glamor is overlaid with shadows of premonition" (151).

12 Million Black Voices: The Vast Tragic School That Swims Below

In 1940, Wright accepted an invitation from Edwin Rosskam, a former Farm Security Administration (FSA) photographer, to compose the text for an illustrated book about Black Americans based on FSA photographs by, among others, Dorothea Lange, Walker Evans, Russell Lee, Ben Shahn, and Rosskam. That summer, Rosskam and Lee accompanied Wright to Chicago to take photographs of the South Side for the book's final two chapters. According to Rosskam, Wright opened doors for the white photographers to the everyday lives of Black Chicagoans they likely would never have discovered on their own: "Dick Wright really knew that stuff cold. He knew where everybody was, and he knew everybody in the Negro world of Chicago.... I don't know if many white men had the opportunity to see it the way we saw it. Man, that was an experience. We did everything from the undertaker to the gangster."[64] Wright's intimate knowledge of the streets and people of the South Side, documented and partly obtained through his IWP research, was indispensable for the second half of the book. The same racial boundaries he had mapped in the IWP essays necessitated his authorization for the white photographers with whom he was collaborating. Liberating for him personally, this interracial solidarity sprang from the CPUSA's incisive analysis of racism as a key principle for organizing class struggle.

However, as Wright clearly expressed in "Blueprint for Negro Writing," Black nationalism was a necessary stage of development that would ultimately have to be transcended by mass, multiracial struggle in order to achieve its own aims. As he put it, "A nationalist spirit in Negro writing means a nationalism that knows its origins, its limitations; that is aware of the dangers of its position; that knows its ultimate aims are unrealizable within the framework of capitalist America."[65] The broad socialist vision that inspired his generation rested on three pillars: a view of race as produced by historical rather than natural or biological forces; a Marxist analysis of the primacy of class division and class conflict in revolutionary struggle that also recognized the right to self-determination of oppressed nations; and a dialectical method responsive to "the interest of the working class."[66] For Wright, these principles guided a practical approach to dialectical thought rooted in his experience as a working-class Black southerner transported to the urban North and in the proletarian vanguard that drew him into its midst. In a letter to his editor Edward Aswell in 1955, he wrote: "I was a Communist because I was a Negro. Indeed the Communist Party had been the only road out of the Black Belt for me. Hence Communism had not been for me simply a fad, a hobby; it had a deep functional meaning for my life." He goes on to observe that without it, he "no longer had a protective barrier" between himself and "a hostile racial environment." Moreover, for him, "the racial situation was a far harder matter than the Communist one and it was one that I could not solve alone."[67]

Nor was the Party or any other organization or movement able to resolve this dilemma, which Wright sought to the end of his life to address through the tension between the "racial situation" and the "Communist one." As Cedric Robinson puts it, "His work thus constituted an inquiry"—an inquiry responsive to the contradictions of his times.[68] While the CPUSA could not answer this question to Wright's satisfaction, it gave him the analytical tools and camaraderie to go beyond its limitations and to grapple with the elusiveness of revolutionary change. His interrogation of the dilemma foresaw persistent, vexing problems of race, Black nationalism, and white supremacy in relation to class struggle. By engaging in a dialectical search for answers, stranded in a "No Man's Land," Wright leaves us not with answers that continue to elude us nearly a century later, but with more questions, such as those he poses in his letter to Kwame Nkrumah at the end of *Black Power*: how to move African nations from tribalism into modernity as they threw off the yoke of colonialism; how to overcome the psychic and socioeconomic trauma of exclusion from expanded opportunities that consolidated middle-class aspirations and norms in the West; and how emerging nations like Ghana could navigate the promises and threats of both existing Communist states and Western capitalist powers. In closing, Wright notes, "You have taken Marxism, that intellectual instrument that makes meaningful the class and commodity relations in the modern state," but counsels, "The moment that that instrument ceases to shed meaning, drop it. Be on top of theory; don't let theory be on top of you. In short, be *free*, be a living embodiment of what you want to give your people."[69]

Applying this same process of dialectical inquiry more than a decade earlier to his post-FWP collaboration with Rosskam for *12 Million Black Voices*, Wright documents the trauma of slavery and the punctured dreams of the Great Migration in the four chapters of the book, which was longer than anticipated because of the epic story he wanted to tell, but still under 150 pages. In *12 Million Black Voices* he presents his slant on a Marxist interpretation of human history in the specific form it took for African Americans, captured, enslaved, and shipped to the Americas, from slavery to feudalism to industrial capitalism. As Marx and Engels wrote in *The Communist Manifesto*, each epoch wrestles with the central contradiction of class antagonisms that ultimately break free of the fetters of the existing order to usher in revolutionary change. In feudal society, the "relations of property became no longer compatible with the already developed productive forces; they became so many fetters. They had to be burst asunder; they were burst asunder."[70] But as Wright conveys in the sermonic overtones of the Black church, these stages of development are uneven and contingent rather than linear and teleological. As a Marxist, he understood that history unfolds according to concrete material forces and relations of production that assume various forms in which the outcome of class struggle is never predetermined. In *12 Million Black Voices*, he shifts the documentary gaze from Black laborers as objects to a collective subject that speaks in the plural first person as a class in and potentially for itself. In the first sentence, he declares, "Our history is far stranger than you suspect, and we are not what we seem."[71]

He thus creates a tension between text and image that challenges mainstream assumptions about Black history, asserting not only a right to self-determination but also a capacity to resist the gaze of the dominant culture. This counternarrative is enabled by the conditions of modernity experienced by Black urban workers catapulted into industrial capitalism as a result of the mass exodus from the South to northern cities. Crucial to the reversal of roles of the observer and the observed is Wright's use of the first-person plural in telling "our" history, complicated by the first image in the book, a close-up of a tenant farmer's dirt- and sun-darkened hands that calls racial categories into question even before the pronouncement that "we [Black Americans] are not what we seem." As Wright argues in his blueprint for Black writers, the vanguard role is for the most ruthlessly oppressed who, "chafing under exploitation, forge organizational forms of struggle to better their lot." Unhindered by "false ambition and property, they have access to a wide social vision and a deep social consciousness" that enables their organizations to "show greater strength, adaptability, and efficiency than any other group or class in society."[72]

While nobody, Rosskam included, expected Wright to tell the story of the photographs, by signaling their unreliability in the opening lines of the text, he called into question both the pictorial impetus for the project and the seemingly neutral, objective character of the image in relation to history. At the same time, he established a point of view that rendered the reader, ambiguously named "you," beguiled by appearances. As Benjamin Balthaser points out, Wright takes a satirical swipe at the documentary aesthetic of seeing in his characterization of the wealthy heiress and Communist Mary Dalton, who declares, as Bigger Thomas chauffeurs her boyfriend Jan and her through the South Side, "I've long wanted to go into these houses . . . and just *see* how your people live."[73] The tropes of sight, blindness, and misrecognition appear throughout Wright's fiction and nonfiction, reflecting the dialectics of structure and content, history and place, time and space, subject and object. In *12 Million Black Voices*, this consciousness takes the form of invoking and destabilizing stereotypes to uncover the essential relations hidden from sight, an ambiguity that at once insists on the crucial significance of Black history and inverts it by asserting, "We black folk, our history and our present being, are a mirror of all the manifold experiences of America. . . . The differences between black folk and white folk are not blood or color and the ties that bind us are deeper than those that separate us."[74]

By the time Wright was working on 12 *Million Black Voices*, the overlapping, contradictory politics of the radical left, the Popular Front, and the New Deal's WPA projects had produced a tangled skein of documentary approaches to "looking" that reflected conscious and unconscious racial, class, and ideological biases, raising questions about the politics of representation that surfaced despite the objective, neutralizing technologies that simulated the real. Associated with police reports, crime scenes, and mugshots, on the one hand, and pseudoscientific eugenics and classification studies on the other, documentary photography served to categorize, scrutinize, and objectify its subjects, whose otherness was established by the documentarian for a variety of purposes, from the moralizing gaze of Jacob Riis's *How the Other Half Lives* to James Agee's decentered shame in *Let Us Now Praise Famous Men*. In the latter, Agee interrupts the narrative to confess that when confronted with "the depths of a subject"—white southern sharecroppers and their families, strangled by economic depression and ecological depredation—he can only let it "stand as the image it is" in relation to his "verbal part of this book as a whole"; all he can do is give "an image of the very essence of their lives: that is, of the work they do."[75]

The liberal legacies of the New Deal's FWP have profound implications for the documentary form. As Daniel Schiffman puts it, "Wright's text revises the rags-to-riches immigrant story touted as quintessentially American" by challenging the Depression era's "discourses proclaiming that individual immigrant success stories represent American promise."[76] That revision, like Wright's conclusion to the *New York Panorama* essay, casts American history in a radically different light than the FWP's "rediscovery" of the nation or the New Deal's appeal to unity and class concessions, both of which, in some respects, undermined struggles for civil rights by placing patriotism, even in the service of antifascism, before the devastating impact of Jim Crow in the South and the North.

THE QUESTIONS WRIGHT RAISES in 12 *Million Black Voices* about Black migration place it in a broad historical context of Western conquest, slavery, and Jim Crow by tracing the migrants' path through the stages of capture by slave traders in Africa, the Middle Passage, and the nation's uneven and unequal economic development. His position as a Black documentary writer from and of the southern Black peasantry and working class enabled him simultaneously to speak in the plural first person and to distance himself from the story he narrates. This double consciousness of seeing and being seen, speaking as and speaking about, is existentially and ideologically available to him not solely because of his racial and class background or his political consciousness but also through the dialectic he forges between them in his capacity to fuse experiential and theoretical knowledge in a ceaseless, restless search for meaningfulness. It is precisely this double vision that enabled him to criticize the very grounds of the projects that he most passionately embraced—whether telling the story of millions of his Black countrymen or working through the relationship of the Black Belt thesis to a blueprint for Black writers or analyzing anticolonial movements in a diasporic world dominated by capital and torn asunder by modernity's intensifying contradictions.

In *12 Million Black Voices*, his affiliation with those from whom he came and for whom he spoke recasts American history in the voice of the oppressed at the same time the "you," the reader, is not only the implied white American who must recognize that the fate of the nation is inextricably bound up with the fate of its most oppressed population but also the nonwhite reader who must learn the same lessons of racial solidarity in the struggle to liberate human potential. The story he tells is of Black and white workers divided not by biological or even cultural difference but by the Lords of the Land and the Bosses of the Buildings who profited from racial competition and the animosity of white southern farmers and northern workers toward their Black counterparts with whom they should have been naturally allied (and in fact, at times had been). As Wright puts it, "To protect their delicately balanced edifice of political power, the Lords of the Land proceeded to neutralize the strength of us blacks and the growing restlessness of the poor whites by dividing and ruling us, by inciting us against one another."[77] As an African American who was born to a sharecropper and a schoolteacher in Mississippi and who joined millions of Black southern migrants fleeing Jim Crow and then became a literary luminary and card-carrying Communist, Wright shone a brighter light on his subject matter than many of his contemporaries. He not only came from a racially oppressed class but also retained his identification with it and theorized its origins, depredations, and potential liberatory power. Echoing his premonition at the end of "Portrait of Harlem" and Marx's declaration that we make our own history, but only under already existing circumstances transmitted from the past, he warned in the final section of *12 Million Black Voices*: "What we want, what we represent, what we endure is what America is. If we black folk perish, America will perish."[78]

In his short preface to the book, Wright elaborates his argument more directly. He begins by acknowledging that the history he presents is not about Du Bois's "talented tenth," the elite, educated Black bourgeois leadership who "like single fishes" leapt above the surface of the sea. Instead, it is about the

Black masses with whom Wright identified and understood as "that vast, tragic school that swims below in the depths, against the current." Wright neither romanticizes "the plight of the humble folk" nor explains their suffering in racial or nationalist terms, but rather aims "to place within full and constant view the collective humanity whose triumphs and defeats are shared by the majority, whose gains in security mark an advance in the level of consciousness attained by the broad masses in their costly and tortuous upstream journey." Moreover, these materials of Negro life are "basic and centrally historical," not given or universal.[79] In other words, it is the dialectic of the material forms of racial oppression and their concealed essential social relations that produces both the immense suffering of the Black peasantry and laboring classes and the revolutionary role into which history has cast them.

For all its buoyant "rediscovery" of America and unmatched federally supported, public documentation of American history, the FWP's pluralistic vision was founded on the quicksand of centuries of racial division and class exploitation that pitted white and Black workers against one another. The FWP chronicled the story of 1930s America as it unfolded in an era of great suffering. It gave support to emerging writers like Richard Wright, boosting their careers and training them in methodologies many would appropriate for their own uses. But the absorption of radical left demands into the Popular Front and the cultural goals of the WPA arts and writing projects crippled what had been a militant labor movement, undermined a civil rights movement that increasingly feared association with Communists, assented to Cold War ideology, and left masses of people vulnerable to the ravages of capitalism and its ever-deepening crises. Wright's ethnographic writing, from his essays on Chicago to the portrait of Harlem to *12 Million Black Voices* straight through to his late travel books, delineates a very different America from the FWP's portrait of the nation as united against fascism, celebrating its diversity. Wright's America is divided, its people at a crossroads, caught up in the wings of history, the din of modernity, neither doomed nor redeemed, uncertain of its future: "Print compels us. Voices are speaking. Men are moving. And we shall be with them."[80]

CHAPTER FIVE

Seeing Deeper
Writing with Marxist Lenses

Contrary to standard interpretations of ideological rupture in Wright's life, clouded by the ambiguity of his politics after he quietly left the CPUSA in 1942, Marxist thought can be seen in his writing throughout the arc of his career, albeit sometimes protectively wrapped in pro-Western rhetoric. He experimented with literary forms in dialectical interrogations of poiesis and praxis, consciousness and materiality, race and class. His insight into social relations and his personal and political vulnerability pushed him to choose exile in what his biographer Michel Fabre called his "unfinished quest" for "humanity," "ideological elucidation," and "truth and certainties."[1] That quest was rooted in his experience growing up in the Jim Crow South, reseen through the lens of Marxist theory in a deeply rooted, evolving critique of capitalism that remained steadfast even as he grew critical of the CPUSA and the Soviet Union. Particularly in the postwar era, critics of the 1930s literary left who saw him and other Communist writers as puppets of the Comintern also tended to set modernist against naturalist or proletarian writing in order to elevate the former as universal high art and dismiss the latter as hackneyed and provincial. But Wright was neither bound by Party dictates nor hostile to Marxism or modernism.

Wright's Transcontinental Revolutionary Thought

Fabre asserts that "the anchor lines of [Wright's] thoughts were cut in a transcontinental and then intercontinental journey, toward ever-widening horizons" in which the driving force for him as a Black man was his need for "personal survival." His description of Wright's intellectual journey across America and the world as enabling him to grasp a global totality and its multiple fractures contests a widespread opinion that his expatriation derailed his career. However, Fabre also rehearses some standard views of Wright—that his "philosophy" (in quotation marks) was more "intuitive" than "bookish"; that "his lack of formal education" left him with an "exaggerated reverence for books" and "too much faith in ideas"; that his quest was "solitary" and that he was searching for "a definition of man."[2] On the contrary, he positioned himself as an outsider out of necessity, chose solitude and exile as a public figure while building an exceptionally social, global network, and participated intensely, often as a leader, in more than one cutting-edge political and/or literary milieu. He sought to illuminate the political economic material conditions of life in an artistic pursuit of truth and social transformation that assumed all literature is protest. Rather than embodying a static, individualistic definition of man, he was engaged in a highly politicized, Promethean search for existential meaning and revolutionary change.

His early poems fuse Marxist ideology with his experience growing up in the South and his disciplined habits of reading into sensual, modernist, vernacular, poetic forms, inflected with humor, bitter irony, and radical élan. The first two poems he published in the JRC's *Left Front* in early 1934 were "A Love Red Note" and "Rest for the Weary," both of which warn a vulgar, useless ruling class that it is "wise to tremble"; there will no longer be any postponements or continuations, and when the revolution comes, "It'll be like love / It'll be a red clap of thunder rising from the very depths of hell." The poem "Child of the Dead and Forgotten Gods" points more directly to the "innocent liberal," the "naïve darling," to whom the speaker declares, "Do show us the magic talisman you use in dispelling the blood and stench of history!," condemning this "poor lost child" whose "soft talk of peace and brotherhood" is drowned out by "the pounding of police clubs on the skulls of strikers / and the scream of the riot-siren to disperse the unemployed / And the noise and clamor of slaughter and rapine and greed."[3]

Other poems in this period, published in *Left Front, New Masses, Partisan Review*, and other left-wing magazines, assert the power of collective protest. In "Strength," millions of comrades become "a raging hurricane vast and powerful, wrenching and dredging the rottening husks of the trees of greed." Similarly, in "Everywhere Burning Waters Rise," a "chafing multitude... wait[s] to build on the cleared and conquered grounds" left by a "red stream of molten anger" that burns a temple with "golden pillars of oppressive privilege" to black ashes. One of his best-known poems, "I Have Seen Black Hands," reiterates the theme of collective struggle of African Americans, whose Black hands are finally "raised in fists of revolt, side by side with the white fists of white workers," articulating both the superexploitation of Black workers and the principle of interracial working-class solidarity at the heart of Depression-era Communism. This poem turns on the Marxist concept of overaccumulation and the periodic crises of capitalism produced by its systemic internal contradictions. The Black hands are "jerked up and down in the throbbing machines massing taller and taller the heaps of gold in the banks of bosses"; they "stacked goods higher and higher until there was too much to be used," leaving those same "black hands [to hold] trembling at the factory gates the dreaded lay-off slip." In other words, Black workers overproduced goods and then got laid off in the resulting economic slowdown. Though dismissed by many critics as propagandistic, Wright's early poems begin to fuse idea with image, theory with experience, abstractions with concrete material existence, anticipating characteristic features of his writing.[4]

He was also drafting the novel "Cesspool," published posthumously in 1963 as *Lawd Today!* Despite—or because of—its modernist, Joycean inflections, experimentation with techniques such as literary newsreels borrowed from John Dos Passos, and repetitious phrases inspired by Gertrude Stein, *Lawd Today!* drew harsh criticism as an apprentice novel marred by "excessive realism." Nick Aaron Ford called it a "dull, unimaginative novel," as well as a "melodramatic, disjointed" story "padded with a multitude of hackneyed episodes." Ford claimed that it was anomalous for Wright in not having "made the white man or the white man's society the predominant villain."[5] However, Wright's depiction of dehumanizing white surveillance and control of Black postal workers against the ironic backdrop of radio broadcasts on Lincoln's birthday suggests otherwise. Like *Native Son*, *Lawd Today!* invokes class conflict and racial oppression that produce working-class alienation and the potential to recruit individuals to fascism or socialism, here in the main character Jake, an older, selfish, abusive postal worker trapped in a demeaning, repetitive, exhausting job, who has ruined his wife's life by seducing and impregnating her as a teenager, then forcing her to get an abortion, which was botched, and then refusing to pay her medical bills. Like Bigger, Jake rebels against the constraints of a white, supervisory culture that immiserates him, and, also like Bigger, he sees no options, endorsing capitalism, condemning "Commoonists," and flirting with fascist ideology. As Brannon Costello argues, defending the novel's modernist themes and citing Wright's comments in *Black Boy* on the gap between the Communist Party and the working people—especially Black workers—they seek to organize, "A fuller consideration of the first part of Wright's plan—to 'tell Communists how common people felt'—is appropriate to help us better understand *Lawd Today*."[6]

During this same period, Wright wrote his novellas, eventually published as *Uncle Tom's Children*, many of which he shared in draft form with the South Side Writers Group. The first edition of *Uncle Tom's Children* in 1938 contained four stories: "Big Boy Leaves Home," "Down by the Riverside," "Long Black Song," and "Fire and Cloud," to which the 1940 edition added the essay "The Ethics of Living Jim Crow," which was denounced by Representative

Martin Dies, head of the House Un-American Activities Committee (HUAC), and the brilliant story "Bright and Morning Star." The unevenly expanding political consciousness of the characters from the first to the last novella reflects Wright's literary genius in melding abstract knowledge with the everyday experience of ordinary people he had known in the South. The stories also display his pioneering explorations of previously unexplored themes, probing the most violent, tragic elements of Jim Crow history for Black and white southerners and their revolutionary potential for social transformation. Enacting the radical and literary principles he lays out in Part Two of *Black Boy* and, earlier, in "Blueprint for Negro Writing," he fuses experience and theory, image and word, respecting nationalist impulses in relation to the need to transcend them through interracial, international class struggle.

As he wrote in his autobiography after describing his mother's horrified response to what she saw as grotesque covers of *New Masses*, "I reread the magazine and was convinced that much of the expression embodied what the artists thought . . . would gain recruits. They had a program, an ideal, *but they had not yet found a language*" (emphasis added). It was from his unique position as a Black southerner with working-class roots who became a Communist and was proving himself as a writer that he could correct the Party's oversimplification of "the experience of those whom they sought to lead." They had "missed the meaning of the lives of the masses" and thus "conceived of people in too abstract a manner."[7] Each story in *Uncle Tom's Children* illustrates Wright's refusal to idealize or simplify complex realities, insisting instead on concretizing political themes in the actual "lives of the masses." From the first story in the 1940 edition, Wright moves from the innocent verbal and physical play of four teenage boys to the heroic act—or tragic mistake—of an older Black woman involved in a local, interracial Communist cell, betrayed by a new white recruit. Both stories end in violent tragedy, and both show signs of rising collective consciousness. Nascent in "Big Boy Leaves Home" in distressed calls to family friends to gather at Big Boy's house to help him escape after having accidentally killed the son of a prominent white landowner, a belief in collective struggle in "Bright and Morning Star" has spread across generations and the color line. That faith, however, is challenged by Aunt Sue's struggle to reconcile her Christian values with her newfound revolutionary commitment, and her feelings of racial dehumanization with her deep affection for Reva, the young white Communist in love with her son Johnny-Boy.

In "Memories of My Grandmother," Wright describes a literary technique in which he strives "to get to a certain point" in a story, a crisis, at which the character is "broken" or "rendered fluid . . . a point in life where the past falls away and the character must, in order to go on living, flesh himself upon the face of the formless night and create a world, a new world in which to live."[8] One of several examples of a breaking point is Aunt Sue's realization in "Bright and Morning Star" that "she has unwittingly betrayed her comrades."[9] The consequences of her actions slowly dawn on her as the white sheriff and his posse who break into her house in the middle of the night interrogate her about Johnny-Boy's whereabouts and she resists, refusing to talk, consumed by a "bitter pride." Just as she has resolved to die rather than comply, her thoughts abruptly shift with the phrase "And then it was," as she tasted her own warm blood: "She gave up Johnny-Boy, gave him to the white folks... because they had come tramping into her heart demanding him [and] because she wanted them to know that they could not get what they wanted by bluffing and killing." When the new white recruit Booker, whom she already suspects is the traitor, finds her unconscious on the floor and presses her for names, pretending to be loyal to the comrades, "all the horror of it flashed upon her: she saw flung out over the rainy countryside an array of shacks where white and black comrades were sleeping; in the morning they would be rising and going to Lem's [Reva's father's house and the site of the planned meeting]; then they would be caught. And that meant terror, prison, and death."[10]

Just as the suffering of Black men became her Jesus and the Party "another Resurrection," Reva's "trust and acceptance," like the airport beacon Sue sees from her window, confirms her sense of humanity, becoming a "refuge from shame and degradation" and defeating the force of the "cold white mountain"—her image of "the white men and their laws." Yet neither Reva's love for her nor the beacon of light can save her or Johnny-Boy from their tragic fate. Oscillating between hatred of her white oppressors and Johnny-Boy's insistence as a Communist revolutionary that "Ah cant see white n Ah cant see black.... Ah sees rich men n Ah sees po men," she retreats into an understandable but fatal need to prove her own worth and protect her son from the posse of white men, betraying their comrades and possibly destroying their growing organization.[11] As Joseph Ramsey aptly observes about the shaft of light from the Memphis airport and the religious symbolism of "bright and morning star" that suffuse the story, "What appears to be a beacon of hope may turn out to be the headlights of doom."[12]

None of the characters in *Uncle Tom's Children* can elude white southern terror except by going North, as Big Boy does—though not without first watching his friend Bo get tarred, feathered, and burned to death in the middle of a dark rainy night. The rest, except Reverend Taylor in "Fire and Cloud," suffer brutal deaths or despair. In "Long Black Song," Sarah watches the walls of her house collapse as her husband Silas "stayed on to burn." Claustrophobic settings, rage, and a sense of dread compete with an emergent revolutionary consciousness that standing together, Black and white, can enable not just resistance but change to the system of racial and class oppression that pits races against each other and holds them down. Wright tells these stories through stark imagery, southern dialect, verbal play, and explosive, retributive anger welling up in response to the savage degradation and killing of Black people by white men and frenzied lynch mobs. Big Boy imagines killing two white men in self-defense: "Then the whole mob swirled around him, and he blazed away, getting as many as he could." In "Long Black Song," Silas exclaims, "Ef Ah run erway, Ah ain got nothin. Ef Ah stay n fight, Ah ain got nothin. It don make no difference which way Ah go. Gawd! Gawd, Ah wish alla them white folks wuz dead! *Dead*, Ah tell yuh! Ah wish Gawd would kill em all!" Aunt Sue, confronting the white sheriff and the posse about to lynch her son, the gun tucked away under her winding sheet, thinks to herself, "Mabbe Ah kin shoot em both! Mabbe Ah kin shoot *twice*!"[13]

In these stories, Wright succeeded in finding a language to speak to multiple audiences across racial, class, and national lines, conveying the experience of masses of the world's people informed, as he noted in "Blueprint for Negro Writing," by "a consciousness which draws for its strength upon the fluid lore of a great people, and molds this lore with the concepts that move and direct the forces of history today."[14] He is referring specifically to the "Negro writer" depicting "Negro life," but the broader connotations for the working class and the oppressed as a whole can be extrapolated. As he notes in "How 'Bigger' Was Born," not only were there many Biggers in his childhood, but he had come to discover that "Bigger Thomas was not black all the time; he was white, too, and there were literally millions of him, everywhere," and that Bigger "carried within him the potentialities of either Communism or Fascism," that "he is a product of a dislocated society; he is a dispossessed and disinherited man." Because of the effects of racial oppression and educational restrictions, the formation of solidarity among Black Americans was "still in a state of individual anger and hatred. Here, I felt was *drama*," Wright exclaims. "Who will be the first to touch off these Bigger Thomases, white and black?"[15]

Responding to the political economic conditions that subjugated Black Americans in particular, complicating calls for revolutionary class struggle, Wright took up key Marxist concepts: (1) a dialectical historical materialist explanation of history in which class conflict and the law of value assume specific social relations under successive modes of production; (2) commodity fetishism in which economic value inheres in relations between things rather than relations between people; (3) the oppression and exploitation of subaltern populations defined by race, ethnicity, nation, gender, or other identities; and (4) imperial and colonial forces as keys to global capitalist development that simultaneously oppressed and united the dispossessed. Although his international focus sharpened after his expatriation, it can be seen as early as Part Two of *Black Boy* in statements such as "It was not the economics of Communism, nor the great power of trade unions, nor the excitement of underground politics that claimed me; my attention was caught by the similarity of the experiences of workers in other lands, by the possibility of uniting scattered but kindred peoples into a whole."[16]

Dialectical Historical Materialism

Dialectical historical materialism stems from an understanding that social relations correspond to evolving productive forces that usher in different stages of history, from the earliest human settlements to what Marx and Engels called "primitive communism" to the advent of agriculture, private property, class and slave societies, and beyond. Although the idea of primitive communism has been disputed by anthropologists, there is widespread agreement that the rise of class society and private property marked a distinct turning point in human history from a collective focus on obtaining food for survival to the production of surplus, leading to the division of classes and the domination of one class over another. Wright explicitly traces part of this history through the Great Migration of the Black tenant farmer in the de jure Jim Crow South to the Black industrial urban dweller in the de facto segregated North in *Native Son*, *12 Million Black Voices*, *Black Boy*, "Black Hope," and *Lawd Today!* In *Black Boy*, he describes his father in their poignant last visit as an old man "standing alone upon the red clay of a Mississippi plantation, a sharecropper, clad in ragged overalls, holding a muddy hoe in his gnarled, veined hands . . . a black peasant who had gone to the city seeking life, but who had failed in the city; a black peasant whose life had been hopelessly snarled in the city, and who had at last fled the city—that same city that had lifted me in its burning arms."[17] The narrative shifts in *Native Son* to the industrial urban North and the second generation of southern Black migrants on Chicago's South Side in his story of Bigger Thomas.

Bigger's mother is deeply religious, moral, law-abiding, and stoical, but his generation of Black urban youth has been transformed; they are conscious of their disenfranchisement and cut off from the southern traditions, religious beliefs, and accommodations to white rule that sustained their parents. But it is in *12 Million Black Voices* that Wright draws his most vivid portrait of Black southerners swept up in an epochal transition. Writing in the plural first person, he declares, "Vast changes engulf our lives," propelled by new machines—tractors and cotton-pickers—that force poor Black southerners to become migrant farm factory workers and "render our labor useless," as well as by deforestation, soil erosion, and loss of soil fertility that "drain the land and leave it a hard yellow mat, a mockery to the sky and a curse to us." Lords of the Land and Bosses of the Buildings compete for cheap Black labor, the latter luring them north where they will live in brick buildings, be able to vote, and send their children to school. Wright observes that this migration to the urban North is a worldwide phenomenon: "All over the world men are leaving the land for the streets of the city," including thousands of poor whites, because the land will no longer "give life to her sons and daughters, black or white." He reflects, "Perhaps never in history has a more utterly unprepared folk wanted to go to the city; we were barely born as a folk when we headed north for the tall and sprawling centers of steel and stone." This passage north is "the beginning of living on a new and terrifying plane of consciousness."[18]

Wright's most precise expression of a historical materialist understanding of the Great Migration, augmented by his lifelong effort to work through the dialectic between class struggle and racial oppression, comes in the final section of the book, in which he declares:

> Imagine European history from the days of Christ to the present telescoped into three hundred years and you can comprehend the drama which our consciousness has experienced! Brutal, bloody, crowded with suffering and abrupt transitions, the lives of us black folk represent the most magical and meaningful picture of human experience in the Western world. Hurled from our native African homes into the very center of the most complex and highly industrialized civilization the world has ever known, we stand today with a consciousness and memory such as few people suggest.
>
> We black folk, our history and our present being, are a mirror of all the manifold experiences of America. What we want, what we represent, what we endure is what America is. If we black folk perish, America will perish.[19]

After his departure from the Party in 1942, the United States in 1947, and his "former attitudes as a Negro and a Communist" in 1952, Wright's Marxist account of the stages of history became more ambiguous. As he put it to William Gardner Smith in *Ebony* magazine in July 1953, four months after *The Outsider* was published to mixed reviews, "I was trying to grapple with the big problem—the problem and meaning of Western civilization as a whole and the relation of Negroes and other minority groups to it."[20] Cross Damon's lengthy discourse on human history in *The Outsider*, like Boris Max's closing defense of Bigger in *Native Son*, was criticized for its clumsy didacticism and "quasi-philosophical prose," elicited by Comrade Blimin's accusation of murder and command to *"talk for your life."* Refusing to defend himself against crimes he insists he did not commit, Damon confesses "not as Blimin wanted him to but as he felt it . . . trying to clarify his predicament in his own eyes."[21] Blimin's questions serve as a counterpoint to Wright's own struggle to think through the consequences of uneven global development, the weaknesses and failures of actually existing capitalist and communist states, and the psychological and emotional barriers to human liberation that conditioned masses of people to accept "the total and absolute in modern life."[22]

Reiterating Wright's earlier treatments of Marx's theory of stages of history, Damon argues that what catapulted human beings from traditional agrarian to modern industrial societies was material productive forces rather than ideas or ideological banners, be they capitalist or communist. His long-winded speech, however, is fraught with logical inconsistencies and dubious political claims, including misrepresentations of Marx conflated with Soviet Communism and pseudo-philosophical pretensions, mixed with some genuine insights into the relationship of ideas to the material forces that propel human history. Absent from Damon's diagnosis of the ills of Western society and the threat of totalitarianism is the role of collective agency in altering the course of history through revolutionary breaks from the past that according to Marx are never predetermined or guaranteed but rather emerge from class struggle at particular historical conjunctures. Wright's condemnation of Damon's worldview is expressed in the character's dying words in response to district attorney Eli Houston's questions about why he chose to live as he did—"I wanted to be free"—and then what he found: "Nothing. . . . The search can't be done alone. . . . Alone a man is nothing."[23]

In *Native Son*, Boris Max also offers a Marxist perspective on Black history, interrupting the limited third-person point of view of the rest of the novel that sees the world through Bigger's eyes. Though criticized by many readers, Max's quasi-legal arguments spoke for Wright at the time, enabling him to give voice to a political analysis that he still found persuasive but wanted to represent through the lens of African American experience. In contrast, shot through with ambivalence, Damon's long-winded history of humanity in *The Outsider* simultaneously exposes his own corruption and criminality and doubles for Wright as he wrestles with Comrade Blimin's dogmatic Marxist principles. Max, speaking for Wright, contends that his defense of Bigger Thomas concerns more than one man, or one people, criminally enslaved for centuries to "[touch] the destiny of an entire nation." Although critics have faulted Wright for his portrayal of a radical defense attorney who failed to fight for Bigger's acquittal, as was the practice of ILD, it is more important to the logic of the novel that Max expresses a Marxist worldview on the devastating impact of dislocations suffered by millions of African Americans. He goes on to explain how historical material forces created those conditions through "the imperial dream of a feudal age that made men enslave others ... [men who] could not have built nations on so vast a scale had they not shut their eyes to the humanity of other men whose lives were necessary for the building."[24]

And yet, despite Damon's logical fallacies, arrogance, and brutality, his lecture contains the essence of Wright's application of Marx's theories of history to earlier work. To sum up Damon's main points in brief:

- Some nations in the West have "already exhausted their industrial potentials of development and are industrially overripe," while China, India, and "vast stretches of Africa ... have hardly begun this journey toward industrialization."
- The undeveloped nations that constitute half the human race and more than half the planet have been stimulated and deformed by the impact of Western imperialism. Through its extraction of natural resources, the West "awakened black, red, brown, and yellow men from their long slumber and sent them, willy-nilly, hurtling down the road of industrialization."
- The process of modernization was quickened by the "marriage of scientific knowledge and industry." But humans are irrational, driven by fear, and reliant on myths to quell fears of a "clamoring world of storms, volcanoes, and heaving waves." Science and industry tore away primitive myths, driving masses of people into "vast, impersonal cities" and causing a split consciousness between reality and "totems and taboos ... in the world of myths."
- Liberals were "kindhearted atheists" who acted like good Christians without believing in Christianity and had gone so far down a "godless road" that they saw a "black nothingness looming as its end." Retreating in fear, "they helped to undermine the old world, but *they discovered that the building of a new world was much harder than they had suspected*" and called for "new systems of ideas" but instead got "programs for wars and revolutions."[25]

Wright's study in exile of Marxist theory alongside Husserl, Heidegger, Hegel, and other Western philosophers suggests that he was no longer relying on characters in *The Outsider*—neither Damon nor Houston—to speak for him. Rather, employing a double-voiced narrative like that which inflected Bigger's constricted point of view with his own keen perceptions, Wright identifies with the characters' outsiderness even as he criticizes their failures of analysis and the ideologies into which they are interpellated. When Damon asserts that it is power, not ideologies, that determines historical outcomes, he mistakenly locates power in the realm of ideas rather than the material forces of production that drive human history. As Marx put it, "It is not the consciousness of men that determines their existence, but their social existence that determines their consciousness. At a certain stage of development, the material productive forces of society come into conflict with the existing relations of production.... From forms of development of the productive forces these relations turn into their fetters. Then begins an era of social revolution."[26]

Yet, Damon's insistence that "the essence of life is psychological" also reflects Wright's growing interest in psychological barriers to human liberation, including the contradictory role of religion. He channels his own ambivalences and anxieties through Damon to reveal the sophistry and cynicism of the postwar convergence of totalitarianism, nihilism, and undefeated fascism, accentuated by a loss of faith in revolutionary movements, intensifying anticolonial struggles, and Cold War political and cultural crackdowns worldwide. Wright was rightly concerned with the psychology of mass movements and the double-edged sword of religion as a radicalizing and conservatizing force. In "Fire and Cloud," Communist organizers, his congregants' hunger, and their increasing militancy persuade Reverend Taylor to join with Black and white protestors who march defiantly through town to demand food. Instead of putting them all in jail as threatened, a chastened Mayor Bolton appeals to Taylor, who triumphs over the mayor's savage attempts to silence the protesters and directs him to speak to the assembled masses himself. As Bolton timorously addresses the crowd, a "baptism of clean joy swept over Taylor" as he watched the "sea of black and white faces" and thought "This is the way! . . . Gawd ain no lie! . . . *Freedom belongs to the strong!*"[27]

The psychological aspects and political challenges of radical mass movements can also be seen in Aunt Sue's conversion from faith in Jesus to faith that the Party was "another Resurrection." For her, "the wrongs and sufferings of black men had taken the place of Him nailed to the Cross."[28] This exchange of one idol for another functions as a hopeful sign of Sue's growth as a revolutionary and a person, but it is also a political quagmire, mired in ambivalent substitution of one "god" for another that, by the mid-1940s for Wright, had indeed failed. At the time he was writing *The Outsider*, his disillusionment with the CPUSA and consternation over the impact of industrialized, commodified, totalitarian societies on human freedom can be seen in Damon's assertion that "modern man still believes in magic ... [and] lives in a rational world but insists on interpreting the events in terms of mystical forces."[29] As Jamall A. Calloway puts it, "For Wright, theology is not just a means of indoctrinating Black slaves in the south. It is the foundation of indoctrinating a slave consciousness throughout the world.... For Wright, God was not assassinated 'in the north' or in Europe; God was replaced."[30] This political theology not only impoverishes the human spirit but also has serious consequences for political salvation for the dispossessed masses.

Commodity Fetishism and Alienation

These psychological and religious problems started to preoccupy Wright as early as 1941, as he was drafting *The Man Who Lived Underground*, challenging and reshaping but not supplanting the Marxist worldview that suffused his earlier work and continued to inform his engagement with postcolonial and nonaligned movements, his travel writing, and his fiction. In addition to explaining social realities through the lens of historical materialism, especially the traumatic leap by Black migrants from feudal to capitalist conditions of life and the parallel leap of colonial subjects of color from Western subjugation to nominal independence, he took up concepts of alienation and commodity fetishism. Starting with *Lawd Today!* he had begun to theorize and portray in increasingly complex characters a Marxist psychoanalytical theory of the logic of racism that emasculated Black men who unconsciously wanted both to kill the Oedipal white father and to become him, internalizing patriarchal racist structures of feeling that fostered Black nationalism in a regressive escape to the womb of the "motherland." This backwardness was a condition that had to be overcome, Wright argued, in order to allow for "the emergence of a new culture in the shell of the old." He understood that once that process was set in motion and "a people begin to realize *meaning* in their suffering, the civilization that engenders that suffering is doomed."[31] As Anthony Dawahare incisively notes in his comparison of postal worker Jake Jackson in *Lawd Today!* to Bigger Thomas in *Native Son*, "Dialectically, then, in Wright's urban fiction, the path to socialism involves retracing and understanding the hazardous, regressive missteps people may take in hope to be free from the pain of social inequality. The novel ends where revolutionary action may begin."[32]

Wright denounced the commodification of human existence, probing the conditions in 1930s Chicago of alienated Black workers denied access to social goods and services reserved for white people. Later, he focused on their African and Asian counterparts oppressed by the same Western forms of exploitation and racial fetishism that turned nonwhite bodies into salable commodities and tribal lands into gold mines for colonial powers. Marx's concept of commodity fetishism, borrowed from the anthropological term for the belief that godly powers reside in things, explains that commodities under capitalist production take the form of relations between things, concealing the social relations among people, which then appear as inherent qualities of the things themselves. In a capitalist mode of production defined by private property and private enterprise, exchange value dominates use value through a process of abstraction that creates a "fantastic form" of the commodity and mystifies the exploitative system resulting in surplus value. In order to accrue profits, the owner needs to maintain and modernize tools, machinery, physical plants, and other capital assets, and to appropriate surplus value created by workers in excess of their wages. These social relations, for Marx, are concealed within the commodity, obscuring the exploitative process by which owners accumulate profit and thereby impeding a rational understanding of reality—precisely the psychological barrier to revolutionary consciousness that Wright sought to address.

In *Lawd Today!* his critique of the commodification of everyday life materializes in Jake Jackson's obsession with playing the numbers. As Jake leaves his building for the single Joycean day the novel chronicles, he stops in the vestibule to pore over "multicolored circulars and advertisement throwaways" in his mailbox that promise "a mountain of gold dollars" at no risk; incense that when burned, reveals numbers in the ashes, leading to "ASTONISHING$$$$$$"; various bottles of impotency castigator for men and women; and "surefire" treatments for drunkards, an ad Jake tears into "tiny pieces" and drops to the floor, pocketing the circulars he prefers. Wright's experimental, modernist stylistic choices appear in this chapter as reproduced circulars, preparing the reader for the scene that follows at the Black Gold Policy Wheel, where Jake enters a crowded, smoky room after a dream the previous night signaling that he should answer "the call of the numbers." Wright describes the game in detail as a "kind of lottery," explaining that the object is for the player to supply three numbers that will win a "gig" that pays 100 to 1. "And who would not take a chance like that?" Jake plays and loses, as he almost invariably does, squandering two dollars and leaving him *"almost dead broke."*[33] This extractive practice aimed at poor and working-class people as a promise of getting rich through luck further impoverishes and delimits their existence.

It also divided generations of working-class, Black southerners catapulted into modernity as memories of a slower, more rural, religious South faded for successive generations. Wright's sensitivity to the transformation of time in industrial capitalist economies from reliance on natural signs and social ritual to clocked, factory hours can be seen in a comical conversation in the story "Long Black Song" in which a farmer's young wife, Sarah, and a white graphophone salesman are mutually perplexed by one another's attitudes toward time. Surprised that Sarah is quieting her baby by letting her bang an old clock with a stick, he is more amazed to discover that she feels no need to tell time. "We git erlong widout time," she says. How do they know when to get up or when it's dark? "We jus git up, thas all.... We git up wid the sun." How can anyone live without time? "We jus don need no time, Mistah."[34] In Damon's speech to Blimin, he compares this timeless, cyclical, agrarian existence to new modes of oppressive urban industry, a process that simultaneously freed masses of rural migrants from "the veil of myth-worlds" and constituted a "kind of war against mankind."[35] These conditions were especially fraught for Uncle Tom's children who migrated to northern cities to confront a harsh, new world.

The depth of Bigger's alienation in *Native Son* is revealed in his conversation with Gus outside the pool hall when they see the plane skywrite the words "USE SPEED GASOLINE," evoking a new reliance on fuel to power emerging forms of transportation. The distance between Bigger's assertion that he could fly and the reality of his life on the South Side can be measured by Gus's sarcastic remark, "If you wasn't black and if you had some money and if they'd let you go to that aviation school, you could fly a plane." Later, they buy tickets to see the 1931 film *Trader Horn*, in which two white traders in 1870s Africa find a missionary's daughter captured as a child and now worshiped as a pagan goddess. The news short preceding the film reports on heiress Mary Dalton's shocking flirtation with a "well-known radical" while on vacation in Florida. After her father denounces her "Communist friend," Gus asks Bigger, "What's a Communist?" Says Bigger, "Damn if I know. It's a race of people who live in Russia, ain't it?" He adds, "Rich people don't like Communists." Diverted from the film's "pictures of naked black men and women whirling in wild dances," he imagines the chauffeur's job for which he is applying will give him access to "smart people" who make millions of dollars. "Maybe if he were working for them ... he would get some of it." He goes on to reflect that "rich white people were not so hard on Negroes; it was poor whites who hated Negroes ... because they didn't have their share of the money."[36]

These early scenes in *Native Son* encapsulate the same story Wright tells about his own life and the lives of voiceless Black boys and millions of migrants, of the shock of modernity and the oppressive conditions of poverty and racism that Black southerners confronted in the urban North. There is potential both for interracial class solidarity, explicitly described in *12 Million Black Voices*, and for disenfranchised African Americans to identify with the ruling class—capitalist and fascist alike, as Wright makes clear in his essay about Bigger—accepting a system of class stratification into which they will not be allowed to assimilate. Bigger, as we have seen, is potentially drawn to fascism or communism, disoriented by social dislocations that leave him "dispossessed and disinherited ... amid the great possible plenty on earth ... looking and feeling for a way out." Whether he follows "some gaudy, hysterical leader" or stands "with the millions of his kindred fellow workers under trade-union or revolutionary guidance depends upon the future drift of events in America."[37]

As Wright observes in *12 Million Black Voices*, the first generation of migrants mourned the loss of their children, many of whom scorned them: "They say that we still wear the red bandanna about our heads, that we are still Uncle Toms." They bear witness to the alienated youth who drop out of school, lured by city lights, taverns, automobiles, and poolrooms; they say they are beaten, while their children are "bitter and frustrated at the sight of the alluring hopes and prizes denied them," dying on city streets as the "courts and morgues become crowded" with them. Meanwhile, educated Black leaders become ashamed of these young Black city dwellers and white people become afraid of the Black proletariat, "fearing that we may rise up against them." Wright makes explicit the dominion of the capitalist class—both the Lords of the Land in the South and the Bosses of the Buildings in the North—so that migrants go from tenant farmer shacks in Mississippi to subdivided kitchenettes on Chicago's South Side, passing from a world of people in the Jim Crow South where "men spoke to you, cursed you, yelled at you or killed you" to Jim Crow in the urban North where "cold forces hit you ... It is a world of *things*."[38] This deepening alienation, he warned yet again, could push Uncle Tom's children to the political left or the political right, revolution or reaction, communism or fascism.

Gender Oppression and Wright's Treatment of Female Characters

Wright's analysis of racism is woven throughout the fabric of his life and work, typically earning him accolades for his early publications and complaints that he lost touch with his roots when he left America. His treatment of female characters and his relations with women, on the other hand, have been subject to damning critique. Even in writing that he explicitly claimed went beyond the "straight black-white stuff," like *The Man Who Lived Underground*, he tells a story of a Black man falsely accused of murder and savagely beaten and killed by police. The persistence of his interrogation of racial oppression is evident in a lecture delivered in 1956, "The Psychological Reactions of Oppressed People," in which he declared, "Today, as the tide of white domination of the land mass of Asia and Africa recedes, there lies exposed to view a procession of shattered cultures, disintegrated societies, and a writhing sweep of more aggressive, irrational religion than the world has known for centuries." With the rise of a new postcolonial, academic literature, he argued, "one enters a universe of menacing shadows where disparate images coalesce—white turning into black, the dead coming to life, the top becoming the bottom." Of this devastating legacy, he observed, "Imperialism turns out to have been much more morally foul a piece of business than even Marx and Lenin imagined!"[39] His position on the "woman question" is not so clear-cut.

Wright's Feminist Critics

A wave of scathing feminist criticism in the 1970s depicted Wright as sexist, misogynistic, and narcissistic, declaring that he had "contempt for black women" and created Black female characters who were "dull," "mindless," and "passive," reduced to "flat, one-dimensional stereotypes." According to Trudier Harris, the female characters in *Native Son* are "in league with the oppressors of black men." Sherley Anne Williams declared that Wright's portraits of Black women "place him at the extreme end of the [African American literary] tradition in a position that is both extremely sexist and racist." She locates the crux of his misogyny in the absence of any central women characters or "women's questions" in his fiction, adding, "When they appear at all, they are subsumed under larger political and philosophical themes."[40] These larger political themes of the historical material conditions that produce oppression are indeed central to his writing, enunciated in the line in "How 'Bigger' Was Born" that he "had put on a pair of spectacles whose power was that of an x-ray enabling [him] to see deeper into the lives of men"—a line to which I keep referring because it so aptly invokes the Marxist lens through which he could see the essential relations of class, race, *and* gender obscured by reified social structures of class rule and its inherent inequalities.

This critical attention to Wright's treatment of women, absent or negligible in earlier assessments of his work and life, reflects the rise of second-wave feminism and the welcome arrival of more Black female writers and critics to literary and academic scenes. Since then, his portrayal of female characters and his attitude toward women have been further reconsidered. At issue in more recent interpretations of his writing is not whether he was sexist in some respects—he no doubt was—but whether his life and work reflect the (sometimes contradictory) antisexist, feminist views attuned to the CPUSA's position on the "woman question." Sylvia Keady argues that many of Wright's female characters serve more as foils for male action than as fully developed individuals. She depicts *The Outsider*'s underage lover Dot Powers, whom Damon impregnates, and the unhappy white artist Eva, with whom he falls in love and whose husband Gil Blount he murders, as "childlike, helpless, and devoted."[41] However, Barbara Foley, Shana Russell, Sondra Guttman, and Cheryl Higashida, among others, have reevaluated Wright's treatment of women based, in part, on his unpublished novel "Black Hope," initially titled "Little Sister."[42] Along with explicating the feminist content of its macabre story of racial passing, human trafficking, 1930s slave markets, murder, mayhem, and fascism in America, rewritten almost entirely in a substantially different second version and finally abandoned in 1948, these critics reinterpret Wright's published work, including his journalism, placing his perspective on women in the context of his politics and his activities as an editor, speaker, and participant in left-wing, Pan-African, and nonaligned movements in the United States and abroad.

Some feminist critics have also objected to Wright's primary relationships with white women, including his two marriages. Trepidations about interracial coupling of Black men and white women are rooted in complex sexual alliances that ironically emerged as part of the CPUSA's heroic, if flawed, multifront, antiracist program adopted after the 1928 Sixth Congress of the Communist International. An unintended consequence of antilynching campaigns was the construction of a triangular relationship of white and Black men courting white women, even as they bonded in vilifying those who accused Black men of rape, such as the two working-class white women in the Scottsboro case whom the defense sought to discredit as prostitutes.[43] It was the tendency to exclude Black female comrades rather than insist on their equality that resonates with Harris's critique of Wright for casting Black female characters as oppressors of Black men. In fact, Black female Communists mounted a significant challenge to the Party's reproduction of a system that relegated Black women to the bottom of the social hierarchy.

Even as the Party sought to establish itself as the only truly egalitarian, antiracist organization in the United States that accepted and encouraged sexual intimacy among Black and white couples, there were far more relationships between Black men and white women than vice versa, which elevated homosocial bonding between Black and white male Communists in a mutual bias against Black female partners and derogation of working-class white women, particularly in the South. Interracial relationships among ardently antiracist radicals during this period were thus complicated by Black men's internalization of "white" male desire combined with their defiance of Jim Crow segregation laws that criminalized Black male relations with white women and terrorized Black communities. Although intimate relationships between Black men and white women were as complex as those of any other couple, the nearly ubiquitous pattern of interracial coupling in the Party and the radical and bohemian left revealed a tendency of Black men to assert a fearless masculinity and insist on racial equality through sexual conquest of white women. Black women in the Party spoke out against this flagrant, if inadvertent, reproduction of gendered racism and sexism, and the topic was openly debated to the extent that some Black comrades started a "movement back to the race," ditching white wives and girlfriends, while Harlem organizers gave dance lessons to white men to help them "break the ice with black women." Mike Gold might have even taken a few dance classes before he jitterbugged at the Savoy Ballroom in 1937 with a Black social worker who, he declared, "could dance like a dream . . . and was a Communist!"[44]

Wright's personal history and writing reflect these gendered psychosocial and political responses to Jim Crow racism and the Party's antiracist program. He would have been privy to internal debates on the "woman question" that evolved partly through the crucial role of the mothers of the Scottsboro Boys in making their case a cause célèbre. Together with white and Black female Communists, they challenged the initial rhetoric of the defense campaign that denigrated the boys' white female accusers as prostitutes, advancing instead a feminist call for interracial solidarity among workers on the basis of untenable conditions that made working-class white women pawns of the same Jim Crow laws that oppressed Black women and terrorized Black communities. Having joined the Party in 1934, two years after the boys' arrests, Wright would have closely followed the Scottsboro case. It was only at the insistence of his editor Whitt Burnett at *Story* magazine in 1938 that he omitted direct references to the case in "Bright and Morning Star." The boys' mothers had by then become heroic international spokeswomen, especially Ada Wright, mother of Roy and Andy Wright—and one prototype for Aunt Sue—whose European tour in 1932 helped transform the campaign into a "central episode in the global racial politics of the 1930s."[45]

Wright's relations with women were shaped by these political discussions of racial and gender oppression as well as by his secular and what might now be described as anti-essentialist values—that is, values based on the belief that race is not biological except in its most superficial traits, but rather is produced by historical material forces and relations of production. He spoke frankly about his need for intellectual and sexual satisfaction in intimate relations with respect to the harsh conditions that oppressed Black women in his lifetime, which restricted their access to education and the sort of cultural and consciousness-raising political experience that benefited many more white women. In describing his "long, tortured affair" with a young, unwed Black mother whose ten-cent insurance premium he paid weekly in exchange for sex, he portrays himself as a callow young man, irritated by her illiteracy and childish behavior yet jealous of other men she sees. When she laughs at his effort to teach her to read, he snaps, "The hell with you," to which she reasonably chides, "Don't you go and cuss me now. . . . I don't cuss you." Some readers view this episode as evidence of Wright's contempt for Black women, but he is clearly aware in retrospect of his meanness toward the young woman and rebukes other insurance agents who treated their "bought girls" as property. "Some of the agents were vicious," he recalls, trading sex for claim money, to which he understood "the average black woman would submit because she needed the money badly."[46] Correspondingly, his relations with white women were arguably based on the quality of their companionship rather than their skin color.

As with other Marxist concepts, a throughline can be seen in Wright's engagement with the "woman question," his understanding of the oppression of women, particularly Black women, and, contrary to the view of many critics, his relative attunement to sexual politics in his female characters. From his early short stories to his meditation on women's status in *Pagan Spain*, published in 1957, a politically conscious, if not always nonsexist, understanding of gender infuses his writing, especially his abandoned novel "Black Hope" and his journalistic and ethnographic reporting. Like other critics, feminists have tended to conflate him with his protagonists—Bigger Thomas, in particular—mistaking his demystification of oppressive social conditions and the unflattering, negative behaviors they produce for his identification with his male characters' misogynistic anomie. At the same time, characters like the Communist heiress Mary Dalton in *Native Son* and the abstract painter Eva Blount in *The Outsider* reveal a more nuanced portrait of women shaped, like men, by myriad social and historical contexts never wholly determined by gender.

Inverting the Image: From Mary Dalton to Sarah Hunter

For Marx, the phenomenal form or surface manifestation of reality is often the inverse of its essence, a principle which, he notes, "is pretty well known in every science except political economy."[47] Wright's female characters often appear in negative or inverted form as one-dimensional, shadowy, undeveloped figures rather than being sharply delineated through the lens of his narrative techniques, including his use of limited third-person point of view, irony, and double vision. In "How 'Bigger' Was Born," Wright explicitly invokes the metaphor of photography in explaining that the conditioning he saw in the many Biggers he knew growing up was not as "blatant or extreme . . . [but] was there, nevertheless, like an undeveloped negative."[48] In Mary Dalton, he was concerned not only with her gender but also with her facile left-wing politics. He took the name from the CPUSA member Mary Licht, who had used it as a pseudonym. In 1936, Licht was arrested in Atlanta, Georgia, with Wright's friend Herbert Newton and four others, all charged with attempted insurrection and seditious activity for organizing a defense meeting for two arrested comrades. In a letter to Michel Fabre, Jane Newton recalled, "Dick didn't know [Licht] very well but rather disliked her on principle and felt very mischievous using her name."[49] Wright could assume that such a recognizable name would irk Party members like his nemesis Harry Haywood. In her naive, overly familiar, seductive behavior, the fictional Mary Dalton embodies Wright's increasingly bitter view of the Party's organizing efforts on the South Side, the origins of which he describes in *Black Boy* in his response to his mother's abhorrence of the covers of *New Masses* issues.

In *Native Son*, Mary Dalton and her Communist boyfriend Jan Erlone enact the CPUSA's missteps in recruiting Black workers, which Wright saw as a failure of radical publications like *New Masses* to understand "the passions of the common people. . . . They had a program, an ideal, but they had not yet found a language." This lack of a "language" also interfered in interpersonal relations across class and racial barriers that white Communists like the fictional Mary and Jan attempted, however clumsily, to cross. Still mired in the racist ideology they sought to overcome, they thrust Bigger into what Wright calls—not for the first time—a "No Man's Land," "a shadowy region . . . the ground that separated the white world from the black that he stood upon." On his first evening as a chauffeur for the Dalton family, he is told to drive Mary to her lecture at the university, but she directs him to pick up Jan instead and drive to the South Side. Impervious to the distress caused by their physical closeness and uncomfortably familiar tone, they push Bigger to the breaking point. Says Jan, "We want to eat at one of those places where colored people eat," pressing Bigger to take them to Ernie's Kitchen Shack. Like a slum tourist, Mary tells him she wants to visit the "tall, dark apartment buildings" on the South Side "and just *see* how your people live."[50]

Wright describes the lives of Bigger's "people" in part through Black female characters, who are routinely and at least to an extent wrongly seen as evidence of Wright's sexism and misogyny, especially toward Black women. While there is some justification for criticism of his Black female characters, who tend to be uneducated, powerless, sexually objectified, and deeply religious, there is also a historical basis for such portrayals. The working-class Black women Wright knew and fictionalized were racially and sexually oppressed, consigned to harsh, proletarian, if not lumpenproletarian lives, and subjected to domination by Black as well as white men. At the same time, his mother's family had petit bourgeois roots and he knew middle-class, educated, politicized Black women in and beyond Chicago's literary and political milieus, especially in the CPUSA, including Margaret Walker, who writes about her complicated relationship with him in *Richard Wright: Daemonic Genius*. But his interest as a writer was mainly in depicting the Black working class, not the bourgeoisie, the intelligentsia, or the radicalized few, but the many; and even though he married two white women, he had friendships and sexual relations with women of color, including fellow writers, editors, and activists. While by his own admission he at times treated some of those women as reprehensively as his sexist male characters, he was on the verge of marrying others.

The Black female characters in *Native Son*—Bigger's mother Mrs. Thompson, his sister Vera, and his girlfriend Bessie—reflect his shortcomings and thwarted dreams. Bigger understands that Bessie's seven-day workweek in the kitchen of a white employer forms "the narrow orbit of her life." There are two Bessies, Wright tells us in Bigger's voice: "one a body that he had just had and wanted badly again; the other was in Bessie's face; it asked questions; it bargained and sold the other Bessie to advantage."[51] The second Bessie is routinely erased in critiques of Wright's treatment of women. Shana Russell points out that this second Bessie "is a refuge for Bigger . . . but, more than that, she gives the reader important insight into the oppression and suffering that underlies the protagonist's rage at white society."[52] Wright treats Mary Dalton more disparagingly than any of his Black female characters. Mary's naive, overfriendly behavior precipitates a crisis for Bigger, whose deep distrust of white people heightens his awareness of the deadly ramifications of close proximity to the wayward daughter of his wealthy, white employer. In contrast, his petulant, adolescent interactions with his mother and sister, even after Mary's murder, reveal ordinary family tensions and hostilities in which the two women talk back, counteracting his point of view and revealing Wright's understanding of them as yearning "to see life in a certain way," unable to escape their distorted "picture of the world" in which Vera "showed a fear so deep as to be an organic part of her."[53]

Nevertheless, Wright admits in an early draft of *Black Boy* that he occasionally "took up with some Negro girl slut, the extent of such relations growing to fantastic and ludicrous proportions as the years passed."[54] This confession resonates with the pornographic references to women by male characters in *Lawd Today!* as "meat" or "stallions" and "bicycles" to be ridden. The offensive language echoes in Damon's repeated allusion in *The Outsider* to "woman as the body of woman," a strangely oblique objectification of the female body interchangeably describing the young prostitute Jenny, a "tart," and Eva, whom he professes to love. Yet, even if one accepts critiques of his male characters' misogyny, his Black female characters as subservient, childish, overly religious, or sluttish, and his own liability to sexist attitudes, Wright's portrayal of women also serves as critical commentary on gender relations and sexual oppression. Rather than glorifying sexism, which would contradict his political consciousness, Wright stands outside his characters' actions as well as his own to illuminate, for example, Bigger's immature, rebellious, cold-blooded desperation as he flees from the law and the lynch mob, to whom he is only a Black rapist of a white woman. What we see in *Native Son* in Bigger's contempt for his mother, sister, and Bessie is that he becomes increasingly exasperated with them because they mirror his own oppressive conditions and shortcomings. But it is the contempt and irritation of the character, not the author.

A Communist by marriage, Eva Blount has a tenuous allegiance to the Party in *The Outsider* that is further weakened by her comrades' treatment of Damon and Bob Hunter, the Black Caribbean waiter Damon meets on the train to New York City who turns out to be a union organizer and Party member. The antithesis of Mary Dalton, Eva is an amalgam of significant women in Wright's life and his own aesthetic interests and conflicts with the Party. Unlike Mary, who arouses and enrages Bigger, entangling him in a relationship that ends in both their deaths, Eva is a sympathetic if weak character. Although she and Damon meet the same fate, Eva functions as a mouthpiece for Wright's disenchantment with the Party as well as a love object and a symbol of his creative process and vision: "In her work she seemed to be straining to say something that possessed and gripped her life; she spoke tersely, almost cruelly through her forms. Her painting at bottom was the work of a poet trying to make color and form sing in an absolute and total manner."[55] According to Keady, although Eva is "slightly more articulate" than many of Wright's other female characters, her "main purpose is to enhance Damon's entrapment." She is helpless, childlike, and oppressed in order for Damon "to experience the necessity of human involvement and love."[56] Likewise, Floyd W. Hayes acknowledges that Damon has a "strange kind of love and pity" for Eva but argues that "Wright often fashions positive representations of the white female and generally constructs negative images of the Black feminine."[57]

Sylvia Keady sees Sarah Hunter, Bob's wife, along with Aunt Sue in "Bright and Morning Star," as exceptions to Wright's other portraits of women like Damon's mother, who is "emotional and revengeful," and his underage, pregnant lover Dot, who is depicted as "childlike" and "intellectually inferior." Their primary function, along with that of his wife Gladys, whom Keady concedes is "slightly more articulate," is to entrap and entangle Damon.[58] However, viewing Black female characters in *The Outsider* through the gaze of the narrator, who simultaneously speaks as and through Damon, arguably recasts them as critics rather than merely passive victims of misogyny. In protesting Damon's treatment of them, each woman addresses his narcissistic, deceitful, destructive behavior, especially toward those closest to him, including his young sons. When he denies that he seduced Dot and lied to her, his mother insists, "You *did*! . . . You let her hope for what you couldn't do, and that's lying. I'm no fool!" As he imagines "slapping her to the floor," enraged and ashamed, a "poignant pity for her" seizes him in a flood of Oedipal projections of her "incestuously-tinged longings." Sympathetically drawn as a Black female Communist, Sarah Hunter decries the Party's desertion of her husband Bob when he no longer serves its interests. When Bob accepts Party discipline, exclaiming, "This is the *Party*!" Sarah cries, "What in hell did I marry, a Marxist or a mouse!" Later, she insists, "Read your Marx and organize."[59] She represents a new generation of strong, radicalized Black women, a literary daughter of Aunt Sue in "Bright and Morning Star."

Uncle Tom's Daughters

In his defense of Wright's often misunderstood intellectual legacy, Paul Gilroy insists that attempts to make sense of the "complex misogyny" in his work should include "his path-breaking inauguration of a critical discourse on the construction of black masculinity" and his "feminist and proto-feminist" consciousness.[60] Joyce Ann Joyce argues that the protagonist Sarah in "Long

Black Song" "emerges as the center of consciousness through which we come to understand the misplacement of emotional vulnerability and its ensuing dangers in a racist society."[61] Wright establishes her positionality through the use of limited third-person point of view to tell the story from her perspective rather than that of her husband Silas. At home for over a week with a crying baby, lonely and unsatisfied by her husband, who has gone to town to sell cotton and buy provisions, she daydreams about her true love Tom, a soldier at war, wondering if her life would have been different with him than it is with Silas. Filled with desire, she hears an approaching car. Her visitor is a young white graphophone salesman who initiates sexual contact with her as she protests, "Naw, Mistah!... Naw, naw.... Mistah, Ah cant do that!... Please.... Lemme go!... Naw, naw," repeatedly saying to herself, "But he's a white man! A white man!"[62]

In keeping with other critics of Wright's misogyny, Sherley Anne Williams describes Sarah as "childish," even "infantile," and "wanton," while Silas is "a good man" who has "succeeded in acquiring the legitimate economic means to care for his family, almost as well as the average white man," living up to the "collective dream" of economic stability and upward mobility.[63] However, as Joyce suggests, reading the story from Sarah's point of view flips that interpretation: as the protagonist, she expresses her sensual and sexual being; her ambivalence toward motherhood, her husband, and the salesman; and her horror and fear when Silas kills the salesman and threatens his companion, avenging his wounded masculine pride. She resists the salesman's sexual advances because he is white and because she "cant do that," ultimately succumbing to desire but also to his whiteness, which overpowers and disarms her despite his youth, what she calls his "childishness." The tension Wright creates between her rape and her desire signals not his hatred of Black women but his grasp of their triple oppression. Nor is he unsympathetic to Silas, who grimly tells Sarah to leave with their child when the white vigilantes descend on their house and burn it to the ground with him inside. Talking out loud just before their arrival, Silas recites the facts of his life: "The white folks ain never gimme a chance! They ain never give no black man a chance! There ain nothing in yo whole life yuh kin keep from em! They take yo lan! They take yo freedom! They take yo women! N then they take yo life.... N then Ah gits stabbed in the back by mah own blood!"[64]

But it is Sarah, despite her betrayal of Silas, who has the wisdom to plead with him to leave: "We kin both go! Git the hosses." She envisions the possibility of a world free of racial hatred, linking human survival to the rhythms of nature and reflecting sorrowfully that the "killing of white men by black men and killing of black men by white men went on in spite of the hope of white bright days and the desire of dark black nights and the long gladness of green cornfields in summer and the deep dream of sleeping grey skies in winter." She feels sorry for Silas, who "followed the old river of blood, knowing that it meant nothing," and she struggles to understand the links between "black men and white men, land and houses, green cornfields and grey skies, gladness and dreams . . . all a part of that which made life good." And it is Sarah, after watching the house burn, the roof cave in, and the walls collapse, the house "hidden by eager plumes of red," who runs with her baby, horror-struck but alive, refusing to die for nothing. Her liminal consciousness, as yet inexpressible (like those of so many of Wright's characters), points to her own latent capacities and to the collective work that must be done to turn incipient dreams into reality and utopian fantasies into actual egalitarian societies in which people across racial lines coexist peaceably with one another and with nature.[65]

Wright distances himself from his characters, putting them in situations that, as he notes in "Memories of My Grandmother," bring them to the breaking point, rendering them fluid, like a jazz improvisation when "the character, hard put upon from within or without, forgets his habits, his backgrounds, his censor, his conditioning and, feeling free, acts with a latitude which he could not and did not possess in the narrow context of daily life." In other words, the character faces contingencies, alternate histories, "if this, then what" scenarios that signal the possible, the imaginable, that on a larger scale of collective rupture can also render world history fluid, enabling masses to act "with a latitude [they] could not and did not possess in the narrow context of daily life." In this same essay, Wright identifies Sarah's breaking point in her "sexual restlessness [which] forms the pivot upon which the story can swing in any direction."[66]

He would have been aware of debates on the "woman question" and representations of women in proletarian fiction like Agnes Smedley's *Daughter of Earth* in which "sexual passion is not a respite from the class struggle but embedded in it, and sexual egalitarianism is integrally related to the fight for a better world."[67] Rather than being wanton or childish, Sarah's "sexual restlessness"—her loneliness, regrets, longings, and desires—accord her a degree of sexual liberation and autonomy from her husband even as it sets in motion her rape/seduction by a stranger whose whiteness and maleness simultaneously threaten and arouse her. This trauma is followed by a chain of tragic events in which she, Silas, and the salesman are swept into a deadly pattern of intertwining racial and gender conflicts that only Sarah survives. It is not a return to "the natural order of things" that Sarah's stream of consciousness represents, as Joyce Ann Joyce suggests, but rather an as yet inarticulable impulse toward a necessary social transformation of the historically specific conditions of capitalism.[68] As Wright well knew, this system of exploitative appropriation of surplus by the capitalist class was established and maintained by pitting racially and sexually oppressed groups against one another to quell discontent and defuse and neutralize working-class solidarity.

Of all Wright's female characters, Aunt Sue is judged most favorably by feminist critics like Keady, who sees her more positively because she kills Booker, the white traitor to the comrades. But then she immediately discredits Sue as "a motherly figure, desexualized by her age and appearance."[69] Similarly, Williams appreciates that Sue rises above the figure of the stereotypical Black "mammy" and acts courageously in killing Booker but asserts that "Wright never creates so complex and dynamic a female figure" again in his writing.[70] These ambivalent interpretations of Aunt Sue by critics who take issue with Wright's depiction of women have been challenged and deepened by numerous scholars, including Cheryl Higashida, Shana Russell, Greg Meyerson and Joseph Ramsey. Aunt Sue is modeled not on the "mammy" stereotype but on the "radical Black mother" that emerges in the Popular Front era in figures like the mothers of the Scottsboro Boys—Janie Patterson, Ida Norris, Viola Montgomery, Mamie Williams Wilcox, and Ada Wright. These women not only stood up for their own children but also allied with women across racial lines and pushed back against masculinist rhetoric produced by an interracial alliance of male workers, Communists, and sympathizers. Their homosocial camaraderie vilified as prostitutes the two white women who charged the boys with rape, sparking internal Party debates as the mothers and other radical women, Black and white, objected to stigmatizing the accusers—one of whom, Ruby Bates, recanted her testimony and joined the defense team. This feminist analysis of the Scottsboro case held that working-class solidarity across racial *and* gender lines was necessary. It served the interests of the capitalist class not only when white women accused Black men of rape but also when Black and white male comrades bonded in their disparagement of working-class white women as prostitutes, subverting the potential for interracial unity and the liberation of women and Black Americans.

Another inspiration for Aunt Sue came from Black female comrades Wright reported on for the *Daily Worker* after moving to New York City in 1937 and assuming the editorship of the Harlem bureau under the leadership of Ben Davis. Chief among them was Mother Ross, a seventy-one-year-old woman born in slavery in 1865 who worked in a tobacco factory in Virginia until she was thirty-nine years old and then as a domestic worker in Harlem, where she and her family migrated in 1904. Frustrated by "Negro" organizations that wanted her money but didn't take action, she joined the CPUSA-sponsored Unemployed Councils in 1930 and soon thereafter the Communist Party, becoming a "day-to-day worker" organizing support for the Scottsboro Boys, Angelo Herndon, and locals for the Workers Alliance as she "spread the message of Communism among Negro women." In sharp contrast to his negative depiction in Black Boy of a Black Communist unit meeting in Chicago in which he felt ridiculed as a bourgeois, out-of-touch "intellectual," Wright praised Mother Ross for her stamina and courage, noting, as he would do time and again, the historical transformation to which she had borne witness in her lifetime: "This woman has seen the face of her country changed more than once during her 71 years, and she has the strength, the courage and faith to fight and wait for still another change."[71]

Contesting the widespread view of Aunt Sue as heroic, Meyerson argues that any heroism is undone by her fatal mistake of acting individually rather than collectively. When she decides to keep the truth from Reva that Johnny-Boy has been captured and thus cannot warn the comrades that the sheriff knows about their meeting, she compromises not only their survival but that of the local Party branch. Wright's story pivots on "false consciousness," in Meyerson's view, a failure to put the collective good above personal need or desire. The key passage comes after the sheriff beats Sue unconscious and she wakes to see "a vast white blur" standing over her as the traitorous new white recruit Booker tells her the sheriff and his posse took Johnny-Boy to the woods to pump him for information, and she fully realizes that she has unwittingly subjected her comrades to "terror, prison and death." Her mistakes are compounded first by taunting the sheriff to satisfy a self-absorbed sense of personal pride and loyalty, resulting in a violent blow that knocks her unconscious; next, against her better judgment, by giving Booker names, having overcome her suspicions of white people, in keeping with Johnny-Boy's refusal to see race as a factor in building a revolutionary movement; and last, by failing to tell Reva when she returns to the house what happened to Johnny-Boy, protecting her partly because she "had a deep need for Reva to believe in her" and cannot let the girl see her frailties.[72]

Meyerson's discovery of what he sees as critics' crucial misreading of the story's political lesson—that "Sue's actions do not guarantee the survival of the party; they all but guarantee its destruction"—complicates her character, he notes, adhering to the educational theme that runs throughout the collection. However, we never know what transpires the next morning—whether the sheriff raids the meeting and, as Sue fears, arrests or kills the comrades, or whether the local Party organization survives. This reexamination of the complexity of Sue's response to events underscores Wright's respect for the anguish and heroism of Black women. It also shows his concern, expressed in recollections of his encounters with the John Reed Club, about the Party's lack of understanding of the people they sought to organize, particularly Black Americans, their religious and cultural affiliations, and their psychological barriers to political action, rooted in their unique oppression and the triple oppression of Black women, all of which he sought to illuminate and dismantle in his search for political and literary forms.

Black Hope: Women and Global Struggles for Freedom

At the end of his essay on Bigger Thomas, Wright alludes for the first time publicly to a novel in progress "about the status of women in modern American society," variously titled "Little Sister," "Slave Market," and, ultimately "Black Hope," and inspired by what he learned from writing *Native Son* "with all of its unrealized potentialities."[73] He sent a 961-page manuscript, started in 1939, to his agent Paul Reynolds on February 6, 1940, and continued to work on the novel, off and on, until 1948. During his most fertile years from 1939 to 1945, he not only published *Native Son* and drafted "Black Hope" but also wrote *The Man Who Lived Underground*, *12 Million Black Voices*, and *Black Boy*. Three drafts of the first version of "Black Hope" were followed by a second, uncompleted version that shifted the focus from a middle-class, educated Harlemite to a young, southern, working-class woman, a total revamping of the novel that reflected his intensive research on "slave markets" in New York City, begun prior to his marriage to the Russian Jewish dancer Dhima Rose Meadman in 1939 and continuing during his three-month stay in Mexico with her in the spring of 1940.

In 1935, Ella Baker and Marvel Cook reported in *The Crisis* that "the Simpson [A]venue block exudes the stench of the slave market at its worst. Not only is human labor bartered and sold for slave wage, but human love also is a marketable commodity ... [and] economic necessity compels the sale."[74] Widespread unemployment drove Black women workers in industrial and stable domestic jobs and housewives outside the labor force into low-paying streetcorner markets in the Bronx and Brooklyn. Joined by desperate southern Black women fleeing north in search of employment, they were subjected to horrific working conditions and abuses, cheated out of wages, and lured into prostitution. Wright saved news clippings from the left-leaning paper

PM and the *New York Amsterdam News* about slave markets, interviewed dozens of domestic workers and activists, and collected reports, including one filed by the "Committee of 'Street Corner Markets,'" submitted to Frieda S. Miller, Industrial Commissioner, State of New York, in April 1940. Committee members represented city offices and agencies as well as organizations like the Domestic Workers Union, the NAACP, and local groups such as the Bronx Citizens' Committee for the Improvement of Domestic Employees and the Social Justice Committee of the Rabbinical Assembly of America.[75]

His focus on Black female domestic workers, extraordinary at the time, attests to his awareness of the oppression of women, particularly Black women. Yet, in a June 6 letter to his agent Paul Reynolds, he explained that although he had begun envisioning a book about Black female workers, the racial theme had become secondary to the novel as a "study of the personality and consciousness of *any* modern woman." He also declared at the end of a five-page synopsis of what was then called "Slave Market" that it was "*not* a novel with a "feminist" theme!" What he meant is ambiguous given his *Daily Worker* articles about women like Mother Ross and the Scottsboro case together with his presumed familiarity with feminist comrades and ideology. Moreover, his denial of a feminist theme is set apart parenthetically, occurring in a sentence in which he states the purpose of the novel as dramatizing "in a symbolic manner the potentially strategic position, socially and politically, which women occupy in the world today." That strategic position resonates with the CPUSA's Black Belt thesis that saw African Americans as the most oppressed sector of the working class and thus potentially a revolutionary vanguard. As he had done in creating Bigger as a flawed antihero, he portrays Maud Hampton's liminal political consciousness of her oppression as "a dramatic picture of woman from feudalism to fascism." This idea of the acceleration of historical stages of development with ever-increasing potential for fascism, which runs throughout his work, also illuminates the failure of Maud's self-centered struggle to overcome obstacles of race and gender that prevent her from achieving what she sees as success in life.[76]

She lightens her skin to pass for white and rebuffs the advances of her boyfriend Freddie (renamed Tommy), at once attracted to and repelled by him because he is "lost" and "too much like herself in this sharp and jagged world." He can never achieve what he wants as a writer (Wright's avatar), but nevertheless seems undaunted, forging ahead "like a child fascinated by a flame"—a simile conjuring the scene in *Black Boy* in which four-year-old Richard sets fire to his grandmother's curtains. Just as Wright drew a portrait of Bigger to educate readers about the consequences of racial oppression for Black urban youth—products, as his attorney Boris Max puts it, of "the monstrous and horrible crimes flowing from [racist] hate"—he sought in "Black Hope" to trace the path of Black women from the Jim Crow South to the urban North, lured by false promises of good pay into working for dishonest employment agencies. He spoke with investigators who documented the illegal transportation and low wages of southern Black women victimized by various kinds of wage theft. Depression-era financial strains on the labor market, including lost wealth among more affluent white women seeking cheap household help, further drove down wages and exacerbated joblessness among Black domestic workers, many of whom were forced into prostitution.[77]

A "Mr. G." told Wright about his investigation of human trafficking and his discovery of a man named Frasier who drove some dozen women from South Carolina to New York. Mr. G. also located a house at 950 Fulton Street in Brooklyn with a clientele of 250 customers in need of domestic help. Frasier worked with pimps "to get the girls as drunk as possible and take their money" and withheld their pay for as long as a month. In his notes on the slave market, Wright works through what the phenomenon revealed about the status of women in a society in which they were "psychological outcast[s]," enslaved by domestic work, biology, and the "mental and physical limits of life," and forced to accept conventional social arrangements. He interviewed other investigators and men in the business, as well as dozens of women who reported both the abuse they suffered and their resistance to it. "Mrs. C.," for example, recalled an employer who dictated arbitrary terms of employment, kept her waiting for an hour later than she had agreed to work, and then summarily fired her. The employer called her to apologize, but Mrs. C. told Wright, "I wouldn't go back. There are millions of jobs. It wasn't such a good job, only $45. That wasn't much." At forty-five dollars a month, she was among the highest paid domestic workers, many of whom got as little as ten dollars.[78]

Both versions of the novel involve slave markets, the second more centrally, including nightmarish descriptions of impoverished young Black women riding north in crowded cars, seeking better jobs and wages under false pretenses. Tricked into working for low-paying, dishonest, domestic staff agencies, they congregate on city street corners, waiting to be picked up by white women in search of cheap household labor or by pimps and johns. In this second version of "Black Hope," Wright depicts the slave markets through the eyes of Maud Wilson in a more radical portrayal of female proletarian struggle. Maud comes to understand the psychology by which the trafficker Ed Basin is empowered by white people who demean and control him to treat other Black people inhumanely. When she flees with the money he owes her, intending to never return, he finds and brutally rapes her. He then forces her, under the fiendish supervision of Granny Butts, to ingest arsenic to lighten her skin because, he says, men like white women. The manuscript breaks off as Maud begins to consider the benefits of her fair complexion and to imagine a new life resembling the billboard poster that she sees from her window showing a white woman diving into blue water. Deeply ambivalent about her prospects, Maud would rather negate this new reality, sympathizing with Basin's suffering and bitterness as she realizes that he hates the world and everyone in it because of his own subjugation. Through the second sight of double vision—or double consciousness—theorized by both Wright and Du Bois, she realizes that Black people see the roots of their oppression by virtue of their "twoness" as outsiders in a society that denies their humanity.[79]

The first version of the novel, however, anticipates the proletarian turn of version two in the character of Ollie Knight, the young, working-class Black woman Maud Hampton imports from the South to work for Cleveland Spencer. In a series of character descriptions on note cards, Wright gives background information about Ollie, who is from his hometown, Natchez, Mississippi, and is "19, brown, tall, strong, fifth grade, reads well, has sense of life going on about her; dreams, yearns; highly sexed; thinks that somewhere someway somehow there's something for her."[80] He begins the novel by introducing us to Eva, a university-educated social worker who has to take a leave of absence from her job due to health problems and lightens her skin color by taking arsenic in order to pass for white and have a better chance of survival in a racist society. Reinventing herself as Maud Hampton, a white woman, she finds work as a housekeeper for Cleveland Spencer, an invalid millionaire banker and widower who lives in a Brooklyn mansion with his mentally ill adult daughter Lily. In her supervisory role, Maud hires and dismisses household workers, including Ollie, who has been transported north by Mr. Downy, a prototype for the even crueler Ed Basin in version two of the novel. Brutally exploited by Downy's illegal employment agency, Ollie is a victim both of wage theft by Maud, who arranges with Downy to pocket half of her monthly payment, and of a horrific sex crime in which Downy forces her at gunpoint to let a dog sexually assault her as he masturbates, a scene based on an actual case reported in one of Wright's interviews with domestic workers.

When Spencer's lawyer Henry Beach and the Black servants hired by Maud discover her true identity, Beach uses the information to blackmail her, encouraging her to murder Spencer, who has fallen in love with her, designated her as his daughter Lily's caregiver after his death, and written her into his will. After she poisons Spencer with arsenic, Maud is held hostage by Beach, who forms a new fascist organization, the National American Union for Rehabilitation, in an unhinged response to his sociopathic son Junior's impending execution for murder. Beach's racist, antisemitic, anti-Catholic, anti–Wall Street, misogynistic rhetoric—none of which he personally believes—resonates not only with the fascism of Wright's time but also with that of rising twenty-first-century fascism worldwide. Afraid that her complicity in Downy's slave market operations will be revealed if Ollie reports him to the police, Maud tries to shame her into silence, bribing her with $100. Despite her seeming passivity, Ollie is convinced by Tommy (aka Freddie) to join the Domestic Workers Union Local 567 (a fictional stand-in for Domestic Workers Local 149, which by 1940 had become a magnet for New York's superexploited domestic workers), where white female organizers protect her from Maud's desperate attempts to shut her up. Knowing she is pregnant with Tommy's child, Maud commits suicide, leaving Spencer's house to the union in a final act of radical solidarity. As the union organizers and Tommy take inventory, Ollie interrupts to exclaim that she knows every inch of the mansion from having cleaned it so often. In an optimistic note that places the emerging Black female proletariat center stage, Wright ends the novel: "Ollie talked on; she had the floor."[81]

WRIGHT'S AWARENESS OF the triple oppression of Black women is clearly expressed in the first version of "Black Hope," in which he describes Maud Hampton as "poor," "black," and "a woman," and in *12 Million Black Voices*, in which he declares that "surrounding our black women are many almost insuperable barriers: they are black, they are women, they are workers; they are triply anchored and restricted in their movements within and without the Black Belts." Even more telling is the preface to his speech at the First International Congress of Negro Writers and Artists in Paris at the Sorbonne on September 19–22, 1956, in which he observes that there are

> no women functioning vitally and responsibly upon this platform helping to mold and mobilize our thoughts. This is not a criticism of the conference, it is not a criticism of anyone, it is a criticism that I heap upon ourselves collectively. When and if we hold another conference—and I hope we will—I hope there shall be an effective utilization of Negro womanhood in the world to help us mobilize and pool our forces. Perhaps some hangover of influence from the past has colored our attitude, or perhaps this was an oversight. In our struggle for freedom, against great odds, we

cannot afford to ignore one half of our manpower, that is, the force of women and their active collaboration. Black men will not be free until their women are free."[82]

That year, he was also revising his manuscript for *Pagan Spain*, in which he conveyed deep sympathy for oppressed Spanish women in a totalitarian "man's world" and brilliantly used a Falangist catechism, *Formación Politica: Lecciones para las Flechas*, to convey the full weight of Franco's authoritarian regime on a country still recovering from the deep wounds of civil war. To be allowed to leave the country, his informant, a young woman named Carmen, tells him that she has to complete her "social service" by memorizing the entire book, which, Wright explains, "was the real thing; it had been designed to inculcate the principles of Fascism in young girls ranging in age from nine upward."[83]

The lessons Wright learned from the catechism, like those he absorbed throughout his life, led him repeatedly to conclude that the way forward to a more humane, egalitarian world—absolved from the crimes of enslavement, conquest, colonization, empire, and extractive industrialization—was through collective struggle. From Aunt Sue and Reverend Taylor in *Uncle Tom's Children* to Cross Damon in *The Outsider* to the Bandung Conference in *The Color Curtain*, the necessity of collective action—and the psychological and political barriers to it—shimmers like a distant star on the horizon. Among his most optimistic visions of the future is Ollie Knight's radicalization as a union activist, affirming his belief that women, Black women in particular, are crucial to the formation of a revolutionary vanguard. That vision would expand during his life as an expatriate to investigations of ecologies of empire that had subjugated African and Asian peoples for centuries and forged his own anticolonial, proto-ecological, political consciousness as the grandson of enslaved Black Americans.

CHAPTER SIX

Ecologies of Empire
Worlds Being Born, Worlds Dying

Disillusioned with the Communist Party, critical of the Soviet Union, in voluntary exile from the United States, Wright sought new literary and political avenues of pursuit in Paris, where he and his family permanently moved in 1947. His entrée to French intellectual life through Sartre, Beauvoir, and fellow American expatriate Gertrude Stein, among others, brought him into contact with Francophone anticolonial writers from Africa and the Caribbean, including Aimé Césaire, Léopold Sédar Senghor, and Alioune Diop, who founded *Présence Africaine* the same year Wright's family settled in at 14 rue Monsieur le Prince. As the voice of *le monde noir*, the quarterly journal *Présence Africaine*, on whose editorial board Wright was invited to sit, played a crucial role in anticolonial struggles and the emergence of the nonaligned Third World. Sponsored by the journal, Black intellectuals from Africa, the Caribbean, and the United States, including Wright, assembled at the First International Congress of Negro Writers and Artists in Paris in 1956. The widening orbit of his work as he undertook the study of global systems of conquest that had dehumanized and impoverished masses of people worldwide led him to remark in his essay on the psychological reactions of oppressed people: "Imperialism turns out to have been much more morally foul a piece of business than even Marx and Lenin imagined!"[1]

At the 1956 congress, he presented a paper titled "Tradition and Industrialization: The Plight of the Tragic Elite in Africa."[2] Three years previously, in 1953, he had traveled to the Gold Coast, encouraged by his friends Dorothy and George Padmore. His six-week visit to the African colony on the verge of independence from Great Britain resulted in his first travel book, *Black Power*, in 1954. That same year, on advice given by his fellow expatriate Gertrude Stein on her deathbed in 1946, he made two of three trips to Spain at a time when he felt compelled to write nonfiction about "so many more exciting and interesting things happening now in the world."[3] Stein had told him to go to Spain because "you'll see the past there. You'll see what the Western world is made of."[4] His third trip to Spain, from February 20 to April 10, 1955, in which he finished his research for the book, immediately preceded his flight to Jakarta, Indonesia, to attend the first conference of twenty-nine nonaligned

Richard Wright with Dorothy and George Padmore. The Langston Hughes Collection, Beinecke Rare Book and Manuscript Library, Yale University. Courtesy of the Estate of Richard Wright. Reprinted by permission of John Hawkins and Associates, Inc.

Asian and African countries, held in Bandung. These trips culminated in the publication of *The Color Curtain* in 1956, followed by *Pagan Spain* and *White Man, Listen!*, a collection of lectures and essays, in 1957. Variously defined as travel writing, literary journalism, and "merely good journalism," the books got mixed reviews and never sold as well as his earlier works. Until recently, despite their relevance to postcolonial and Afro-Asian studies, they were mostly viewed as inferior, evidence of his declining talent as a writer and his loss of contact with Black America, which many critics saw as his natural and only subject matter as an African American writer.[5]

Contrary to the standard evaluation of Wright that his career as a writer was derailed by his break from the CPUSA and his choice of exile abroad, his persistent quest to make sense of a fast-changing world suffuses and enhances his literary and political activity during this period. His late travel books and novels deepen themes from his earliest, best-known works through the lens of ecologies of empire, or postcolonial ecologies, (de)formed by European conquest and colonization of 80 percent of the world's peoples and the lands they occupied in a centuries-long extractive system of exploitation and plunder. While some scholars have begun to explore Wright's treatment of nature and the environment in his writing, contributing to efforts to expand the scope of ecocriticism rooted in nineteenth-century nature writing that routinely omitted Black writers, the linkage between his environmental consciousness and his abiding commitment to freedom struggles in the United States and the colonized world has yet to be fully established. Connecting environmental literature to postcolonial ecologies, Elizabeth DeLoughrey and George B. Handley observe that nature has been redefined by "the globalization of the environment, a process that has been formulated by a long and complex history of empire"—to which can be added the rise and global domination of capitalism. Conversely, they point out, "the decoupling of nature and history has helped to mystify colonialism's histories of forced migration, suffering, and human violence."[6]

Together with his radical contemporaries in the 1950s, particularly those from the Global South (then known as the Third World), Wright was beginning to theorize the ravages of empire in relation to human and nonhuman life. This emergent critique of empire's dual assault on nature and oppressed peoples was forged in rebellions against slavery and colonization, born out of human subjugation and the effects of global land use practices on agricultural workers and nature. Capitalist imperatives disrupted traditional subsistence farming and dispossessed colonized and formerly enslaved people under the thumb of Jim Crow and its global counterparts through policies of enclosure and widespread deforestation and desertification. Shaping this critique was the world-shaking October Revolution in Russia in 1917, which demonstrated that workers could rise up and establish state power, posing a direct challenge to capitalism and enlisting anticolonial Pan-Africanists like George Padmore and Aimé Césaire in the international communist movement. Although Padmore left the Communist Party in 1935—nearly a decade before Wright's official break from the CPUSA in 1944 over the Comintern's failure to support anticolonial struggles against the French and British governments— he remained "a Marxist and a revolutionary," according to C. L. R. James in a memorial tribute in *The Nation* in 1959.[7]

The impact of capitalist expansion on the environment was also evident to Marx, who closely followed the research of the German chemist Justus von Liebig on soil depletion and Britain's desperate need by 1830 for fertilizer. The degradation of soil resulted from the replacement of arable land with sheep pastures and increased, mechanized agricultural production, driving peasants off the commons through a process of enclosure and privatization starting in the seventeenth century and turning people who had once been producers into deracinated, propertyless vagabonds. Just as British enclosure acts persisted into the twentieth century, sharecropping in the Jim Crow South continued after Reconstruction, trapping Black farmers in poverty and forcing many of them to migrate north as landlords hoarded profits in a vicious circle of debt servitude. These same political economic forces drove deforestation and soil degradation in European colonies, expanding farmland and monocrop agriculture to supply coffee, cocoa, sugar, cotton, and other cash crops to colonial powers, and requiring colonized peoples to import expensive goods no longer locally produced. In "Silt" and "Down by the Riverside," Wright documents the impact of the 1927 flood on Black Mississippians and the despair of sharecroppers whose indebtedness imprisoned them in a system of legal bondage. Although he died too early to see the formation of ecosocialist thought and ecological critiques of empire, he and his contemporaries wrote about these intensifying crises and their intertwining histories and geographies, anticipating ecocritical studies and environmental social movements that arose in response to them.

Earlier dismissal of Wright's late work as inferior has been challenged by scholars like Cedric Robinson and Paul Gilroy who have revalued Wright's contributions to world literature and radical, antiracist, anticolonial political economic thought, influencing a raft of criticism following them that reconsiders his legacy. His chief biographers agree that he remained a Marxist but barely skim the surface of what that meant in relation to his life abroad, his travels, and his associations with *Présence Africaine*, the Congress of Negro Writers and Artists, and other political and cultural formations. Neither do they explicate his critique of imperialism, a key theme in his exilic nonfiction and fiction, or the impact of having to appear to be pro–United States to elude harassment from US agencies that had kept increasingly strict tabs on him since 1942. As Frances Stonor Saunders observes about America's "cultural cold war," the Congress for Cultural Freedom—the CIA front group that courted Wright and countless other writers and artists—disseminated US propaganda "to nudge the intelligentsia of western Europe away from its lingering fascination with Marxism and Communism towards a view more accommodating of 'the American way.'"[8] Acutely aware of the power of the state to limit his freedom and restrict his activities, or worse, Wright relied on the same double-voiced discourse evident in his fiction to embed inverse meanings in language and escape detection and censorship by FBI "ghostreaders," as William J. Maxwell called them.[9]

Unnatural Forces: Like a Mute Warning

The Great Mississippi Flood of 1927 was among the worst floods in US history, ripping through 27,000 square miles of land across eleven states, leaving 250 people dead and displacing hundreds of thousands. The flooding started in the summer of 1926 with exceptionally heavy rains, breaking through the levees upriver from Greenville, Mississippi, on April 21, 1927, and subsiding only in August of that year. According to the final report of the Colored Advisory Committee of the Red Cross and the President's Committee for Relief Work in the Mississippi Valley Flood Disaster, "The Great Mississippi Flood of 1927 will go down in history as one of America's greatest peacetime disasters."[10] Like so many (un)natural environmental tragedies, this one disproportionately affected African Americans, more than half a million of whom lost their homes. At the time, Wright was living in Memphis, Tennessee, 150 miles from Greenville. Largely unaffected because of its elevation, the city served as a hub for relief and rescue efforts. The 1927 flood goes unnamed in two of his stories: "Silt," originally published in *New Masses* in 1937, republished posthumously as "The Man Who Saw the Flood" in *Eight Men* in 1961, and "Down by the Riverside" in *Uncle Tom's Children*. But Wright is clearly denoting the actual event, which he would have followed closely in local Memphis and national Black newspaper accounts of what was a major topic of conversation for months, inspiring, among other responses, Bessie Smith's "Back Water Blues." Relatedly, "The Ethics of Jim Crow," first published in 1937 in a WPA writers' anthology, and "Long Black Song" delineate the stark racial and class divides in various permutations of socially mediated natural and built spaces.

As Susan Scott Parrish points out in her brilliant study of the cultural history of the 1927 flood, Wright would have been reading the news of the flood while in Memphis but only composed these stories years later in Chicago. By then, he had encountered multiple theoretical currents, including the Chicago school of sociology and Marxist thought. Countering Carla Cappetti's contention that he replaced his Marxist worldview with sociology after his slow break from the CPUSA, Parrish argues that despite the intellectual community the Chicago school offered him, he was uncomfortable with the "reification that seemed to accompany institutionalized empiricism" and diverged from Robert Park's normalizing theory of society in which "the social organism was patterned much like the apparently self-stabilizing ecology of the natural world."[11] The 1927 flood exposed the devastating impact of natural disasters on communities of color, turning Black victims into an army of surplus labor. It also lay bare the effects of reliance on levees that changed the flow of the river and combined with centuries of deforestation and monocrop agriculture to increase the potential for the historic flood. Although some observers saw it as an unavoidable natural disaster, others denounced industrial practices that destabilized the Mississippi delta ecology. Wright focuses on the federal and local authorities' abuse of the flood's individual Black refugees, who had limited means of escape from the rising waters and were then forced into what amounted to slave labor in Red Cross concentration camps. But he recounts the ecological disaster as well.

In "Silt," published a decade after the flood, an omniscient narrator follows the return of a family of three—Tom, May, and their daughter Sally, introduced archetypally as "a black father, a black mother, and a black child"—to their destroyed home. All they have left is their cow, the stove, a box of matches, and some tobacco. Unlike most of Wright's stories told from an interior character's viewpoint, "Silt" is a distanced, third-person narrative, more ethnographic than fictional in tone, documenting the impact of the flood on one Black family. Starting with their survey of the damage from eight-foot-high floodwaters to the exterior of their wood shack house, the family's tour of the wreckage reads like the viewing of a crime scene as they discover they have been robbed of their possessions and livelihood. Except for their damaged, mud-filled house and their cow, all else is gone: the henhouse, the pigpen, their horse, and the next-door neighbor Miz Flora's house—Miz Flora and her family's whereabouts are unknown. The road is gone; all that remains is "just a wide sweep of yellow, scalloped silt." The steps to the house gone, too, Tom lifts May and Sally to the porch. The now bicolored siding, gray at the top and yellow from the soaking rainwater below, looks "as though its ghost were standing beside it."[12]

Inside, a dingy light falls on layers of silt and mud. The "wavering floodmark" high up on the interior house walls sends a "mute warning" as they survey the wreckage: "A dresser sat cater-cornered, its drawers and sides bulging like a bloated corpse. The bed, with the mattress still on it, was like a casket of mud. Two smashed chairs lay in a corner as though huddled together for protection." The smashed chairs bear witness to a desolate scene of death and decay in the wake of ravaging floodwaters—more than robbery, it is a symbolic murder, signified by the dresser like a bloated corpse and the mud-filled bed, a casket. In what follows, Wright reveals a third, even more distressing crime: the family's imprisonment by debt to the storeowner Burgess, whose insistence that Tom pay back the $800 he owes is seconded by May. Burgess impassively warns Tom that he expects no trouble from him, which is to say that if he were to attempt to leave town with his debt unpaid, Burgess would have to turn him over to the sheriff, as he had already done to two debt dodgers. Attentive to Sally's gnawing hunger and the flood's unforgiving impact on their lives, May, too, vehemently urges him to get up on the white man's buggy: "Yuh got t go on, Tom. We ain't got nothin here."[13]

This racialization of social space is documented as well in "Down by the Riverside," in which the protagonist Mann struggles to bring his pregnant wife Lulu to safety as dangerously high waters rise outside their home, threatening to wash away the steps and trap them. Mann is tense with exhaustion and fear of not only the rising water but also the "white folks," including National Guard troops, who had begun to conscript Black men to shore up the levee and who, Mann thinks, "in times like this shoota nigger down jus lika dog n think nothin of it."[14] This double threat of the flood and dehumanizing Jim Crow relations built on centuries of enslavement and the resurgence of white supremacist rule after Reconstruction puts Mann in a precarious if not insoluble bind. Assuming the water would recede, he had turned down a government offer of evacuation; his friend Bob, charged with selling Mann's mule in exchange for a boat, could get only half as much for the mule as a boat would cost, so he steals one from the Heartfields. Faced with his wife's difficult labor and urgent need for medical care, Mann feels he has no option but to take Lulu, her mother, Granny, and his small son Peewee in the stolen boat, even though he knows they may all drown in the dark roiling water or be killed on the spot for stealing a white man's property.

These sociological and ecological forces coalesce in what Marxist ecosocialists have called "second nature," the socially mediated world created by human production, as distinct from "first nature," the natural world that preceded and gave rise to the human species.[15] Evidence that Wright confronted this interrelationship of racial (and class) oppression and environmental depredation appears in much of his writing, illuminating not only the ecological implications of colonial and capitalist enslavement, conquest, and expropriation in the periphery but also their effects in the centers of global power. The conditions of survival that Wright describes in "Down by the Riverside" reappear in his late nonfiction chronicles of his travels to the Gold Coast (Ghana), Spain, and Indonesia. He probes the connection between political economic dominance and dispossession from his earliest poems to the rhetorical question he asks in *Black Power* about the meaning of the industrial world in light of his conversation with the Akan chief Nana Kwame Dua Awere II: "Must he leave behind him his humanity, such as it was, as he moved into that industrial world, as he built his Volta Projects?" While modern technology could improve life in the chief's village, Wright observes, it had also by then unleashed atomic energy, leaving Parisians in his adopted home "huddled together in indecision, numbed with despair, facing a myriad of possibilities."[16]

Mann, as his name suggests, is tragically human in his confused, desperate response to the worst flood in US history and the racially charged social relations that endanger him and his family as much as if not more than the rising floodtide. It is these intersecting environmental and political economic forces that propel his doomed, heroic efforts to save his family, forcing him to navigate both the river and the "white folks" whose humanity he questions but about whom he nevertheless holds out hope that they "would *have* to take [Lulu] in." Less hopefully, Bob reports, returning with Heartfield's stolen boat: "Everwhere Ah looked wuznt nothin but white men wid guns."[17] Wright's awareness of representations of the flood in mainstream media, including blatantly racist cartoons, and his grasp of the social determinants that made it so disastrous can be seen in his characters' names—Heartfield, Mann, Burgess, and Burrows (the doctor who pronounced Lulu dead in the Red Cross hospital)—which not only suggest heartlessness, humanness, and the bourgeoisie's greediness but also refer literally to the Dada artist John Heartfield, whose agitprop appeared in radical publications and book covers; the sociologists Delbert Mann and Ernest Burgess; and the Freudian psychologist Trigant Burrow.[18]

As Parrish notes, according to Burrow's theory of "biological recoil," human "self-consciousness" had "recoiled away from the continuous biology of life."[19] The emergence of consciousness had split the self from society, privileging the individual over the social in "a fallacy of *a self as over and against other selves*."[20] Burrow's explanation of ecological survival at the species level foresaw a higher level of consciousness that mended this rift in consonance with the fundamentally social nature of human existence, an insight that resonates with Marx's understanding, recovered by contemporary ecosocialists, of a metabolic rift between nature and society. Similarly, Wright's critique of racism in and beyond the Jim Crow South flows dialectically from his belief in an underlying common humanity fractured by the West's twisted history of conquest, enslavement, colonization, and expropriation. Just as he delineates how the geography of Jim Crow policed Black southerners' access and mobility to green spaces and safe harbor through strictly enforced racial codes, depicted in Mann's failure to save his family, his travel narratives expose the impact of colonial and postcolonial monocrop sugar and tobacco plantations on indigenous land use practices, transforming the earth in an "ecological remaking" that produced an "*imperialist second nature*."[21]

Paralleling the Great Migration in the United States was an exodus of working-class West Indians to North American and European cities in the postwar period, followed a few decades later by accelerated African emigration. A much more selective Black migration abroad included American expatriate writers and performers like Wright, Josephine Baker, Chester Himes, and James Baldwin, and African and Afro-Caribbean intellectuals like Léopold Senghor and George Padmore. The same forces of oppression and dislocation that drove these migrations can be seen in Wright's work ranging from "Down by the Riverside," in which Mann's family survives slavery only to be victimized by a resurgent white supremacy, to his travel narratives of the Gold Coast, Indonesia, and, less obviously, Spain. The imperialist second nature of a prevailing global capitalist economy, despite revolutionary socialist movements and victories, polluted and degraded the nonhuman environment while exploiting the world's masses for profit. In 1927, the swelling Mississippi River defied the arrogant engineers who insisted the levees would hold, causing widespread suffering that disproportionately affected Black southerners, but it was Jim Crow racism that conscripted the exhausted Mann in Wright's story to the hard physical labor of Red Cross rescue efforts, compelling him under martial law to work in what was essentially a "slave camp."[22]

Brought to the general in command in a makeshift tent in the hills, where he had helped transport Heartfield's wife and son to safety, Mann is found guilty of theft and murder and taken away by soldiers who shoot him in the back when he attempts to flee amid "waves of green, wet grass" and falls, "face buried in the wet, blurred green."[23] This overlay of environmental degradation onto racial and class oppression is also evident in "Long Black Song," "The Ethics of Living Jim Crow," *Black Boy*, and *12 Million Black Voices*, all of which can be read through a socioecological lens. Faced with self-abnegation or suicidal rage, Silas in "Long Black Song" enacts the logic of Jim Crow when he kills the young white salesman who raped his wife Sarah and then returns the next morning to sell him a graphophone. Notably, at the time of the salesman's visit, Silas was in town selling cotton and buying the red cloth that Sarah wanted and ten more acres of land from a man named Burgess—the same name Wright gives to the storeowner in "Silt," signifying the bourgeoisie's role in enforcing Jim Crow.

Staring at the dead body, Silas expresses his "deep and final sense that now it was all over" and inventories everything white people take from him: "The white folks ain never gimme a chance! Thay ain never give no black man a chance! There ain nothin in yo whole life yuh kin keep from em! They take yo lan! They take yo freedom! They take yo women! N then they take yo life!"[24]

It is Sarah who sees beyond Silas's despair, in a lyrical if inchoate expression of the good life: "Somehow, men, black men and white men, and land and houses, green cornfields and grey skies, gladness and dreams, were all a part of that which made life good. Yes somehow, they were linked.... She felt they were... but she could not say how." This vision of harmony among white and Black people, and built and natural environments, is shattered by the approach of a caravan of cars, a shootout, and a burst of flames as the white men burn the family's house with Silas in it, engulfing him in "eager plumes of red."[25]

The mute warning of the 1927 flood in "Silt" and Silas's rage in "Long Black Song" reverberate in the racist codes that Wright learns to recognize, evade, and resist in "The Ethics of Living Jim Crow." First published in 1937 in *American Stuff: An Anthology of Prose & Verse by Members of the Federal Writers' Project*—which was denounced, ironically, by the House Un-American Activities Committee for promoting racial hatred—and later included in the 1940 edition of *Uncle Tom's Children*, the essay educates Wright's white readers in particular about the geography of racism in the American South. Just as pastoral scenes of innocence turn deadly in the first story in the collection, "Big Boy Leaves Home," lessons on the evils of Jim Crow begin with a memory of boyhood play in Arkansas in which two gangs, one Black, one white, face off against each other. Wright's "skimpy yard" is full of black cinders. "Nothing green ever grew in the yard," he recalls. "The only touch of green we could see was far away, beyond the tracks, over where the white folks lived." This lack of greenery was nothing he missed, until he and his friends had nowhere to hide when the white boys started hurling broken bottles at them and then retreated "behind trees, hedges, and the sloping embankments of their lawns."[26] Drilled into him by a gash from broken glass that landed behind his ear and required three stitches, this first lesson was followed by many more on how to survive Jim Crow—including the one his mother taught him when she got home that evening from working in the white folks' kitchen and, rather than comforting him as he had expected, beat him into a feverish delirium.

The same year as the flood, Wright migrated to Chicago, where he bore witness to severe droughts in the Great Plains and dust storms that blew as far as Chicago and deposited 12 million tons of dust on the city. The drought lasted from 1930 to 1940, causing extensive ecological damage and intensifying economic hardship across the country as a result of decreased supplies of midwestern wheat and grain. Speculative banking and farming in the 1920s increased the amount of arable land throughout the affected areas, and dryland farming methods relying on rainfall and groundwater left the Great Plains even more vulnerable to natural, periodic droughts and wind and soil erosion. Wright would have thus been well aware of the impact of human and natural forces on the Dust Bowl. In *Native Son*, he presciently invokes the ecology of empire in Bigger Thomas's yearning to fly a plane, an opportunity denied to him as a young Black man growing up in 1930s Chicago. The quintessential symbol of modernity driven by the expansion of capitalist markets and concomitant plunder of nature and workers, the scene signals what Gregory Rutledge calls Wright's "eco-critical perspective on American urbanity and modernity—including spaces like Harlem [and Chicago]—as an ecological disaster unfolding on a global scale."[27]

Rutledge establishes a link between the rapidly expanding, gas-fueled car industry and Wright's insistent representation of the Great Migration as a broken promise to Black southern migrants whose dreams of a better life were destroyed by the racially divided, impoverished conditions of life in the urban North that shackled them almost as harshly as the Jim Crow South. Unlike Ellison and some other Black writers who followed Wright and embraced the ethos of American capitalism, celebrating the migration north and interpolation of Black workers into the booming postwar industrial era of rising US global hegemony as an "obvious redeeming recourse," Wright understood the burden on Black workers, in particular, of the environmental costs of capitalist expansion.[28] Those costs appeared in the soil depletion of southern farmland, the slums of northern cities, many of which became Black ghettos, and the depredation of natural resources that further polluted both regions. Unlike Ellison, Wright saw the Great Migration as a continuation of the racial oppression that Black migrants sought to escape. In his insightful essay on the ecocritical dimensions of *Black Boy*, Rutledge considers the oft-ignored epigram, a Negro folk song, that prefaces Part Two, "The Horror and the Glory":

> Sometimes I wonder, huh,
> Wonder if other people wonder, huh,
> Sometimes I wonder, huh,
> Wonder if other people wonder, huh,
> Just like I do, oh, my Lord, just like I do![29]

Based on the linguistic, syntactic, and rhythmic parallels between the folk song and Archibald McLeish's poetic *Land of the Free*, published in 1938, Rutledge assumes that Wright knew of this "book of photographs illustrated by a poem," as McLeish described it, which featured FSA photographs just as *12 Million Black Voices* would do three years later.

Like the wondering of the narrator in the folk song that Wright strategically and without explanation inserts between the stories of his childhood in the Deep South and his early adulthood in Chicago, McLeish wondered "whether the dream of American liberty / Was two hundred years of pine and hardwood / And three generations of the grass / And the generations are up: the years over / We don't know."[30] This same wondering can be seen in the work of other contemporaries, including James Agee and Walker Evans, Erskine Caldwell and Margaret Bourke-White, Robert Cantwell, and John Steinbeck, all of whom documented the degeneration of the American dream into a wasteland of infertile land, polluted air, impoverished cities, and widespread unemployment during the Depression. They wrote about rural farmland laid to waste and "the flat black stretches of Chicago" that greeted Wright on his arrival, left him "depressed and dismayed," and "mocked all [his] fantasies."[31] As Donald Worster remarks, some of the writers lamented the "diffused moral values" associated with capitalism in general, while others, like Cantwell and Wright, specifically critiqued capitalist modes of industrial production.[32]

It is only in Wright's wide-eyed childhood discovery of the teeming world of Mississippi fauna and flora, described in *Black Boy*, and in his late haiku, written in the last year of his life, that he evokes a natural world at least somewhat insulated from the racialized geography of Jim Crow. That safe space of his youth all but vanishes once he becomes racially conscious, a moment poignantly captured in the barrage of questions he asks his mother about the nature of race and his own family's mixed racial background—Irish, Scotch, French, Negro, Indian, white—finally demanding to know, "Then what am I?" to which she teasingly, knowingly, replies, "They'll call you a colored man when you grow up.... Do you mind, Mr. Wright?"[33] He signals his preliterate sense of being in the world by referring to events that speak to him in a "cryptic tongue" filled with wonderment, delight, a sense of intimacy, nostalgia, desire, yearning, disdain, "aching glory," "incomprehensible secrets," panic, "speechless astonishment," and love, but also, inescapably, with violence, "a hint of cosmic cruelty," and "quiet terror." The more clearly the "days and hours" spoke to him over the years, the more determined he was to escape American racism and McCarthy's witch hunts when he moved to Paris in 1947 and stepped out on the "stage of the world" as an expatriate, a self-proclaimed outsider, and a world citizen in a rapidly shifting global order.[34]

Lonely Outsiders: Taking the Hard Path

Wright dedicated his last nonfiction book, *White Man, Listen!*, to his friend Eric Williams, the author of *Capitalism and Slavery* and chief minister of Trinidad and Tobago, and to "the Westernized and tragic elite of Asia, Africa, and the West Indies—the *lonely outsiders* who exist precariously on the clifflike margins of many cultures ... who seek desperately for a home for their hearts ... [that] could be a home for the hearts of all men." In his introduction to the book, what he called the "why and wherefore," he describes himself as "a rootless man" who prized "the state of abandonment, of aloneness ... [which] seems the natural, inevitable condition of man," a condition he welcomed, declaring, "I can make myself at home almost anywhere on this earth and can ... easily sink myself into the most alien and widely differing environments."[35] That theme recurs in *Pagan Spain*, in which he tells a young, unhappy, Spanish Catholic woman, "I have no religion in the formal sense of the word. . . . I have no race except that which is forced upon me. I have no country except that to which I'm obliged to belong. I have no traditions. I'm free. I have only the future."[36] This conundrum of rootlessness and the capacity to make a home anywhere on earth has confounded critics who interpret rootlessness to mean psychosocial detachment rather than an internationalist ethos that expanded his literary and political spheres of travel, engagement, and influence. Others lamented his decision to live as an expatriate far from his first home, the Deep South, portraying him as alienated from American realities and disconnected from his ostensibly natural subject matter of race and racism. In his review of *The Long Dream*, J. Saunders Redding concluded, "Wright has been away too long. Severing his cruel intimacy with the American environment, he has cut the emotional umbilical cord through which his art was fed, and all that remains for it to feed on is the memory."[37]

Despite its generally unfavorable critical reception, *The Outsider*—his first novel published abroad, thirteen years after *Native Son*—broke new artistic and political ground that has been obscured by early judgments of it. The quintessential outlaw in Wright's fiction, the novel's protagonist Cross Damon is a Chicago postal worker who moves to New York City. In addition to the parallel to Wright suggested by these locations, Damon, like Wright, is also an atheist, a restless man who once studied philosophy in search of life's meaning. To conflate the author with the character, however, is to commit the same error that critics made about *Native Son*'s Bigger Thomas. Far more rootless than Wright, Damon severs all ties with his past when he escapes unscathed from a subway crash to a cheap hotel, taking on a dead rider's identity. After encountering and murdering a fellow Black postal worker whose betrayal he fears, he quietly leaves the hotel, abandons his wife, young sons, elderly mother, and pregnant, underage girlfriend, and flees by train to New York, feeling adrift in a godless world that he finds increasingly meaningless. There, he becomes involved with a Communist cell and accepts an invitation from a Party leader to move in with him and his wife, an abstract painter, to challenge their racist landlord, a "dyed-in-the-wool Negro hater."[38] The rather belabored plot climaxes in a symbolic assault on totalitarianism—seen as twin evils of communism and fascism—when Damon intercedes in a deadly fight between the two men and bludgeons them to death. Adding to the three murders he has by then committed, he kills a fourth man, also a Communist, whom he suspects knows too much about his crimes.

The Outsider was written between 1947 and 1953 as Wright worked through his break from the CPUSA and his exile abroad. In the wake of ruptures in the global order and his own dislocations, the novel can be read as a philosophical meditation on rapidly transforming postwar realities in which, as he put it in The Color Curtain nearly a decade later, "worlds were being born and worlds were dying."[39] He was drawn to existential philosophy, which came intuitively to him, as Michel Fabre notes: "Far from being alien to the black experience, existentialism is a world philosophy so appropriate to it that Wright held an existential view of life long before he had even heard the word."[40] Although he read Sartre and Camus, according to Fabre he was more influenced by the works of Russian and German existentialists, especially Heidegger's Existence and Being, and he evoked Kierkegaard and Nietzsche in The Outsider more than his coterie of French writers. Less apparent to most critics, then and now, was that he was becoming a serious student of Marx and Engels, adding to his library works he had not previously read, including the second and third volumes of Capital, The Manifesto of the Communist Party, The Civil War in the United States, Hegel's The Phenomenology of Mind, and various exegeses of them. Rather than contradicting his break from the CPUSA, his deepening interest in Marxism points to the continuation of his pursuit of historical materialist explanations of unfolding global events and conditions of life. It is this perspective that he wrestles with in The Outsider both through and beyond Damon's nihilistic logic, examining and critiquing rather than endorsing not only communism but also existentialism, individualism, and universalism. Ultimately, the novel reaffirms Wright's belief in collective action as the only path to freedom, and rejects political economic equivalencies, amoral self-aggrandizement, and despair.

Another outsider by virtue of his hunched back, the character Ely Houston, the New York district attorney, meets Damon by chance on his New York–bound train and expresses a profound if patronizing interest "in the psychological condition of the Negro in this country." Rooted in his politics as well as his deformity, this sensitivity gives him "insight into the problems of other excluded people." He engages Damon in a couple of wide-ranging conversations about "the question of the Negro" and the human condition that also serve as a plot device to reintroduce him later. After confessing that he "feel[s] outside of the lives of men" but he is required to "enforce the law against the outsider who breaks that law," he turns out to be the district attorney investigating Damon's murders. Although critics often counterpose Wright's belief in individual freedom to his revolutionary politics as a young Communist, he consistently rejected bourgeois individualist ideologies and embraced collective struggle against the oppressive yoke of capitalism and imperialism. In other words, he went beyond liberal conceptions of freedom based on property rights to work through the contradictions of historically specific social relations, especially, but not limited to, racial subjugation rooted in chattel slavery and colonization. Nor was it his intent in *The Outsider* to promulgate a theory of totalitarianism linking communism to fascism, but rather to question the easy equation of the one to the other and insist on the need for collective struggle to overcome the alienation that destroys Cross Damon.[41]

Although Damon sympathizes with oppressed Black Americans, he defines his own "decisive life struggle ... [as] a personal fight for the realization of himself." After he is shot, most likely by a Party member, it is Houston who asks why he chose to live as he did and who provokes his dying words: "I wanted to be free ... to feel that I was worth." Houston persists: "And what did you find?" Damon: "Nothing.... The search can't be done alone.... *Never alone*.... *Alone a man is nothing*."[42] His last words to Houston are "It was ... horrible.... Because in my heart ... I'm ... I felt ... I'm innocent."[43] This paradoxical confession of guilt echoes both Kurtz's famous last words in *The Heart of Darkness* ("The horror! The horror!") and Bigger's declaration to his attorney, a mystified Boris Max: "I didn't want to kill! ... But what I killed for, *I am!*"[44] Neither Bigger nor Damon sees himself as guilty of the crimes they committed. Murdering Mary Dalton and Bessie Mears gives meaning to Bigger's life, releasing him from a future with no options, no possibilities, except the kitchenettes and dead-end jobs reserved for Black Chicagoans whose migration north crushed their dreams of freedom; he is only reiterating in more direct language Max's legal defense of him as a product of America's racist history. Damon's nihilistic and reactionary tendencies envelope him in a color-blind, bourgeois liberal illusion that he can act as a free agent, immune not only from the law but also from the conditions of racial conflict that trap other Black people. The opposite of who he says he is, warped by his pseudo-intellectual identification as an outsider, he remains unable to perceive the system that produced him even as he ultimately recognizes the need for collective action.

By 1935, Wright had bought and presumably read Kenneth Burke's *Permanence and Change*, whose "poetics of action" resonated with his own efforts to fuse experience and theory and forge meaning through the press of literary form—a politics of literature evident in "Blueprint for Negro Writing," published in 1937 and preceded by a year or two in his unpublished essay "Personalism." In "Personalism," Wright opposes the proletariat, as the vehicle for "the fulfillment of the individual through struggle, through the attainment of the scientific hopes of the 18th century," to the fascist, who conceives of "the social order as changeless and eternal ... infused with religious ideology [that] seeks to lull and pull the individual back to the past."[45] He was drawn to Burke's attempt to cut across debates between right-wing Southern Agrarian writers allied with emerging New Critics and their left-wing counterparts by "falling on the bias"—that is, insisting on the necessity of the writer's engagement with the world through symbolic action but avoiding the propagandistic conformity dictated by some elements of the CPUSA. While Wright appreciated Burke's aesthetic theory of art's real-world efficacy, he was disappointed by his conflation of communism and fascism on the one hand and Communist doctrine and Marxist method on the other.

Burke was denounced at the 1935 Congress of American Writers for proposing to replace the term "worker" with what he saw as a less rigid, positive symbol of "the people," defusing his sense of a schematic, Marxist logics with a reconfigured Communist poetics stripped of Marxist concepts—particularly class struggle. As Konstantina Karageorgos notes, Wright appropriated only what was useful to him in Burke's theory, turning to the "poetic Marx," as he studied Marxism more seriously, to sharpen his own dialectical imagination through a capacious reading of Marxist thought as a "poetic conception of life." This Marx is akin to the philosophical investigations of human nature of the young Marx, or the only truly orthodox Marxism of dialectical materialism that Lukacs calls "the road to truth"—not uncritical acceptance of Marx's theses, but a "revolutionary dialectic whose "methods can be developed, expanded and deepened only along the lines laid down by its founders."[46]

The outlaws in *The Outsider*—Damon, Communists, fascists, and the disabled district attorney, all of whom appeared to many critics to be caricatures of Wright's own supposed existential crisis, embodying his estrangement as an expatriate and his disillusionment with Communism—are deformed by their interpellation into fast-changing postwar realities. They are caught up in contradictions intensified by the provisional defeat of fascism, the start of the Cold War, and struggles of people of color in the United States and the colonized world to achieve racial equality under the banners of civil rights and national liberation, leaving intact the economic misery of masses of Black Americans and decolonized populations of color still under the control of former colonizers. It was this global upheaval of mid-twentieth-century history that Wright interrogated through a cast of characters alienated from mainstream society and cast adrift by dimming prospects for salvation in a godless, industrialized world, transformed by new technologies to the point of cataclysmic destruction with the creation of the atomic bomb. His deep concern about the threat of nuclear war presaged the equally destructive (if not yet apparent) impact of increased fossil fuel extraction in rapidly expanding, postwar, global economies, which we now know resulted in a climate crisis endangering all life on earth.

In response to Blimin's accusations of espionage and murder, Damon holds forth on human history, which is "moving away from traditional, agrarian, simple handicraft ways of life toward modern industrialization," a recurring theme for Wright in works from *Black Boy* and *12 Million Black Voices* to his speech at the First International Congress of Negro Writers and Artists in Paris in 1956. Some nations in the West, Damon proclaims, have "already exhausted their industrial potentials of development and are industrially overripe," while other countries—China, India, and nations on the African continent—are just beginning to industrialize. The undeveloped nations, comprising "more than one half of the human race and more than one half of the territory of the earth," have been stimulated and retarded by the impact of Western imperialism. When "the hands of the West reached out greedily for the natural resources," they inadvertently awakened "black, red, brown, and yellow men from their long slumber and sent them, willy-nilly, hurtling down the road of industrialization." Damon's critique of the extraction of natural resources from the colonies contradicts the view of nature he conveys to Party leader Gil Blount's wife Eva in relation to her nonobjective art: "Nature's not us; it's different. A part of us is nature, but that part of us that's human and free is opposed to nature."[47] Contradicting this universalization of humanity's oppositional relationship to nature, Damon tells Blimin that a few powerful imperialist nations plundered half the earth's natural resources and half the human race comprising the undeveloped world. Despite the novel's ambiguities and inconsistencies, Wright's appreciation of the natural world and his sympathy for the underdog, inscribed in his earliest memories of "the verdant bluffs of Natchez," suggest that far from universalizing humanity, he tirelessly interrogated the relation of the exploiter and the exploited.

Just as early works like "The Ethics of Living Jim Crow" reveal the racial geography of second nature's physical and social transformations of the natural world, the clue to Damon's double murder in *The Outsider* is hidden in plain sight by the racist assumptions of detectives who ignore his fingerprints on the door handle that opens to the room where he murdered both the racist landlord Langley Herndon and Gil Blount. While such assumptions often led to savage treatment of African Americans ranging from verbal abuse to mob violence and murder, they sometimes enabled a protective shield of invisibility that both Wright and Ellison played on in *The Man Who Lived Underground* and *Invisible Man*, respectively. As Rachel Watson points out, the crimes committed by Bigger Thomas in *Native Son* and Cross Damon in *The Outsider* go undetected because the white police miss clues to the identity of culprits they assume, for various reasons, are not Black.[48] In Bigger's case, his ransom note attests to his literateness and cunning deception of the Daltons, who "would think that white men did it; they would never think that a black, timid Negro did that." Instead, they would blame Mary's Communist boyfriend Jan Erlone, as Bigger plots, having signed the note "Red" and drawn a clumsy hammer and sickle on it.[49] Similarly, Damon counts on the assumption that the police won't suspect him despite his fingerprints on the doorknob because he is *"just a Negro roomer* who had gone down at the suggestion of Mrs. Blount to see what was happening and had seen them fighting" (emphasis added).[50]

These racial codes are mapped, metonymically, onto a culturalization of nature, or second nature: "To Bigger and his kind white people were not really people; they were a sort of great natural force, like a stormy sky looming overhead, or like a deep swirling river stretching suddenly at one's feet in the dark."[51] As Murray Bookchin explains, the movement away from first nature to second nature produces one of the "searing questions of human history," that of "the social burden that we begin to develop at the same time we move away from a largely nature-based form of life with nature-based institutions into specifically cultural and political structures." According to Bookchin, the rise of social institutions such as the patriarchal family, the church, and the nation, along with processes of industrialization, urbanization, and migration from country to city, incite practical and political demands to address problems of agriculture, ownership, and social hierarchies, all driven by the central "issue of class rule—those who control or own property, and those who are placed in an oppressive and exploitative relationship to the owners of property."[52] Wright sharply delineates those relationships through the spatial logistics of Jim Crow in the Deep South and the urban North that segregate Black communities from mainstream society and mete out varying degrees of punishment from humiliation to lynching for people of color who cross racial lines in the wrong place at the wrong time.

In "The Ethics of Living Jim Crow," he educates readers with lessons on the unethical distribution of land, wealth, and power in the American South. As a young child, he learns the "appalling disadvantages" of waging war against white boys from the other side of the tracks, with nothing but cinders to hurl in defending against their broken bottles, and no cover to hide from their attacks when they retreated behind trees and hedges in their landscaped yards. His efforts to learn the optical trade as he dreams of "working his way up" are derailed by white coworkers' racial hatred and fear of competition, expressed in violent threats of retaliation for his alleged disrespect, a Jim Crow lesson compounded by his family calling him "a fool" for not staying in his place as dictated by white employers and employees. Yet another lesson occurs as he makes deliveries on his bicycle after sundown when the police stop and roughly search him, warning him menacingly to tell his boss not to send him out on deliveries at night.[53] He exposes these same if somewhat more subtle racial codes and maps of Black life in his long-awaited second novel, the first written in exile, *The Outsider*.

In general, Wright sought to educate readers, not in a didactic or moralistic sense, but by breaking existing codes of silence and crossing geographical boundaries, particularly with respect to racial trauma, laying bare the relentless dehumanization of white supremacy in its myriad forms, naturalized by centuries of exploitation. His dialectical approach to writing enabled him to fuse thought and feeling, idea and image, action and speech, through a Marxist analysis that could, as he put it in "Blueprint for Negro Writing," "buttress [the young Negro writer] with a tense and obdurate will to change the world."[54] Despite his assertion that he was going beyond the question of race in *The Outsider*, a claim he made as well in *The Man Who Lived Underground*, he inverts Damon's refusal to be racially defined to reveal the failure of rights-based legal remedies focused on civil liberties that leave the structures of racism intact. As Watson observes in her discussion of *The Outsider* as a crime novel, "A discourse of 'individual rights' can counterintuitively serve to push the deprivation of black humanness further beneath the ideological surface."[55]

To argue that Wright's evocation of the lonely outsider is metaphorical and affiliative rather than literal is not to deny that he suffered from isolation, especially in the last two years of his life, heightened by severe bouts of amoebic dysentery and anxiety about Cold War surveillance and his suspicions that his own milieus had been infiltrated by spies. But he was also closely associated with various left and Black diasporic circles—*Présence Africaine*, the African American colony in Paris, Rassemblement Démocratique Révolutionnaire, the Franco-American Fellowship, the Bandung Conference, the

Richard Wright with Leopold Senghor and others at the First International Congress of Negro Writers and Artists in Paris in 1956. Keystone-France via Getty Images.

International Conference of Negro Writers and Artists, gatherings at the Café Tournon and elsewhere in Paris—and with a wide circle of associates and friends, including European and expatriate writers such as Sartre, Beauvoir, Gertrude Stein, Chester Himes, and Ollie Harrington, as well as Pan-Africanists like George Padmore, C. L. R. James, Frantz Fanon, Léopold Senghor, and Aimé Césaire. Far from an antisocial loner, Wright was a highly sociable, collaborative, if iconoclastic, participant in multiple political and literary scenes after he left the CPUSA. His alleged loss of connection to the United States misinterprets his self-described outsiderness as an expression of anguish rather than a paradigmatic plight of African Americans who left their country of origin, disillusioned by its failure to live up to its promises, to join a diasporic community abroad of Black and other anticolonial artists, writers, and intellectuals. It was this collective sense of homelessness that united them in seeking to remake a world that, as Wright put it, could be a home for the hearts of all men. He stood in solidarity with intellectual and political outcasts and the world's dispossessed.

Disappointed by the CPUSA's subordination of antiracist and labor struggles to antifascist unity, especially after the Nazis invaded the Soviet Union, and by doctrinaire Marxist theory that inadequately addressed the predicament of racial oppression in global contexts, Wright sought with other displaced Black writers, intellectuals, and activists to work through contradictions of class and race that had eluded actually existing left-wing parties and socialist states as well as the Western bloc, especially the United States. Far from losing touch with the political pulse of the postwar era, he was on its cutting edge, expanding his own geographical, cultural, and intellectual compass as he sought to confront "the quicksands of cataclysmic historical changes." Rather than losing sight of America from his perch abroad, he saw the country through a wider-angle lens. In public lectures, travel books, fiction, and poetry he experimented with modernist and surrealist techniques, ethnographic descriptions, new journalism, and haiku, always seeking to wed content to form through a dialectical process that allowed him to see deeper into people's lives and find "that fixed point in intellectual space where a writer stands to view the struggles, hopes, and sufferings of his people," neither too close, resulting in "*blurred vision*," nor too far, resulting in "neglect of important things" (emphasis added).[56] He sought to clarify the image through a critical lens sharpened by intensive studies across disciplines, ethnographic research practiced as a federal writer, and the dialectical method of discerning the material conditions and contradictions of the social relations of production, which he had learned as a young Communist. In reply to a young woman's query as to whether his ideas would make people happy, he quipped, "My dear, I do not deal in happiness; I deal in meaning."[57]

Take the Hard Path! Rereading Wright's Travel Narrative of the Gold Coast

It was perhaps just this need of Wright's to make meaning of his experience that explains why James Baldwin's dismissal of *Native Son* as a protest novel so deeply irked him, and why he tore into the younger writer in Paris at the Brasserie Lipp about the just published essay, unapologetically snapping, "*All literature is protest*. . . . Here you go again with all that art for art's sake crap."[58] For Wright, to grasp the meaning of life was political *and* personal, a protest that took shape in literary investigations of the specific historical material conditions of his life and times. The larger cultural context for his reaction to Baldwin's betrayal was the emergence in the mid-twentieth century of New Criticism as the dominant literary method and theory—which we now know, and he suspected, had ties to the CIA and the Congress for Cultural Freedom—and the political chill of the Cold War.[59] A steady rightward drift of former Communists like Philip Rahv, the founding editor of *Partisan Review*, echoed New Critical attacks on proletarian literature on aesthetic grounds, disparaging sociopolitical content as poorly written polemic. Its "art for art's sake" focus on close reading of internal elements of a text and rejection of sociohistorical contexts as irrelevant to the study of literature obviously had implications for Wright's work. In addition to the combativeness of younger writers like Baldwin and critiques of his widely read books *Native Son* and *Black Boy*, the motivation to dethrone him as America's foremost Black writer came from the threat he posed to the status quo through the clarity and acuity of his linkage of Jim Crow in its different guises in the South and the North with European enslavement and colonization of the world's masses. It was thus not only a case of Baldwin's having "used [Wright's] work as a springboard into [his] own," as Baldwin later confessed, but also a larger broadside against Wright and other left-wing writers, intended to silence and defang their radical vision and struggles.[60]

Wright's deepening involvement in anticolonial movements and steadfast, if muted, criticism of the imperial West presaged postcolonial ecologies deformed by the economic, cultural, and environmental destructiveness of capitalist expansion. He was part of a wider group of intellectuals, artists, and activists attempting to enact a dialectics of liberation that theorized class and race from African, Asian, and diasporic African perspectives. This posture allied him with what he referred to as the Westernized, tragic elite of colonized countries, the young men and some women, including many friends and associates, educated abroad in the Soviet Union, Europe, or the United States—a perspective that Franz Fanon harshly criticized in his review of *White Man, Listen!* For Fanon, who had previously expressed deep admiration for Wright's portrait of Bigger Thomas, the psychology of racism rooted in Nietzsche's "frog perspective," always gazing up at the predator, represented a banal analysis of racial oppression, while Wright's appeal to the "White Man" naively sought to persuade the ruling classes to act against their own interests.[61] However, Wright typically wrote in two registers in his travel books, as a straight spokesperson appealing to the West's benevolence on behalf of the decolonizing masses and as "something of a trickster" undercutting any trust in the West's goodwill by calling its very possibility into question.[62]

Despite his affinity with the Westernized elite, with whom he had much in common as a Black, left-wing intellectual, Wright consciously identified with the colonized masses, the poor, and the proletariat, as well as lumpen criminals, vagabonds, and prostitutes worldwide, and he aimed to "lend his tongue" to them as he had done for the "voiceless Negro boys" of his youth whom he vowed not to disown.[63] Nevertheless, his travel narratives drew criticism as well as praise for seeming to side with the West and the Westernized elite and for denigrating traditional African and Asian cultures. Many readers were irritated by his expressions of dismay, distance, and even horror in relating his Third World encounters. Critics like Kwame Anthony Appiah, whose father was Ghanaian, understandably condemned what he saw as Wright's ethnocentric, condescending rejection of African traditions, religion, and values.

But his friend George Padmore, who enabled his visit to the Gold Coast, defended *Black Power* for portraying "the challenge of the barefoot masses against the black aristocracy and the middle class."[64] As a test of existential philosophy's limitations, *The Outsider* clarifies Wright's embrace of outsiderness as a critical standpoint from which he could survey what he presciently saw as the death and rebirth of a new world order defined by the Cold War, the atomic bomb, and the rise of national liberation movements challenging centuries of colonial rule and plunder. Rather than endorsing nihilism or substituting European existentialism for a Marxist worldview, he rejected bourgeois conceptions of freedom and, however subtly and critically, reinscribed the call for collective action that defined his involvement with the CPUSA from 1934 to 1944. *The Outsider* enabled him to come to terms with his own crisis of identity as an expatriate and ex-Communist and "step out onto the stage of the whole world."[65]

Wright's first major stop on the world stage was the Gold Coast in 1953 at the invitation of Prime Minister Kwame Nkrumah. His account of his visit, controversial as it was, represented a turning point in global history and an early radical analysis by a then world-famous African American author of anticolonial struggles and the future of postcolonial states. He was uniquely positioned—part deliberately, part deservedly, part by pure chance—to join forces with key transnational, literary, political, and intellectual figures of his time and to play a significant role in theorizing, bearing witness to, and narrating major historical events and currents. To have been able to undertake such a journey is in itself remarkable given that Wright was just one generation away from slavery, his formal education cut short by the conditions of life in the Jim Crow South. His brilliant capacity for melding experience with ideas, stories with plots, launched him on this path, but his brilliance alone does not explain his trajectory before or after he catapulted to international fame. Inspired to write as a boy, learning to "fuse experience and make articulate the experiences of men [sic]" in literary expression as a young Communist in order "to buttress him[self] with a tense and obdurate will to change the world," he came of age as a writer poised to pursue his desire to write not in tension with the political formations and exigencies that defined him, but enabled by his education as a CPUSA member to grasp the significance of unfolding anticolonial struggles in all their fraught complexity.[66] But some of his clarity as a Communist was lost in the ambiguities and anxieties of the postwar period as, unmoored from the certitudes of the Party and the revolutionary zeitgeist of the 1930s, he wrestled with the internal contradictions of colonization produced by hundreds of years of Western conquest and colonial rule.

Several critics, including Appiah, point out Wright's seeming obsession with women's breasts—elongated, exposed, disfigured—and with nudity in general as he fixed an outsider's gaze on culturally different practices with a mixture of dismay and fascination. For Wright, nudity was a sign of "utter asexuality," an "absolute otherness" that caused him "a vague sense of mild panic, an obsessive burden of alertness." Another insensitive response, according to Appiah, occurred on Wright's first night in Accra in the British-built bungalows where the government put him up. As he looked out from a screened balcony at the "swarming, far-off, faint yellow lights of Accra twinkling in the valley below," a steward appeared and asked, "Massa want chop?" in a pidgin English that Wright could not understand and that elicited a shudder from him. "I resented it," he complained, "and I vowed that I'd never speak it." Rather than sympathizing with the steward, whose dialect he associated with racial degradation, "a tradition left here for a hundred years by English housewives," Wright expressed contempt for him and two other men who served his dinner. Yet, in a self-deprecating story of a "magnificent woman . . . nursing a fat black baby" whose picture he asks to take and who asks for a "penny, Massa," the joke is on Wright. He gives her a shilling and she runs with her baby to her mud hut. He writes, "A howl of black laughter echoed through the compound. I stood looking like a blundering fool. She had outwitted me. I laughed too. She had won."[67]

In his introduction to *Black Power*, he promises to reveal his "prepossessions" and provide his "working frame of reference." He claims to have written "a first-person, subjective narrative," which he also describes as an "intensive study," an attempt "to subject a slice of African life to close scrutiny in terms of concepts that one would use in observing life anywhere." Signaling his awareness of debates about "African survivals" and negritude, he notes, "Some conclusions arrived at in these pages might well startle or dismay those who like to dote on 'primitive' people."[68] Likewise, his caveats about subjectivity and objectively "close scrutiny" suggest that he understood the unavoidability of the one and the necessity of the other. It was his subjective response to Africans that Appiah condemns as a "failure of sympathy," a criticism that was warranted perhaps but also hostile, or impervious, to the nuances of his portrait of Ghanaian people and the historical materialist basis for his critique of the legacy of imperialism.[69] Reinforced by his rejection of religion, his materialist worldview had evolved by then into a dialectical approach to art as an expression of human history that is always economic and political, material and ideological, subjective and objective.

Commenting on other critics of Wright's complicated involvement in Pan-Africanist intellectual and activist circles, Babacar M'Baye cites the Nigerian scholar Femi Ojo-Adi's contention that Wright's internalized, Eurocentric "self-hate, resulting from White racism and Black rootlessness, pushes him to become the *Outsider* . . . [who] deep down, hungers for America." While acknowledging the legitimacy of such complaints, M'Baye insists that they "overlook the significance of Wright's attitudes toward Africa in Pan-African and transnational explorations of the consequences of imperialism and colonialism in Africa and the Black Diaspora," and goes on to insist that he "was committed to Africa's liberation from Western exploitation."[70] In this light, it is possible to see, without dismissing them, how objections to Wright's Eurocentrism overlaid or misread, but did not negate, his self-doubt or his critique of religion, superstition, illiteracy, and backwardness in the wake of centuries of Western subjugation and the devastation it wreaked on colonized peoples.

If he drew different conclusions than some anticolonial leaders with whom he debated these matters, he also questioned his own assumptions. For example, about the necessity of industrialization and literacy learning for Ghanaians, he wondered if the desire for it was his or theirs: "I was literate, Western, disinherited, and industrialized and I felt each day the pain and anxiety of it. Why then must I advocate the dragging of these people into my trap?"[71] John Reilly calls Wright's Gold Coast trip a "secular salvation" enabling him to recreate himself and his intellectual persona through "his discovery of the Third World."[72] But even if he was attempting to salvage his identity and career, he was also aiming to theorize and support anticolonial struggles as he reoriented himself to a fast-changing world that included the dramatic rise of the Ghanaian and other independence movements.

He sought always to "see" what had been hidden or mystified, to bring to light meanings eclipsed by the historical processes of struggles to survive, first in nature and then in the conflict between owners and producers that has structured human history in all epochs. He wrestled dialectically with aesthetic considerations as a writer using a method that, as he reminded Baldwin, was always political. Unafraid of offending readers who could not face the harsh truths he aimed to tell, he struggled to see through the appearances of things to their essential relations. This determination forged the sympathetic yet critical narrative persona he assumed in *Black Power*, an amalgam of the traveler, the American-born Black writer visiting Africa for the first time, the former Communist, and the anticolonial activist and thinker, all introduced in the front matter of the book. Following the letter of invitation from Nkrumah are facing pages with a map of Northwest Africa and the Gold Coast on one side and Wright's dedication "to the Unknown African" on the other, followed by three epigraphs by Countee Cullen, Walt Whitman, and Robert Briffault, a contemporary novelist and anthropologist.

The dedication attributes to the unknown African a "primal and poetic humanity" that caused white men to treat him as property, "a 'thing' to be bought, sold, and used as an instrument of production." In what could be construed either as a stereotype of Africans or a condemnation of their colonizers' inhumanity, Wright describes the Africans' vision of life prior to colonization as simple, terrifying, and "irreducibly human." Cullen's poem "What Is Africa to Me?" poses the question at the core of the book as Wright grapples with his ambivalence about his "'racial' heritage" and supposed "racial qualities" in conflict with his "habitual kind of thinking that had no 'race' in it" and that "was conditioned by the reaction of human beings to a concrete social environment."[73] Whitman's line from "To a Common Prostitute," "Not till the sun excludes you do I exclude you," expresses the sympathy of the poem's speaker ("Walt Whitman") for inclusivity and for the girl—or in this case, perhaps, the African. What sort of prostitution colors Wright's report on his Gold Coast trip? How does it relate to European commodification of the African, or to the definition of the African as "primal and poetic" or "simple and terrifying"? Through whose gaze is the African so seen? Finally, his repudiation a few pages later of so-called racial qualities, such as a "*special gift* for music, dancing, rhythm and movement"—an idea of his "defensive-minded Negro friends"—is amplified by Briffault's comment that "the entire course of development of the human race . . . [is] coincident with those of transmitted *social* heredity" (emphasis added).

This front matter maps his voyage to the Gold Coast onto the antinomies and ironies that increasingly characterized his writing in exile amid mounting global tensions and crises, an emerging new world order, and the intensification of the Cold War. He understood the idea of race as central to the history of Jim Crow in the United States and European colonization, but he firmly rejected it as a defining category of his own life and of human existence; he valued indigenous folk culture as a source of collective wisdom that "arose out of a unified sense of a common life and a common fate," but he also saw it as an impediment to his own literary aspirations and a symbol of the racist brutality of the South that could entrap Black Americans or colonized Africans and Asians in demeaning social roles.[74] As was true of his most widely read books, *Native Son* and *Black Boy*, his travel narratives are complex, double-voiced, political mediations of his experience that reflect his position as a former Communist living in Paris under US surveillance, constantly in fear of losing his passport and deportation to the United States, where he almost certainly would have been called to testify before Senator Joseph McCarthy's Senate subcommittee investigating known or suspected Communists. He was also spied on by the British and French and forced to remain silent on the Algerian War.

Wright's late work has been interpreted as pro-Western and anticommunist. However, given his anti-imperialist politics and his debt to tricksterism, his overt praise for the West can be seen as a means of outmaneuvering Cold War surveillance. Every appeal he makes to the West for support is undermined by a sober assessment of the unlikelihood that it would be voluntarily and generously given. After announcing his intent in *Black Power* "to pose this problem anew," he admits, "Let me be honest; I'm not too hopeful." Likewise, at the end of *White Man, Listen!* he approves the West's "secular, rational base of thought and feeling" but makes clear that "new terms will have to be found," a challenge that would have to be met "openly and selflessly." He thus calls on the non-Western nations—the "rest" of the world—to modernize and embrace rational, secular, scientific discourse, and on the West to let colonies verging on independence "finish that job" with the same industrializing tools with which it exploited them.[75] Accused of distancing himself from his African roots and identifying with the West, he explains he was shaped by the culture into which he was born, reiterating Briffault's point that human beings are mainly conditioned by social heredity. Far from believing in the natural superiority of the West over Africa and Asia, he presents a view of a postwar world order ruled by Western wealth and power built on the backs of exploited global masses, arguing that the tools of the West could liberate colonized peoples in a dialectical process by which the contradictions of colonialism would create the conditions for independence and equality for all.

He is neither deriding African cultures nor disputing the destructiveness of colonization, but rather reckoning with a nascent postcolonial future when he asks, "Can the African overcome his ancestor-worshipping attitudes and learn to doubt the evidence of his senses as Descartes taught the Europeans to do, and master the techniques of science and develop a spirit of objectivity?"[76] This apparent bias in favor of the West offended readers who saw it as contempt for indigenous African traditions rather than belief in a common humanity. Further complicating his travel narratives, he needed to assert his loyalty to the United States to FBI spies and "ghostreaders"—that is, agents assigned to surveil Black writing for signs of political protest, who ironically became some of its best readers—while navigating the contradictions of Western imperialism.[77] His double-voiced prose veiled a radical critique of imperial domination and racist ideology with appeals for Westernizing a backward, tribalized people. Turning to the West to support postcolonial nations allowed him to call openly for a more egalitarian world, free of racism and class exploitation, predicated on a secular understanding of reality and dictated not by superstition, religion, or racial identity but by objectivity, reason, and science, a worldview that in turn clashed with some anticolonial conceptions of negritude.

His letter to Nkrumah at the end of *Black Power* surprised readers who saw it as a failure of communication or a strange U-turn from his revolutionary politics to a totalitarian call to militarize the Gold Coast. But it was a revolutionary militantism that Wright implored Nkrumah to enact, "not for war, but for peace, not for destruction, but for service; not for aggression, but for production; not for despotism, but to free minds from mumbo-jumbo." He goes on to explicitly clarify for those who would "misconstrue [his] words" that he means not a "military dictatorship" but "a militarization of the daily, social lives of the people" to give "form, organization, direction, meaning, and a sense of justification to those lives." Only a militant commitment to modernization and equitable global development, he argued, could overcome entrenched irrational forces militating against the future of humanity. Even as he called on the West to support national struggles for self-determination, Wright told Nkrumah to reject Western intervention for the sake of his people's future and "take the hard path!" to win freedom and escape foreign domination. As he prophetically observed in 1956 in "Tradition and Industrialization," his lecture at the First International Congress of Negro Writers and Artists, "The truth is that our world—a world for all men, black, brown, yellow, and white—will either be all rational or totally irrational. For better or worse, it will eventually be one world."[78]

All of the Human Race: Looking Back to Look Forward

Looking back on this prophesy from the third decade of the twenty-first century makes visible the crossroads of history at which Wright stood—a time when national liberation movements held great promise even as the threat of imperial domination of former colonies was already emerging. Today, we know the direction history took: US-sponsored destabilizations of newly independent African, Asian, and Latin American nations, including, among other anticommunist, covert, and military operations, the 1965 deployment of the first 3,500 US combat troops to South Vietnam, to join the 25,000 military advisers already there; the 1966 assassination of the leader of Democratic Republic of Congo, Patrice Lumumba; mass killings in 1965–66 of as many as 1 million suspected Indonesian communists and communist sympathizers, culminating in the ouster of President Sukarno in 1967, followed by Suharto's thirty-two-year dictatorship; the military coup d'état that deposed Ghanaian president Kwame Nkrumah in 1966; and the overall underdevelopment of emerging nations, plundered for natural resources and trapped in cyclical poverty and onerous debt repayment programs. The promise of a more egalitarian international order grew dimmer with the post–Cold War globalization of mid-to-late-twentieth-century capitalism as it tightened its tentacles on the world. Although Wright lived to see only the first decade and a half of this new world order, his prophetic warnings continue to resonate in the twenty-first century.

In *The Color Curtain*, Wright reported on the historic April 1955 Bandung Conference of twenty-nine African and Asian countries, a watershed event in postcolonial history that led to the formation of the Non-Aligned Movement (NAM) in 1961. Today, despite criticisms of the book and his interactions with conference attendees and his Indonesian hosts, he is considered by scholars across the disciplines as having been "clearly ahead of his time." He had glimpsed "a vision of anticolonial cosmopolitanism" as the "keenest observer" from the United States of this unfolding history, authoring a book that "went on to influence much anticolonial and antiracist thought" and "remains the most influential perspective" on the conference.[79] He was "no stranger to the dynamic that would unfold at Bandung" given his connections to the Black Atlantic, negritude, and Pan-Africanism.[80]

In Paris for Christmas between trips to Spain, he recalls spotting a story about the conference in the evening paper. Setting the stage for his three-week visit to Indonesia, he remarks on Bandung's momentous appeal to billions of Third World peoples, "ex-colonial subjects ... whom the white West called 'colored,'" dominated by Europe for centuries and now led by revolutionary nationalists and former political prisoners. The meeting, he declared, was at the "main geopolitical center of gravity of the earth," an event that "smacked of tidal waves, of natural forces." World leaders at the conference were to include Indonesian prime minister Ali Sastroamidjojo, Indian prime minister Jawaharlal Nehru, prime minister of the Gold Coast Kwame Nkrumah, and Chinese premier Zhou Enlai, among others: "The despised, the insulted, the hurt, the dispossessed—in short, the underdogs of the human race were meeting." When he handed the article to his wife Ellen to read, she exclaimed, "Why, that's the human race!" "Here," Wright understood, "were class and racial and religious consciousness on a global scale" of the most populous nations on earth.[81]

Like *Black Power*, Wright's book on Bandung drew both praise and criticism. Initial reviewers were mostly positive, calling it a "book that needs to be pondered," "a vivid and illuminating job of reporting," a problem of great "magnitude" to which Wright brought "amazing clarity," and "a good journalistic account of an extraordinary and significant event." Abner W. Berry, writing for the *Daily Worker*, declared that the report "can be considered as a warning to the West to mend its ways in Asia and Africa" and that Wright saw "no chance of imperialism coming to terms with its former subjects," a failure that accounts for his "doleful tone."[82] Recent scholars have praised *The Color Curtain* as "an unprecedented postmodern, postcolonial travelogue" indicative of Wright's "expanding consciousness as a global humanist."[83] More problematically, with the solidification of postcolonial and Afro-Asian studies, *The Color Curtain* has taken on mythic status as an "ur-narrative" that may have generated more commentary than documentation, as Brian Russell Roberts and Keith Foulcher observe, threatening to supplant "an archivally verifiable Bandung Conference" with "what people wanted to believe had happened."[84] In their excellent sourcebook on Wright and Bandung, they counterpose his report with Indonesian critics of both the conference and Wright. These sources reflect the complex politics of Indonesia from 1955 to 1960, as Sukarno and other conference participants sought to establish Third World unity and solidarity beholden to neither superpower amid intensifying CIA support for regional military forces critical of Sukarno's central government. Ultimately, these forces would extinguish the "Bandung spirit" in a US-backed slaughter of suspected communist sympathizers followed by decades of Suharto's authoritarian rule.

Among Wright's critics was Beb Vuyk, a Dutch writer whose father was half Indonesian. Born in Rotterdam, Vuyk moved to Indonesia in 1929 at age twenty-four, married, raised two children, and remained there until fierce anti-Dutch sentiment forced her to return to the Netherlands in 1957. In 1960, five years after meeting Wright in Indonesia, she published a two-part article about him in a left-wing Dutch magazine, *Vrij Nederland*, in which she depicts strained relations and miscues between him and his Indonesian hosts, including

Mochtar Lubis, the founder and editor of *Indonesian Raya*; Sutan Takdir Alisjahbana, the editor of *Konfrontasi*; and the emerging novelist Sitor Situmorang. These writers were associated with universal humanism and the journal *Konfrontasi*, which was affiliated with Sutan Sjahrir's Partai Sosialis Indonesia (PSI, Indonesian Socialist Party) and edited by Takdir after the dissolution of a popular 1930s magazine that he helped found. They were also members of the Konfrontasi study group, with whom Wright spent several days. The publication of the second installment of Vuyk's article coincided with the last days of Wright's life as he lay in a hospital bed in the Eugène Gibez Clinic, where he had gone for a routine checkup and tragically died of an apparent heart attack two days later. His Dutch translator Margrit de Sablonière had corresponded with him about the first part of Vuyk's article, which he bitterly disputed, and she was ready to issue a public response on his behalf at the time of his death, but it was never published.[85] The circumstances surrounding his interactions with the Konfrontasi group were rife with political tensions over nationalism and communism, racialism and colonialism, and cultural debates reflective of mounting Cold War pressures. Like the attacks by New Critics in the United States on the literary left's definition of literature as a "class weapon," the universal humanism espoused by the Konfrontasi group rejected the socialist realism of the People's Cultural Front (Lekra) that was linked to the Indonesian Communist Party (Partai Komunis Indonesia, PKI) and professed individual freedom over collective struggle.

The CIA-funded Congress for Cultural Freedom (CCF) had sponsored Wright's trip to Bandung and travel by several Konfrontasi members to Europe and the United States to participate in CCF-sponsored events. It was also the CCF that arranged for Mochtar Lubis to meet Wright at the Jakarta airport and plan his itinerary, lectures, and contact with other writers, all of whom were associated with universal humanism and Konfrontasi. Wright might have gotten a different sense of the politics of the Indonesian literary community had he met with Pramoedya Ananta Toer, a novelist and admirer of his work. Pramoedya had no contact with him other than possibly attending one of his lectures at the cultural center Balai Budaja and had already begun to move away from universal humanism to embrace socialist realism and the PKI. As Roberts and Foulcher note, the lack of records of any encounter between the two writers "serves as a reminder that Wright's interactions were culturally limited"—likely by the CCF, to which Wright had reluctantly turned for financial backing after exhausting other potential funding sources for his trip to Bandung and after his longtime publisher Harper and Row refused to publish the proposed book.[86]

Despite terms that released Wright from official coverage of the conference, the CCF obliged him to publish articles in transcontinental CCF magazines, including *Encounter*, a British magazine founded by Stephen Spender and Irving Kristol, former leftists on the CIA payroll. One of the CCF's earliest activities was to distribute Arthur Koestler's *The God That Failed*, which featured Wright's "I Tried to Be a Communist." By this point, as has been well documented, US anticommunist operations were well underway abroad, including in Indonesia, as the Bandung Conference aroused fears of a leftward, anti-Western, antiwhite turn among the assembled nations. Unbeknownst to Wright, Michael Josselson, the CCF director who had arranged his travel to Bandung, was a CIA agent, underscoring the role Wright played and counterplayed in shaping "the contours of a specific approach that the United States took in attempting to intervene in the Bandung Conference and its representation to an international readership."[87]

Other issues of misrecognition and misrepresentation described in Vuyk's article center on complaints about Wright's ignorance of Indonesian history, including the oppressiveness of the Japanese occupation during World War II, of which he seemed to be unaware, and what they saw as his racialization of both the conference and their own attitudes. According to Vuyk, Mochtar thought Wright was "color crazy" and denied hating or feeling inferior to whites. In Wright's account, an unnamed Indonesian writer who appears to be Sitor Situmorang replies to a question about his racial identification that yes, he sees himself as "colored" because as a member of a backward nation he feels inferior to the advanced white Western world. Wright characterizes him as holding "the most violent attitudes toward the Japanese," referring to them as "*yellow* monkeys," as opposed to "*brown*" Indonesians, comments that Wright saw as "feelings of race consciousness."[88] Vuyk reports that Sitor, too, denied any feelings of racial inferiority and believed that Wright took his remark about the Japanese out of context. It was not he but rather a village head, an ordinary Indonesian reacting to a plan for a Japanese factory, who complained, "Those yellow monkeys here in our village?" Similarly, in a letter to the editor of *Encounter*, the UK magazine that published "Indonesian Notebook," Wright's first report on Bandung in August 1955, Mochtar accused Wright of looking through "coloured-glasses." Indonesians had no "colour or racial problems," Mochtar declared. In his public reply, Wright referred Mochtar to the full, soon to be published account of his trip in *The Color Curtain*, assuring him that he had found "racial feeling" among Asians generally and admonishing him to "think hard" about their conversations driving through the Java mountains.[89]

When Vuyk asked Mochtar, en route to pick up Wright from the airport, what the American author was doing in Indonesia, he replied, "Covering the Bandung circus." Later, responding to Wright's remarks that Sukarno was a "great man" whose idea it was to convene "for the first time in human history ... the colored races in an international conference," and that the conference held "great historical significance," the Indonesians fell silent and Mochtar explained that the ulterior motive for the meeting was to cover up the "weaknesses and blunders" of the administration. When Wright asked his companions to name the most important historical fact of the century, they all agreed it was "the liberation of the colonies" and that the commonality among African and Asian peoples was their colonial past rather than their color.[90] Wright would not have disagreed with part of their answer, but he understood that racism had been produced by and helped sustain colonial rule, just as it had enabled the economic development of the Americas through slavery and the African diaspora. It was precisely this dialectical relationship between class struggle inherent in capitalist expansion and racial oppression vis-à-vis national liberation that he sought to understand. Notwithstanding the Konfrontasi group's more or less hostile reaction to him, Sukarno, and the conference, Wright's clarity about the historical significance of Bandung and his fears of imperial resubjugation have been borne out by history.

At the same time, Wright's anxiety about Cold War surveillance and dependence on CCF funding necessitated a degree of self-censorship that permeated his exilic writing. Carefully worded in the "enforced duplicity" required to evade censorship and Cold War retribution, his report on Bandung supports yet questions Pan-African reliance on the West.[91] Like George Padmore, he "played the Cold War game," criticizing Communist states and arguing that Pan-Africanism posed little threat to the West while warning that anticolonial leaders would turn to Moscow if necessary.[92] Explaining that colonial oppression was primarily an economic rather than a "racial matter" and that Western supremacy would only be broken when the West no longer controlled raw materials in Africa and Asia, he declared, "To have an ordered, rational world in which we all can share ... the average white Westerner ... either accepts [de-Occidentalization] or he will have to seek for ways and means of resubjugating these newly freed hundreds of millions of brown and yellow and black people." If he accepts it, "he will also have to accept ... *a much, much lower standard of living*" because such a process would "*result in a need for radical reconstruction of the social and economic systems of the Western world*" (emphasis added).[93] These contingencies undercut his pro-Western avowals in light of references to the achievements of the Communist bloc and his anticapitalist critique of colonialism. Acknowledging the past, foreseeing the future, he condemned the West's broken Enlightenment promises and knew it would never cede its economic interests in a capitalist world order.

On his country's Independence Day in 1963, President Sukarno pointed to the revolutionary demands of Black Americans as a beacon for postcolonial freedom and proclaimed that the Indonesian Revolution was linked with global aspirations in satisfying material needs but also in achieving ideals of equality and solidarity. Wright repeatedly declared, echoing the CPUSA's position on Black liberation, that African Americans formed the vanguard of revolutionary change not by virtue of their race but because history had assigned them that role as the most oppressed group in America. In his lecture "American Negro Writing," delivered at Takdir's villa, he expanded that thesis of "what America *is*" to the whole world: "The voice of the American Negro is rapidly becoming the most representative voice of oppressed people anywhere in the world today." All the human race, he prophesied in *12 Million Black Voices*, would move forward with this "new tide ... into the sphere of conscious history" or perish. As he left the airport and drove through Jakarta with Mochtar Lubis, Wright reflected on ecologies of empire, as I am calling them, created by Dutch imperialism, observing that as factory and financial relations replaced family relations, the teeming city "presents to Western eyes a commercial aspect, naked and immediate, that seems to swallow up the entire population in petty trade." The human savagery and ruinous environmental cost of Dutch rule was evident in the canals it dug "in this hot mudhole of a city" in which Wright saw "a young man squatting, defecating in broad daylight" as children bathed and brushed their teeth and women washed clothes in the dirty water.[94]

CHAPTER SEVEN

Yearning for What Never Was

The question of whether Wright remained a Marxist is complicated by his renunciations of Communism and, at times, Marxism, his evasive politics during the Cold War, and the myriad conflicting representations of his political outlook. Wrapped in the ironies of living Jim Crow and writing about it, his "bitter truths" were indecipherable to many readers. Although reviewers mainly hailed *Native Son* as a masterpiece, "the Negro *American Tragedy*," and compared Wright to Dreiser, Dostoevsky, Steinbeck, and Dickens, even Peter Monro Jack's favorable review was mired in racist assumptions—what he saw as the immutability of blackness—about Bigger Thomas, trapped in slums, his family on relief, representing "an *impasse* rather than a complex, [whose] tragedy is to be born into a black and immutable minority race." Far from reaffirming "blackness" as an immutable category, Wright meant Bigger's monstrous murders of white Communist heiress Mary Dalton and his Black, working-class girlfriend Bessie Mears to shock readers into awareness of the social and psychological consequences of American racism. His inversion of ingrained racial stereotypes exposed the structural causes of Bigger's crimes, explaining his justification of the murders as necessary and his lawyer Boris Max's extralegal defense of his client as the legacy of America's sinful history of slavery and racial terror. It is just this point that Fanon makes in *Black Skin, White Masks*, observing, "In the end, Bigger Thomas acts. To put an end to his tension, he acts, he responds to the world's anticipation."[1]

Wright, too, is answering a world—Chicago's South Side, 1930s America, fraught by global economic depression as it catapulted toward World War II—in which millions of Black southerners fled Jim Crow terror for northern cities in search of "the warmth of other suns," as he put it in his revised ending to the first edition of *Black Boy*. These Black migrants' hopes, chronicled in *12 Million Black Voices*, were punctured by new, urban realities not as debilitating as the long nightmare of slavery and peonage they left behind in the South but no less malevolent and often just as deadly. Some joined forces with radicals, especially Communists, across racial lines and ideological differences; others participated in cultural and political fronts. They imagined a socialist future of world peace, economic and racial equality, and freedom. That dream dimmed for many radicals, including Wright, disillusioned by Soviet policy and silenced by intensifying Cold War repression, but he continued to pursue it throughout his career. His life and times coincided with a historical crossroads that could have led to an alternative future for emerging independent nations and their diasporic descendants hoping to achieve social equality worldwide. As much as that world has changed eighty-five years after Bigger entered the annals of world fiction, it remains eerily the same.

Subject to persistent racial, gender, and class inequality, masses of people today are also vulnerable to catastrophic environmental conditions. Neither Wright nor his comrades could have foreseen the ecological breakdown of the planet in this century or fully apprehended the incompatibility of economic growth and industrial development with the survival of human and other species. But if the apocalyptic consequences of carbon-fueled industrial development were not yet apparent, Wright and his fellow Pan-Africanists nonetheless were demarcating the racial geography of imperialism in relation to the depredation of soil, forests, and other natural resources, all funneled unidirectionally to the centers of empire away from the colonized masses. In addition to perceiving racial codes in the US South and the Western empire, Wright looked to nature, which spoke to him in a "cryptic tongue," to reveal its "coded meanings," from his early writing to the more than 4,000 haiku composed toward the end of his life. Long before he left the United States in search of a place where he could live relatively free of racial discrimination, he had linked the rise of capitalism to the slave trade, colonization, and extraction of human labor and natural resources from mineral- and soil-rich continents. His political education in Chicago, including the principles of internationalism and working-class solidarity, informed his thinking about racial and class exploitation before and after his break with the CPUSA.

These insights enabled him to demystify social realities that appeared as natural, inevitable, and universal rather than historically specific conditions of life. It was the explanatory power of Marxist theory that bolstered his intuitive understanding of race and assertions of racial superiority or inferiority as being produced by historically specific social relations rather than being given, fixed categories. His aesthetic practice fused the social theory he learned in the John Reed Club and *New Masses*, the covers of which had so horrified his mother, with literary techniques that mixed modernist and naturalist elements with gothic, pulp, detective, crime, and horror genres. When he said in his essay on Bigger that he had learned to see with X-ray vision into the inner lives of men (and women), he was rehearsing the dialectical method he would practice from then on, by which he grasped the hidden substratum of phenomena that, as Marx put it, "appear directly and spontaneously as current modes of thought."[2] His critique of systemic racism, which was maintained by urban slumlords no less than white southerners, incensed white liberal and Black bourgeois critics alike, while his withering depiction of white Communists in *Native Son* irked CPUSA leaders. What they saw as gross misrepresentations of the Party and its many Black leaders, comrades, and fellow travelers missed Wright's point that white cadre like Mary Dalton who exoticized Bigger were oblivious to the profound discomfort, bewilderment, and alienation they caused, embodying the Communists' failure to speak to ordinary people.

Fellow Traveling: "The Dead Author Was Anything but Anti-Communist"

Most recent scholars agree that Wright retained a Marxist worldview, but the publication of "I Tried to Be a Communist" in *The Atlantic* in 1944 and in excerpted selections elsewhere, culminating in the fully restored text of *Black Boy* in 1991, left a lasting impression that he had abandoned left politics. According to the standard narrative of his involvement in the CPUSA, he naively joined the Party to escape Jim Crow and get a boost as a writer, never acquiring more than shallow knowledge of its political programs. This demeaning portrait of him as a young Communist corresponds with assessments of his literary style as course, flat, prolix, and didactic; both his politics and his writing are seen as spontaneous, if not "miraculous," instead of rooted in conscious, diligent study of history, theory, and literature. Fabre points out that by 1945 Wright had learned from Leo Cherne, an economist and anticommunist liberal, that the Party had tried to prevent the Book-of-the-Month Club from sponsoring *Black Boy* at the same time he heard that it had ordered the assassination of his friend Hank Johnson, a packing house worker organizer and executive secretary of the Chicago chapter of the National Negro Congress. This chilling news, which I have not been able to corroborate, along with "other experiences and impressions," further disillusioned Wright about the CPUSA and informed the plot twists of *The Outsider*. Although Fabre maintains that Wright remained a Marxist, he substantiates the view that he renounced the Party and the USSR, noting that he "was satisfied to find an irrefutable criticism of the Soviet Union" in a report on the Russians by W. L. White, a journalist from Emporia, Kansas, who went from conservative to progressive politics, supporting both Theodore and Franklin Delano Roosevelt.[3]

Contesting that narrative, the cartoonist and journalist Ollie Harrington called the 1971 publication of *American Hunger* (Part Two) in its entirety "the mugging of a dead genius." He remembers a conversation at a bar in a Parisian hotel with E. Franklin Frazier, Chester Himes, and Wright that touched on Black youth and, inevitably, *Black Boy*, and insists that it was Wright who decided not to publish Part Two "because it obviously detracted from its anti-racist, anti-fascist message." One of Wright's closest friends in the last years of his life, Harrington maintains that *American Hunger* was "written in a burst of frustration and bewilderment by a young black genius" and was thus seen as "anti-communist," insisting that "*the dead author was anything but anti-Communist*" (emphasis added). He also remembers Wright telling him at his flat on rue Regis in 1956 that he had refused to write a new essay for Richard Crossman's planned tenth anniversary edition of *The God That Failed*. Instead, dripping with irony, Wright said he would give Crossman an essay on racism and "cloak and dagger terrorism" on the West Bank, gleefully declaring, "They can publish that in their goddamned 10th anniversary issue."[4]

Along with contradictory assessments of Wright's political insights and literary skill, there are also depictions of him as lonely, alienated, and bitter. In her foreword to Harrington's book, Julia Wright notes that one of her father's biographers described him as "unable to keep his friends for very long," an assertion that she contests on the basis of her memories of her parents' solid friendships creating an "affective soil" that nurtured her "belief in the possibility of trust." In particular, she recalls that Ollie Harrington and George Padmore, her father's closest friends in Paris, were always "around" and served as her "intellectual and ethical mentors."[5] At various times, Wright no doubt felt like the persona of the lonely outsider he assumed in his travel books: as an African American, a writer, and a Marxist, he was at odds with the Communist Party; and as an expatriate, he was caught between the antipathies of communism and Western imperialism. He told his Dutch translator Margrit de Sablonière that to the Americans, he was "worse than a Communist, for my work falls like a shadow across their policy in Asia and Africa."[6] Although the CPUSA continued to champion Black freedom and Black nationalism as necessary, vanguard aspects of class struggle during and after World War II—through the National Negro Congress, the Civil Rights Congress, and the Southern Negro Youth Congress, in particular—Wright and other Black Communists were disillusioned by what they saw as a choice that the country as a whole but also, to a lesser extent, the Party had made between fighting fascism and fighting racism.

Adding to these tensions, he was plagued by right-wing attacks, starting with Congressman Martin Dies's denunciation in 1938 of "The Ethics of Living Jim Crow" as "filthy" and "disgusting," and of the FWP anthology *American Stuff* in which it was published as "reeking with Communism."[7] From then on, long after he left the CPUSA, he was under surveillance by US counterintelligence operatives, making it increasingly difficult to know what he really thought. In *The Outsider*, he portrays Communists as a group of scurrilous despots and lackeys who mindlessly obey Party dictates no matter how brutal, hiding their thirst for power in rhetorical appeals to the historic role of the working class. His accounts of his trips to the Gold Coast, Spain, and Bandung similarly seemed to look to the West for solutions and regard Communism negatively. Cross Damon, however, is an unreliable narrator whose dying words express remorse for his amoral, apolitical individualism. Rather than representing a turn to existentialism, *The Outsider* allowed Wright to test theories of history, power, and being in a philosophical novel that ultimately rejected and mocked Damon's half-baked existential nihilism. Additionally, like most American leftists abroad during the McCarthy era, Wright was under constant duress, afraid he would be deported back to the United States and called to testify before the House Un-American Activities Committee. To protect himself from anticommunist witch hunts, in his travel narratives—funded partly by the CIA-sponsored Congress for Cultural Freedom—he employed the double-voiced discourse he had learned as a child to survive Jim Crow. His books were thus laced with pro-Western and anticommunist rhetoric to evade his American censors.

One tantalizing, if not wholly verifiable, possibility is that he was more than a fellow traveler in Paris. Joe Sims, cochair of the CPUSA, told me in 2023 that according to George B. Murphy Jr., Wright remained a clandestine Party member in exile. A comrade and journalist who served as editor-in-chief of the Washington, DC, *Afro American* in the late 1950s, Murphy was in touch with Wright throughout his self-exile. In 1980 or 1981, Sims recalls telling Murphy that he was unhappy with Wright because of his departure from the CPUSA, "and George scolded me, 'Young man you don't know anything about Richard Wright. You want to know about him, you ask me. I paid his dues all the while he was in Paris.'" Harrington, too, alludes to Wright's political afterlife in the Party. Shortly before the construction of the Berlin Wall, Harrington sought refuge from US surveillance in East Berlin, where he got a job illustrating American classics with Aufbau Verlag. Though circumspect about his CPUSA membership, he apparently joined in the 1930s or early 1940s.[8] In his essay on Wright's death, he praised socialist countries as the only places that had eliminated the cynical, corrupt state of affairs that existed in the United States, which had "throttled ... decency and democracy" and permitted anything in "the race for profit." Socialism, he declared, "represents a real danger to a broken-down system" that fueled America's anticommunist crusade. It was in this context that he claimed that Wright, despite having written *American Hunger*, was anything but anticommunist. As Joe Sims put it, however, his only evidence that Wright remained a dues-paying member of the CPUSA in Paris is George Murphy's "sterling reputation and word."[9]

In either case, Wright was expanding his orbit from the "ethics of Jim Crow" to Pan-Africanist and incipient postcolonial thought. He embarked on this path with some of the great socialist leaders and thinkers of his time, including his friend George Padmore, a top adviser to Ghanaian president Kwame Nkrumah. From 1945 to 1947, when Nkrumah returned to Ghana, he and Padmore worked together as joint secretaries of the organizing committee of the Pan-African Congress. They reunited in 1951 after Nkrumah's Convention People's Party (CPP) won its first general election and he formed his first government for the Gold Coast under colonial rule. That July, he invited Padmore to visit the Gold Coast "to chronicle the remarkable history of postwar events."[10] It was Padmore who urged Wright to visit two years later and obtained an official letter of invitation from Nkrumah. Wright's contributions to Pan-Africanist and Third World movements bolstered his denunciation of racism in America and increased his vulnerability to US surveillance. He was actively involved in several US civil rights cases at the same time, including the defenses of Willie McGee, wrongfully charged with rape of a white woman, and Henry Winston, a Black Communist and fellow Mississippian convicted of espionage under the Smith Act in 1948.

His antiracist politics also led him to reject essentialist theories of race, including that aspect of negritude that his friend John Gibbs St. Claire Drake described in 1965 as pseudoscientific, rife with "antiquated notions of biology and instinctual psychology." Weighing the value of negritude for its appreciation of African cultures against its reinforcement of racial stereotypes, Drake judiciously called the concept an important "subsidiary myth" that helped unify scattered descendants of the African diaspora with their African counterparts on the basis of shared suffering and hope for the future. Echoing Wright's sociological explanation of race, he added, "It is this common fate, not genes, which binds them together and reinforces the struggle against racism."[11] For African American intellectuals, Drake argued, the concept of negritude as a complex of African traits, known as "African survivals" in the United States, too closely mirrored white supremacist justifications of slavery, segregation, and inequality that African Americans had strived for centuries to overcome. As Robert Reid-Pharr more recently observed, the idea of a "black tradition," in which blackness is an inviolable category, supports the "same ideas [that] underwrite logics of segregation and apartheid."[12] Drake's essay situates Wright's critique of negritude in the context of the wider Black and Pan-African intellectual communities that informed it. Though accused of Western insensitivity toward Africans and Indonesians, Wright's concerns reflected these larger debates; like Drake, he sympathized with the appeal of negritude but insisted on a common humanity across racial lines and identified more and more strongly with the world's disinherited across national boundaries.

His portraits of Bigger Thomas in *Native Son* and Fishbelly (Rex) Tucker in *The Long Dream*—the one a lumpen, Black teenager whose father was lynched in the South and whose mother migrated to Chicago, the other a Mississippi-born son of a petit bourgeois undertaker, rentier, and pimp, Tyree Tucker, making regular payoffs to the town's corrupt white police chief—delineate not only the course of twentieth-century Jim Crow but also, prophetically, the "New Jim Crow," a term popularized by Michelle Alexander in her widely read 2010 book about mass incarceration in the age of color blindness. Wright understood that the Black bourgeoisie was subject to the same racial codes that trapped Bigger in Chicago slums, squeezed by a system in which "niggers ain't got no rights but them they *buy*," and that those who accrued property and wealth like Tyree extracted it from lower-class Black "whores and gamblers" in the form of rent and brothels like the one in which forty people died in a devastating fire, including Fish's girlfriend, Gladys. When he learns that Tyree is half-owner of the Grove, Fishbelly realizes that "he and his family had been living off the immoral earnings of Gladys! The money he had paid her for the right to sleep with her had found its way back into his own pocket! . . . He was a kind of superpimp." The brothel fire ultimately leads to Tyree's execution by police gunfire and Fish's imprisonment for two years on trumped-up rape charges. Finally set free from the local jail, Fish finds that the system by which Tyree collected fees for Police Chief Cantley is back in place; nothing has changed. Resolving to flee before Cantley kills him for refusing to give him Tyree's canceled checks, which implicate him in a bribery scheme, Fish debates whether to go North and, once there, whether to return to school or start a business. But when he receives a letter from his friend Zeke in France, he decides to join him, exclaiming, "Goddammit . . . he would go, go, go!" As Zeke writes from his army station in Orleans, not far from Paris, "France ain't no heaven, but folks don't kill you for crazy things. These white folks just more like real human beings."[13]

Objecting to the racial terror in *The Long Dream*, including scenes of public castration and lynching, many readers accused Wright of losing touch with a changed America, especially after *Brown v. Board of Education of Topeka*. Although he repeatedly expressed interest in going beyond race, he persisted in tracing Jim Crow through the 1940s into the 1950s and examining the psychologically complex, brutal form it took in the South in *The Long Dream* as well as the "historical roots and the emotional problems of western whites which make them aggressive toward colored peoples" in *Savage Holiday*, a 1954 crime novel with an almost entirely white cast of characters that critics routinely viewed as his only "nonracial novel."[14] However, in a 1956 interview, Wright told Roland Barthes that, in *Savage Holiday*, he had "attempted to deal with . . . the most important problem white people have to face: their moral dilemma," and had thus created a white New Yorker as the novel's protagonist. More than half a century later, Alexander's history of the New Jim Crow bears out Wright's definition of racism as a white problem that could have been resolved if federal troops had remained in the South to protect Reconstruction. But they did not, and Wright told *La Nef*, in response to a question about the malevolent white mob barring nine Black students from entering Little Rock High School in 1957, "Today racism has sunk deep roots in the United States, both in the North and in the South."[15] In an unfinished article from the early 1950s on the limits of civil liberties, he wrote, "It must be recalled that, despite a few single gains, the vast majority of Negroes are downright poor, and when a minority of that group, having the talent and the duty to express themselves, decide to remain silent to protect their private holdings, then the rest of the Negroes are left defenseless. . . . That is the stark truth of the situation." A rights-based strategy without deep structural change would empower only a handful of Black Americans, leaving the rest mired in poverty and de facto racism while creating a "moral problem" for the minority who might feel "bought" by a good job and hide that truth "in gratitude for what white US has given him."[16]

Wright's critique of liberal civil rights reforms reflects a Marxist analysis of the relationship of race and racism to class struggle, a theoretical perspective that emerges early in his career in "Blueprint for Negro Writing" and periodically resurfaces, often obliquely, recognizing class struggle and international solidarity as the driving forces in revolutionary change across racial, ethnic, and national identities and boundaries. He appreciated the primacy of class struggle in the CPUSA's antiracist programs but was critical of what he saw as its retreat from full support for Black freedom—particularly with respect to the Double V campaign to end fascism abroad and racism at home. Having early on criticized the Communists' knowledge of "common people," he challenged their class analysis with lumpen types like Bigger—unemployed, consigned to low-paid, nonindustrial, domestic jobs, engaged in crime—who have the potential to swing toward fascism or socialism. Like many fellow Black intellectuals and activists, he prioritized opposition to racism in all its forms, turning to Pan-African and Third World perspectives on class struggle for a more expansive definition of transnational labor.

In "Blueprint," he distinguished between Black bourgeois writers, "parasitic and mannered," who believed they could escape racial oppression by dint of individual merit, and the "unwritten and unrecognized" Black workers, whose embrace of religion, folktales, blues, and spirituals constituted forms of resistance to the inhumane conditions of slavery that had produced a distinctive, mass Black culture. It was necessary, he argued in "Blueprint," for Black Americans—especially writers, whose expressive capacities obliged them to do more than plead for justice from white America—to acknowledge the "nationalist character" of the struggle against Jim Crow and give voice to the majority's collective suffering, needs, and aspirations. However, it was equally necessary to "accept the nationalist implications of their lives, not in order to encourage them, but to change and transcend them." He further argued that the goals of Black nationalism could not be realized in capitalist America, and he called on Black writers to achieve "the highest pitch of social consciousness" to explain the "wider social connotations" and "revolutionary significance of these nationalist tendencies"; otherwise, they would "do a rank injustice to the Negro people and alienate their possible allies in the struggle for freedom."[17]

Although his later writing loses some of the clarity of "Blueprint" on the question of Black nationalism and class struggle, his grounding in Marxist dialectics shaped his perspective on race and racism not as natural or universal categories but as historically specific social divisions of labor in modern capitalism created by chattel slavery in the Americas. Works like *12 Million Black Voices* and his travel books suggest he understood that class struggle takes different forms throughout history, and it has manifested since the sixteenth century in the combined and uneven patterns of the global development of capitalism. A revolutionary program had to cut across national, ethnic, and racial differences to emancipate, as Marx and Engels put it, "the great mass of the people [who] are more and more falling into the proletariat, their situation becoming more wretched and intolerable in proportion to the increase in wealth of the bourgeoisie."[18] Through this lens, adjusted by firsthand knowledge of racial terror, Wright and other Black socialists focused their attention on anticolonial struggles for independence of peoples whose brutal oppression, like that of African Americans, according to the CPUSA's Black Belt thesis, made them a vanguard revolutionary force.

X-Ray Vision: A Predilection for What Was Real

Restless, unbroken, and driven by his Promethean talent, Wright found it impossible as a young Black man "to calculate, to scheme, to act, to plot all the time." He confessed to his classmate Gibbs that he "would remember to dissemble for short periods" but then he would "forget and *act straight and human again*" (emphasis added).[19] His insights into racial and class exploitation in his writing proceeded from his most notorious character, Bigger Thomas, to his least likable one, Cross Damon in *The Outsider*, and from Fishbelly (Rex) Tucker in *The Long Dream* and "Island of Hallucination" to police captain Ruddy Turner and fifteen-year-old Johnny Gibbs in the posthumously published novels *A Father's Law* and *Rite of Passage*. Together with his nonfiction works, these narratives stretch across stages of history and geographical distances, from the feudal South to Chicago slums to New York to Paris to the Gold Coast and beyond. *A Father's Law*, drafted in a burst of energy in 1960, and *Rite of Passage*, written in 1945 after the publication of *Black Boy*, reflect his lifelong preoccupation with racial injustice, class conflict, juvenile delinquency, and the consequences of social inequality and deprivation for both victims and perpetrators of crimes. He excelled in puncturing normalized views of individual criminality to expose the crimes of the state and its complicity in systemic oppression of the working-class, poor, white, and colored masses of people worldwide. Credited with first using the phrase "Black power"—as the title of his 1954 book on the Gold Coast—he spent his life deciphering the psychic and social costs of racism in relation to capitalist expansion on the backs of the multitudes.

By 1940, he had determined that neither white liberal sympathizers nor Black bourgeois reformers understood the Black working-class protagonist that was his primary subject in *Native Son*. With *Uncle Tom's Children*, he explains, "I had made an awfully naïve mistake. I found that I had written a book which even bankers' daughters could read and weep over and feel good about." But if white liberal catharsis over his short stories had convinced him to write a book "so hard and deep that they would have to face it without the consolation of tears," he also found fault with the CPUSA's organizational strategies, which "had missed the meaning of the lives of the masses, had conceived of people in too abstract a manner." He worried that his portrait of Bigger would confirm white reactionaries' racist stereotypes of Black people or convince them that he was "preaching hate against the whole white race," as Congressman Martin Dies had asserted in his denunciation of "The Ethics of Living Jim Crow"; it would cause Black and white comrades in the CPUSA to see him as an "individualist and dangerous element"; or it would incur the anger of the Black bourgeoisie, who would protest that he had portrayed the race negatively, representing its "anger and bitterness" rather than its "*best* traits."[20]

Thirteen years after *Native Son*, in his long-awaited second novel *The Outsider*, he created Bigger's intellectual doppelganger, Cross Damon, an educated Black Chicago postal worker entangled in domestic conflict and infidelity and consumed by Kierkegaardian dread and desire. In the opening scenes of the novel, after bantering with coworkers, Damon confronts his underage mistress Dot and his beleaguered, disapproving mother. Later, eating a hamburger at a luncheonette, he overhears a group of young Black men joking about scared white people hushing up colored men in flying saucers from Mars and Jupiter. "White folks in America, France, England, and Italy," they joke, "are the scaredest folks that ever lived on this earth. They're scareda Reds, Chinese, Indians, Africans, everybody...'cause they're guilty.... For four hundred years these white folks done made everybody on earth feel like they ain't human, like they're outsiders."[21] But the plot soon turns to Damon's nefarious murders and his own faked death. As an educated man who deliberately kills his adversaries, he is even more culpable than Bigger, expressing the same logic of racial oppression but reflecting Wright's disillusionment with the CPUSA, which also serves as a foil for the author's critique of the hollowness of his character's quasi-philosophical beliefs.

No more able than Bigger to escape from the circumstances that made him, Damon gasps on his deathbed, "I wanted to be free... to feel what I was worth... what living meant to me." Asked what he found, he tells District Attorney Ely Houston, "The search can't be done alone.... Alone a man is nothing."[22] Both *Native Son* and *The Outsider* reflect Wright's grasp of a dialectical materialist analysis of individuals and the sociohistorical conditions into which they are born. Five years after *The Outsider*, he applied the same Marxist analysis of class to Fishbelly Tucker and his father, Tyree, in *The Long Dream*, the last novel that appeared before Wright's death in 1960 and the prequel to "Island of Hallucination," his penultimate, unfinished book. If Damon is an apolitical, cynical pseudo-intellectual who engages even more coldly and abstractly in violent acts than Bigger, then Fishbelly is more akin to the young Richard Wright: a Black Mississippian growing up in an inhumane world of corruption, racial terror, police brutality, and betrayal. Fishbelly enjoys the bourgeois comforts of his father's lucrative, shady businesses, and although Wright was poor and often hungry, he similarly benefited from his maternal grandparents' middle-class status, aspirations, and values.

While Bigger and Cross Damon resonate with Wright's life in Chicago and New York, Fishbelly is drawn both from his creator's primal experience growing up in the Jim Crow South and from his exhilarating escape to Paris. The savage cruelty inflicted on Fishbelly by white townspeople, though greater than any Wright suffered, pervades his account of his own youth in *Black Boy*. Similarly, Fishbelly's florid interior monologue as he flies through the night sky over the Atlantic—derided by critics for its grandiloquence—expresses Wright's immense sense of desire, hope, and relief on his arrival in Paris in 1946. Awed by the city's beauty and welcomed by the American expatriate Gertrude Stein and the French intellectuals Sartre, Beauvoir, Camus, and others, he felt for the first time free of the racial oppression of mid-twentieth-century America. Many critics panned *The Long Dream* when it was published a little over a decade later in 1958, declaring that Wright had lost his bearings as an American writer in exile. As J. Saunders Redding put it in an unfavorable *New York Times* review, the novel "proves that Wright has been away too long.... He has cut the umbilical cord through which his art was fed and all that remains for it to feed on is the memory, fading, of righteous love and anger."[23]

More recent revelations about extensive CIA operations during the Cold War suggest that the bad reviews and Wright's difficulty finding publishers had less to do with the quality of his writing than with the climate of ideological conformity and fear instigated by anticommunist propaganda. Despite CIA surveillance and the political shift from the radical 1930s to the conservative 1950s, Wright refused to be silent about persistent racism in the United States, linking African American human rights to anticolonial struggles worldwide. His understanding of race and ethnicity as culturally produced and riven by class interests drew criticism from both "poets of negritude" invested in racial solidarity and the essential elements of a "Negro ethos" and Western imperialists happy to promote a primitivist racial ideology that minimized class conflict. Meanwhile, he strove with other Pan-African activists and intellectuals to forge a Marxist analysis of the development of capital based on centuries of accumulated wealth created by European colonization and the transatlantic slave trade. This viewpoint informed his critiques of the attribution of racial traits to "Negro" identity in conceptions of negritude; of racial consciousness, "deprived of historical perspective" at the Bandung Conference; and of the capacities of tribal Africa to achieve the modernization and industrialization of colonized nations quickly enough to sustain newly won or soon to come independence and join an international world order as equals.[24]

It was his consciousness of class conflict in relation to his firsthand experience of racial oppression that enabled him to imagine a sequel to *Native Son* that would take up the "woman question" and consider the racial geography of subjugation in that and other works in ways that are only beginning to be understood. He documented the human trafficking of poor Black women from the South to "slave markets" in Harlem and Brooklyn in the 1930s in his unpublished novel "Black Hope" about "the status of women in modern American society," and he punctured the myth of the Black rapist in other works, exposing the vulnerability of Black men to false charges of rape. Such charges concealed the neurotic desires and aggressions of white men *and* women while maintaining control over Black male and female bodies. In 1951, after the execution of Willie McGee for allegedly raping a white woman in Mississippi six years previously, Wright explained to a French audience in *La Droit de Vivre* that the problem was rooted in the political economy of plantation slavery, disposing of the question of McGee's guilt in a sentence. The "Negro press" had reported that McGee had been having a four-year, intimate relationship with a white woman, Wiletta Hawkins, when her traveling salesman husband discovered them together—"hence," Wright observed dryly, "the charge of rape."[25]

A year previously, Wright had helped found the French-American Fellowship (FAF), whose goals were "to promote social and cultural relations" and "heighten the consciousness of its members in relation to the urgent issues confronting the world today." Under his leadership, the FAF advocated for McGee as well as the Martinsville Seven, condemned to death for raping a white woman in Virginia. Like the Scottsboro Boys, these accused men became cause célèbres, both cases attracting widespread calls for clemency from supporters, including Sergei Prokofiev and Dmitri Shostakovich for the Martinsville Seven, and Albert Einstein, Jessica Mitford, and William Faulkner for McGee. Meanwhile, the NAACP and the CPUSA-affiliated Civil Rights Congress (CRC) vied to lead McGee's defense team, led by a young Bella Abzug. Capable of mounting an international campaign on McGee's behalf as it had done for the Scottsboro Boys, it was the CRC that pressured the United States to adhere in the postwar era to its purported democratic values. As Wright put it, reassuring French readers their protests had not hurt McGee's case, "Today the whites of Mississippi will hesitate and think hard and long before staging another McGee legal lynching. They now realize that the tide of world opinion is definitely against them and their criminal race code." A "moral victory," the campaign to save McGee underscored deeply rooted racism at the height of the Cold War as America pursued foreign policy and economic interests under a banner of democracy, badly stained by Jim Crow, in emerging independent nations.[26]

The stereotype of the Black rapist haunts Wright's work. We see it in his portrayal of Bigger Thomas, whose fear of being accused of rape turned him into a brutal murderer, and in Fishbelly Tucker, who eats a picture of a white woman in his wallet and faints because he is so terrified that the police will castrate him. Wright invokes this theme again, albeit humorously, in "Man of All Work," written in 1959 as a radio play and posthumously published in *Eight Men*. Unemployed cook Carl Owens and his wife Lucy, also jobless, have a young son, a newborn baby, and a mortgage to pay. Desperate for work, Carl searches through want ads, finding no jobs for Black men but many for female cooks, including one for a "Negro" who can also clean and care for children—work that Carl proves he can do by feeding his newborn daughter and caring for his bedridden wife and young son. This depiction of a racialized economy that emasculates and marginalizes Black male workers mirrors McGee's plight. According to the Black press, McGee, a domestic worker, had been seduced by his white employer Wiletta Hawkins, who threatened to accuse him of rape if he refused her sexual advances.

Determined to apply for the cook's job, Carl tries on his wife's dress, which fits him perfectly, and over her strenuous objections, he slips out of the house early the next morning dressed as a woman. Hired by Dave and Anne Fairchild as "Lucy Owens," Carl learns from Mrs. Fairchild that her husband is a lecherous drunkard whose sexual abuse of the former cook—their precocious daughter Lily calls it "wrestling"—led to her dismissal. When a drunken Dave pursues "Lucy" in the same unrestrained manner, his wife Anne surprises them. Hurt and jealous, she grabs a rifle and shoots Carl, quickly regretting that she had not shot her husband instead. A brother-in-law doctor determines that "Lucy" is still alive and reveals that she is a man. After devising scenarios to lay blame on Carl—he was caught stealing; he was threatening to rape Mrs. Fairchild—the couple is convinced by the doctor to negotiate a deal with Carl to keep silent in return for a sum of money, which he cleverly sets at $200 plus medical expenses, just enough to pay off his mortgage.

In addition to exposing the structural economic disadvantage experienced by working-class Black men in comparison to both white and Black women, Wright's story suggests that despite the power of the "white paternal order," Black men resisted rather than imitated white male sexual violence against Black men (and women), even as they were "castrated by white racism, existing only as an emasculated (negation) of white masculinity."[27] While this interpretation of the story by Tommy J. Curry insightfully tracks the complex political economic and psychosexual elements of the oppression of Black men—countering stereotypes undergirding cases like McGee's—another reading of "Man of All Work" is that what appears to be a story of emasculation is also, if not more so, an antiracist, feminist appreciation of women's work and oppression. The opening scenes of Carl feeding baby Tina and caring for his wife Lucy after the exhausting labor of childbirth demonstrate his kindness, gentleness, and domestic talent, all traits that could be seen as emasculating, but—truer to a textual reading of his rejection of gender stereotypes—signal Wright's feminist consciousness and perhaps his own observations as a father of two daughters. Thus, while the idea of Carl wearing a dress mortifies Lucy, he has no qualms about it; he also declares that gender differences are not so great as they may seem, in the way men and women walk, for example.

Finally, in the story's denouement, Lucy exacts a promise from Carl that he will never again dress in her clothes to which he replies,

— Ha, ha, Lucy you don't have to ask. *I was a woman for almost six hours and it almost killed me.*
— But Carl, I warned you. *It's not easy for a man to act like a woman.*
— Gosh, Lucy, *how do you women learn it? . . . I didn't know it was so hard.* (emphasis added).[28]

Wright's interrogation of structural and sexual exploitation of Black men is complemented by his support for women's rights and awareness of the triple oppression of Black women. He understood the interrelationship of race and gender within and between class differences in hierarchical social relations. One element of "Man of All Work" missed by many readers, including Baldwin, whose praise for the story focused on "the humiliation the Negro male endures," is the egalitarian sweetness of Carl and Lucy's relationship and Carl's staunch determination to protect his family from financial ruin. Like the assumptions about race that render Wright's meanings opaque to those who read his works through the lens of their own biases, this aspect of the story is important to uncover in addressing the unresolved question of his perspective on women's rights and status and as a counterpoint to critiques of his misogyny and sexism.

The sociogeographical mapping of these gendered and racial histories occurs throughout his writing as he moves from the Jim Crow South to Chicago to New York City to Paris and traces the oppression of African descendants and colonial subjects in a world of expanding markets and superexploitation of Black labor—enslaved, penal, and low waged. Released from the hell of Clintonville, Mississippi, into the heavens above as his plane crosses the Atlantic,

Fishbelly beholds, however fleetingly, the "vast, wheeling populations of ruled stars swarming in the convened congresses of skies anchored amidst nations of space."[29] Demarcating Wright's proto-ecological premonitions, Fish's flight to Paris at the end of *The Long Dream* was for Bigger an unattainable dream, symbolized by the skywriting plane high above Chicago's South Side that he and Gus watch spell out "USE SPEED GASOLINE." Says Bigger wistfully to Gus, "I *could* fly a plane if I had a chance. . . . God, I'd like to fly up there in the sky," to which Gus retorts, "God'll let you fly when He gives you your wings up in heaven."[30] This consciousness of the contradictory utopian promises of modernity suffuses *Native Son*'s portrayal of both excluded Black youth like Bigger and, presciently, the ecological destruction wreaked by Big Oil.

Wright's appreciation of nature can be seen in his paean to the Mississippi delta in *Black Boy* and in the 4,000 haiku he wrote, many at Le Moulin d'Anduve, a writing community in the French countryside toward the end of his life. The Promethean energy he drew from nature as a small boy, however, was refracted by the racial codes and unequal environmental impacts of disasters like the Great Flood of 1927 on the Black Belt communities in which he lived. Such forces of "second nature" demarcated African American activity, especially but not only in the South. By linking industrial development and pollution to oppressed working-class Black Americans in early stories like "Silt," Wright anticipates Bigger's murderousness in his confession that maybe white people were right in not allowing Black people to fly, "'cause if I took a plane up I'd take a couple of bombs along and drop 'em as sure as hell."[31] The racial barrier to flying infuriates Bigger even as he admires the industrial economy that enabled aviation's invention, production, and increasingly widespread use, relying on oil and gas extracted from the earth, destroying the environment, and restricting access for Black youth like Bigger and Gus to the spectacular achievements and devastating consequences of capitalist modernity. With the economy of poetry, the words USE SPEED GASOLINE underscore what Wright described in "I Choose Exile" as America's "desire for materialistic power that dominates us all."[32] While he could not have anticipated the existential threat posed by climate change, gasoline as an advertised commodity represents Bigger's unattainable desire to fly a gas-fueled plane as well as America's emergence as a world power and the intensifying contradiction between development and sustainability.

Hungry for books as a young man, for "new ways of looking and seeing" at twelve years old, he had a precocious "conception of life that no experience could erase, a predilection for what was real that no argument could ever gainsay . . . a notion as to what life meant that no education could ever alter . . .

that the meaning of life came only when one was struggling to wring a meaning out of meaningless suffering."[33] Through disciplined reading and engagement in radical politics from 1932 to the end of his life, he struggled to wring those meanings from suffering he knew firsthand. For better or worse, he never toed any party or political line uncritically. This trueness to his own vision was born at least in part in the clarity of pubescence recalled by the renowned writer in his mid-thirties, reinforced by having by then become the putative father of African American literature and a very public Communist who broke with the Party and took refuge in Paris with other Black expatriates fleeing US racism and the political chill of the Cold War.

Paris Noir: Cold War Spies and Illusions of Freedom

According to official reports, Richard Wright died of a heart attack on November 28, 1960, at the Eugène Gibez Clinic. It was rumored, then and now, that he was assassinated, but Fabre found not the "slightest bit of proof" to substantiate that. Nor did he believe that Wright posed a sufficient threat to US national security interests to make him a "marked man." Nevertheless, he "could not automatically conclude that Wright had *not* been the victim of the 'evil designs' of the CIA" (emphasis added).[34] More than thirty years after Wright's death, giving voice to long-held suspicions, Ollie Harrington declared in a talk at Wayne State University that he had "never met a Black person who did *not* believe that Wright was done in. By whom, I don't know. I've no idea. There are so many possibilities."[35] As Cold War tensions heightened, Wright "was almost continuously under surveillance and they [US operatives] were hostile to him."[36] According to a CIA report filed in 1969 by Paul Chalemsky, a young mathematician named Ed Dubinsky told a CIA agent codenamed Petunia that he had met Julia Herve-Wright in Ghana, where he had been teaching, and that she accused "his best friend" at that time of killing her father, Richard Wright. Initially doubtful, Dubinsky came to believe Julia because the unnamed friend, almost certainly Richard Gibson, never denied the charge and had admitted to being a CIA agent. Chalemsky's report concludes, "Wright was killed by the CIA because he had just finished a manuscript on the use of American blacks abroad by the government."[37] That manuscript was "Island of Hallucination."

Arriving in Paris in 1954, Gibson was one of the young African American writers whom Wright suspected of spying; another was William Gardner Smith, who had already published three novels and would go on to publish a fourth, *The Stone Face*, set in Black Paris during the final years of the Algerian struggle for independence in 1960–61. Both Smith and Gibson worked at Agence France-Presse (AFP), and both were at the center of what came to be known as the Gibson affair. The plot of "Island of Hallucination," Wright's unpublished sequel to *The Long Dream*, hinges on the affair and half-satirizes, half-retaliates against the spy-ridden Black expatriate café community. As one observer described this scene of escalating Cold War tensions, "Everybody thought everybody else was spying on someone or other for somebody."[38] Wright's characters are composites of real people, including Harrington, Gibson, Smith, Baldwin, and C. L. R. James, which are sufficiently recognizable that Ellen Wright restricted access to the manuscript, which was opened to researchers at Yale's Beinecke Library only in 1996. Set against the backdrop of the Cold War in 1951, three years before the outbreak of the Franco-Algerian War, the unfinished manuscript is haunted by the question of support for the Algerian National Liberation Front (Front de Libération Nationale, FLN) and how it fractured Black Paris, puncturing the illusion of France as a refuge from racism and triggering the Gibson affair.

The real-life cloak-and-dagger story began in 1956 when Harrington sublet his apartment in the rue de Seine to Gibson, who refused to leave on Harrington's return to Paris from the Côte d'Azur. Afraid of drawing attention to his ties to the Communist Party, Harrington took no legal action but verbally confronted Gibson at the Café Tournon and beat him badly enough outside the apartment to land him in the hospital. A year later, Gibson forged Harrington's signature on a letter published in *Life* and the *London Observer* that criticized French policy in Algeria. Appearing a few weeks before the United Nations Security Council was planning to discuss the question of Algerian self-determination, the letter put Harrington at risk of deportation for meddling in French politics as a nonresident. Wright believed a CIA plot against him was driving the affair, and he counseled Harrington to seek legal representation. Whether Gibson was arrested and convicted of forgery, as Fabre reports, or not, as Gibson claimed, the affair heightened suspicions that he was a CIA agent and divided *Paris Noir* amid a sea of accusations and shifting loyalties. Adding to Wright's worries, the following November, *Time* published "Amid the Alien Corn," an article about Black expatriates that quoted him declaring, "The Negro problem in America has not changed in 300 years." Having denied *Time*'s request for an interview, Wright was outraged by the attribution and threatened a lawsuit for what he saw as another case of forgery and character defamation.

The Franco-Algerian War was the crucible in which these internal battles were fought. Forced to withdraw from Vietnam after the Battle of Dien Bien Phu in 1954, France became embroiled in the Algerian war, seeking to retain its last colony as the newly formed FLN, inspired by Ho Chi Minh and other revolutionary leaders, launched its war of independence. It was the Franco-Algerian War that Gibson said motivated him and William Gardner Smith to concoct the scheme of publishing letters with Black expatriates' forged signatures to build support for the FLN. As a light-skinned African American easily mistaken as Algerian or North African, Gibson believed he had experienced French racism in ways that Wright and other African Americans had been spared. But Smith broke relations with Gibson and disavowed any connection to the affair after it became public, even as Gibson insisted, somewhat contradictorily, that their plan was to give plausible deniability to other Black radicals silenced by their precarious status in France by forging their names to shield them from reprisal. According to Gibson, Smith was supposed to notify the signatories in advance, but never did so.

In April 2018, the National Archives released thousands of documents related to John F. Kennedy's assassination, including three CIA files confirming that Gibson was an agent from at least 1965 to 1977. Gibson got a job in 1957 at CBS News in New York; in 1960, he cofounded the Fair Play for Cuba Committee (FPCC). He was a person of interest to the FBI because he knew FPCC member Lee Harvey Oswald, who was arrested for Kennedy's assassination and murdered in detention two days later by the nightclub owner Jack Ruby. Gibson claims to have left the FPCC in 1962 to protect its reputation after he was called to testify before the Senate Internal Affairs Subcommittee as a suspected foreign agent. In Algeria, where he was alleged by FPCC and FLN associates to be a CIA agent, he worked for the FLN newsletter *Révolution Africaine*. In her groundbreaking study of the Congress for Cultural Freedom (CCF), Frances Stonor Saunders observes that few Western intellectuals escaped the CIA-sponsored anticommunist network of cross-cultural and funding opportunities; although Wright, too, was rumored to be a State Department mole, his fears of persecution were well founded.[39] As early as 1951, the US Information Service solicited an essay by Baldwin on racial injustice for *France-USA*, intended to defuse Wright's dogged condemnation of American racism. As Fabre notes, US propaganda operations in Paris "felt they must disprove Wright's picture of the racial situation."[40]

Criticism of Wright's failure to speak out in support of the Algerian revolution has persisted. In a mostly insightful essay about the relationship between the Black expatriate community and the *Paris Review*, Craig Lanier Allen refers to Wright's "deafening silence on the Algerian Question," asserting that he "was a committed 'race man' in the traditional mold" who argued that "the world was no longer divided between left and right but black and white."[41]

A number of sources, however, including Wright's daughter Julia, maintain that he chose silence out of necessity while quietly supporting the Algerian forces.[42] Contrary to portrayals of him as indifferent to the racial oppression of North Africans in France, or complacent in his somewhat privileged role as an African American expatriate, Julia Wright insists that he "wholeheartedly condemned the colonial war conducted by France in Algeria" and recalls Beauvoir visiting her family's apartment bearing the "latest news" about FLN activities.[43] Harrington likewise affirms that both Wright and he "were sympathetic to the Algerians, but we couldn't mention it." Wright wrote to Sablonière on August 28, 1957, that "France is sinking each day, each hour. We may have a dictatorship here before the year is over. A Fascist one! It is strange. And it will now have to happen. Poor mankind."[44]

Whether or not Wright died of natural causes, he was exhausted from bouts of dysentery, Cold War espionage, internecine betrayals, and left sectarian politics, beleaguered by "a fake Stalinist or Trotskyist by day [and] . . . a G-man at night."[45] He was anxious about attacks on his reputation, negative book reviews, fast-depleting finances, and difficulty publishing new work. He was also, Saunders observes, "the first casualty in the Kulturekampf," quietly cast out of the "Non-Communist Left" (NCL), as it was known, an informal group of ex-Communists and left-leaning intellectuals cultivated to convey anticommunist propaganda in the CIA's ideological war against the Soviet Union. In 1949, the Soviet Cominform (Communist Information Bureau) held the World Congress for Peace in Paris. Despite the CCF's propaganda campaigns, including its distribution that same year of *The God That Failed*, to which, of course, Wright had contributed, the World Congress was attended by 2,000 delegates from seventy-five countries and endorsed by well-known writers and artists including Paul Robeson, Pablo Picasso, and Charlie Chaplin. In response, the CCF organized a counterconference, sponsored by the NCL newspaper *Franc-Tireur*, which backfired. A dismal affair whose "barely concealed anti-Americanism" disappointed the organizers, the International Day of Resistance to Dictatorship and War resulted in Wright's unofficial expulsion from the "*The God That Failed* gang . . . because his break with Stalinism was made 'more on personal than on political grounds,' and he showed 'no understanding of its true nature.'"[46]

Gibson's induction into the cultural cold war began during his undergraduate studies at Kenyon College, home of the *Kenyon Literary Review*, founded by the New Criticism pioneer John Crowe Ransom and funded by the CIA. In 1951, Gibson published "A No to Nothing" in the magazine, attacking "Negro literature" as artistically deficient and warning young Black writers not to join the "motley band of puerile imitators of Richard Wright," whom he derided as "a doubtless sincere but defective thinker."[47] Meanwhile, the *Paris Review*, established in 1953 by Peter Matthiessen, Harold L. Humes, and George Plimpton, was a center of CIA-sponsored cultural influence in 1950s Paris. A photograph of Wright in front of Notre-Dame with Matthiessen, who had been recruited to the CIA by the Yale professor Norman Holmes Pearson, and fellow *Review* editor Max Steele appears to affirm the city as a refuge for African Americans escaping US racism. The supposedly apolitical stance of the *Review*—a journal that Wright helped launch but never liked, according to Steele—can be traced to New Criticism's study of literature through ahistorical, self-contained, "close readings" of texts, rooted in the Southern Agrarians' defense of southern traditions.[48] In addition to its covert ideological agenda, the well-funded, preeminent literary magazine displaced many small rival journals by denigrating political literature and punishing authors like Wright who persisted in telling "bitter truths."

On the other hand, according to Irwin Shaw, *Paris Review* editors "went off on no crusades, . . . did not seem to be tempted by the Left, either French, American or Russian," and "might be termed capitalists, [but] were not intense about the system which cradled them." Defending this stance in his preface to the first issue of the *Review*, William Styron declared, "I think that if we have no axes to grind, no drums to beat, it's because it seems to us—for the moment, at least—that the axes have all been ground, the drumheads burst with beating."[49] These "White Collar Bohemians," as *Harper's Bazaar* had called them, seemed impervious not only to the intensification of civil rights struggles in the United States but also to the significance of the 1956 Bandung Conference and the burgeoning anticolonial movement. In an oft-cited, withering comparison of American racism to French universalism, Wright had written in 1951: "I tell you frankly that there is more freedom in one square block of Paris than there is in the entire United States of America."[50] It was this Paris that he entered in 1946 on his first visit to France and that persuaded him to return to live there permanently a year later.

But by 1953, as Allen points out, the photograph of the three men in front of Cathédrale Notre-Dame could already be read as evincing a "specter of surveillance" in which Wright was standing next to one man, Matthiessen, paid to surveil him, and another whose associations with the *Paris Review* made him suspect. The freedom of one square block of Paris had become severely compromised by pervasive US counterintelligence operations attacking the Soviet Union and unrepentant Marxists like Wright. And by the time he embarked in 1958 on "Island of Hallucination," the second of a trio of novels that began with *The Long Dream* and would conclude with a third novel to be set, not surprisingly, in Algeria, France's romance with African American intellectuals and artists had revealed its racial hypocrisies and brutalities as Paris became a center for Cold War espionage—an ideological battleground between communism and capitalism in which socialist revolutions and national liberation movements were rocking the world order, and the West, led by the United States, was covertly and overtly combatting them.

Wright's gnawing desire for freedom in a deracialized world and his initial enjoyment of it in Paris resonates with his aspirations as a nineteen-year-old leaving the terror of the Jim Crow South for Chicago "in search of the warmth of other suns." Just as the hopes and dreams of southern Black migrants were at best deferred by the racial oppression and harsh conditions they encountered in the urban North, the French universalism that had given Wright a sense of belonging in Paris had succumbed to Cold War antagonisms in the midst of intensifying anticolonial struggles, pitting the West against colonized masses of peoples of color. Leaving Memphis in 1927 for the promise of freedom and a better life in Chicago, Wright had been dismayed by the *"flat black stretches"* of the city, lined with crowded, rat-infested, South Side kitchenettes. A quarter of a century later, the Paris that he had once described as civilized, "a land of refuge," had become a treacherous island of hallucination swarming with spies and counterspies as France engaged in a brutal war in Algeria and oppressed Algerian migrants, who suffered under second-class citizenship and intense racial discrimination in Parisian slums.

This pattern of hopeful transit "between the shores of dread and desire"—South to North, Midwest to East Coast, America to Europe—recurs at the end of *The Long Dream* in Wright's description of Fishbelly's departing flight to Paris. On board the plane, surrounded by white passengers, he feels a roiled sense of freedom from the racial terror that led to his father's murder by police and to his own imprisonment for more than a year on false rape charges, which he experiences as "a free gesture of faith welling up out of a yearning to be at last somewhere home." But even before he arrives at Paris Orly Airport in the opening pages of "Island of Hallucination," the limits of French republican values are tested by racial slurs and stereotyping from other passengers, such as "That nigger's being spoilt as sure as God made green apples and when he gets back home he'll be fit for only tar and feathers." Next, at a stopover in Shannon, Ireland, French con artists swindle him out of $2,000 with promises of cheap rent and sex. Although he knew about the confidence game, "he had never heard of its being used against black men with sex as the bait, with racial balm as the lure, and sympathy as the comeon." The methods and stakes were different, but the wellspring of racism was the same.[51]

Growing up Black in Mississippi had not prepared Fish for Paris, where underlying France's color-blind ethos of racial equality were stereotypes of Black people as primitive, exotic, and gullible—patronizing attitudes that crystallized for Wright as racial discrimination and repressive policing of North African migrants on the outskirts of Paris increased in response to the intensifying guerrilla activity of the FLN in Algiers. Wright's 1957 radio play "Man, God Ain't Like That," written a year before he embarked on "Island of Hallucination," and published as a story in *Eight Men*, skewers a white jet-setting couple's exoticizing degradation of Babu, an African man they run over with their car on a dark, rainy night in the jungle in an unspecified location in Africa. Babu becomes a model for the husband John's paintings and a devoted servant who asserts that John is God. When the couple takes him back to Paris like a trophy, Babu ends up murdering John, evoking Melville's mutinous Babo in *Benito Cereno*. He openly confesses to the murder, but the detectives refuse to believe him and decide to reopen the case as a crime of passion committed by Odile Dufour, John's illicit lover. Along similar lines, in "Island of Hallucination" Wright "ridicules the infatuation with blackness in French culture, even as he will praise the indifference of French legal institutions toward race."[52]

Fishbelly tours Parisian nightlife, replete with pimps, prostitutes, criminals, and spies, guided by Mechanical, a queer Black writer and Trotskyist at the heart of the novel who is a blend of Gibson, Smith, and, most infamously, if least true to fact, Baldwin. It is Mechanical, while working with French police to expose Stalinists, who writes a militant letter to *Life* denouncing Ned Harrison as a "commy." Bearing a resemblance to both Ollie Harrington and Wright, Ned Harrison is a rotund, older Black lawyer who also mentors Fishbelly. As Mechanical types the letter, he crows, "Ned's cooked!," then forges Bill Hart's signature and brazenly rejoices that Harrison will be deported from France. According to Gibson, "I turn up as Hart, 'the superspy from Rome who spied on spies.'"[53] Although Gibson denied he was a CIA operative, he was accused of involvement in US counterintelligence efforts to destabilize Black and Third World radical movements in the United States, France, Africa, Cuba, and Algeria by contemporaries including Wright, Harrington, and other regulars at the Café Tournon, along with E. Franklin Frazier, Julian Mayfield, and Shirley Graham Du Bois. As Charisse Burden-Stelly puts it, Gibson and other Black spies who "supplied government agencies with a multitude of information about Black and Third World radical

An animated Richard Wright at the Café Tournon. Dominique Berretty via Getty Images.

movements, organizations, and activism reveal the treacherous terrain freedom fighters were forced to navigate."[54]

Mechanical and Ned Harrison introduce Fishbelly to the Tournon community of African American, African, and Caribbean writers, artists, and intellectuals and Black GIs. The dreams and nightmares that haunted Fish in *The Long Dream* persist in Paris, with a phantasmagorical mix of coffins, his father, and white temptresses in one nightmare and, in another, Police Chief Cantley burying a coffin filled with coins that Fish opens to find Mechanical dressed as a woman. One of Fish's first sexual encounters is with Anita, a doll-like prostitute with paraffin-inflated breasts and an invisible navel. Through Anita, he meets a troupe of stripteasers who take advantage of him until, like Tyree, he starts doing business with them at the GI base in Évreux, where Wright had been collecting interviews with Black American soldiers. He falls in love with Yvette, a French communist from an affluent family, reminiscent of Mary Dalton, who exoticizes Black men as "wholesome and brimming with life."[55] The story of intrigue climaxes in Part Four, "Parenthood," in which Fish has to choose between Yvette, who disappears after her brother denounces Fish as a Communist, and Marie-Rose, the girl he seduces in

Yvette's absence. Meanwhile, having been charged with the crime of forging the revolutionary letter, Mechanical spectacularly commits suicide by leaping off the top of Notre-Dame. Anticipating the third, unwritten novel set in Algeria, in which Fish assumes adult commitments and responsibilities, Harrison tells him, "When you can accept responsibility for what you do, then you are starting to grow up, to be free."[56]

Echoing Damon's dying words in *The Outsider*, Harrison also tells Fishbelly, "No man can stand absolutely alone and make any meaning out of life."[57] Had Wright lived to write the third book in the trilogy, he had planned to tell the story of Fish's travels with Yvette and their soon-to-be born child from Paris to Algeria to West Africa to New York, depicting his liberation from the racial stigma of his youth to his political education abroad to his embrace of adulthood and its responsibilities. Against the backdrop of the escalating Franco-Algerian War and the global implications of Wright's works from his earliest militant poetry to his nonfiction books about colonialism and fascism, "Island of Hallucination" can be seen not as tell-all, pulp-fiction revenge but rather as a cautionary tale of the poisonous influence of CIA informers and provocateurs on Black Paris and the necessity of building a transnational revolutionary consciousness. As Maxwell observes, "'Island of Hallucination' is a guidebook to an international black metropolis inescapably molded by state surveillance and thereby forced toward self-renovation."[58] Beyond "self-renovation," Wright sought to work through intensifying mid-twentieth-century contradictions of global capitalist expansion.

No Race, No Country: Spinning Poems of Light Out of Gathering Darkness

In her introduction to the posthumous publication of her father's haiku in 1998, Julia Wright notes that the Cold War was an "onslaught against the deepest springs of his genius," but he continued "to spin these poems of light out of the gathering darkness." He began writing haiku in the summer of 1959, inspired by a young South African friend, the writer Peter Abrahams, who lent him R. H. Blythe's four-volume study of the art form. Coping with illness that often confined him to bed in Paris, he had written 4,000 poems by March 1960. He did not know he was nearing death, but he had suffered from amoebic dysentery and was weak and in pain. Julia Wright recalls that he took his binder of haiku everywhere he went during the last months of his life as he worked on revisions of "Island of Hallucination" and a new novel, *A Father's Law*. She describes the room where he wrote before the poems were typed and bound, where "he would hang pages and pages of them up, as if to dry, on long metal rods strung across the narrow office areas of his tiny sunless studio in Paris."[59] Fascinated by the modernist tenor of haiku, diligently studying its traditional forms, he shivered with familiar creative impulses as he set out "to bring the life and consciousness of a black American" to the centuries-old poetic practice.[60]

The thousands of poems echo his paeans to nature in *Black Boy*, in which he expressed his wonderment as a child at the fierce beauty of his surroundings in rural Mississippi. But even as the haiku reaffirm his appreciation of nature, they demarcate the geographical and social ecologies of racial segregation and the global history that shaped the experience of African Americans and peoples of emerging and newly independent Third World nations, whose mutual fate he understood was intertwined and indissoluble. Writing haiku enabled him to dwell in the solitude and quiet of nature, and to keep writing in the throes of pain and fever, but it was not primarily a retreat from racial oppression or revolutionary politics. Instead, haiku gave him a new aesthetic form in which to interrogate interanimated social and natural worlds, recovering the place of human existence in nature and the nature of human existence in poems about tenements, rats, Black workers, and paying rent. With this proto-ecological consciousness, he saw that the same forces of history that alternately trapped and freed him as an African American from the US South were ravaging the lands of the global dispossessed with whom he identified and for whom he believed that another world was possible.

The 817 poems in *Haiku: The Last Poems of an American Icon* invoke themes of nature, illness, loneliness, trains, ships, dolls (perhaps those of his daughters), scarecrows, anger, grief, and loss. They are "hymns to nature" but also cartographies of natural cruelties and ironies and social histories—tenements and jazz, blackness and nakedness, quiet country fields and desolate cityscapes in a unity of opposites, spirit and matter, present and future, reflecting and breaking from the idealism of traditional haiku. Following the classical Japanese form of three lines, seventeen syllables, the where, when, and what, and a syllogistic epiphany or insight, Wright rigorously practiced writing haiku even as he transformed it, reclaiming the nature of his boyhood that gave him solace and stirred his imagination while resisting the depoliticization of Japanese haiku in his intuitions of the essence of a moment. As he had done in his early poems, he mapped the forces and relations of production that drove human history, dividing the world into a dominant few who plundered the wealth and natural resources of the disinherited many. He wrote about cats, dogs, bees, sparrows, snails, consumptive men, blind men, corpses, crows cawing, music, summer sunsets, autumn sunlight, and cold winter seas. Like Japanese poems inspired by nature and seasonal change, many of his haiku return to the "coded meanings" of events he witnessed as a boy in verdant Mississippi gardens, on bucolic country roads, and at the Mississippi River that swirled below the bluffs of Natchez and "spoke with a cryptic tongue":

> 240
> In a red sunset
> A frog commands the night wind
> To roll out a moon.
>
> 261
> A night of spring stars:
> Waves breaking beyond the wall
> Have a dark blue sound.[61]

In her biography of Wright, based partly on her friendship with him in the 1930s, Margaret Walker described his sense of humor as "ribald, risqué, and clever." She recalls Arna and Alberta Bontemps' recollection of him in Paris in late September 1960, two months before his death, as "the same jovial Dick" with "infectious laughter, good humor, and contagious charm."[62] That wry humor surfaces in his haiku as tongue-in-cheek commentary on human interactions with insects and other animals, and a funny, urbane image of a dog's territorial marking of a tree:

> 11
> You moths must leave now;
> I am turning out the light
> And going to sleep.
>
> 22
> With a twitching nose
> A dog reads a telegram
> On a wet tree trunk.
>
> 514
> "Say, Mr. Beetle,
> Are you taking a detour
> Crawling on my knee?"

The theme of blackness signals his aesthetic intent to master haiku and find solace in nature as he convalesced, often in the French countryside, and to bend the form to fit the arc of his life and work. Rather than breaking from the past or retreating from politics, the poems reflect the continuity of his artistic vision. He portrays the hard labor of Black women and men conditioned by the elements of sun, water, and snow that connect them to nature's beauty and expose them to its harshness.

60

Sun is glinting on
A washerwoman's black arms
In cold creek water.

609

Black men with big brooms
Sweeping streets in falling snow
Are absorbed by flakes.

Black children play naked in the streets, innocent yet subjected to alleyways instead of landscaped yards, chasing a gray cat that might under other circumstances have been a rat, a rodent that appears throughout the collection, like the one Bigger kills at the beginning of *Native Son*. In another poem, green cockleburs in a boy's "wooly hair" offer a potentially bucolic image except that, as Wright probably would have known, the plant is poisonous.

429

Naked black children
Chasing down an alleyway
After a gray cat.

455

The green cockleburs
Caught in the thick wooly hair
Of the black boy's head.

In haiku about cities, he fuses the traditional form with the artistic focus of his earliest work, such as the terrain of the war between Black and white boys hurling cinders at each other, or Bigger's flight from the law, during which he sees a sign—THIS PROPERTY IS MANAGED BY SOUTH STREET REAL ESTATE COMPANY—and observes that Mr. Dalton owned both the company and the house in which the Thomas family paid "eight dollars a week for one rat-infested room."[63] Wright pushed the boundaries of haiku to include scenes of urban tenements, lice, and rats, signifying their relation to nature just as crows caw in a cornfield or frogs croak at sunset, and demarcating lines of class and race that set them apart from bourgeois households.

253
From a tenement,
The blue jazz of a trumpet
Weaving autumn mists.

356
An Indian summer
Heaps itself in tons of gold
Over Nigger Town.

459
I am paying rent
For the lice in my cold room
And the moonlight too.

453
The sound of a rat
Gnawing in the winter wall
Of a rented room.

The motif of illness weaves throughout the collection, reflecting his own bouts of illness and empathy with others, learned by bearing witness to his mother's deteriorating health, her suffering "a symbol ... of the meaningless pain and the endless suffering" that "set the emotional tone of my life."[64]

224
While convalescing,
The red roses have no smell,
Gently mocking me.

243
Leaving the doctor,
The whole world looks different
This autumn morning.

He hints at his profound grief at the loss of his mother, two months after the death of his editor Edward Aswell—a man, he wrote to Paul Reynolds, "the like of which, as an editor and friend, I don't think I shall find again soon in this life."

186
From these warm spring days,
I can still see her sad face
In its last autumn.

565
A slow autumn rain:
The sad eyes of my mother
Fill a lonely night.

Along with loneliness and life's ephemerality, the haiku express a philosophical primacy of social and natural collectivity over individual ego, echoing Dickinson here:

1
I am nobody:
A red sinking autumn sun
Took my name away.

508
It is September,
The month in which I was born;
And I have no thoughts.

After her father's funeral at Père Lachaise Cemetery on December 3, 1960, where he was cremated holding a copy of *Black Boy*, Julia Wright read through his haiku and picked the poem below as emblematic of his life and work.

647
Burning out its time,
And timing its own burning,
One lonely candle.

In a photograph of Wright by Harriet Crowder shortly before his death, the light chisels his cheeks, defining his hairline and the corners of his mouth, molding his lips, eyes alive, one side of his face dark, the other illumined. He looks into the camera lens with a frank, intimate, knowing expression, as if he is gazing back at us as we study the photograph, speaking to us across time, echoing Whitman's rapturous call to future generations: "I am with you, you men and women of a generation, or ever so many generations hence."[65] In one haiku, he gestures to a wider world in the simple act of selling cows and giving the pasture back to the commons.

778
Having sold his cows,
His wide green pasture becomes
A part of the world.

In another, he reminds us of what never was but still might be. It is #308 that speaks powerfully and poignantly of an America—and a world—that he yearned for but never had and that never was.

> 308
> A sleepless spring night:
> Yearning for what I never had,
> And for what never was.

WRIGHT HAD OTHER LONGINGS that kept him awake that sleepless spring night—his illness, anxiety about his daughters, his faltering marriage, a rather unappealing, demeaning lover (according to Hazel Rowley's description of her), his financial straits, continuing obstacles to publishing his work, and always the swirling, fast-changing state of a world he sought to change, a world in which the Silent Generation, as Styron put it, had "no axes to grind, no drums to beat ... because it seems ... that the axes have all been ground."[66] Wright never stopped grinding axes. Nor did he abandon America, as many of his critics maintained, though he fled from its systemic racism and J. Edgar Hoover's ever watchful FB Eyes, only to realize by the late 1950s that Paris was no refuge from either one. The America he cared about, the promise of its earliest declarations of freedom and equality, was a nation inextricably bound to the fate of the world. Back in New York in early 1947 after his first trip to Paris, he told *PM's Sunday Picture News*, "The Negro problem of America is not an American problem. It is a world problem of colonials all over the world." Asked why he had returned to the United States, he replied, "I live here.... My work is here. My main job is in this country.... I belong here.... I was fashioned in this particular kind of hell." But half a year later, having gone back to Paris for an indefinite stay, he would tell *Nuit et Jour*, "To be American in the United States means to be white, protestant, and very rich" and declare, "I am happy to be back [in Paris]. I feel more at home here than where I was born."[67]

It is perhaps in *Pagan Spain* that he most clearly expressed his view of religion, race, and nationalism as fetters on the revolutionary change immanent in the anticolonial movements sweeping around the world. "I have no religion in the formal sense of the word," he told a young woman he met in Barcelona. "I have no race except that which is forced upon me. I have no country except that to which I'm obliged to belong. I have no traditions. I'm free. I have only the future."[68] The future writ large was increasingly uncertain in the 1950s, fractured by left sectarianism and Cold War espionage as the old world was dying and the new one was being born. As Wright put it in *Black Power*, "History is a strange story. Men enact history with one set of motives and the consequences that flow from such motivated actions often have nothing whatsoever to do with such motives."[69] In that period of dueling superpowers, worldwide anticolonial struggles for independence, and fierce imperial backlash, he might have had in mind Marx's oft-quoted pronouncement that "men make their own history, but they do not make it as they please; they do not make it under self-selected circumstances, but under circumstances existing already, given and transmitted from the past."[70] At the same time, Wright's sense of his own freedom and his own future were anything but certain.

The record of his voyage to his ancestors' homeland in *Black Power* conveys this ambivalence about the collective fate of the Gold Coast, the world, and his identity as he interrogates race, class, and the depredations of colonialism that fueled the development of global capitalism and the revolutionary forces it unleashed. He imagined a postcolonial future that could honor but transcend primal cultural, religious, and folk traditions eviscerated by centuries of European colonization. Through the lens of his secular, scientific, modernist worldview, he saw how slavery and colonization transmuted Africans, Asians, and their descendants into racialized "others" suffering from what Fanon called "internalized racism," and he yearned for a more egalitarian world that even before it was born seemed to have been menaced with signs of a postcolonial future of recolonization and economic dependence. He could see the aftermath of hard-won independence in the form of Western investments, Third World indebtedness to rich countries, and ever-deepening extraction of surplus wealth and natural resources, and he sought to warn Nkrumah to resist it. In his last days on the Gold Coast he visited Elmina Castle, built by the Portuguese in 1482, where captured Africans were imprisoned before boarding a slave ship to the Americas, and where he imagined that instead of the buried gold dust that the natives liked to believe was there, the only treasure was "a tiny, pear-shaped tear that formed on the cheek of some black woman torn away from her children, a tear that gleams here still, caught in the feeble rays of the dungeon's light."[71]

Marx and Engels make clear the dialectic of creative and destructive capacities of capitalism whose forces and relations of production would produce its own gravediggers. Wright expressed an appreciation of that dialectic on topics ranging from the transatlantic slave trade and the rise of capitalism in the Americas to the expropriation and destruction of peoples and lands worldwide. He understood that it was these same forces that created the conditions for antiracist and anticolonial movements that, at least for a time, promised to set in motion a global transformation for the betterment of humankind. That promise has not been met. The failure of postcolonial nations to achieve economic freedom has had dire consequences for the nonaligned nations that met at Bandung in 1956 and about which Wright presciently wrote in *The Color Curtain*. That book, together with *Black Power*, established him as a founding theorist of postcolonial studies and an inspiration to generations of writers and revolutionaries who emerged in the 1960s and later. What might he have thought of the heartbreaking reports in 2023 of lithium and cobalt mining in the Democratic Republic of the Congo, or the first year of Israel's war on Gaza in which Israel unleashed its full, US-backed military might in what many refer to as the second Nakba, killing more than 44,000 Palestinians, including tens of thousands of children, destroying hospitals, schools, and universities, and risking irreversible damage to natural ecosystems?[72]

Born in 1942 to Communist parents whose involvement in radical politics continued after they officially left the CPUSA, Julia Wright followed in their footsteps not only in her resolute efforts to free the Black activist and journalist Mumia Abu-Jamal, imprisoned since 1982 after having been wrongfully convicted of murdering the police officer Daniel Faulkner, but also in her involvement with Ellen Wright in the Black Panther Party, Black Lives Matter, and other social movements. More recently, Julia Wright has been working to establish the Elaine Museum and Richard Wright Civil Rights Center in Elaine, Arkansas, where Wright's uncle Silas Hoskins was lynched in 1916, a terrifying event in Wright's life that he writes about in chapter 2 of *Black Boy*, and where hundreds of Black people were killed in 1919 by a racist, union-busting white mob in what became known as the Elaine Massacre.[73] In 2006, Abu-Jamal described Julia as "a strong presence in peoples' movements for generations on three continents . . . not just a proud daughter of a pioneering writer and activist, but an activist and writer in her own right."[74] Along with continuing to question the circumstances of her father's death as she attempts to set the record straight about his life and work, she carries on his political journalistic legacy of reporting on social movements and explaining how seemingly disparate struggles are linked. For instance, she recently connected the battle for Algerian independence—which her father supported quietly, given the risk that he would be deported, or worse, for speaking out—to twenty-first-century state surveillance, repression, and assassination of radical activists and people of color.[75]

Like her father, whose proto-ecological awareness enabled him to critique imperialist environmental depredation and social demarcations of where one could go, what happened if one crossed color, class, and gender lines, and how one stood in relation to land and property, Julia Wright reports on the use of repressive tactics to respond to a new generation of environmental activists who see the climate crisis as inextricably linked to racism, social inequality, and militarism. She writes about the fatal shooting of seventeen-year-old Algerian-Moroccan Nahel Merzouk by French police on June 17, 2023, and the ensuing weeks of rioting and looting by French youth, relating that case to hundreds of other police murders, including that of George Floyd in the summer of 2020, and Manuel Esteban Paez Terán, also known as Tortuguita, in Atlanta, Georgia, on January 23, 2023. An Indigenous, queer, nonbinary Venezuelan, Tortuguita was protesting the construction of Cop City—officially named the Atlanta Public Safety Training Center—in the South River Forest area at the Defend Atlanta Forest / Stop Cop City encampment in Atlanta, Georgia. Citing the intergenerational, transcontinental trauma of these attacks, Wright notes that Tortuguita's mother, Belkis Terán, led an Atlanta Forest march in memory of her son just one day before the Nanterre march in honor of Nahel on June 29.[76]

Richard Wright's last years were marked by loneliness, illness, and loss. Unable to find publishers for his work, panned by critics, besieged by spies, grieving over the deaths of Ed Aswell, George Padmore, and his mother Ella, he was in the midst of a midlife crisis the resolution of which we will never know. But even in this period of recurring illness and self-questioning so severe that he considered giving up writing and finding other means of supporting himself and his family, he was feverishly working on multiple projects, including a planned trip to French West Africa at a historical turning point for imperial France and its African colonies. Unlike Indochina and Algeria, which fought prolonged, bloody wars with France, the French West African colonies transitioned peacefully to independence in what French officials viewed as "successful decolonization." A more complex reading of history, however, reveals "a complicity between France's governing élites and African leaders" that enabled France "through the creation of a network of client states, to continue to punch above its weight . . . [and] played a central role in the maintenance of France's status as a world power."[77] In 1959, Wright published a special introduction for French readers in *Écoute, homme blanc!* (*White Man, Listen!*) in which he made a similar point: "Current popular observation tends to regard what is taking place in Africa—the creation of republics and federations under French rule and the rapid assumption of constitutional authority under British guidance—as indicating the end of imperial domination and, thus, the beginning of an epoch of stabilization for 'free' Africans. This point of view oversimplifies the complex reality involved in the African problem."[78]

In September 1960 he returned to Paris to meet Julia and was closely watching Patrice Lumumba's rise to power in the Congo as signaling an end to European dominance, even as he anticipated the stranglehold of neocolonial relations that would lead to the reconquest of Africa. This analysis of world affairs and his keen desire to report on newly independent and emerging states firsthand present a different Wright than the gloomy, defeated man he was purported to be. According to Bontemps, who saw Wright when he and his wife Alberta passed through Paris en route to Uganda in September 1960, he was "more outgoing and joyous" than ever. In October, Wright wrote to Langston Hughes that he had been ill for a year with amoebic dysentery, "but at last I'm back to work in full swing," adding, "I'm hankering to get back to Africa. That place haunts me." Two months later, Hughes visited Wright the same afternoon he entered Eugène Gibez Clinic. Initially taken aback by Wright's corpselike appearance, lying in bed, fully clothed to go to the hospital, Hughes found that he quickly revived, becoming much like the Dick Wright he had known in Chicago—"vigorous, questioning, very much alive, and with a big, warm smile."[79] He handed Hughes the radio play script he had been working on, "Daddy Goodness," to take to New York, hoping he would find a little theater to produce it. According to Harrington, "When he left his apartment to enter the clinic for that last check-up, his work table was covered with manuscripts, essays, and writings of the most astute musicologists in the field of jazz."[80] In addition to planning his French West Africa trip and researching liner notes for Barclay jazz records, Wright was revising "Island of Hallucination," drafting *A Father's Law* in a burst of creative energy, preparing his collection of stories, *Eight Men*, for publication, and writing haiku.

In the last lecture he gave, on November 8 at the American Church in Paris, Wright railed against US policy in the Congo and the divisions sown by CIA spies and the white publishing industry among Black writers, intellectuals, and activists. Alluding to the Gibson affair, he described it as a "nightmarish jungle ... a deadly fight in which brother is set against brother, in which threats of mystical violence are hurled by one black against the other, where vows to cut or kill are voiced." He made two more crucial points: first, that "the ideology seeping into the Black Belts cannot be completely controlled" as racial boundaries became more porous and books, mass media, and tourism passed more freely in and out of Black communities; and second, that revolutionary Black Americans "were not talking; they were wary," and "hence Negroes who would talk Communism were sent into the Black Belts" as informers and spies, a degree of infiltration, he declared, that went so far that "most revolutionary movements in the Western world are government sponsored . . . launched by agent provocateurs to organize the discontented so that the Government can keep an eye on them."[81]

How to sum up the measure of the man and make a dent in the tens of thousands of pages of conflicting impressions and assessments that have been written about Richard Wright—a brilliant, iconoclastic, African American writer whose candle burned brightly, an autodidact with a ninth-grade education, a "race man," a Communist, a traitor to the Party turned informant, a founder of postcolonial studies, a committed Marxist? His politics later in life were obscured by evasive tactics to avoid Cold War persecution, an experience shared by tens of millions of people of color and hundreds of thousands of Communists and fellow travelers who went underground, channeling their activism into aboveground organizations like the National Lawyers Guild, or else dissembled, eluding detection by speaking in two registers, as Wright did, denouncing communism as he blasted Western imperialism. Rather than derailing him, his break with the Party and refuge to Paris, alleged to have cut him off from his source of creativity, inspired new modernist, ethnographic, and poetic forms, philosophies, and geographies, undermined not by a failure of imagination or vision but by Cold War surveillance and barriers to publishing in a vast, networked, well-funded cultural war against the left that influenced presses, foundations, literary critics, and readers, extolling apolitical art that conformed to the apathy and smugness of the Silent Generation, pitting one Black writer against another, and denouncing the "protest novel."

Rather than abandoning the conclusions he had come to about race and class in "Blueprint for Negro Writing," he deepened and refined them in the widening world he claimed as a world traveler and American expatriate in Black Paris investigating racial oppression and colonial devastation in relation to an international, interracial working class. Together with other African American, Caribbean, and African intellectuals, he honed his analysis of the impact of colonialism and capitalism on peoples of color, whose intense exploitation had to be factored into revolutionary theory and practice. His refusal to postpone antiracist and anticolonial priorities in the name of class struggle or to narrow the issue to only race offers us a model for revolutionary theory and action, education and practice.

He passed forward to his daughters, grandchildren, readers, revolutionaries, and the dispossessed his yearning for another world—a world beyond the militant authority he advised Nkrumah to assert in the emerging nation-state of Ghana, a world premised on peace and human need rather than endless war and profit. Youths like Tortuguita and Nahel would have renewed his faith in battles for a more just, egalitarian, peaceful future for humankind. Given his incipient ecological awareness, he, like Julia, would have spoken out in support of environmental activists defending the earth, opposing the construction of police training sites like Cop City in Atlanta and its French equivalent, the National Training Center for Gendarme Forces. He would have linked the struggle to avert the climate crisis to movements to end the carceral state, racial oppression, the military-industrial complex, the exploitation of debt-ridden neocolonial countries, and the immiseration of workers everywhere. He would have continued to interrogate US empire, global capitalism, and deepening, worldwide, social inequality. The world that Richard Wright fought to bring about is a world that never was but could and still must be.

Acknowledgments

This book has been many years in the making, through two sabbaticals, trips to New Haven to pore over Richard Wright's papers at the Beinecke Library, reading and rereading his work, a visit to Paris in 2014 to retrace his footsteps, and an intensive period of writing from 2020 to late 2023. As my collection of Wright's books and mountains of biographical, critical, and personal writing about him outgrew my shelves and sat in piles on my desk and floor, I bought a small metal case to keep within arm's reach the most well-worn volumes, especially Wright's works and biographies about him, many color-coded with tabs and sticky notes marking passages to which I continually referred, the spines of the books breaking, the pages heavily marked. It is to these authors of these writings—chiefly Wright, but also his many interlocutors, critics, biographers, and protégés—that I am immeasurably indebted.

I am also deeply grateful to Julia Wright for her kindness and generosity in corresponding with me as I prepared the final manuscript for publication, and to the Richard Wright Estate for granting permission to use two photographs, reproduce some of his haiku, and quote some longer passages from his writing. As a red diaper baby whose parents found their way to Marxism in the late 1930s at the University of Michigan in Ann Arbor, not far from Chicago, I thought often of Julia Wright in relation to her father insofar as her life's work as a journalist, poet, and activist seemed to bear the mark of his influence, confirming my sense of him as a revolutionary thinker—someone who both rejected the essentialization of race and, as a socialist and Marxist, fiercely opposed all forms of racism and identified with the disinherited worldwide.

Of the biographical writing on Wright, Michel Fabre's many books and articles about him, especially *The Unfinished Quest of Richard Wright*, have been indispensable guides to his life and work. Constance Webb, his first biographer and the only one who knew him personally, interviewed him extensively and shared a political world with him and her husband C. L. R. James. She provided a more familiar, firsthand account of Wright, from his childhood, including extensive portraits of his grandparents and parents, to his exilic friendships with French philosophers and Caribbean and African anticolonial leaders. Wright's most recent major biographer, Hazel Rowley, helped reframe his legacy and correct misconceptions about his life and work, noting her gratitude not only to Fabre and Webb but also to Ellen Wright, each of whom she interviewed. By the time I began this book, all three as well as Rowley had passed, as successive generations of researchers, scholars, and critics take up new lines of inquiry, adding to our collective knowledge of his life, times, and writing, indebted to the labors of those who came before us.

In addition to his biographers, I have relied on a plethora of Wright scholars and scholars of African American literature, including a few who have begun to discuss him in relationship to the intersection of ecocriticism and Black literature and culture. To fill gaps in my own knowledge and correct standard narratives of Wright, I also sought out and now thank scholars of the CPUSA, the cultural front, the Black cultural front, the Federal Writers' Project, the Popular Front, and the *Daily Worker*, as well as the Cold War, the Congress for Cultural Freedom, and histories more generally of the US left, the international left, Pan-African anticolonial movements, and the Bandung Conference in Indonesia in 1955.

Heartfelt thanks, too, to those who supported the book more directly. Alan Wald wrote me recommendations for grant applications and gave me advice about publishers. Barbara Foley provided feedback on early drafts and encouraged me to change my working title to something more indicative of his internationalist perspective. Jim Smethurst, a reviewer who chose not to be anonymous, offered to read chapters as I wrote them and was enormously helpful, giving me notes and a tip about Wright's having been a dues-paying member of the Communist Party in Paris. I am grateful to Joe Sims, national CPUSA cochair, for answering my queries on that front and telling me the story he had heard about Wright's ties to the Communist Party in France. And I thank an anonymous reviewer whose suggestions for revision in the early stages of the book helped reshape it and whose endorsement of the final draft affirmed I had achieved at least some of what I had set out to do.

Sara Rutkowski, who included my chapter on Wright and the FWP in her edited volume *Rewriting America: New Essays on the Federal Writers' Project*, also read and responded to the manuscript as a whole, always encouraging, critical, and editorially gifted. Other friends and colleagues who read parts of the book in progress include Mady Schutzman, Brenda Edwards, Andrea Phillips-Merriman, and Shannon Carter. I thank Jonathan Alexander and Nancy Welch for inviting me to submit a chapter on the relevance of *Native Son* to twenty-first-century protest movements to their edited volume *Unruly Rhetorics: Protest, Persuasion, and Publics*. Thanks go as well to Joe Ramsey and other members of the Richard Wright Society for inviting me to join a panel at the 2024 American Literature Association Conference, for continuing to make space for me to talk about Wright to a wider audience, and for carrying on the important work of the Richard Wright Circle, which was convened by Wright scholars Maryemma Graham and Jerry W. Ward, Jr. in 1991.

I am grateful to Long Island University for approving two sabbaticals and research funds to visit the Beinecke Library and to travel to Paris in 2014; to my former, longtime dean of liberal arts and sciences, the late David Cohen; and to my current dean Maureen Tuthill, whose unstinting generosity helped me obtain permissions and complete the final stages of the project. Thanks, too, to Beinecke librarians who helped me locate archival material and obtain digitized images of Wright, and to a librarian at New York Public Library's Schomburg Center for the Study of Black Culture, who in the midst of the pandemic sent me a digitized copy of Wright's notes for "Biography of a Bolshevik," abandoned after Party leaders put his subject, David Poindexter, on trial for "class collaborationist attitudes" and "ideological factionalism."

Many thanks also to my editor Debbie Gershenowitz whose faith in this project gave me the confidence to press forward even in the most challenging, daunting moments of doubt that I could do justice to Wright's literary and historical significance and contemporary relevance. I am especially grateful to Debbie for echoing Barbara Foley's advice to replace my original title with *No Race, No Country: The Politics and Poetics of Richard Wright*, which now seems to have guided the logic of the book all along. Thanks as well to Alexis Dumain for answering my many questions as I finalized the manuscript, and to the editorial and marketing teams who were always thorough, gracious, and quick to respond to my queries.

Finally, I thank John Sandman, Jacob Mutnick Sandman, and Barbara Mutnick for their patience and support—for putting up with me during the throes of writing and letting me read them passages that finally seemed to have clicked late into the night. To my parents, George and Margaret Mutnick, who left this world too soon to see even a flicker of the book, it would not have come to be without your love, guidance, humor, and radical spirit.

Notes

Introduction

1. Irving Howe, "Black Boys and Native Sons," *Dissent*, Autumn 1963, 366. See also Howe's oft-cited declaration, "The day *Native Son* appeared American culture was changed forever" (354).

2. James Baldwin, "Everybody's Protest Novel," in *Notes of a Native Son*, 22; Baldwin, "Alas, Poor Richard," in *Nobody Knows My Name*, 612.

3. Ayana Mathis and Pankaj Mishra, "James Baldwin Denounced Richard Wright's 'Native Son' as a 'Protest Novel' : Was He Right?," *New York Times Book Review*, March 1, 2015. See also Baldwin, "Everybody's Protest Novel."

4. See Henry Louis Gates's analysis of the sexual tensions contributing to the enmity between Wright and Hurston. Henry Louis Gates, "Why Richard Wright Hated Zora Neale Hurston."

5. Ta-Nehisi Coates, "Native Sonned," *The Atlantic*, June 7, 2012; Hannah Giorgis, "An Arty but Superficial Take on *Native Son*," *The Atlantic*, April 6, 2019; Monica Castillo, review of *Native Son*, April 5, 2019, www.rogerebert.com/reviews/native-son-2019; Troy Patterson, "A New Adaptation of 'Native Son' Reaches the Limits of What the Text Has to Offer," *New Yorker*, April 5, 2019; *Native Son*, directed by Rashid Johnson (Los Angeles: Bow and Arrow Entertainment, 2019).

6. Eagleton, *Literary Theory*, 43.

7. Walhout, "New Criticism," 870. See also Maxwell, *F. B. Eyes*.

8. Foley, *Radical Representations*.

9. Wright, "Blueprint," 59–60.

10. Wright, "Blueprint," 59.

11. Baldwin, *Notes of a Native Son*, 21; Hazel Rowley, "Framing Richard Wright," *Yale University Library Gazette* 73, no. 1/2 (1998): 63.

12. James T. Farrell, review of *Uncle Tom's Children*, by Richard Wright, in Gates and Appiah, *Richard Wright*, 4–5; Clifton Fadiman, review of *Native Son*, by Richard Wright, in Gates and Appiah, *Richard Wright*, 6–8; Louis Menand, "The Hammer and the Nail: Richard Wright's Modern Condition," *New Yorker*, July 13, 1992.

13. Wright, *Native Son*, 174.

14. Fadiman, review of *Native Son*, 6–8.

15. Nick Aaron Ford, review of *The Long Dream*, by Richard Wright, in Reilly, *Richard Wright*, 335–36.

16. Howe, "Black Boys and Native Sons," 354, 357–59; Henry Seidel Canby, qtd. in Fadiman, review of *Native Son*, 6.

17. See, e.g., Stepto, *From Behind the Veil*; Barnett, "Politicizing the Personal"; Wright, *Native Son*, 420.

18. Wright, *12 Million Black Voices*.

19. Here I am questioning the very concept of autodidacticism rather than suggesting that Wright was not exceptionally self-motivated and, in some respects, self-taught.

20. Deborah Brandt theorizes the concept of "literacy sponsorship" in "Sponsors of Literacy," 166–67.

21. Foley, "Politics of Poetics," 197.

22. Wright, "Blueprint," 59.

23. Rutledge, "Wonder," 255–65.

24. Julia Wright, "Richard Wright's Legacy and Remembering George Floyd—Part 1," *History of Black Writing*, September 16, 2020, https://hbw.ku.edu/blog/richard-wrights-legacy-remembering-george-floyd-part-1; Malcolm Wright, qtd. in Victoria Garcia Unzueta, "Richard Wright's Legacy and Remembering George Floyd—Part 2," *History of Black Writing*, September 17, 2020, https://hbw.ku.edu/blog/richard-wrights-legacy-and-remembering-george-floyd-part-2; Maxime Desirat, qtd. in Victoria Garcia Unzueta, "Richard Wright's Legacy and Remembering George Floyd—Part 3," *History of Black Writing*, September 18, 2020, https://hbw.ku.edu/blog/richard-wrights-legacy-and-remembering-george-floyd-part-3-final.

25. Rowley, *Richard Wright*, 250.

26. See, e.g., Thaddeus, "Metamorphosis."

27. Douglass, *Narrative of the Life of Frederick Douglass*, 33.

28. For critiques of communism and assertions that Wright rejected Marxism when he broke from the CPUSA, see, e.g., Baldwin, *Notes of a Native Son*; Ellison, "Richard Wright's Blues"; Cruse, *Crisis of the Negro Intellectual*; Gayle, *Richard Wright*; and Robinson, *Black Marxism*. For new perspectives on Wright in relation to the CPUSA and Marxism, see, e.g., Gilroy, *Black Atlantic*; Wald, *Exiles from a Future Time*; Foley, *Radical Representations*; Maxwell, *New Negro, New Left*.

29. Wright, *Black Boy*, 317. See also M'Baye, "Richard Wright"; Roberts and Foulcher, *Indonesian Notebook*.

30. Arna Bontemps, "Three Portraits of the Negro," *Saturday Review*, March 28, 1953, 15. See also Webb, *Richard Wright*.

31. Wright, *12 Million Black Voices*, 146.

32. Buell, *Environmental Imagination*, 86.

33. Rutledge, "Wonder," 257–58. See also Hicks, "W. E. B. Du Bois," 202–22; Hutchinson, "Literary Ecology."

34. Fanon, *Black Skin*, 139.

35. Julia Wright, introduction to *Haiku*, xi.

36. Fabre, *Unfinished Quest*.

37. Wright, *Haiku*, 305.

Chapter One

1. Wright, *Native Son*, 454.
2. "Note on the Texts," in Wright, *Man Who Lived Underground*, 222.
3. "Note on the Texts," 223.
4. Imani Perry, "The Bleak Prescience of Richard Wright," *The Atlantic*, June 2021.
5. Ward, "*Uncle Tom's Children* Revisited," 352.

6. See, e.g., Foley and Ward, "Richard Wright"; and Wald, "He Tried to Be a Communist."
7. Wright, "Blueprint," 59.
8. Letter from Wright to Paul Reynolds, December 17, 1943, along with the complete manuscript of *Black Boy*, then titled "American Hunger," in Fabre, *Unfinished Quest*, 253.
9. Wilkerson, *Warmth of Other Suns*.
10. Wright, *Black Boy*, 261–63.
11. JanMohamed, *Death-Bound-Subject*, 2.
12. Wright, *Man Who Lived Underground*, 163, 166.
13. Wright, *Black Boy*, 461.
14. Wright, 441.
15. Wright, 344.
16. Wright, 461.
17. JanMohamed, *Death-Bound-Subject*, 2.
18. Robinson, *Black Marxism*.
19. Adrienne Westenfeld, "Eighty Years Later, Richard Wright's Lost Novel about Police Brutality Speaks across Decades," *Esquire*, April 20, 2021. In her review of the novel, Westenfeld writes, "Wright saw *The Man Who Lived Underground* as a creative breakthrough: an allegorical and existential novel that stood in stark contrast to the literary naturalism of his name-making bestseller, *Native Son*."
20. Wright, *Man Who Lived Underground*, 201, 274.
21. Wright, 5–6.
22. Wright, 37, 43, 48.
23. Ridenour, "Critique," 54. See also Fabre, "Richard Wright."
24. Morrison, *Playing in the Dark*, 59.
25. Wright, *Man Who Lived Underground*, 6–26.
26. Wright, 28–29, 44–45, 47.
27. Fabre, *Unfinished Quest*, 240.
28. Douglas Field, "Going Underground," *Times Literary Supplement*, April 23, 2021.
29. Wright, *Man Who Lived Underground*, 204–5.
30. Wright, 196, 173.
31. Fabre, *Unfinished Quest*; Rowley, *Richard Wright*; Kiuchi, "Kay Boyle."
32. See, e.g., Reginald Dwayne Betts, "Richard Wright's Newly Restored Novel Is a Tale for Today," *New York Times*, April 26, 2021; Aaron Coats, "Nearly Eighty Years Later, Richard Wright's *The Man Who Lived Underground* Emerges," *Chicago Review of Books*, April 21, 2021; Lauren Michele Jackson, "What We Want from Richard Wright," *New Yorker*, May 12, 2021; Scott McLemee, "Notes from the Underground," *Inside Higher Education*, April 23, 2021.
33. Ford, "Long Way from Home," in Reilly, *Richard Wright*, 436.
34. Alexander, *New Jim Crow*, 3.
35. Colin Asher, "When Richard Wright Broke with the Communists," *New Republic*, April 19, 2021; Joseph Ramsey, "Did Cancel Culture Drive Richard Wright Underground?," *The Nation*, May 20, 2021; Alan Wald, "Protesting the Protest Novel: *The Man Who Lived Underground*," *Against the Current* 216 (January–February 2022).
36. Arna Bontemps, qtd. in Wright, *Man Who Lived Underground*, 222; 205–9.
37. Wright, *Man Who Lived Underground*, 205, 209; Wright, *Black Boy*, 381.

38. *Jet* review of *The Outsider*, in Reilly, *Richard Wright*, 42; Kent Ruth, "An Outsider Queries Why?," in Reilly, *Richard Wright*, 206.

39. Cossu-Beaumont, "Richard Wright," 83. See chapter 6 for a closer analysis of Wright's "tricksterism."

40. See Marx on the phenomenal forms. *Capital*, vol. 1, chap. 19.

41. Tuttleton, "Problematic Texts," 264; Arna Bontemps, "Review of *The Outsider*," 106.

42. Troy Patterson, "A New Adaptation of *Native Son* Reaches the Limits of What the Text Has to Offer," *New Yorker*, April 5, 2019.

43. Smethurst, "After Modernism," 15.

44. Wright, *Black Boy*, 287.

45. Bone, "Richard Wright," 448; Ford, "Fire Next Time?," in Reilly, *Richard Wright*, 367.

46. See Fabre, *Books and Writers*.

47. Sutherland, *Gertrude Stein*, 54; Wright, *Man Who Lived Underground*, 181–82; Wright, "Blueprint," 102.

48. Richard Wright, "Not My People's War," *New Masses*, June 17, 1941, 8.

49. Folsom, *Days of Anger*, 242.

50. Wright, *Man Who Lived Underground*, 176; Wright, "Blueprint," 59–60.

51. Asher, "When Richard Wright Broke."

52. Ramsey, "Cancel Culture."

53. Wright, *Native Son*, 4–9; Wright, *Man Who Lived Underground*, 59. Hereafter, in this section these two novels are cited in text.

54. This male chauvinist dialogue, mocking the blue-eyed girl, seems to suggest Wright's position on the "woman question" and the emancipation of women from male domination and marriage. See chapter 3 for a fuller discussion of perspectives on Wright's sexual politics.

55. For an insightful discussion of Wright's use of the concept "No Man's Land," see Entin, *Sensational Modernism*, 215–55.

56. See, for example, commentary on the name "Bigger Thomas" as a portmanteau for "bad nigger" and the antithesis of an Uncle Tom, as well as one of Uncle Tom's uprooted children set adrift in the urban North. Darryl Lorenzo Wellington, "Native Son: One Hundred Years after His Birth, Richard Wright's Dramatic Journey Continues," *The Crisis* 115, no. 2 (Spring 2008): 22–25; Dinerstein, "Uncle Tom Is Dead."

57. Callahan and Conner, *Selected Letters*, 487; Ellison, *Shadow and Act*, 120.

58. Ellison, "Richard Wright's Blues," 211.

59. See Foley, *Wrestling with the Left*.

60. Ellison, "Richard Wright's Blues," 198, 201.

61. Ellison, "World and the Jug," 108, 114.

62. Wright, *Black Boy*, 349.

63. Rowley, *Richard Wright*, 255, 558.

64. Wright, *Black Boy*, 100.

Chapter Two

1. Baldwin, *Nobody Knows My Name*, 161.

2. Rolo, "This, Too, Is America," 28, 30.

3. Rowley, *Richard Wright*, 250.

4. Rolo, "This, Too, Is America," 28.

5. Wright discusses his theory of brokenness in "Memories of My Grandmother," stating that the breaking point in a character comes at a point "where the character is rendered fluid... where the author can do anything with him, where everything fits." In Bigger's case, the "breaking point came after Bigger committed his first murder; from that point on the story could have gone in any number of directions with ease." Thus, although the breaking point determines Bigger's tragic fate, his life could have gone in another direction. Wright, *Man Who Lived Underground*, 191, 192.

6. James, "*Native Son* and Revolution," 92–93.

7. Brandt, "Sponsors of Literacy," 165–85; Williams, *Self-Taught*. Also see the digitized archive of interviews at the Library of Congress, *Born in Slavery: Slave Narratives from the Federal Writers' Project, 1936 to 1938*, www.loc.gov/collections/slave-narratives-from-the-federal-writers-project-1936-to-1938/about-this-collection/.

8. Ella's role in Wright's life can be seen in other stories of the educational, political, and emotional support Black mothers gave their children in the long struggle for freedom and equality in America. See, e.g., Tubbs, *Mothers of Martin Luther King*.

9. Rowley describes the John Reed Club as Wright's university, but it was arguably a constellation of literary and political organizations—the JRC, the CPUSA, the South Side Writers Group, and the Federal Writers' Project, as well as the Chicago Post Office, according to Nelson Algren—that gave him a richer education than most college students receive. See Rowley, *Richard Wright*, 78.

10. Wright, *Black Boy*, 24–25.

11. Wright, *Black Boy*, 74–77; *Native Son*, 16–17.

12. Wright, *Black Boy*, 90–101.

13. Wright, 100–101.

14. Wright, 104.

15. Wright, *Man Who Lived Underground*, 164, 169; *Black Boy*, 102.

16. Asher, "When Richard Wright Broke"; Wright, *Man Who Lived Underground*, 203.

17. Wright, *Man Who Lived Underground*, 178; *Native Son*, 388, 392.

18. Wright, *Man Who Lived Underground*, 183; *Black Boy*, 122.

19. Wright, *Black Boy*, 133, 148.

20. Wright, 174.

21. Webb, *Richard Wright*. The only one of Wright's biographers to note this detail about his grandfather, whom Wright describes at some length in *Black Boy* but without any mention of Douglass, is his first, Constance Webb, wife of the Trinidadian Marxist historian C. L. R. James, both of whom were Wright's close personal friends. A large part of Webb's biography is based on conversations with Wright—many of which are not footnoted, she states, so as not to burden the reader. Webb thus would have drawn her portrait of Richard Wilson from stories Wright told her between 1945 and 1960. Neither Wright nor his other biographers refer to Douglass, though the two authors are often discussed in relation to each other.

22. Wright, *Black Boy*, 22–23.

23. Williams, *Self-Taught*, 2, 5; Morrison, "Site of Memory."

24. Proefriedt, "Immigrant or 'Outsider' Experience," 84–85.

25. Brandt, "Sponsors of Literacy," 166. See also Anyon, "Social Class and the Hidden Curriculum" and "Social Class and School Knowledge"; and Kozol, *Savage Inequalities*.

26. See Kozol, *Savage Inequalities*.

27. Qtd. in Fabre, *Unfinished Quest*, 252.

28. Wright, *Black Boy*, 129–32. Although Wright does not refer to the family friend by name, Fabre identifies him as Essie Ward's father. See Fabre, *Unfinished Quest*, 40.

29. Wright, *Black Boy*, 318. This perspective on Wright's literacy development as fundamentally social rather than individual is rooted in Russian psychologist Lev Vygotsky's pioneering cognition studies in the 1920s and '30s and social theories of literacy that followed. See, e.g., Vygotsky, *Thought and Language*.

30. Lewis Gannett reviewed *Black Boy* for the *New York Herald Tribune* on February 28, 1945; a few days later, on March 4, 1945, W. E. B. Du Bois reviewed the book in the *Tribune's Weekly Book Review*. Horace Cayton, with whom Wright stayed in Chicago while collecting images and information for *12 Million Black Voices*, wrote a more extended, critical review of the book in a double issue of the journal *Twice a Year* published in 1945. Reprinted in Reilly, *Richard Wright*, 119–20, 132–33, 184–88.

31. Qtd. in Fabre, *Unfinished Quest*, 251. See, e.g., Hakutani, "Creation of the Self," 70–75.

32. Wright, *Black Boy*, 38–39.

33. Wright was reflecting on the talk he gave on April 9, 1943, at the Commemorative Chapel at Fisk University in Nashville. Qtd. in Fabre, *Unfinished Quest*, 249.

34. Fabre, *Unfinished Quest*, 251, xxxiv.

35. Webb, *Richard Wright*, 16–17.

36. Webb, 7, 17.

37. Webb, 23; Wright, *Black Boy*, 7.

38. Wright, *Black Boy*, 3, 8–9, 2; Freire and Macedo, *Literacy*, 29.

39. Wright, *Black Boy*, 10–11.

40. Wright, 12–14.

41. hooks, *Talking Back*, 158.

42. Wright. *Uncle Tom's Children*, 2.

43. Louis Menand, "The Hammer and the Nail: Richard Wright's Modern Condition," *New Yorker*, July 20, 1992, www.newyorker.com/magazine/1992/07/20/the-hammer-and-the-nail.

44. Wright, *Black Boy*, 40–44.

45. Wright, 45–46.

46. Wright, 23–24.

47. Wright, 46–49.

48. Wright, 65–68.

49. Wright, 71–73.

50. Wright, 73–74. For more on Lenin's distinction in *What Is to Be Done?* between spontaneous worker riots and destruction of machinery and class consciousness, see Au, "Vygotsky and Lenin," 276, 278.

51. Wright, *Black Boy*, 37. This first parenthetical interjection is cited by many readers whose entire critique of the book stems from Wright's characterization of Black life as essentially bleak and culturally barren. See also Wright, "How 'Bigger' Was Born," in *Native Son*, 441.

52. Wright, *Black Boy*, 302.

53. The reference to "Western civilization" is made in the first set of parenthetical comments in *Black Boy*, 37; the reference to the ruling class is in the fourth set of parenthetical

comments, 302. Wright's critique of materialism is from a letter to Dorothy Norman, March 9, 1948, qtd in Fabre, *Unfinished Quest*, 325.

54. The citations from *Black Boy* are in Part Two, chap. 17, 301–2. The essay on Harlem in *New York Panorama*—unsigned, as was the case for all FWP materials—was begun by Claude McKay and completed by Wright, who took over the WPA work on Harlem in 1937 when he moved to New York City. Federal Writers' Project, *New York Panorama*, 151.

55. Wright, *Black Boy*, 233 (second set of parenthetical comments), 265–67 (third set), 345 (fifth set), and 228–33 (references to Shorty, the white northerner, and the white "superworld").

56. The term "No Man's Land" occurs in *Black Boy* (265–67), *Native Son* (347), and "How 'Bigger' Was Born," the essay about *Native Son* appended to the 2005 Harper Perennial Classic edition (451).

57. Wright, *Black Boy*, 345.

58. Wright, 345.

Chapter Three

1. Hansberry, review of *The Outsider*, in Reilly, *Richard Wright*, 220.
2. Harrington, *Why I Left America*, 21.
3. Robinson, *Black Marxism*, 289.
4. See, e.g., Reilly, "Richard Wright's Apprenticeship"; Foley, *Radical Representations*; and Mills, "Marxism, Communism," 58–73.
5. Brièrre, "R. Wright," in Kinnamon and Fabre, *Conversations*, 210.
6. Denning, *Cultural Front*.
7. Wright, "Blueprint," 54.
8. Wright, 54.
9. Webb, *Richard Wright*, 205.
10. Du Bois, "Richard Wright Looks Back," in Reilly, *Richard Wright*, 132; Wright, "Letters to Joe C. Brown."
11. If, at times, Wright represented himself as a "lonely rebel," others who wrote about him helped create the impression that he was isolated and cut off from society in Paris. See, e.g., Gaines, "Revisiting Richard Wright in Ghana," 182.
12. Wald, "He Tried to Be a Communist," 87–97. See also Keith, "Richard Wright, *The Outsider*, and the Empire of Liberal Pluralism," *Black Scholar* 39, no. 1–2 (2009): 51–58.
13. Walker, *Daemonic Genius*, 69.
14. Webb, *Richard Wright*.
15. Fabre, *Unfinished Quest*, 97.
16. Wright, *Black Boy*, 257.
17. See, e.g., Mullen, *Popular Fronts*.
18. For a more in-depth but concise history of the CPUSA, see Michael Goldfield, "100 Years of American Communism," *Jacobin*, December 10, 2019, https://jacobin.com/2019/12/communist-party-usa-history.
19. See Solomon, *Cry Was Unity*.
20. Solomon, 7.

21. In his detailed analysis of the Black Belt thesis, Solomon observes that the power of the Party's evolving line on Black liberation was its identification of an alternative to assimilation and segregation, "based on unqualified equality and self-determination, grounded in the distinct, historically evolved nationality of the Negro people." Solomon, *Cry Was Unity*, xix.

22. Wright, *Black Boy*, 334–35. Wright's reference to Stalin demonstrated both his loyalty to the CPUSA at that time and his appreciation of Stalin's analysis of oppressed nations.

23. Wright, 346, 353.

24. Wright, 359.

25. Wright, 338, 336, 340, 351–52. Rowley points out the loss to the historical record of Wright's abandoned profiles of Black Communists, noting that Law, who commanded an interracial battalion in the Spanish Civil War, died in 1937. Rowley, *Richard Wright*, 97.

26. Wright, *Black Boy*, 358.

27. Claude Lightfoot, interview with Michael Solomon, in *Cry Was Unity*, 269. Although Solomon dates the trial as happening in 1932, it took place in 1934, the year Haywood arrived in Chicago. See also Randi Storch's account of Poindexter's trial in Storch, *Red Chicago*, 64–65.

28. Patterson, *Man Who Cried Genocide*, 149, 140, 148.

29. Wright, *Black Boy*, 373.

30. Rowley, *Richard Wright*, 100.

31. Wright, *Black Boy*, 373, 374.

32. Wright, 315–18.

33. Goldfield, "100 Years of Communism," 7.

34. Charlie Post, "The New Deal and the Popular Front," *International Socialist Review* 108 (Winter 2016–17), https://isreview.org/issue/108/new-deal-and-popular-front/index.html; and Post, "The Popular Front Didn't Work," *Jacobin*, October 17, 2017, https://jacobin.com/2017/10/popular-front-communist-party-democrats.

35. Paul Buhle and Dan Georgakas, "Communist Party USA," in *Encyclopedia of the American Left* (New York: Oxford University Press, 1998), 150.

36. Post, "Popular Front," 3.

37. Wright, *Black Boy*, 344.

38. Folsom, *Days of Anger*, ix.

39. Wright, "Not My People's War."

40. Richard Wright, "Two Million Black Voices," *New Masses*, February 25, 1936, 15.

41. *Chicago Defender*, February 22, 1936.

42. Walker, *Richard Wright*, 71; Davis, *Livin' the Blues*, 240.

43. Wright, *Black Boy*, 360–62.

44. See, e.g., Patterson, *The Man Who Cried Genocide*; and Davis, *Livin' the Blues*.

45. Post, "New Deal," 3.

46. "The Communist Election Platform," campaign document of Browder-Ford campaign for president and vice president of the United States, Workers Library Publishers, July/August 1936, 14.

47. Qtd. in Mangione, *Dream and the Deal*, 309.

48. Wright, *Black Boy*, 35.

49. Bone, "Chicago Renaissance," 446–68.

50. See Hine and McClusky, *Black Chicago Renaissance*; and Courage and Reed, *Roots of the Black Chicago Renaissance*.
51. Wright, *Black Boy*, 296.
52. Fabre, "Richard Wright's First Hundred Books."
53. Wright, *Black Boy*, 320.
54. Walker, *Richard Wright*, 73–74.
55. Fabre, *Unfinished Quest*, 101.
56. Richard Wright, "I Have Seen Black Hands," *New Masses*, June 26, 1934, 16.
57. Cappetti, "Sociology of an Existence," 25, 40, 28.
58. See, e.g., Jaynes et al., "Chicago School."
59. York and Clark, "Marxism, Positivism." York and Clark argue, "A scientific perspective that avoids overly reductionistic, mechanistic, and teleological positions and incorporates the concepts of plasticity, historicity, social gravity, and coevolution can provide the foundation for critical research that is not epistemologically naive, while remaining grounded in materialism and realism. In this, the scientific enterprise, whether Marxist or positivist, can grapple with the dynamic world in which we are immersed." (442).
60. Qtd. in Rowley, *Richard Wright*, 81.
61. Mullen, *Popular Fronts*, 14–15.
62. Platt, "E. Franklin Frazier Reconsidered," 188.
63. Wright, introduction to *Black Metropolis*, xviii; Drake and Cayton, *Black Metropolis*, 86.
64. Drake and Cayton, *Black Metropolis*, 86–87.
65. Horace R. Cayton, "Black Bugs," *The Nation* 9 (September 1931): 255.
66. Wald, "He Tried to Be a Communist," 90; Rideout, *Radical Novel*, 260–61; Bone, *Negro Novel in America*, 114; Louis Menand, "The Hammer and the Nail: Richard Wright's Modern Condition," *New Yorker*, July 13, 1992; Afflerbach, "Liberalism's Blind Judgment," 98.
67. Fabre, *Unfinished Quest*, 230–31.
68. Wright, *Black Boy*, 345.
69. Wright, 345.
70. Richard Wright, "Ah Feels It in Mah Bones," *International Literature* 4 (April 1935): 80.
71. Richard Wright, "Transcontinental," *International Literature* 2 (April 1936): 52–57.
72. Record, *Negro and the Communist Party*, 65. Jessica Manry speculates that the author of the unsigned editorial "Disturbing 'Good' Race Relations," in *The Crisis*, October 1935, might have been George Padmore, whose ambivalence toward the CPUSA and Marxism resonates with Wright's and whose revolutionary vision likewise can be seen in his later writings despite his rightward drift. Manry, "Reading Backward," n66.
73. White, review of *The Negro and the Communist Party*.
74. Gayle, *Way of the New World*, 155–56. Gayle quotes Wright but omits the source, "The Literature of the Negro in the United States," originally given as an invited lecture. Wright, *Black Power*, 734.
75. Cruse, *Crisis of the Negro Intellectual*, 188.
76. Wald suggests that given the ambiguity of Wright's post-CPUSA politics, he might be called a "free radical." "He Tried to Be a Communist," 92; Cruse, *Crisis of the Negro Intellectual*, 182.
77. Bone, *Negro Novel in America*, 116.

78. Aaron, *Writers on the Left*, 1–2. In his preface to Aaron's book, Wald describes it as a Kuhnian paradigm shift and calls it "*the* pivotal text" in establishing the study of American literary radicalism (xiii–xiv).

79. Irving Howe and Lewis Coser, qtd. in Alan Wald, preface to *Writers on the Left*, by Daniel Aaron, xxi.

80. Irwin Granich (Mike Gold), "Towards Proletarian Art," *The Liberator*, February 1921, 23. Irwin Granich had yet to assume the Party name "Mike Gold."

81. Granich, "Towards Proletarian Art," 22.

82. Mike Gold, "A New Program for Writers," *New Masses*, January 1930, 21.

83. Homberger, "Proletarian Literature," 226.

84. Le Sueur, *Worker Writers*.

85. Kazin, introduction to *Jews without Money*, 5.

86. Foley, *Radical Representations*, 443–44.

87. Qtd. in Fabre, *Unfinished Quest*, 256; Cayton, *Long Old Road*, 249; Sam Sillen, "Richard Wright in Retreat," *New Masses*, August 29, 1944, 25–26; Davis, *Livin' the Blues*, 243; James W. Ford, "The Case of Richard Wright: A Disservice to the Negro People," *Daily Worker*, September 5, 1944, 6; George Breitman, review of *American Hunger*, in Reilly, *Richard Wright*, 392.

88. Wright, "I Tried to Be a Communist."

89. Ellison, *Shadow and Act*, 120.

90. Webb, *Richard Wright*, 208; Joseph Gollomb, review of *Black Boy*, in Reilly, *Richard Wright*, 392.

91. Rowley, *Richard Wright*, 320.

92. Davis, *Livin' the Blues*, 244.

93. Mullen, *Popular Fronts*, 22–25.

94. Hartman and Wilderson, "Position of the Unthought," 192.

Chapter Four

1. Jackson, *Indignant Generation*, 51.

2. Fabre, *Unfinished Quest*, 73; Richard Wright, *Black Boy*, 414. The phrase "the warmth of other suns" is in the first 1944 edition of *Black Boy*, published without Part Two, "The Horror and the Glory," at the request of the Book-of-the-Month Club.

3. Fabre, *Unfinished Quest*, 82.

4. Typically, for example, the historical research evident in *12 Million Black Voices* is attributed to Horace Cayton, whom Wright acknowledges in the book's preface. But Wright had contributed as a federal writer to Cayton's files, and his ethnographic essays contain detailed histories of Black Chicago.

5. Wright, *Black Boy*, 300.

6. Wright's scathing account of his hospital job and Jim Crow racism in the urban North culminates in a hilarious episode in which he and three Black male coworkers inadvertently knock over lab animal cages and then return the escaped animals to the right cages as best they can, only to find that none of the researchers ever notice the repopulated cages. In Wright, *Black Boy*, 304–14. Apropos of Wright's educational experiences in Chicago, it was in 1940 that Louis Wirth gave him a "program of readings in sociology that Wright conscientiously followed" (Fabre, *Unfinished Quest*, 232).

7. Wright, *Black Boy*, 341.
8. Mangione, *Dream and the Deal*, 121.
9. Walker, *Richard Wright*, 81.
10. Mangione, *Dream and the Deal*, 34.
11. *New Masses*, November 1929, 21, www.marxists.org/history/usa/pubs/new-masses/1929/v05n06-nov-1929-New-Masses.pdf.
12. Wright, *Black Boy*, 321.
13. Denning, *Cultural Front*, 227.
14. Wright, "Blueprint," 102.
15. Dolinar, *Negro in Illinois*, ix–x.
16. Wright and McKay, "Portrait of Harlem," 151.
17. Fox, "Achievement of the Federal Writers' Project," 3.
18. Wright, *Black Boy*, 320.
19. See, e.g., Hathaway, "Native Geography"; Balthaser, "Killing the Documentarian"; Butts, "New World A-Coming."
20. See, e.g., Bryant, *Byline, Richard Wright*.
21. Wright, *Black Boy*, 384.
22. Wright, "Blueprint." See Baldwin's "Alas, Poor Richard," in which he quotes Wright as responding to the younger writer's attack against him in "Everybody's Protest Novel," "What do you mean, *protest*! . . . *All* literature is protest." Baldwin, "Alas, Poor Richard," 157.
23. Stryker is quoted in Rankin, "Looking and Telling," 5–6.
24. Rankin, 8.
25. In *Let Us Now Praise Famous Men*, Agee reflects on his struggle to represent "an image of the very essence" of the lives of the poor white sharecroppers: "To come devotedly into the depths of a subject, your respect for it increasing in every step and your whole heart weakening apart with shame upon yourself in your dealing with it: To know at length better and better and at length into the bottom of your soul your unworthiness of it: Let me hope in any case that it is something to have begun to learn." Agee and Evans, 319.
26. Wright, *Black Boy*, 318.
27. Wright describes at length his attempt to write biographies of Black Communists in chapter 19 of *Black Boy*. His notes on the project, which was derailed by CPUSA leadership suspicious of his motives, are in his papers at the Schomburg Center for Research in Black Culture. Box 2, folder c3, reel 2: "Biography of a Bolshevik," Richard Wright Papers, Schomburg Center, New York Public Library.
28. Wright, *Black Boy*, 318–20.
29. Coles, *Doing Documentary Work*, 249.
30. Coles, 318.
31. Coles, 294–97.
32. Coles, 332.
33. Wright, *Uncle Tom's Children*, 17.
34. Wright, "Blueprint," 102.
35. Wright, *Native Son*, 454. These reflections are in the essay "How Bigger Was Born," now appended to the novel.
36. Wright's story about interracial union organizing efforts among southern tenant farmers, "Bright and Morning Star," was inspired by his interview for a *Daily Worker* article

with the Southern Negro Youth Congress leader Edward Strong. See Richard Wright, "Negro Youth on March, Says Leader," *Daily Worker*, October 1937, 3.

37. Rowbotham, *Hidden from History*.

38. Caldwell and Bourke-White's exposé of tenant farming in the South exemplifies unconscious racism in left photodocumentary works. Despite their sympathies for exploited farmers, Black and white, they invented captions for the photographs, including the unfortunate description of Black children as "coming along like watermelons in the summer." Caldwell and Bourke-White, *You Have Seen Their Faces*, 22.

39. Wright, *Black Boy*, 354.

40. Both Hathaway's essay, "Native Geography," published in 2008, and Dolinar's "The Illinois Writers' Project," a year later, paved the way for my interpretation of Wright's FWP reports and their impact on his literary career.

41. Fabre, *Unfinished Quest*, 571; Horace Cayton, qtd. in Kiuchi and Hakutani, *Richard Wright*, 41.

42. In addition to Dolinar's edited volume *The Negro in Illinois*, see his article "Radicals on Relief." Unless otherwise indicated, all in-text page references in this section are to Dolinar, "Illinois Writers' Project Essays."

43. Wright, *Native Son*, 22.

44. Hathaway, "Native Geography," 93.

45. Hirsch, *Portrait of America*, 17.

46. Wright, *Native Son*, 30.

47. Wright, 48.

48. Wright, *Black Boy*, 281; Alexander, "Richard Wright," in Ray and Farnsworth, *Richard Wright*, 55.

49. Wright, *12 Million Black Voices*, 106.

50. Wright, *Black Boy*, 341.

51. Wright, 341.

52. Wright, *Native Son*, 441.

53. Wright, 16–17. This scene of the novel also opens a line of inquiry into Wright's ecological consciousness, which I take up in chapter 6, "Ecologies of Empire."

54. Qtd. in Rowley, *Richard Wright*, 543n82.

55. Fabre, *Unfinished Quest*, 165.

56. Naison, *Communists in Harlem*, 206.

57. "About the New York Historical Society 'Slavery and the Making of New York,'" *Slavery in New York*, www.slaveryinnewyork.org/about_exhibit.htm. *Slavery in New York*, a major exhibition at the New York Historical Society on the history of slavery in the state, can be accessed online at www.slaveryinnewyork.org/index.html.

58. Wright and McKay, "Portrait of Harlem," 132. Unless otherwise indicated, all in-text page references in this section refer to this essay.

59. A plaque marking the site of an eighteenth-century slave market in lower Manhattan at the corner of Wall Street and Water Street, which operated from 1711 to 1762, was unveiled in the summer of 2015.

60. "Police End Harlem Riot; Mayor Starts Inquiry; Dodge Sees a Red Plot," *New York Times*, March 21, 1935, 1.

Notes to Chapter Five   263

61. Recent criticisms of New Deal policies, particularly with respect to the Federal Housing Administration and racist mortgage programs that denied loans in Black neighborhoods, make clear the racial biases that created segregated, unequal neighborhoods across the United States. However, as Paul Heideman argues, such views fail to account for the New Deal's enormous, far-reaching "egalitarian impact on workers of all races, including black workers." See Heideman. "Jim Clyburn Is Wrong about FDR and the New Deal," *Jacobin*, April 15, 2021, https://jacobin.com/2021/04/jim-clyburn-fdr-new-deal-joe-biden-black-workers.

62. Wright, *Black Boy*, 384.
63. Wright, "Blueprint," 99.
64. Qtd. in Rowley, *Richard Wright*, 249.
65. Wright, "Blueprint," 101.
66. Mayer, "Lenin," 42.
67. Fabre, *Unfinished Quest*, 230–31.
68. Robinson, *Black Marxism*, 190.
69. Wright, *Black Power*, 418–19.
70. Marx and Engels, *Manifesto of the Communist Party*.
71. Wright, *12 Million Black Voices*, 10.
72. Wright, "Blueprint," 98.
73. Wright, *Native Son*, 357.
74. Wright, *12 Million Black Voices*, 146.
75. Agee and Evans, *Let Us Now Praise Famous Men*, 319.
76. Shiffman, "Richard Wright's *12 Million Black Voices*," 444–45.
77. Wright, *12 Million Black Voices*, 17.
78. Wright, 146.
79. Wright, xx–xxi.
80. Wright, 147.

Chapter Five

1. Fabre, *Unfinished* Quest, 529.
2. Fabre, 528–30.
3. All poems cited here are in Fabre, *World of Richard Wright*.
4. One other widely cited early poem that deserves mention is "Between the World and Me," Wright's unsparing description of the remains of a lynching victim that the narrator stumbles across and empathizes with so completely that he seems to merge into the victim's body and imagine his own brutal murder. Ta-Nehisi Coates borrows the title for his best-selling book *Between the World and Me*, paying homage to Wright and James Baldwin.
5. Nick Aaron Ford, "The Fire Next Time?," reprinted in Reilly, *Richard Wright*, 367.
6. Costello, "Richard Wright's *Lawd Today!*"
7. Wright, *Black Boy*, 320.
8. Wright, *Man Who Lived Underground*, 191.
9. Wright, *Black Boy*, 191–92.
10. Wright, *Uncle Tom's Children*, 239, 244.
11. Wright, 229, 234.

12. Ramsey, "Makings of a Heroic Mistake," 74.
13. Wright, *Uncle Tom's Children*, xx.
14. Wright, "Blueprint," 59.
15. Wright, "How 'Bigger' Was Born," in *Native Son*, 514, 521, 522.
16. Wright, *Black Boy*, 317–18.
17. Wright, 33–34.
18. Wright, *12 Million Black Voices*, 78, 93, 99.
19. Wright, 146.
20. Fabre, *Unfinished Quest*, 366; Wright, *Outsider*, 473.
21. Steven Marcus, "The American Negro in Search of Identity: Three Novelists: Richard Wright, Ralph Ellison, and James Baldwin," *Commentary*, November 1953, www.commentary.org/articles/steven-marcus/the-american-negro-in-search-of-identitythree-novelists-richard-wright-ralph-ellison-james-baldwin/; Wright, *Outsider*, 474.
22. Wright, *Outsider*, 491. Damon repeats the same phrase five times in a single paragraph—either an editorial oversight or emphatic reiteration of the point.
23. Wright, 584–85.
24. Wright, *Native Son*, 389. Though critical of the novel's politics, Ben Davis Jr. praised its "literary excellence," acknowledging that Boris Max shows some of "the responsibilities of capitalism for Bigger's plight" but arguing that he "should have argued for Bigger's acquittal," or else "the first business of the Communist Party or the I.L.D. would have been to chuck him out of the case." Davis, review of *Native Son*, reprinted in Reilly, *Richard Wright*, 74–75.
25. Wright, *Outsider*, 474–92.
26. Marx, preface to *Contribution to the Critique*.
27. Wright, *Uncle Tom's Children*, 220.
28. Wright, 225.
29. Wright, *Outsider*, 476.
30. Calloway, "Wright and Religion," 158.
31. Wright, "Blueprint," 57.
32. Dawahare, *Nationalism, Marxism*, 131.
33. Wright, *Lawd Today!*, 38–39, 44–45, 49–50.
34. Wright, *Uncle Tom's Children*, 131.
35. Wright, *Outsider*, 480–81.
36. Wright, *Native Son*, 16–17, 32–33.
37. Wright, 446–47.
38. Wright, *12 Million Black Voices*, 100.
39. Wright, *Black Power*, 655–66.
40. Keady, "Richard Wright's Women Characters," 124; DeCosta-Willis, "Avenging Angels and Mute Mothers," 540; Williams, "Papa Dick and Sister-Woman," 395.
41. Keady, "Richard Wright's Women Characters," 127.
42. Foley, "Dramatic Picture," 43–54; Russell, "Wright and African American Women," 77–86; Guttman, "What Bigger Killed For," 169–93; Higashida, "Aunt Sue's Children," 395–425.
43. See William J. Maxwell's insightful discussion of interracialism and the homosocial rhetoric of the Scottsboro case. Maxwell, *New Negro, Old Left*, 125–51.
44. Naison, *Communists in Harlem*, 137.

45. Miller, Pennybacker, and Rosenhaft, "Mother Ada Wright," 387–430.
46. Wright, *Black Boy*, 289–93.
47. Marx, *Capital*, vol. 1, chap. 19.
48. Wright, *Native Son*, 440.
49. Qtd. in Beasley, *Life in Red*, 105.
50. Wright, *Black Boy*, 320; *Native Son*, 67–69.
51. Wright, *Native Son*, 140.
52. Russell, "Wright and African American Women," 79.
53. Wright, *Native Son*, 106, 109.
54. Rowley, *Richard Wright*, 64.
55. Wright, *Outsider*, 276.
56. Keady, "Richard Wright's Women Characters," 127.
57. Hayes, "Richard Wright and Black Women," 15.
58. Keady, "Richard Wright's Women Characters," 127.
59. Wright, *Outsider*, 26, 257–58.
60. Gilroy, *Black Atlantic*, 176.
61. Joyce, "Richard Wright's 'Long Black Song,'" 380.
62. Wright, *Uncle Tom's Children*, 136.
63. Williams, "Papa Dick and Sister-Woman," 398, 408, 409.
64. Wright, *Uncle Tom's Children*, 152.
65. Wright, 153–56.
66. Wright, *"Man Who Lived Underground*, 191–92.
67. Foley, "Woman and the Left," 163.
68. Joyce, "Richard Wright's 'Long Black Song,'" 385.
69. Keady, "Richard Wright's Women Characters," 124.
70. Williams, "Papa Dick and Sister-Woman," 404.
71. Wright, "Unemployed Councils" and "Soviets in the U.S.," in Bryant, *Byline, Richard Wright*, 186–87.
72. Wright, *Uncle Tom's Children*, 244, 249.
73. Wright, *Native Son*, 461.
74. Ella Baker and Marvel Cook, "The Bronx Slave Market," *The Crisis* 42, no. 11 (November 1935): 330.
75. Committee of "Street Corner Markets," 1940. "Black Hope," box 119, F. 1928, Richard Wright Papers, Beinecke Rare Book and Manuscript Library, Yale University. Hereafter referred to as RWP.
76. Richard Wright to Paul R. Reynolds, February 6, 1940, box 18, F. 292, RWP.
77. Wright, "Black Hope," MSS 3, box 17, F. 284, p. 21, RWP; Wright, *Native Son*, 387.
78. Wright, "Black Hope," synopsis and notes, box 21, F. 329 and F. 332, RWP.
79. Wright, "Black Hope," new version, early draft corrected, box 21, F. 323, RWP.
80. Wright, "Black Hope," Ollie Knight, notes and interviews, box 22, F. 331, RWP.
81. Wright, "Black Hope," MSS 3, box 21, F. 320–22, RWP.
82. Wright, "Black Hope," MSS 3, box 17, F. 284, RWP; Wright, *12 Million Black Voices*, 131; Richard Wright, "Tradition and Industrialization: The Plight of the Tragic Elite in Africa," *Presence Africaine*, September 1956, 356.
83. Wright, *Pagan Spain*, 21.

Chapter Six

1. Wright, *Black Power*, 656.
2. Fabre, *Unfinished Quest*, 489.
3. Wright to Paul Reynolds, qtd. in Fabre, 407.
4. Wright, *Pagan Spain*, 4.
5. Fabre, *Unfinished Quest*, 415.
6. DeLoughrey and Handley, *Postcolonial Ecologies*, 4.
7. James, "Notes on the Life of George Padmore," 288.
8. Saunders, *Cultural Cold War*, 1.
9. Maxwell, *F. B. Eyes*.
10. Colored Advisory Commission, *The Final Report of the Colored Advisory Commission Appointed to Cooperate with The American National Red Cross and the President's Committee on Relief Work in the Mississippi Valley Flood Disaster of 1927* (Washington, DC: American Red Cross, May 21, 1929).
11. Parrish, *Flood Year*, 251, 244.
12. Wright, "Silt," *New Masses*, August 24, 1937, 19.
13. Wright, 19–20.
14. Wright, *Uncle Tom's Children*, 64.
15. See, e.g., Bookchin, "Social Ecology."
16. Wright, *Black Power*, 346–47.
17. Wright, *Uncle Tom's Children*, 66, 69.
18. Parrish, *Flood Year*, 244–45.
19. Parrish, 254.
20. Burrow, *Social Basis of Consciousness*, 119.
21. Foster, "Third Nature," 53.
22. Barry, *Rising Tide*, 315.
23. Wright, *Uncle Tom's Children*, 123.
24. Wright, 152.
25. Wright, 152–56.
26. Wright, "Ethics of Living Jim Crow," 1.
27. Wright, *Native Son*, 16–17; Rutledge, "Wonder," 258.
28. Rutledge, "Wonder," 257.
29. Wright, *Black Boy*, 260.
30. Archibald McLeish, qtd. in Rutledge, "Wonder," 260.
31. Wright, *Black Boy*, 261.
32. Worster, *Dust Bowl*, 47.
33. Wright, *Black Boy*, 49.
34. Wright, 7–9, 45; Reilly, "Art of Nonfiction."
35. Wright, *Black Power*, 633, 647.
36. Wright, *Pagan Spain*, 21.
37. J. Saunders Redding, "The Way It Was," in Reilly, *Richard Wright*, 329.
38. Wright, *Outsider*, 263.
39. Wright, *Black Power*, 444.

40. Fabre, "Richard Wright and the French Existentialists," 39.
41. Wright, *Outsider*, 165.
42. Wright, 160–70, 585.
43. Wright, 195, 586.
44. Wright, *Native Son*, 429.
45. Wright, qtd. in Miller, *Voice of a Native Son*, 179.
46. Karageorgos, "Richard Wright's Poetic Marxism," 184; Cox and Nilsen, *We Make Our Own History*, 19; Lukacs, *History and Class Consciousness*, 1–2.
47. Wright, *Outsider*, 474–92, 274.
48. Watson, "Living Clue."
49. Wright, *Native Son*, 187.
50. Wright, *Outsider*, 305.
51. Wright, *Native Son*, 114.
52. Murray Bookchin, "Second Nature" (lecture, Institute for Social Ecology, 1996), https://theanarchistlibrary.org/library/murray-bookchin-second-nature.
53. Wright, *Uncle Tom's Children*, 1–15.
54. Wright, "Blueprint," 60.
55. Watson, "Living Clue," 67–68.
56. Wright, "Blueprint," 61.
57. Wright, *Black Power*, 647.
58. Baldwin, *Nobody Knows My Name*, 157.
59. Saunders, *Cultural Cold War*, 234–51.
60. Saunders, 157.
61. Fanon, *Frantz Fanon*, 101–4.
62. Tuhkanen, "Queer Guerrillas."
63. Fabre, *Unfinished Quest*, 252.
64. George Padmore, qtd. in Gaines, *American Africans in Ghana*, 56.
65. Reilly, "Art of Nonfiction," 519.
66. Wright, "Blueprint," 59–60.
67. Wright, *Black Power*, 57–59, 68, 283–84.
68. Wright, 9, 13.
69. Appiah, "Long Way from Home," 181.
70. M'Baye, "Richard Wright," 30.
71. Wright, *Black Power*, 184.
72. Reilly, "Art of Nonfiction," 519.
73. Wright, *Black Power*, 21.
74. Wright, "Blueprint," 57.
75. Wright, *Black Power*, 11, 608, 728.
76. Wright, 808.
77. Maxwell, *F. B. Eyes*.
78. Wright, *Black Power*, 415, 418, 723.
79. Bevins, *Jakarta Method*, 51; Chakrabarty, "Legacies of Bandung," 59; Lee, *Making a World after Empire*, xix.
80. Prashad, foreword to Raphael-Hernandez and Steen, *AfroAsian Encounters*, xi.

81. Wright, *Black Power*, 437–40.

82. Assorted reviews of *The Color Curtain* in Reilly, *Richard Wright*, *Kirkus Reviews*: Tillman Durdin, 273–75; Ellen Logue, 278–79; Abner W. Berry, 279–81; Paula Snelling, 283–285.

83. Hakutani, "Richard Wright's Journey," 64, 81.

84. Roberts and Foulcher, *Indonesian Notebook*, 5.

85. By the time Sablonière told Wright about the first article, he knew the Congress for Cultural Freedom was a CIA-sponsored organization. He believed that Vuyk was associated with it and was increasingly disillusioned by the "white West" that was "sticking knives into [his] back." See Rowley, *Richard Wright*, 520.

86. Roberts and Foulcher, *Indonesian Notebook*, 16. I am indebted to Roberts and Foulcher's superbly annotated sourcebook of Indonesian counternarratives to Wright's "ur-narrative."

87. Roberts and Foulcher, 17.

88. Wright, *Black Power*, 584.

89. Roberts and Foulcher, *Indonesian Notebook*, 202, 10.

90. Roberts and Foulcher, 192, 196–97.

91. Tuhkanen, "Queer Guerrillas," 616.

92. Theo Williams, "George Padmore Played a Vital Role in the Struggle against Colonial Oppression," *Jacobin*, June 9, 2023, https://jacobin.com/2023/06/george-padmore-anti-colonialism-marxism-color-line-communism.

93. Wright, *Black Power*, 594–95.

94. Wright, qtd. in Roberts and Foulcher, *Indonesian Notebook*, 191; Wright, *12 Million Black Voices*, 147; Wright, *Black Power*, 504.

Chapter Seven

1. Among many comparisons of Wright to other authors, including Dreiser, Steinbeck, Dostoevsky, and Dickens in reviews of *Native Son*, see Henry Seidel Canby, Lewis Gannett, Charles Poore, and Clifton Fadiman, in Reilly, *Richard Wright*, 39–45. Peter Monro Jack, "A Tragic Novel of Negro Life in America," in Reilly, 54. Fanon, *Black Skin*, 118.

2. Marx, *Capital*, vol. 1, chap. 19.

3. Fabre, *Unfinished Quest*, 276.

4. Harrington, *Why I Left America*, 22–23.

5. Julia Wright, foreword to Harrington, *Why I Left America*, ix–xi.

6. Fabre, *Unfinished Quest*, 509.

7. Mangione, *Dream and the Deal*, 309, 324. Dies chaired the House Un-American Activities Committee from 1938 to 1944.

8. Smethurst and Rubin, "Cartoons of Ollie Harrington," 126.

9. Joe Sims, personal correspondence with author, June 28, 2023. George Murphy was the son of the founder and publisher of Baltimore Afro-American Newspapers, a major local and national Black institution and Black left-wing press. Harrington, *Why I Left America*, 22–23.

10. Sherwood, "All African People's Congress," 64.

11. Drake, "Hide My Face?," 94–95.

12. Reid-Pharr, *Once You Go Black*, 14.

13. Wright, *Long Dream*, 273, 234–35, 360, 372.

14. See Lâle Demirtürk, "Mapping the Terrain of Whiteness," 129.
15. Kinnamon and Fabre, *Conversations with Richard Wright*, 167, 177.
16. Qtd. in Watson, "Living Clue," 71.
17. Wright, "Blueprint," 53–65.
18. Marx and Engels, *Manifesto of the Communist Party*.
19. Wright, *Black Boy*, 184.
20. Wright, 454, 320, 448–50.
21. Wright, *Outsider*, 34.
22. Wright, 439.
23. J. Saunders Redding, "The Way It Was," in Reilly, *Richard Wright*, 329.
24. Drake, "Hide My Face?," 86; Wright, *Black Power*, 585.
25. Wright, *Native Son*, 461; Kinnamon and Fabre, *Conversations with Richard Wright*, 155.
26. Fabre, *Unfinished Quest*, 358–60.
27. Curry, "He's a Rapist," 145.
28. Wright, *Eight Men*, 154.
29. Wright, *Long Dream*, 383–84.
30. Wright, *Native Son*, 17.
31. Wright, 17.
32. Submitted to *Ebony* in 1951, "I Choose Exile" was rejected by editor Ben Burns and never published. Box 1, Richard Wright Papers, Special Collections and Archives, Kent State University.
33. Wright, *Black Boy*, 100, 249.
34. Fabre, *Unfinished Quest*, 522.
35. Harrington, *Why I Left America*, 109.
36. Webb, *Richard Wright*, 375. Webb cites the source as "name withheld" (n419).
37. Paul K. Chalemsky, "Dispatch, European Division" (Contact Report, HQS File Number 200-6-387/3), July 11, 1969.
38. James Campbell, "The Island Affair," *The Guardian*, January 7, 2006, www.theguardian.com/books/2006/jan/07/featuresreviews.guardianreview25.
39. Saunders, *Cultural Cold War*; Maxwell, *F. B. Eyes*, 172.
40. Fabre, "Richard Wright's Critical Reception," 314–15.
41. Allen, "Spies Spying on Spies," 37.
42. See also, e.g., Harrington, *Why I Left America*; Rowley, *Richard Wright*; and Ruquist, "Non, nous ne jouons."
43. Julia Wright, "Nahel's France: Neo-colonized and Pan-African Voices Speak Up," *Pan-African News Wire*, July 15, 2023, www.panafricannews.blogspot.com/2023/07/nahels-france-neo-colonialized-and-pan.html.
44. Qtd. in Fabre, *Unfinished Quest*, 458.
45. Qtd. in Maxwell, *F. B. Eyes*, 245.
46. Saunders, *Cultural Cold War*, 57–58; see also "Origins of the Congress for Cultural Freedom, 1949–1950," *Studies in Intelligence* 38, no. 5 (May 8, 2007), www.cia.gov/resources/csi/studies-in-intelligence/archives/vol-38-no-5/origins-of-the-congress-for-cultural-freedom-1949-1950/.
47. Richard Gibson, qtd. in Menand, *Free World*, 395.

48. Max Steele, "Richard Wright: The Visible Man," *Paris Review* 167 (Fall 2003), www.theparisreview.org/letters-essays/169/richard-wright-the-visible-man-max-steele.

49. Irwin Shaw, qtd. in Wilbers, "Author Resurrected, 193; William Styron, qtd. in Wilbers, 194.

50. Richard Wright, "I Choose Exile," box 1, folder 1, Richard Wright Papers, Kent State Special Collections and Archives.

51. Wright, *Long Dream*, 383; "Island of Hallucination," qtd. in William J. Maxwell, *F. B. Eyes*, 246.

52. Ruquist, "Non, nous ne jouons," 292.

53. Campbell, "Island Affair."

54. Charisse Burden-Stelly, "'Stoolpigeons' and the Treacherous Terrain of Freedom Fighting," *Black Perspectives*, September 13, 2018, www.aaihs.org/stoolpigeons-and-the-treacherous-terrain-of-freedom-fighting/.

55. Ruquist, "Non, nous ne jouons," 293.

56. Maxwell, *F. B. Eyes*, 250.

57. Fabre, *Unfinished Quest*, 481.

58. Maxwell, *F. B. Eyes*, 175.

59. Julia Wright, introduction to Wright, *Haiku*, x, viii.

60. Webb, *Richard Wright*, 393.

61. Wright, *Haiku*, 60, 66. Hereafter, numbered haiku in this chapter are from this source.

62. Walker, *Richard Wright*, 309, 337.

63. Wright, *Native Son*, 148.

64. Wright, *Black Boy*, 100.

65. Walt Whitman, "Crossing Brooklyn Ferry," 130.

66. Rowley, Richard Wright, 505; Styron, qtd. in Wilbers, "Author Resurrected," 194.

67. *PM's Sunday Picture News*, "Why Richard Wright Came Back from France" and *Nuit et Jour*, "I Feel More at Home in France Than Where I Was Born," in Kinnamon and Fabre, *Conversations with Richard Wright*, 124, 125, 126–27.

68. Wright, *Pagan Spain*, 21.

69. Wright, *Black Power*, 721.

70. Marx, *Eighteenth Brumaire*.

71. Wright, *Black Power*, 409.

72. Israel's war on Gaza started after Hamas invaded southern Israel on October 7, 2023, killing some 1,200 people and kidnapping 252 others. This reference to it was added as the book was going into production in June 2024.

73. The Elaine Massacre was sparked by a meeting on September 30, 1919, of the Progressive Farmers and Households Union attended by approximately 100 Black sharecroppers. When a group of white men attempted to enter the church where the union was meeting, shots were exchanged and two white men died. A white mob of angry landowners descended on the Black town, culminating in one of the worst massacres in Arkansas history. For a brief history, see https://if-these-walls-could-talk.shorthandstories.com/these-walls-can-talk/index.html#group-section-1919-1946-t7LKr19SjK.

74. "Julia Wright, Daughter of Famed Writer Richard Wright, on Mumia Abu-Jamal," *Democracy Now*, June 23, 2006, www.democracynow.org/2006/6/23/julia_wright_daughter_of_famed_writer.

75. Wright, "Nahel's France."
76. Wright, "Nahel's France."
77. Chafer, *End of Empire*, 235.
78. Richard Wright, *Écoute, homme blanc!* (Paris: Calmann-Levy, 1959).
79. Rowley, *Richard Wright*, 519, 523.
80. Harrington, *Why I Left America*, 17.
81. Fabre, *Unfinished Quest*, 518–19.

Bibliography

Archives

Yale Collection of American Literature, Beinecke Rare Book and Manuscript Library, New Haven, CT
    Richard Wright Papers
The New York Public Library, Schomburg Center for Research in Black Culture, New York, NY
    Richard Wright Collection
Kent State University Libraries, Special Collections and Archives, Kent, OH
    Richard Wright Papers
Library of Congress, Washington, DC
    Born in Slavery: Slave Narratives from the Federal Writers' Project, 1936 to 1938, www.loc.gov/collections/slave-narratives-from-the-federal-writers-project-1936-to-1938/about-this-collection/

Newspapers and Magazines

Against the Current
Atlantic
Black Perspectives
Chicago Review of Books
Commentary
Crisis
Dissent
Esquire
Inside Higher Education
International Socialist Review
Jacobin
Liberator
Nation
New Masses
New Republic
New York Times
New Yorker
New York Times Book Review
Pan African News
Saturday Review
Times Literary Supplement
Yale University Library Gazette

Books and Articles

Aaron, Daniel. *Writers on the Left: Episodes in Literary Communism*. With a new preface by Alan Wald. 1961. New York: Columbia University Press, 1992.

Afflerbach, Ian. "Liberalism's Blind Judgment." *Modern Fiction Studies* 61, no. 1 (Spring 2015): 90–113.

Agee, James, and Walker Evans. *Let Us Now Praise Famous Men*. Boston: Houghton Mifflin, 1941.

Alexander, Michelle. *The New Jim Crow: Mass Incarceration in the Age of Colorblindness*. New York: New Press, 2012.

Allen, Craig Lanier. "Spies Spying on Spies Spying: The Rive Noire, the *Paris Review*, and the Specter of Surveillance in Post-war American Literary Expatriate Paris, 1953–1958." *Australasian Journal of American Studies* 35, no. 1 (July 2016): 29–50.

Andrews, William L., and Douglas Taylor, eds. *Richard Wright's Black Boy (American Hunger): A Casebook.* New York: Oxford University Press, 2003.

Anyon, Jean. "Social Class and School Knowledge." *Curriculum Inquiry* 11, no. 1 (1981): 3–42.

———. "Social Class and the Hidden Curriculum of Work." *Journal of Education* 162, no. 1 (1980): 67–92.

Appiah, Kwame Anthony. "A Long Way from Home: Wright in the Gold Coast." In *Modern Critical Views: Richard Wright*, edited by Harold Bloom, 173–90. New York: Chelsea House, 1987.

Au, Wayne. "Vygotsky and Lenin on Learning: The Parallel Structures of Individual and Social Development." *Science & Society* 71, no. 3 (July 2007): 273–98.

Baker, Ella, and Marvel Cook. "The Bronx Slave Market." *The Crisis* 42, no. 11 (November 1935): 330–31.

Baker, Houston A. "Race, Displacement, and Richard Wright's Transatlantic Real Estate." *Obsidian* 11, no. 2 (2010): 107–14.

Baldwin, James. *Nobody Knows My Name: More Notes of a Native Son.* 1961. New York: Vintage International, 1989.

———. *Notes of a Native Son.* New York: Beacon Press, 1955.

Balthaser, Benjamin. "Killing the Documentarian: Richard Wright and Documentary Modernity." *Criticism* 55, no. 3 (2013): 357–90.

Barnett, Timothy. "Politicizing the Personal: Frederick Douglass, Richard Wright, and Some Thoughts on the Limits of Critical Literacy." *College English* 68, no. 4 (2006): 356–81.

Barry, John M. *Rising Tide: The Great Mississippi Flood of 1927 and How It Changed America.* New York: Touchstone Books / Simon & Schuster, 1997.

Beasley, David. *A Life in Red: A Story of Forbidden Love, the Great Depression, and the Communist Fight for a Black Nation in the Deep South.* Winston-Salem, NC: John F. Blair, 2015.

Bevins, Vincent. *The Jakarta Method: Washington's Anticommunist Crusade & the Mass Murder Program that Shaped Our World.* New York: PublicAffairs / Hachette Book Group, 2020.

Bone, Robert. *The Negro Novel in America.* 1958. New Haven, CT: Yale University Press, 1966.

———. "Richard Wright and the Chicago Renaissance." In "Richard Wright: A Special Issue." *Callaloo* no. 28 (Summer 1986): 446–68.

Bontemps, Arna. "Review of *The Outsider*." In *The Critical Response to Richard Wright*, edited by Robert J. Butler, 105–8. Westport, CT: Greenwood, 1995.

Bookchin, Murray. "Social Ecology versus Deep Ecology: A Challenge for the Ecology Movement." *Socialist Review* 88, no. 3 (1988): 1–29.

Brandt, Deborah. "Sponsors of Literacy." *College Composition and Communication* 49, no. 2 (1998): 165–85.

Bryant, Earle V., ed. *Byline, Richard Wright: Articles from the "Daily Worker" and "New Masses."* Columbia: University of Missouri Press, 2016.

Buell, Lawrence. *The Environmental Imagination: Thoreau, Nature Writing, and the Formation of American Culture.* Cambridge, MA: Harvard University Press, 1995.

Burrow, Trigant. *The Social Basis of Consciousness*. New York: Harcourt, Brace, 1927.
Butler, Robert J., ed. *The Critical Response to Richard Wright*. Westport, CT: Greenwood, 1995.
Butts, J. J. *Dark Mirror: African Americans and the Federal Writers' Project*. Columbus: Ohio State University Press, 2021.
———. "New World A-Coming: African American Documentary Intertexts of the Federal Writers' Project." *African American Review* 44, no. 4 (2011): 649–66.
Caldwell, Erskine, and Margaret Bourke-White. *You Have Seen Their Faces*. 1937. Athens: University of Georgia Press, 1995.
Callahan, John F., and Marc C. Conner, eds. *The Selected Letters of Ralph Ellison*. New York: Random House, 2019.
Calloway, Jamall A. "Wright and Religion." In *Richard Wright in Context*, edited by Michael Nowlin, 150–60. Cambridge: Cambridge University Press, 2021.
Cappetti, Carla. "Sociology of an Existence: Richard Wright and the Chicago School." *MELUS* 12, no. 2 (Summer 1985): 25–43.
Cayton, Horace R. *Long Old Road: Back to Metropolis*. 1965. London: Routledge, 2017.
Chafer, Tony. *The End of Empire in French West Africa: France's Successful Decolonization Account*. Oxford: Berg, 2002.
Chakrabarty, Dipesh. "The Legacies of Bandung: Decolonization and the Politics of Culture." In *Making a World after Empire: The Bandung Moment and Its Political Afterlives*, edited by Christopher J. Lee, 45–68. Athens: Ohio University Press, 2010.
Coates, Ta-Nehisi. *Between the World and Me*. New York: Spiegel & Grau, 2015.
Coles, Robert. *Doing Documentary Work*. New York: Oxford University Press, 1997.
Cossu-Beaumont, Laurence. "Richard Wright and His Editors: A Work under the Influence? From the Signifyin(g) Rebel to the Exiled Intellectual." In *Richard Wright in a Post-racial Imaginary*, edited by Alice Mikal Craven and William E. Dowe, 83–98. London: Bloomsbury, 2014.
Costello, Brannon. "Richard Wright's *Lawd Today!* and the Political Uses of Modernism." *African American Review* 37, no. 1 (Spring 2002): 39–52.
Courage, Richard A., and Christopher Robert Reed, eds. *Roots of the Black Chicago Renaissance: New Negro Writers, Artists, and Intellectuals, 1893–1930*. Foreword by Darlene Clark Hine. Urbana: University of Illinois Press, 2020.
Cox, Laurence, and Alf Gunvald Nilsen. *We Make Our Own History: Marxism and Social Movements in the Twilight of Neoliberalism*. London: Pluto Press, 2014.
Cruse, Harold. *The Crisis of the Negro Intellectual: A Historical Analysis of the Failure of Black Leadership*. New York: New York Review of Books Classics, 2005.
Curry, Thomas J. "He's a Rapist, Even When He's Not: Richard Wright's Account of Black Male Vulnerability in the Raping of Willie McGee." In *The Politics of Richard Wright: Perspectives on Resistance*, edited by Jane Anna Gordon and Cyrus Ernesto Zirakzadeh, 132–52. Lexington: University Press of Kentucky, 2019.
Davis, Frank Marshall. *Livin' the Blues: Memoirs of a Black Journalist and a Poet*. Edited by John Edgar Tidwell. Madison: University of Wisconsin Press, 1992.
Dawahare, Anthony. *Nationalism, Marxism, and African American Literature between the Wars: A New Pandora's Box*. Jackson: University Press of Mississippi, 2003.
DeCosta-Willis, Miriam. "Avenging Angels and Mute Mothers: Black Southern Women in Wright's Fictional World." *Callaloo* no. 28 (Summer 1986): 540–51.

DeLoughrey, Elizabeth, and George B. Handley, eds. *Postcolonial Ecologies: Literatures of the Environment*. New York: Oxford University Press, 2011.

Denning, Michael. *The Cultural Front: The Laboring of American Culture in the Twentieth Century*. 1996. New York: Verso, 2011.

Dinerstein, Joel. "'Uncle Tom Is Dead!': Wright, Himes, and Ellison Lay a Mask to Rest." *African American Review* 43, no. 1 (2009): 83–98.

Dolinar, Brian. "The Illinois Writers' Project Essays: Introduction." *Southern Quarterly* 46, no. 2 (2009): 84–162.

———, ed. *The Negro in Illinois: The WPA Papers*. Champaign: University of Illinois Press, 2015.

———. "Radicals on Relief: Black Chicago Writers and the WPA." *American Communist History* 14, no. 1 (2015): 27–39.

Douglass, Frederick. *Narrative of the Life of Frederick Douglass, An American Slave*. Warbler Classics Annotated Edition, introduction by Ulrich Baer. 1845. New York: Warbler Classics, 2022.

Drake, John Gibbs St. Clair. "Hide My Face? On Pan-Africanism and Negritude." In *Soon One Morning: New Writing by American Negroes, 1940–1962*, edited by Herbert Hill, 77–105. New York: Alfred A. Knopf, 1965.

Drake, John Gibbs St. Clair, and Horace R. Cayton. *Black Metropolis: A Study of Negro Life in a Northern City*. Introduction by Richard Wright and foreword by William Julius Wilson. 1945. Chicago: University of Chicago Press, 1993.

Eagleton, Terry. *Literary Theory*. 3rd ed. Minneapolis: University of Minnesota Press, 2008.

Ellison, Ralph. "Richard Wright's Blues." *Antioch Review* 5, no. 2 (1945): 198–211.

———. *Shadow and Act*. 1953. New York: Vintage Books, 1964.

Entin, Joseph. *Sensational Modernism: Experimental Fiction and Photography in Thirties America*. Chapel Hill: The University of North Carolina Press, 2007.

Fabre, Michel. "Richard Wright and the French Existentialists." *MELUS* 5, no. 2 (Summer 1978): 39–51.

———. *Richard Wright: Books and Writers*. Jackson: University Press of Mississippi, 1985.

———. "Richard Wright's Critical Reception in France—Censors Right and Left, Negritude Intellectuals, the Literary Set, and the General Public." *Mississippi Quarterly* 50, no. 2 (Spring 1977): 307–25.

———. "Richard Wright's First Hundred Books." *CLA Journal* 16, no. 4 (June 1973): 458–74.

———. "Richard Wright: The Man Who Lived Underground." *Studies in the Novel* 3, no. 2 (1971): 165–79.

———. *The Unfinished Quest of Richard Wright*. 1973. Urbana: University of Illinois Press, 1993.

———. *The World of Richard Wright*. Jackson: University Press of Mississippi, 1985.

Fanon, Frantz. *Black Skin, White Masks*. New York: Grove Press, 1967.

———. *Frantz Fanon: The Political Writings from Alienation and Freedom*. Edited by Jean Khalfa and Robert J. C. Young. Translated by Steven Corcoran. London: Bloomsbury Academic, 2021.

Federal Writers' Project. *New York Panorama: A Comprehensive View of the Metropolis*. American Guide Series. New York: Random House, 1938.

Federal Writers' Project of the Works Progress Administration in New York City. *The WPA Guide to New York City: the Federal Writers' Project Guide to 1930s New York*. Introduction by William H. Whyte. New York: New Press, 1995.

Foley, Barbara. "'A Dramatic Picture . . . of Woman from Feudalism to Fascism': Richard Wright's 'Black Hope.'" *Obsidian* 11, no. 2 (2010): 43–54.

———. *Radical Representations: Politics and Form in US Proletarian Fiction, 1929–1941*. Durham, NC: Duke University Press, 1993.

———. *Wrestling with the Left: The Making of Ralph Ellison's Invisible Man*. Durham, NC: Duke University Press, 2010.

Foley, Barbara, and Jerry W. Ward Jr. "Richard Wright in the Era of Black Lives Matter: Two Views." In *Richard Wright in Context*, edited by Michael Nowlin, 348–57. Cambridge: Cambridge University Press, 2021.

Folsom, Frank. *Days of Anger, Days of Hope: A Memoir of the League of American Writers, 1937–1942*. Niwot: University Press of Colorado, 1994.

Ford, Nick Aaron. "A Long Way from Home." *Phylon Quarterly* 19, no. 4 (1958): 435–36.

Foster, John Bellamy. "Third Nature: Edward Said on Ecology and Imperialism." *Will the Flower Slip through the Asphalt*, edited by Vijay Prashad, 50–57. New Delhi: LeftWord Books, 2017.

Fox, Daniel M. "The Achievement of the Federal Writers' Project." *American Quarterly* 13, no. 1 (1961): 3–19.

Freire, Paulo, and Donald Macedo. *Literacy: Reading the Word and the World*. Westport, CT: Praeger, 1987.

Gaines, Kevin Kelly. *American Africans in Ghana: Black Expatriates and the Civil Rights Movement*. Chapel Hill: The University of North Carolina Press, 2006.

———. "Revisiting Richard Wright in Ghana." In *The Politics of Richard Wright: Perspectives on Resistance*, edited by Jane Anna Gordon and Cyrus Ernesto Zirakzadeh, 181–97. Lexington: University Press of Kentucky, 2018.

Gates, Henry Louis, Jr., and K. A. Appiah. *Richard Wright: Critical Perspectives Past and Present*. New York: Amistad, 1993.

Gayle, Addison. *Richard Wright: Ordeal of a Native Son*. New York: Anchor Books, 1980.

———. *The Way of the New World: The Black Novel in America*. New York: Anchor Press / Doubleday, 1975.

Gilroy, Paul. *The Black Atlantic: Modernity and Double-Consciousness*. Cambridge, MA: Harvard University Press, 1993.

Gordon, Jane Anna, and Cyrus Ernesto Zirakzadeh, eds. *The Politics of Richard Wright: Perspectives on Resistance*. Lexington: University Press of Kentucky, 2018.

Guttman, Sondra. "What Bigger Killed for: Rereading Violence against Women in *Native Son*." *Texas Studies in Language and Literature* 43, no. 2 (Summer 2001): 169–93.

Hakutani, Yoshinobu. "*The Color Curtain*: Richard Wright's Journey into Asia." In *Richard Wright's Travel Writings: New Reflections*, edited by Virginia Whatley Smith, 63–77. Jackson: University Press of Mississippi, 2001.

———. "Creation of the Self in Richard Wright's *Black Boy*." *Black American Literature Forum* 19, no. 2 (1985): 70–75.

Harrington, Oliver W. *Why I Left America and Other Essays*. Jackson: University Press of Mississippi, 1993.

Hartman, Saidiya V., and Frank B. Wilderson. "The Position of the Unthought." *Qui Parle* 13, no. 2 (Spring/Summer 2003): 183–201.

Hathaway, Rosemary. "Native Geography: Richard Wright's Work for the Federal Writers' Project in Chicago." *African American Review* 42, no. 1 (2008): 91–108.

Hayes, Floyd W., III. "Richard Wright and Black Women: Imagining the Feminine in *The Outsider*." In *The Politics of Richard Wright: Perspectives on Resistance*, edited by Jane Anna Gordon and Cyrus Ernesto Zirakzadeh, 107–19. Louisville: University Press of Kentucky, 2018.

Hicks, Scott. "W. E. B. Du Bois, Booker T. Washington, and Richard Wright: Toward an Ecocriticism of Color." *Callaloo* 29, no. 1 (2006): 202–22.

Higashida, Cheryl. "Aunt Sue's Children: Re-viewing the Gender(ed) Politics of Richard Wright's Radicalism." *American Literature* 75, no. 2 (June 2003): 395–425.

Hine, Darlene Clark, and John McClusky, eds. *The Black Chicago Renaissance*. Chicago: University of Illinois Press, 2012.

Homberger, Eric. "Proletarian Literature and the John Reed Clubs 1929–1935." *Journal of American Studies* 13, no. 2 (1979): 221–44.

hooks, bell. *Talking Back: Thinking Feminist, Thinking Black*. Boston: South End Press, 1999.

Hutchinson, George. "The Literary Ecology of *Native Son* and *Black Boy*." In *The Cambridge Companion to Richard Wright*, edited by Glenda R. Carpio, 23–38. Cambridge: Cambridge University Press, 2019.

Jackson, Lawrence. *The Indignant Generation: A Narrative of African American Writers and Critics, 1934–1960*. Princeton, NJ: Princeton University Press, 2013.

James, C. L. R. "*Native Son* and Revolution." *New International* 6, no. 4 (1940): 92–93.

———. "Notes on the Life of George Padmore." In *The C. L. R. James Reader*, edited by Anna Grimshaw, 288–295. Hoboken, NJ: Wiley-Blackwell, 1992.

JanMohamed, Abdul R. *The Death-Bound-Subject: Richard Wright's Archeology of Death*. Durham, NC: Duke University Press, 2005.

Jaynes, Gerald D., et al. "The Chicago School and the Roots of Urban Ethnography: An Intergenerational Conversation with Gerald D. Jaynes, David E. Apter, Herbert J. Gans, William Kornblum, Ruth Horowitz, James F. Short Jr., Gerald Suttles, and Robert E. Washington." *Ethnography* 10, no. 4 (2009): 375–96.

Joyce, Joyce Ann. "Richard Wright's 'Long Black Song': A Moral Dilemma." *Mississippi Quarterly* 42, no. 4 (Fall 1989): 378–85.

Karageorgos, Konstantina M. "Deep Marxism: Richard Wright's *The Outsider* and the Making of a Postwar Aesthetic." *Mediations: Journal of the Marxist Literary Group* 28, no. 2 (2015): 109–27.

———. "Richard Wright's Poetic Marxism." In *Lineages of the Literary Left: Essays in Honor of Alan M. Wald*, edited by Howard Brick, Robbie Lieberman, and Paula Rabinowitz, 180–194. Ann Arbor: Michigan Publishing, 2015.

Kazin, Alfred. Introduction to *Jews without Money*, by Mike Gold, 1–8. 1930. New York: Public Affairs, 2004.

Keady, Sylvia. "Richard Wright's Women Characters and Inequality." *Black American Literature Forum* 10, no. 4 (Winter 1976): 124–28.

Keith, Joseph. "Richard Wright, *The Outsider*, and the Empire of Liberal Pluralism: Race and American Expansion after World War II." *Black Scholar* 39, no. 1–2 (2009): 51–58.

Kinnamon, Keneth, and Michel Fabre. *Conversations with Richard Wright*. Jackson: University Press of Mississippi, 1993.

Kiuchi, Toru. "Kay Boyle and Richard Wright, 1948–1960: A 'Friendship Forever' in a 'Difficult Time.'" *E-Rea* 10, no. 2 (June 2013).

Kiuchi, Toru, and Yoshinobu Hakutani. *Richard Wright: A Documented Chronology, 1908–1960*. Jefferson, NC: McFarland, 2014.

Kozol, Jonathan. *Savage Inequalities: Children in American Schools*. New York: Crown, 1991.

Lee, Christopher J. *Making a World after Empire: The Bandung Moment and Its Political Afterlives*. Athens: Ohio University Press, 2010.

Le Sueur, Meridel. *Worker Writers*. Worker Writer Series No. 4. 1939. Minneapolis: West End Press, 1982.

Lukacs, Georg. *History and Class Consciousness: Studies in Marxist Dialectics*. 1968. Cambridge, MA: MIT Press, 1999.

Mangione, Jerre. *The Dream and the Deal: The Federal Writers' Project, 1935–1943*. Syracuse, NY: Syracuse University Press, 1996.

Manry, Jessica. "Reading Backward with 'The Forgotten Man of History': George Padmore's Revolutionary Theory of Class and Race." *Mediations: Journal of the Marxist Literary Group* 32, no. 2 (Spring 2019): 41–70.

Marx, Karl. *The Eighteenth Brumaire of Louis Bonaparte*. Chap. 1. 1852. Marx/Engels Archive. www.marxists.org/archive/marx/works/1852/18th-brumaire/index.htm.

———. Preface to *A Contribution to the Critique of Political Economy*. 1859. Marx/Engels Archive. www.marxists.org/archive/marx/works/1859/critique-pol-economy/preface.htm.

———. "The Transformation of the Value (and Respective Price) of Labour-Power into Wages." Vol. 1, chap. 19 of *Capital*. 1867. Marx-Engels Archive. www.marxists.org/archive/marx/works/1867-c1/ch19.htm.

Marx, Karl, and Frederick Engels. *Manifesto of the Communist Party*. 1848. Marxists Internet Archive. www.marxists.org/archive/marx/works/download/pdf/Manifesto.pdf.

Maxwell, William J. *F. B. Eyes: How J. Edgar Hoover's Ghostreaders Framed African American Literature*. Princeton, NJ: Princeton University Press, 2015.

———. *New Negro, Old Left: African-American Writing and Communism between the Wars*. New York: Columbia University Press, 1999.

Mayer, Robert. "Lenin and the Practice of Dialectical Thinking." *Science & Society* 63, no. 1 (1999): 40–62.

M'Baye, Babacar. "Richard Wright and African Francophone Intellectuals: A Reassessment of the 1956 Congress of Black Writers in Paris." *African and Black Diaspora: An International Journal* 2, no. 1 (2009): 29–42.

Menand, Louis. *The Free World: Art and Thought in the Cold War*. New York: Farrar, Straus and Giroux, 2021.

Meyerson, Gregory. "Aunt Sue's Mistake: False Consciousness in Richard Wright's 'Bright and Morning Star.'" *Reconstruction: Studies in Contemporary Culture* 8, no. 4 (2008). http://reconstruction.digitalodu.com/Issues/084/meyerson.shtml.

Miller, Eugene E. *Voice of a Native Son: The Poetics of Richard Wright*. Jackson: University Press of Mississippi, 1990.

Miller, James A., Susan D. Pennybacker, and Eva Rosenhaft. "Mother Ada Wright and the International Campaign to Free the Scottsboro Boys, 1931–1934." *American Historical Review* 106, no. 2 (April 2002): 387–430.

Mills, Nathaniel F. "Marxism, Communism, and Richard Wright's Depression-Era Work." In *The Cambridge Companion to Richard Wright*, edited by Glenda R Carpio, 58–73. Cambridge: Cambridge University Press, 2019.

Morrison, Toni. *Playing in the Dark: Whiteness and the Literary Imagination*. New York: Vintage Books, 1992.

———. "The Site of Memory." In *Inventing the Truth: The Art and Craft of Memoir*, edited by William Zinsser, 183–200. 2nd ed. New York: Houghton Mifflin, 1995.

Mullen, Bill V. *Popular Fronts: Chicago and African-American Cultural Politics, 1935–46*. Urbana: University of Illinois Press, 1999.

Naison, Mark. *Communists in Harlem during the Depression*. Champaign: University of Illinois Press, 2005.

Parrish, Susan Scott. *The Flood Year 1927: A Cultural History*. Princeton, NJ: Princeton University Press, 2017.

Patterson, William L. *The Man Who Cried Genocide*. New York: International, 1971.

Platt, Tony. "E. Franklin Frazier Reconsidered." *Social Justice* 16, no. 4 (1989): 186–95.

Prashad, Vijay. Foreword to *AfroAsian Encounters: Culture, History, Politics*, edited by Heike Raphael-Hernandez and Shannon Steen, xi–xxiii. New York: New York University Press, 2006.

Proefriedt, William A. "The Immigrant or 'Outsider' Experience as Metaphor for Becoming an Educated Person in the Modern World: Mary Antin, Richard Wright, and Eva Hoffman." *MELUS* 16, no. 2 (1989–90): 75–89.

Ramsey, Joseph G. "Lunacy and the Left: Learning from Richard Wright's Lost Confessions." *Cultural Logic: Marxist Theory and Practice* 23, no. 19 (2019): 72–86.

———. "The Makings of a Heroic Mistake: Richard Wright's 'Bright and Morning Star,' Communism and the Contradictions of Emergent Subjectivity." *Mediations: Journal of the Marxist Literary Group* 30, no. 1 (Fall 2016): 61–90.

Rankin, Tom. "Looking and Telling, Again and Again: The Documentary Impulse." *Southern Cultures* (Spring 2016): 3–9.

Ray, David, and Robert M. Farnsworth, eds. *Richard Wright: Impressions and Perspectives*. Ann Arbor: University of Michigan Press, 1973.

Record, C. Wilson. *The Negro and the Communist Party*. 1951. Chapel Hill: The University of North Carolina Press, 2011.

Reid-Pharr, Robert. *Once You Go Black: Choice, Desire, and the Black American Intellectual*. New York: New York University Press, 2007.

Reilly, John M. "Richard Wright and the Art of Nonfiction: Stepping Out on the Stage of the World." In "Richard Wright: A Special Issue." *Callaloo* no. 28 (Summer 1986): 507–20.

———, ed. *Richard Wright: The Critical Reception*. New York: Burt Franklin, 1978.

———. "Richard Wright's Apprenticeship." *Journal of Black Studies* 2, no. 4 (1972): 439–60.

Ridenour, Ronald. "*The Man Who Lived Underground*: A Critique." *Phylon* 31, no. 1 (1970): 54–57.

Rideout, Walter B. *The Radical Novel in the United States: 1900–1954*. New York: Hill and Wang, 1956.

Roberts, Brian Russell, and Keith Foulcher, eds. *Indonesian Notebook: A Sourcebook on Richard Wright and the Bandung Conference*. Durham, NC: Duke University Press, 2016.

Robinson, Cedric. *Black Marxism: The Making of the Black Radical Tradition*. Chapel Hill: The University of North Carolina Press, 2000.

Rolo, Charles. "This, Too, Is America." In *Richard Wright's "Black Boy" ("American Hunger"): A Casebook*, edited by William L. Andrews and Douglas Taylor, 25–30. New York: Oxford University Press, 2003.

Rowbotham, Sheila. *Hidden from History: 300 Years of Women's Oppression and the Fight Against It*. London: Pluto Press, 1975.

Rowley, Hazel. *Richard Wright: The Life and Times*. Chicago: University of Chicago Press, 2008.

Ruquist, Rebecca. "Non, nous ne jouons pas la trompette: Richard Wright in Paris." *Contemporary French and Francophone Studies* 8, no. 3 (Summer 2004): 285–303.

Russell, Shana. "Wright and African American Women." In *Richard Wright in Context*, edited by Michael Nowlin, 77–86. Cambridge: Cambridge University Press, 2021.

Rutledge, Gregory E. *The Epic Trickster in American Literature: From Sunjata to So(u)l*. New York: Routledge, 2013.

———. "The 'Wonder' behind the Great-Race-Blue(s) Debate: Wright's Eco-criticism, Ellison's Blues, and the Dust Bowl." *ANQ: A Quarterly Journal of Short Articles, Notes, and Reviews* 24, no. 4 (2011): 255–65.

Saunders, Frances Stonor. *The Cultural Cold War: The CIA and the World of Arts and Letters*. 1999. New York: New Press, 2013.

Sherwood, Marika. "The All African People's Congress (AAPC) called by Kwame Nkrumah—and George Padmore." *Contemporary Journal of African Studies* 8, no. 1 (2021): 63–68.

Shiffman, Dan. "Richard Wright's *12 Million Black Voices* and World War II–Era Civic Nationalism." *African American Review* 41, no. 3 (2007): 443–58.

Smethurst, James. "After Modernism: Richard Wright Interprets the Black Belt." In *Richard Wright in a Post-racial Imaginary*, edited by Alice Mikal Craven and William E. Dowe, 13–25. London: Bloomsbury, 2014.

———. *The New Red Negro: The Literary Left and African American Poetry, 1930–1946*. New York: Oxford University Press, 1999.

Smethurst, James, and Rachel Rubin. "The Cartoons of Ollie Harrington, the Black Left, and the African American Press during the Jim Crow Era." *American Studies* 59, no. 3 (2020): 121–41.

Smith, Virginia Whatley, ed. *Richard Wright's Travel Writings: New Reflections*. Jackson: University Press of Mississippi, 2001.

Solomon, Mark. *The Cry Was Unity: Communists and African Americans, 1917–1936*. Jackson: University Press of Mississippi, 1998.

Stepto, Robert B. *From Behind the Veil: A Study of Afro-American Narrative*. 2nd ed. Urbana: University of Illinois Press, 1991.

Storch, Randi. *Red Chicago: American Communism at Its Grassroots, 1928–35.* Urbana: University of Illinois Press, 2007.

Sutherland, Donald. *Gertrude Stein: A Biography of Her Work.* New Haven, CT: Yale University Press, 1981.

Thaddeus, Jane. "The Metamorphosis of Richard Wright's *Black Boy*." *American Literature* 57, no. 2 (1985): 199–214.

Tubbs, Anna Malaika. *How the Mothers of Martin Luther King, Jr., Malcolm X, and James Baldwin Shaped a Nation.* New York: Flatiron Books, 2021.

Tuhkanen, Mikko. "Queer Guerrillas: On Richard Wright's and Frantz Fanon's Dissembling Revolutionaries." *Mississippi Quarterly* 61, no. 4 (Fall 2008): 615–42.

Tuttleton, James W. "The Problematic Texts of Richard Wright." *Hudson Review* 45, no. 2 (Summer 1992): 261–71.

Vyotsky, Lev. *Thought and Language.* Cambridge, MA: MIT Press, 1986.

Wald, Alan M. *Exiles from a Future Time: The Forging of the Mid-Twentieth-Century Literary Left.* Chapel Hill: The University of North Carolina Press, 2002.

———. "He Tried to Be a Communist." In *Richard Wright in Context,* edited by Michael Nowlin, 87–97. Cambridge: Cambridge University Press, 2021.

Walhout, Mark. "The New Criticism and the Crisis of American Liberalism: The Poetics of the Cold War." *College English* 49, no. 8 (1987): 861–71.

Walker, Margaret. *Richard Wright: Daemonic Genius: A Portrait of the Man, a Critical Look at His Work.* New York: Amistad, 1988.

Ward, Jerry. "*Uncle Tom's Children* Revisited." *Papers on Language and Literature* 44, no. 4 (2008): 343–53.

Watson, Rachel. "The Living Clue: Richard Wright's *The Outsider* (1953)." *Obsidian* 11, no. 2 (Fall/Winter 2010): 55–73.

Webb, Constance. *Richard Wright: The Biography of a Major Figure in American Literature.* New York: G. P. Putnam's Sons, 1968.

White, Walter. Review of *The Negro and the Communist Party*, by Wilson Record. *American Historical Review* 57, no. 1 (October 1951): 193–94.

Whitman, Walt. "Crossing Brooklyn Ferry." *Leaves of Grass* (1881–82), 129–134. Walt Whitman Archive, https://whitmanarchive.org/item/ppp.01663_01750.

Wilbers, Usha. "The Author Resurrected: The *Paris Review*'s Answer to the Age of Criticism." *American Periodicals* 18, no. 2 (2008): 192–212.

Wilkerson, Isabel. *The Warmth of Other Suns: The Epic Story of America's Great Migration.* New York: Random House, 2010.

Williams, Heather Andrea. *Self-Taught: African American Education in Slavery and Freedom.* Chapel Hill: The University of North Carolina Press, 2005.

Williams, Sherley Anne. "Papa Dick and Sister-Woman: Reflections on Women in the Fiction of Richard Wright." In *American Novelists Revisited: Essays in Feminist Criticism,* edited by Fritz Fleischmann, 394–415. Boston: G. K. Hall, 1982.

Worster, Daniel. *Dust Bowl: The Southern Plains in the 1930s.* 1979. New York, Oxford University Press, 2004.

Wright, Julia. Foreword to *Why I Left America and Other Essays,* by Oliver W. Harrington, xvii–xxix. Jackson: University Press of Mississippi, 2010.

———. Introduction to *Haiku: The Last Poems of an American Icon: Richard Wright*, edited by Yoshinobu Hakutani and Robert L. Tener, vii–xii. New York: Arcade, 2012.
Wright, Richard. *Black Boy (American Hunger): A Record of Childhood and Youth*. New York: Harper Perennial Modern Classics, 2006.
———. *Black Power: Three Books from Exile: "Black Power"; "The Color Curtain"; and "White Man, Listen!"* New York: Harper Perennial Modern Classics, 2008.
———. "Blueprint for Negro Writing." *New Challenge* 2, no. 1 (1937): 59–60.
———. *Eight Men: Stories by Richard Wright*. 1961. With an introduction by Paul Gilroy. New York: Harper Perennial, 1996.
———. *Haiku: The Last Poems of an American Icon: Richard Wright*. Edited by Yoshinobu Hakutani and Robert L. Tener. New York: Arcade, 2012.
———. Introduction to *Black Metropolis: A Study of Negro Life in a Northern City*, by John Gibbs St. Clair Drake and Horace R. Cayton, lix–lxxvi. 1945. Chicago: University of Chicago Press, 1993.
———. "I Tried to Be a Communist." *The Atlantic*, September 1944. www.theatlantic.com/magazine/archive/1944/09/i-tried-to-be-a-communis/655979/.
———. *Lawd Today!* 1963. Lebanon, NH: Northeastern University Press, 1993.
———. *Letters to Joe C. Brown*. Edited with an introduction by Thomas Knipp. Kent, OH: Kent State University Libraries, 1968.
———. *The Long Dream*. 1958. Lebanon, NH: Northeastern University Press, 2000.
———. *The Man Who Lived Underground*. New York: Library of America, 2021.
———. *Native Son*. 1940. New York: Harper Perennial Classics, 2008.
———. *The Outsider*. 1953. New York: Harper Perennial Modern Classics, 2008.
———. *Pagan Spain*. 1957. New York: Harper Perennial, 2008.
———. *12 Million Black Voices*. 1941. New York: Basic Books, 2002.
———. *Uncle Tom's Children*. 1936. New York: Harper Perennial Modern Classics, 2008.
Wright, Richard, and Claude McKay. "Portrait of Harlem." In *New York Panorama: A Comprehensive View of the Metropolis*, by Federal Writers' Project, 142–46. New York: Random House, 1938.
York, Richard, and Brett Clark. "Marxism, Positivism, and Scientific Sociology: Social Gravity and Historicity." *Sociological Quarterly* 47, no. 3 (Summer 2006): 425–50.

Index

Italic page numbers refer to illustrations.

Aaron, Abe, 89, 96, 97
Aaron, Daniel, 105
Abraham, Aaron, 30
Abrahams, Peter, 234
abstraction, 22, 26, 38, 145
Abu-Jamal, Mumia, 242
Abzug, Bella, 222
Accent (journal), 23, 43
Act for the Gradual Abolition of Slavery (1799), 132
The Adventures of Huckleberry Finn (Twain), 105
Afflerbach, Ian, 102
African Blood Brotherhood (ABB), 84
Agee, James, 118, 140, 187, 261n25
Agence France-Presse (AFP), 227
agriculture: sharecropping, 65, 179; soil degradation, 178–79; tenant farming, 262n38
"Ah Feels It in Mah Bones" (Wright), 103
"Alas, Poor Richard" (Baldwin), 2
Alexander, Michelle, 27, 48, 216, 217
Algeria, 227–29, 231
Algerian National Liberation Front, 227
Algren, Nelson, 80, 91, 96, 113
alienation, 30, 145, 154–57, 190, 212; No Man's Land, 39, 77, 138, 162
Alisjahbana, Sutan Takdir, 206
Allen, Craig Lanier, 228, 230
Alsberg, Henry, 113, 115, 131
American Guide Series, 106, 115
American Hunger (Wright), 107, 108, 212–13. See also *Black Boy* (Wright)
American Life Series (FWP), 115
American Negro Labor Congress, 97
"American Negro Writing" (lecture), 209

American Stuff: WPA Writers' Anthology, 121, 185, 213
An American Tragedy (Dreiser), 5
American Writers' Congress (1935), 91
Anderson, Lewis, 54
Anderson, Marian, 134
Anderson, Sherwood, 95
anticolonial movements, 197, 200
antifascism, 195–96
antilynching campaigns, 81, 159
Anvil (magazine), 20, 103
Anyplace but Here (Bontemps & Conroy), 115
Appiah, Kwame Anthony, 198, 199, 200
Aragon, Louis, 103
Arbery, Ahmaud, 27
"art for art's sake," 4, 196–97
Asher, Colin, 33
Aswell, Edward, 102, 137, 238, 243
The Atlantic (magazine), 17
Aufbau Verlag (publishing company), 214
Auld, Hugh, 55

"Back Water Blues" (Smith), 180
Baer, Max, 134
Baker, Ella, 170
Baker, Josephine, 134–35, 184
Baldwin, James, 184, 227, 228; "Alas, Poor Richard," 2, 261n22; "Everybody's Protest Novel," 2; on protest novels, 1, 4, 47, 196
Balthaser, Benjamin, 139
Bandung Conference (1955), 194, 204–5, 207, 230, 242. See also Indonesia
Barthes, Roland, 217
Basie, Count (William James Basie), 134

Bates, Ruby, 168
Battle of Dien Bien Phu (1954), 227
Beard, Charles, 124
Beard, Mary, 124
Bearden, Romare, 134
Beauvoir, Simone de, 109, 195, 229
Beavers, Louise, 129
Berry, Abner W., 205
"Between the World and Me" (Wright), 263n4
"Big Boy Leaves Home" (Wright), 17, 120–21, 145, 146
Bilbo, Theodore, 21
"Biography of a Bolshevik" (Wright), 119
"biological recoil" (Burrow), 183
Birmingham, Alabama, 27
Black Belt thesis, CPUSA, 104, 141, 244–45, 258n21
Black Boy (Wright), 43, 73; alternate versions of, 108; author's experiences teaching, 1–2; autobiographical elements of, 81; as bildungsroman, 61–62; and Communist Party, 89; critical reception of, 61–62, 109, 256n30; dialectical historical materialism, 149; ecocriticism of, 186; on education, 50–51; female characters in, 164; fire incident in, 65–66; "Negro Question," 85–86; obscenity in, 21; and race relations in America, 74–77, 171–72; restored version (1991), 212
Blackburn, D. C., 54
Black communities: and clandestine education, 68; and female domestic workers, 20; in Jim Crow South, 54–59, 67–68; informal networks in, 60–61; relationship to America, 75–76
Black diaspora, 200
"Black Hope" (Wright), 20, 44, 159, 170, 172–74, 222
Black Lives Matter movement, 8, 242
Black Metropolis (Drake & Cayton), 96, 100, 115, 122
Black nationalism, 11, 84–85, 99, 104, 137–38, 154, 213, 218

Black Panther Party, 242
"Black power," 219
Black Power (Wright), 78, 138, 198, 199–200, 201, 241, 242
Black Skin, White Masks (Fanon), 210
"black tradition," 215–16
"Blueprint for Negro Writing" (Wright): dialectical theory of composition, 31, 33, 75, 194; Marxist analysis, 4, 7, 16, 107, 146, 148, 191, 217–18; nationalist perspective, 104, 137
blues music, 26. *See also* jazz
Blythe, R. H., 234
Bone, Robert, 96, 102, 105
Bontemps, Alberta, 236, 244
Bontemps, Arna, 15, 79, 92, 96, 100, 115, 134, 236, 244
bonus marchers, 97
Bookchin, Murray, 193
Booker, Perry, 54
Born in Slavery (FWP), 115
Bourke-White, Margaret, 187
Breitman, George, 107
Brièrre, Annie, 80
Briffault, Robert, 201, 202
Briggs, Cyril, 78, 84
"Bright and Morning Star" (Wright), 71, 73, 92–93, 121, 146, 147, 160; Aunt Sue, 153, 165, 168, 169–70
Bronx Citizens' Committee for the Improvement of Domestic Employees, 171
Browder, Earl, 91
Brown, Joe C., 54, 60, 81–82
Brown, Sterling Allen, 114
Brown v. Board of Education, 27, 59
Bughouse Square, 96, 98
Burden-Stelly, Charisse, 232
Burgess, Ernest, 98, 183
Burke, Kenneth, 91, 191
Burley, Dan, 97
Burnett, Whitt, 160
Burrow, Trigant, 183

Caldwell, Erskine, 187
Calloway, Cab, 135

Calloway, Jamall A., 154
Calverton, V. F., 106
Canby, Henry Seidel, 5
Cantwell, Robert, 187
Capital (Marx), 98, 189
capitalism: capitalist expansion, 178–79; critiques of, 7–8; and environmental damage, 8
Capitalism and Slavery (Williams), 187
Cappetti, Carla, 99, 101, 180
Castillo, Monica, 3
Cayton, Horace R., Jr., 9, 62–63, 96, 100–102, 107, 112, 115, 260n4
Cayton, Revels, 101
Central Intelligence Agency (CIA): Congress for Cultural Freedom (CCF), 179, 196–97, 206–7, 268n85; Kennedy files, 228; surveillance, 221, 226
Cerf, Bennett, 24
Césaire, Aimé, 176, 178, 195
"Cesspool" (Wright), 30, 145. See also *Lawd Today!* (Wright)
Chalemsky, Paul, 226
Chaney, James, 27
Chaplin, Charlie, 229
Chappelle, Kitty, 96
Chauvin, Derek, 24
Cherne, Leo, 212
Chicago, IL, 17, 96–99, 110, 185–86; Black Chicago Renaissance, 112; Great Migration, 124–25; Illinois Writers' Project (IWP), 123–30; photographs in *12 Million Black Voices*, 136–37; South Side Boys' Club, 130
Chicago Post Office, 97
Chicago Renaissance, 96
Chicago Urban League, 125–26
Chicago Workers School, 98
"Child of the Dead and Forgotten Gods" (Wright), 144
Church of St. John (NYC), 106–7
Civil Rights Act (1964), 16
Civil Rights Congress (CRC), 213, 222
civil rights movement: classical phase, 27; critique of, 217–18

Civil War in the United States, The (Marx), 189
class struggle: class-based stereotypes, 4–5; class conflict, 221–22; class struggle vs. racial conflict, 26
climate crisis, 243
"close reading," 3, 197, 230
Coates, Ta-Nehisi, 3, 263n4
coded language, 29, 211, 236
Colbert, Claudette, 129
Cold War era, 105, 198, 208, 210–11, 234
"Cold War poetics," 3–4
"The Collapse of Liberalism" (Martin), 98
The Color Curtain (Wright), 110, 177, 189, 204–5, 242
Comintern, 90
Committee for Industrial Organization, 136
commodity fetishism, 154–57
The Communist Manifesto (Marx & Engels), 138. See also *The Manifesto of the Communist Party* (Engels and Marx)
Communist movement, 86–87
Communist Party USA (CPUSA), 1, 6; activities, 88; background and overview, 83–95; Black Belt thesis, 104, 141, 244–45, 258n21; Black communists, 86–87; and Black nationalism, 137–38; during Depression, 90–91; legal defense campaigns, 83–84; "Negro question," 84, 104; Popular Front Strategy and NNC, 94; and race riots, 133; Third Period to Popular Front, 87–90; and "woman question," 19; on World War II, 31–32. See also John Reed Clubs (JRC)
Congo, Democratic Republic of, 242, 244
Congress for Cultural Freedom, 179, 196–97, 206–7, 228, 268n85
Congress of American Writers, 191
Congress of Industrial Organizations (CIO), 94–95
Congress of Negro Writers and Artists, 179
Conroy, Jack, 96, 100, 115
Convention People's Party (Ghana), 215
Cook, Marvel, 170
Cooper, Esther, 94

Cop City (Atlanta, GA), 243, 246
Coser, Lewis, 105
Costello, Brannon, 145
The Crisis (NAACP magazine), 104, 170
The Crisis of the Negro Intellectual (Cruse), 104
Crossman, Richard, 213
Cross-Section (Seaver, ed.), 24
Crowder, Harriet, 239
The Crusader (newspaper), 84
Cruse, Harold, 104
Cullen, Countee, 134, 201
Cummings, E. E., 103
Curry, Tommy J., 223–24

Daemonic Genius (Walker), 83
Daily Worker (newspaper), 9, 45, 79, 117, 130, 205
darkness, imagery of, 24–25, 35, 117, 234
Das Kapital (Marx), 98, 189
Daughter of Earth (Smedley), 167
Davis, Angela, 94
Davis, Ben, 168, 264n24
Davis, Frank Marshall, 92–93, 96, 107, 110, 112
Davis, John P., 86, 93–94
Davis, Sallye B., 94
Dawahare, Anthony, 154
DeLoughrey, Elizabeth, 178
Democratic Republic of the Congo, 242, 244
Denning, Michael, 113
desegregation, 27, 59, 74, 217
Desirat, Maxime, 9
dialectical materialism, 75–76, 149–54, 220
Dickinson, Emily, 239
Dies, Martin, 95, 114, 121, 146, 213, 219
Diop, Alioune, 176
documentary techniques, 118–19, 139–40
Dolinar, Brian, 123
domestic workers, 171
Domestic Workers Union, 171
Dos Passos, John, 113, 145
Dostoevsky, Fyodor, 2, 43, 80
double consciousness, 78, 140

Double V campaign, 95, 217
"double vision," 78
double-voiced narratives, 29, 52–53, 68
Douglass, Frederick, 10, 54, 55, 58, 62
"Down by the Riverside" (Wright), 92, 145, 179, 180, 182–83, 184
Drake, John Gibbs St. Clair, 96, 100, 115, 215–16
Dreiser, Theodore, 5, 48, 80, 91, 117
Drew, Charles R., 95
Dubinsky, Ed, 226
Du Bois, Shirley Graham, 232
Du Bois, W. E. B., 62, 78, 80, 124, 131, 133, 134, 141
Dust Bowl, 8, 11, 186

Eagleton, Terry, 3
Ebony (magazine), 150–51
ecocriticism, 178
ecological crises, 183, 211, 243, 246
Écoute, homme blanc! (Wright), 243. See also *White Man, Listen!* (Wright)
Eight Men (Wright), 24, 180, 223, 232
Einstein, Albert, 222
Elaine, AK, 242; massacre (1919), 71, 270n73
Ellington, Duke, 135
Ellison, Ralph, 39, 43–44, 69, 193
Encounter (magazine), 207
Engels, Friedrich, 83, 138, 241
English language, 53
environmental issues, 211, 243, 246
environmental literature, 178
Equiano, Olaudah, 56
"The Ethics of Living Jim Crow" (Wright): criticism of, 95, 122, 145, 213; on environmental damage, 180, 184, 185, 192–93; land, wealth and power, 194; violence and punishment, 69. See also Jim Crow era racial oppression
"Ethnographic Aspects of Chicago's Black Belt" (Wright), 123
ethnography, 9, 99, 114, 115, 118, 130, 142
Eugène Gibez Clinic, 206, 226, 244
Evans, Walker, 118, 136, 187

Evers, Medgar, 27
"Everybody's Protest Novel" (Baldwin), 2
"Everywhere Burning Waters Rise" (Wright), 144–45
Existence and Being (Heidegger), 189
existentialism, 11, 12, 24, 29–30, 32, 79, 144, 189, 198, 214

Fabre, Michel: on *The Man Who Lived Underground*, 25–26; on Marxism, 83, 162, 189, 212; on US propaganda, 228; on Wright's death, 226; on Wright's literary career and impact, 64, 112, 131; on Wright's mother Ella, 69; on Wright's philosophy, 143–44
Fadiman, Clifton, 5
Fair Labor Standards Act, 94
Fair Play for Cuba Committee (FPCC), 228
Fanon, Frantz, 12, 78, 82, 195, 197, 241; *Black Skin, White Masks*, 210
Farm Security Administration (FSA), 95, 136
Farrell, James T., 5, 80
A Father's Law (Wright), 219, 234, 244
Faulkner, Daniel, 242
Faulkner, William, 222
FBI (Federal Bureau of Investigation), 21, 109, 121, 203, 228
Federal Art Project, 134
Federal One program, 111, 114, 116
Federal Writers' Project (FWP), 1, 6, 11, 90, 106, 111–14; and Black artists, 114–15; contemporary interest and use, 115–16
feminism: feminist critics of Wright, 158–61; women's status, 170–74. *See also* gender roles; women
Field, Douglas, 25
"Fire and Cloud" (Wright), 17, 112, 121, 145, 147, 153
First International Congress of Negro Writers and Artists (1956), 110, 174–75, 176, 192, 195
Fisk University, 63, 117
Floyd, George, 8–9, 24, 27, 243

Foley, Barbara, 7, 105, 106, 159
Folsom, Frank, 32–33, 91
Ford, James W., 107
Ford, Nick Aaron, 5, 27, 30, 145
Formación Política (Falange Española Tradicionalista), 175
Foster, William Z., 83
Foulcher, Keith, 205, 206
Fourth American Congress of Writers, 31
Fox, Daniel M., 115–16
France: Franco-American Fellowship, 194; West African colonies, 243
Franco-Algerian War, 227–29, 234
Franc-Tireur (newspaper), 229
Frazier, E. Franklin, 101, 213, 232
"freedom of action," 53
Freedom Schools, 59
Freire, Paulo, 66
French-American Fellowship (FAF), 222
Front de Libération Nationale (FLN), 227–28

Gaines, Kevin Kelly, 82
Gannett, Lewis, 62
Garvey, Marcus, 97, 126
Gaspar, Sam, 97
Gayle, Addison, 104
Gaza, Palestine, 242, 270n72
Geertz, Clifford, 118
gender roles: female characters in fiction, 157–58, 161, 162–65; gender oppression, 157–58; in "Man of All Work" (Wright), 223–24. *See also* feminism; women
Gibson, Richard, 226, 227–28, 229–30
Gilroy, Paul, 165, 179
Giorgis, Hannah, 3
The God That Failed (Koestler), 108, 207, 213
Gogol, Nikolai, 30
Gold, Mike, 91, 105–6, 113, 160
Gold Coast, Ghana: Nkrumah's leadership, 215, 241; Wright's travels to, 109, 176, 198, 200–201; Wright's travel writing, 182, 200–201, 203, 214
Gollomb, Joseph, 109

Goodman, Andrew, 27
Good Shepherd Community Settlement House, 9
Gorky, Maxim, 98
Gray, Helen, 94
Great Depression, 111–12, 186–87
Great Man theory of history, 117
Great Migration, 1, 6, 59, 111, 124–25, 136, 149–50, 184, 186, 210. *See also* migration
Great Mississippi Flood (1927), 8, 180–81, 225
Great Plains, 185–86
Greenville, MS, 180
Greenwood, MS, 50
Grierson, John, 118
Guttman, Sondra, 159

haiku, 12, 225, 235–40
Haiku (Wright), 12, 235
Hall, Heywood, 84. *See also* Haywood, Harry
Hall, Otto, 84
Hammett, Dashiell, 31–32
Handley, George B., 178
Hansberry, Lorraine, 79
Harlem: culture and art, 134–35; labor unions, 136; "Portrait of Harlem," 131–32; racial tension and riots, 132–33; real estate, 133–34
Harlem Renaissance, 111–12
Harrington, Ollie, 79, 195, 212–13, 214, 226, 227, 229
Harris, Trudier, 158, 159
Harrison Alferdteen, 74
Harsh, Vivian, 126
Hathaway, Rosemary, 127
Hawkins, Wiletta, 222, 223
Haywood, Harry, 15, 84, 85–87, 93–94
Heartfield, John, 183
The Heart of Darkness (Conrad), 190
Hegel, Georg Wilhelm Friedrich, 189
Heidegger, Martin, 189
Henderson, Fletcher, 135
Herndon, Angelo, 80–81, 84, 169
Herskovits, Melville, 98

Hicks, Granville, 95
"hidden transcripts," 10, 58, 60, 61
Higashida, Cheryl, 159, 168
Himes, Chester, 184, 195, 213
Hirsch, Jerrold, 128
history: dialectical historical materialism, 149–54; Great Man theory, 117; "history from below," 58, 116, 122; Lost Cause mythology, 124, 131; views of, 241
Hitler, Adolf, 31, 95
Hitler-Stalin Pact, 91, 94, 95
Ho Chi Minh, 228
hooks, bell, 67, 68
Hoover, J. Edgar, 4, 240
Hooverville camps, 97
Hopkins, Henry, 114
Hoskins, Silas, 49, 71, 242
House Un-American Activities Committee (HUAC), 95, 113, 121, 122, 146, 214
"How 'Bigger' Was Born" (Wright), 34
Howe, Irving, 1, 5, 15, 44, 105
How the Other Half Lives (Riis), 118, 140
Hughes, Langston, 15, 91, 92, 113, 134, 244
Huiswoud, Otto, 78, 84
human trafficking, 172, 222
Humes, Harold L., 230
Hurst, Fannie, 129
Hurston, Zora Neale, 3, 134
Hyman, Stanley Edgar, 43

"I Am the American Negro" (Davis), 93
"I Choose Exile" (Wright), 225
"I Have Seen Black Hands" (Wright), 98–99, 112
Illinois Writers' Project (IWP), 11, 99, 112–13, 116, 118; Chicago work, 123–30
Imitation of Life (film, 1934), 129
Indonesia, 176–177, 204–9; Bandung Conference (1955), 194, 204–5, 207, 230, 242; Konfrontasi group, 206
Indonesian Communist Party (PKI), 206
Indonesian Socialist Party (PSI), 206
International Brotherhood of Sleeping Car Porters, 92, 135

International Day of Resistance to Dictatorship and War, 229
International Labor Defense (ILD), 83, 133
International Literature (journal), 17, 103
International Socialist Review, 107
International Workingmen's Association, 111
interracial alliances and relationships: in Chicago, 19, 30, 89; class struggle, 104–5, 108, 146, 157, 160, 168; CPUSA, 32, 85, 88, 137; personal, 159–60
Interracial Messenger (Urban League), 124
Invisible Man (Ellison), 39, 43, 193
"The Island of Hallucination" (Wright), 44, 226–27, 230, 234, 244
Israel, 242, 270n72
"I Tried to Be a Communist" (Wright), 17, 29, 87–88, 207, 212

Jack, Peter Monro, 210
Jackson, James, 94
Jackson, MS, 61
Jacobs, Harriet Ann, 56
James, C. L. R., 48, 82, 109, 195, 227
JanMohamed, Abdul R., 18, 45
jazz, 135; blues music, 26; liner notes, 244; Wright's interest in, 18–19
Jet (magazine), 29
Jim Crow era racial oppression, 27, 63–64, 69, 119–20, 217, 260n6; educational systems, 58–59. *See also* "The Ethics of Living Jim Crow" (Wright)
John Reed Clubs (JRC), 10, 17, 20, 54, 85, 106, 112; dissolution of, 77–78, 88; and Illinois Writers' Project, 113
Johnson, Fenton, 92, 96
Johnson, Hank, 212
Johnson, Hewlett, 98
Johnson, James Weldon, 131
Johnson, Lyndon Baines, 27
Joint Committee on National Recovery, 93
Jordan, Dick, 54, 60
Josselson, Michael, 207
Joyce, James, 30, 62
Joyce, Joyce Ann, 165–66, 168

Jubilee (Walker), 92–93
Julius Rosenwald Foundation, 9

Kafka, Franz, 30
Karageorgos, Konstantina, 191
Keady, Sylvia, 159, 165, 168
Kennedy, John F., 228
Kent State University Libraries, 82
Kenyon Literary Review, 229
Kerner Commission, 27
King, Martin Luther, Jr., 27
Knipp, Thomas, 82
Koestler, Arthur, 207
Konfrontasi group, 206
Kristol, Irving, 207
Ku Klux Klan, 53, 61

labor unions, 136, 261–62n36
La Droit de Vivre (journal), 222
La Guardia, Fiorello, 133
Land of the Free (McLeish), 186–87
La Nef (journal), 217
Lange, Dorothea, 118, 136
language: Black English, 31; coded, 29, 211, 236; and consciousness, 31; formal vs. vernacular, 53; literal vs. figurative, 67
Larsen, Nella, 134
Law, Oliver, 86, 121–22
Lawd Today! (Wright), 18, 30, 44, 97–98, 107, 145, 154; critique of commodification, 155–56; female characters in, 164
League of American Writers (LAW), 31, 90–91
League of Struggle for Negro Rights, 91–92, 97
Lee, Russell, 136
Left Front (magazine), 17, 89, 103, 112
"Left March" (Mayakovsky), 103
Leibig, Justus von, 178
Lenin, Vladimir, 74
Leopold, Nathan, 34
Lerner, Tillie (Olsen), 91, 113
Le Sueur, Meridel, 106, 113
Let Us Now Praise Famous Men (Agee & Evans), 118, 140, 261n25

Licht, Mary, 15, 162
Lightfoot, Claude, 87
Lincoln, Abraham, 55
literacy, 55–56; importance of, 59; rhetorical literacy lessons, 67; Russian campaigns, 85
literacy narratives, 56–58, 68
"The Literature of the Negro" (Wright), 98
Little Rock Central High School, 27, 217
Locke, Alain, 134
Loeb, Richard, 34
"Long Black Song" (Wright), 84–85, 92, 145, 147–48, 156, 165–67, 180
The Long Dream (Wright), 5, 27, 188, 216–17, 219, 220–21, 231–34
Lost Cause mythology, 124, 131
Louis, Joe, 134
"A Love Red Note" (Wright), 144
Lovett, Robert Morss, 98
Lower Depths (Gorky), 98
Lumumba, Patrice, 204, 244
Lunceford, Jimmie, 135
lynching, 9, 61, 71, 242

Malcolm X, 27
"Man, God Ain't Like That" (Wright), 232
Mangione, Jerre, 113
The Manifesto of the Communist Party (Engels and Marx), 189. See also *The Communist Manifesto* (Marx and Engels)
Mann, Delbert, 183
"Man of All Work" (Wright), 223–24
The Man Who Lived Underground (Wright), 9, 15, 154, 158, 193, 194; abridged versions, 23–24; and Bigger in *Native Son*, 35–40, 44; brutality and trauma, 18–19; complete version (2021), 2, 15, 16; critical reception of, 30, 32, 33–34, 44; graphic content of, 21–22; opening sentence, 25; production and reception of, 16–22; racial and class oppression, 22–28, 44–45; trauma, 45; world events as inspiration for, 33

"The Man Who Saw the Flood" (Wright), 180
"The Man Who Was Almost a Man" (Wright), 18
Martin, Lawrence, 98
Martin, Trayvon, 28
Martinsville Seven, 222
Marx, Karl, 83, 138, 241
Marxism, 4, 96; class consciousness, 74; influence of, 148–49, 151–53; Marxist theory, 96–97; psychoanalytic theory, 154–55; stages of history, 38
materialism, dialectical historical, 149–54
Mathis, Ayana, 2–3
Matthiessen, Peter, 230
Maxwell, William J., 4, 179, 234
Mayakovsky, Vladimir, 103
Mayfield, Julian, 232
M'Baye, Babacar, 200
McCarthy, Joseph, 202
McCarthyism, 3
McClusky, John, 105
McGee, Willie, 215, 222–23
McHenry, Beth, 45
McKay, Claude, 76, 95, 122, 131, 134
McLeish, Archibald, 186–87
McNearner, Sarah, 54
Meadman, Dhima Rose, 21, 170
"Melanctha" (Stein), 31, 53
"Memories of My Grandmother" (Wright), 17, 18–19, 26, 28, 31, 33, 51–53, 146–47, 167, 255n5
Menand, Louis, 5, 102
Mencken, H. L., 47, 54
Merzouk, Nahel, 243, 246
Meyerson, Gregory, 168, 169–70
Midland Left (magazine), 103
migration: internal in United States, 231; US expatriates, 6, 184, 195, 228, 231–32; West Indian immigration, 184. See also Great Migration
Miller, Frieda S., 171
Mishra, Pankaj, 2–3
Mississippi flood (1927), 8, 180–81, 225
Mitford, Jessica, 222

Mochtar Lubis, 206, 207–8, 209
modernist literature, 12, 21, 30–31, 97–98, 145, 155, 211, 241
Molotov-Ribbentrop Nonaggression Pact (1939), 88
Montgomery, Viola, 168
Moore, Richard B., 84
Morris, Nathan, 123
Morrison, Toni, 24–25, 58
Mosley, Jessie Bryant, 74
Mother (Gorky), 98
Mullen, Bill, 101, 110
Murphy, George B., 214–15, 268n9

Naison, Mark, 131
Narrative of the Life of Frederick Douglass, An American Slave (Douglass), 55, 62
Nasanov, Charles, 84
The National and Colonial Question (Stalin), 85
National Association for the Advancement of Colored People (NAACP), 135, 171
nationalism, 204, 206, 240
National Labor Relations Act, 94
National Negro Congress (NNC), 90–93, 101, 135, 213
National Training Center for Gendarme Forces, 246
National Urban League, 135
Native Son (films), 3
Native Son (Wright): alienation, 156–57; Bigger Thomas, 2, 3, 35–40, 44, 48, 254n56; Chicago setting, 129–30; Communist Party, 102; critical reception of, 15, 210, 264n24; dialectical materialist analysis of, 220; female characters in, 161, 162–64; inspiration for, 34–35; Marxist perspectives, 151–52; movie theaters and films, 128–29; as protest novel, 2–3, 196; publication of, 170; racial theories, 63, 216; writing process, 19
nature, 211; appreciation of, 12–13, 225, 235; perspectives on, 66; writing, 178, 187

Nazi Party, 88
The Negro and the Communist Party (Record), 104
Negro Bill of Rights, 92
The Negro in Illinois (Dolinar, ed.), 115, 121, 123
Nehru, Jawaharlal, 205
The New Caravan (Kreymborg et al.), 120
New Challenge (journal), 117
New Critics, 191, 206, 230; form vs. content, 3–4
New Deal, 90, 93, 94, 111, 263n61. *See also* Federal Writers' Project (FWP)
"New Jim Crow," 48, 69, 216, 217
The New Jim Crow (Alexander), 27–28
New Masses (magazine), 9, 31, 83, 89, 92, 113, 146
Newton, Herbert, 19, 45, 131, 162
Newton, Jane, 19, 131, 162
New York African Society for Mutual Relief, 135
New York Amsterdam News (newspaper), 171
New York City, 132
New York City WPA Guide (Federal Writers' Project), 117
New York Daily Tribune (newspaper), 83
New Yorker (magazine), 62
New York Herald Tribune (newspaper), 62; Weekly Book Review, 62
New York Historical Society, 132
New York Panorama (WPA), 76, 115, 117, 118, 131, 140, 257n54
New York Writers' Project, 131–36
Nixon, Robert, 27, 34
Nkrumah, Kwame, 138, 198, 203, 204, 205, 215
No Man's Land, 39, 77, 138, 162
Non-Aligned Movement (NAM), 110, 204
Non-Communist Left (NCL), 229
Norris, Ida, 168
Notes from Underground (Dostoevsky), 43
"Not My People's War" (Wright), 91
"A No to Nothing" (Gibson), 229–30

Obama, Barack, 27
Office of Negro Affairs (FWP), 114
Ojo-Adi, Femi, 200
One Hundred Days That Shook the World (Reed), 98
oral histories, 114, 117
Oral History Research Office (Columbia University), 117
Oswald, Lee Harvey, 228
outsider (theme), 52–53, 187–96
The Outsider (Wright), 29, 44, 79, 102, 151, 188–90, 191–92, 193; alienation, 214, 219, 220; critical reception of, 82; dialectical materialist analysis, 220; female characters in, 161, 164–65

Padmore, Dorothy, 176, 177
Padmore, George: as Black socialist, 109, 178; "Cold War game," 208; as expatriate, 184; First International Congress of Negro Writers, 195; friendship with Wright, 176, 177, 198, 213, 243; and Ghana, 215; and Pan-African movement, 82
Paez Terán, Manuel Esteban (Tortuguita), 243, 246
Pagan Spain (Wright), 161, 175, 177, 188, 240–41
Pan-African Congress, 215
Pan-Africanism, 110, 178, 195, 200, 208
Parish, Susan Scott, 180, 183
Paris Review (journal), 228, 230
Park, Robert E., 9, 47, 100, 101, 180
Parks, Gordon, 118
Partisan Review (magazine), 20, 197
Patterson, Janie, 168
Patterson, Troy, 3, 29–30
Patterson, William, 87
Payton, Philip A., 133
Pearson, Norman Holmes, 230
People's Educational Forum, 84
Perkins, Marion, 92
Permanence and Change (Burke), 191
Perry, Imani, 16
"Personalism" (Wright), 191

The Phenomenology of Mind (Hegel), 189
Picasso, Pablo, 229
Plimpton, George, 230
PM (magazine), 60, 171
PM Sunday Picture News, 240
Poindexter, David, 85, 86–87, 119, 120, 122
police brutality, 23–24, 26–27, 45
Poplar, Ellen, 9, 21, 46. *See also* Wright, Ellen
Popular Front, 90, 91, 94–95, 124
"Portrait of Harlem" (Wright & McKay), 76
Portrait of the Artist as a Young Man (Joyce), 62
postmodernism, 4. *See also* modernist literature
postmodern theory, 4
Powell, Adam Clayton, Jr., 133
Présence Africaine (journal), 110, 176, 179, 194
Proefriedt, William A., 58
Prokofiev, Sergei, 222
Proletkult (proletarian culture), 105–6
protest novels, 4, 105; Baldwin on, 1, 2, 47, 196
"The Psychological Reactions of Oppressed People" (lecture), 158
Thomas, Bigger, 2, 3, 35–40, 44, 48, 254n56

Quinn, Kerker, 16, 18, 23, 43

race: and "black tradition," 215–16; essentialist theories of, 215; race relations in United States, 78; racial and class oppression, 182; racial terror, 216–17, 218; "racial uplift," 80; racial violence, 26–27
racism: Black rapist (stereotype), 223; internalized, 241; during Jim Crow era, 27, 58–59, 63–64, 69, 119–20, 217, 260n6; systemic, 27–28; white supremacy, 138, 194
Rahv, Philip, 197
Ramsey, Joseph, 33, 147, 168
Randolph, A. Philip, 92, 94, 135
Rankin, Tom, 118

Ransom, John Crowe, 229
Rassemblement Démocratique Révolutionnaire, 82, 110, 194
"reading the world," 66
Record, Wilson, 104
Redding, J. Saunders, 188, 221
Redfield, Robert, 101
"Red Front" (Aragon), 103
"A Red Slogan" (Wright), 103
Reed, John, 98
Reid-Pharr, Robert, 215–16
Reilly, John, 200
relativism, 4, 12
religion: alienation from, 34, 39, 198, 200, 240; contradictory role of, 153, 218; Wright's grandmother (Granny Wilson), 19, 22, 26, 51–52
"Rest for the Weary" (Wright), 144
Révolution Africaine (FLN newsletter), 228
Rexroth, Kenneth, 113
Reynolds, Paul, 17, 20, 23, 170, 171, 238; correspondence with Wright, 25–26
Richardson, Willis, 134
Richard Wright: Daemonic Genius (Walker), 163
Rideout, Walter, 102, 105
Riis, Jacob, 118, 140
Rite of Passage (Wright), 219
Roberts, Brian Russell, 205, 206
Robertson, Smith, 74
Robeson, Paul, 134, 229
Robinson, Bill "Bojangles," 134
Robinson, Cedric, 21, 79, 137, 179
"The Role of the Negro Artist and Writer in a Changing Social Order" (panel discussion), 92
Rolo, Charles J., 47–48, 64
Roosevelt, Eleanor, 63
Roosevelt, Franklin Delano, 212
Roosevelt, Theodore, 212
Ross, Mother, 168–69, 171
Rosskam, Edwin, 11, 95, 136, 139
Rowley, Hazel, 4, 87, 240
Ruby, Jack, 228

Russell, Shana, 159, 163, 168
Russian Revolution, 178
Rustin, Bayard, 27
Rutledge, Gregory, 186

Sablonière, Margrit de, 206, 213, 229
Sacco, Nicola, 83
Sartre, Jean-Paul, 109, 195
Sastroamidjojo, Ali, 205
Saunders, Frances Stoner, 179, 228
Savage, Augusta, 92, 134
Savage Holiday (Wright), 217
Schiffman, Daniel, 140
schizophrenia, 22, 52
Schwerner, Michael, 27
Scottsboro Boys, 27, 81, 83–84, 97, 101, 160, 168, 222
Seaver, Edwin, 24
Second New Deal, 90, 94
Senghor, Léopold Sédar, 82, 109, 176, 184, 195
Seventh-day Adventism, 22, 51–52
Shahn, Ben, 136
sharecropping, 65, 179
Shaw, Irwin, 230
Shostakovich, Dmitri, 222
Sillen, Sam, 107
"Silt" (Wright), 179, 180, 181–82, 225
Sims, Joe, 214–15, 268n9
Sitor Situmorang, 206, 207
Sixteenth Street Baptist Church bombing, 27
Sjahrir, Sutan, 206
slave narratives, 56, 115
slavery: impact and legacy of, 78; in New York City, 132; slave markets, 171, 172–73, 222
Smedley, Agnes, 167
Smethurst, James, 30, 105
Smith, Adam, 98
Smith, Bessie, 180
Smith, William Gardner, 150–51, 226–27, 228
Smith Robertson Junior High School, 49, 54, 74

Smith Robertson Museum and Cultural Center, 74
Socialist Labor Party, 83
Socialist Party, 83
Social Justice Committee of the Rabbinical Assembly of America, 171
Social Security Act, 94
sociology, 99–102
The Souls of Black Folk (Du Bois), 133
Southern Agrarian writers, 191, 230
Southern Negro Youth Congress (SNYC), 94, 213
Southern Quarterly (journal), 123
Southern University, 117
South Side Boys' Club (Chicago), 130
South Side Community Art Center, 96
South Side Writers Group, 54, 92, 96, 112
Soviet Cominform, 229
Soviet Power (Johnson), 98
Soviet Union, 85, 95; Proletkult (proletarian culture), 105–6; Russian Revolution, 178; Trotsky's expulsion from, 86–87
Spanish Civil War, 91
Spender, Stephen, 207
Stahl, John M., 129
Stalin, Joseph, 85
Starnes, Joe, 95
Steele, Max, 230
Stein, Gertrude, 30–31, 53, 117, 145, 176, 195, 221
Steinbeck, John, 48, 187
The Stone Face (Smith), 226
Story Magazine, 17, 160; contest, 121
Strachey, John, 98
"Strength" (Wright), 144
Strong, Edward, 94
Stryker, Roy, 118
Styron, William, 230, 240
Suharto (Indonesian president), 205
Sukarno (Indonesian president), 205, 208, 209
systemic racism, 27–28

"talented tenth," 80, 141
Targ, William, 12

Taylor, Breonna, 27
tenant farming, 262n38
Terán, Belkis, 243
These Are Our Lives (FWP), 116
They Seek a City (Bontemps & Conroy), 115, 122
Thirteenth Amendment, 28
Thurman, Wallace, 134
Toer, Pramoedya Ananta, 206
Toomer, Jean, 134
Tortuguita (Manuel Esteban Paez Terán), 243, 246
Trader Horn (film), 129, 156
Trade Union Educational League, 83
"Tradition and Industrialization" (Wright), 176
"Transcontinental" (Wright), 103–4
trauma, 18, 26–27, 45; and racial terror, 20, 194, 216–17
Trotsky, Leon, 86
True Detective (magazine), 34
Turgenev, Ivan, 2
12 Million Black Voices (Wright): dialectical historical materialism, 149–50; FBI inquiry, 21; and Great Migration, 6, 125; Marxist stages of history, 38, 122, 218; overview and background of, 136–40; research and ethnography, 9, 95–96; solidarity, 157; "Two Million Black Voices" article, 92

Uncle Tom's Cabin (Stowe), 105
Uncle Tom's Children (Wright), 5, 44, 71, 120–121, 145, 219; racism as theme, 63
United States foreign policy, 204
Universal Negro Improvement Association, 97
University of Chicago, 96; Sociology Department, 1, 6

Vanzetti, Bartolomeo, 83
Vietnam, 227
Voting Rights Act (1965), 16, 27
Vrij Nederland (magazine), 205
Vuyk, Beb, 205–6, 208

Wald, Alan, 82–83, 102, 105
Walhout, Mark, 3–4
Walker, Margaret, 83, 92, 96, 98, 112, 113, 163, 236
Walrond, Eric, 134
Ward, Essie Lee, 53, 54, 60
Ward, Jerry, 16
Ward, Ted, 92
Washington, Booker T., 80, 100, 133
Washington, Mary Helen, 105
Washington Afro American (newspaper), 214
Watson, Rachel, 193
The Wealth of Nations (Smith), 98
Webb, Constance, 58, 64, 81
West, Nathaniel, 91
West Indian immigration, 184
"What Is Africa to Me?" (Cullen), 201
White, Walter, 104, 131, 134
White, W. L., 212
White Man, Listen! (Wright), 85, 177, 187–88, 243
white supremacy, 138, 194
Whitman, Walt, 106
Wilcox, Mamie Williams, 168
Williams, Eric, 78, 187
Williams, Heather Andrea, 58
Williams, Sherley Anne, 158, 166
Wilson, Margaret (Wright's grandmother), 22, 50, 72; religious beliefs, 19, 22, 26, 51–52
Wilson, Richard, 55
Winston, Henry, 215
Wirth, Louis, 100–101, 112, 123
Wirth, Mary, 112, 121
women: breasts and nudity, 199; mother-child relationships, 69–70; oppression of Black women, 174–75; status of in US society, 19; "woman question," 19, 158, 159, 160–61, 167–68, 222, 254n54. *See also* feminism; gender roles
Woodward, C. Vann, 124
Worker Writers (Minnesota WPA), 106
Workingmen's Party, 83

Works Progress Administration (WPA), 9, 111, 114
"The World and the Jug" (Ellison), 43
World Congress for Peace, 229
World War II, 31, 95
Worster, Donald, 187
WPA Guide to New York City (Federal Writers' Project of the Works Progress Administration in New York City), 131–32
Wright, Ada, 160, 168
Wright, Andy, 160
Wright, Ella (née Wilson), 49, 50, 56, 64–65, 67, 69, 71–72, 243, 255n8
Wright, Ellen Poplar, 227, 242. *See also* Poplar, Ellen
Wright, Julia, 9, 13, 45, 57, 213, 229, 234–35, 239, 242–43
Wright, Malcolm, 9
Wright, Nathaniel, 65
Wright, Richard, fiction of: *American Hunger*, 107, 108, 212–13; autobiographical elements in fiction, 69–70, 71, 81; "Big Boy Leaves Home," 17, 120–21, 145, 146; "Cesspool," 30, 145; characters' breaking points, 146–47; "Down by the Riverside," 92, 145, 179, 180, 182–83, 184; *A Father's Law*, 219, 234, 244; female characters in, 157–58, 161–70; "Fire and Cloud," 17, 112, 121, 145, 147, 153; "The Island of Hallucination," 44, 226–27, 230, 234, 244; "Long Black Song," 84–85, 92, 145, 147–48, 156, 165–67, 180; *The Long Dream*, 5, 27, 188, 216–17, 219, 220–21, 231–34; "Man, God Ain't Like That," 232; "Man of All Work," 223–24; "The Man Who Saw the Flood," 180; "The Man Who Was Almost a Man," 18; *Rite of Passage*, 219; *Savage Holiday*, 217; "Silt," 179, 180, 181–82, 225. *See also Black Boy* (Wright); "Bright and Morning Star" (Wright); *Lawd Today!* (Wright); *The Man Who Lived Underground* (Wright); *Native Son* (Wright); *The Outsider* (Wright); *Uncle Tom's Children* (Wright)

Wright, Richard, lectures and speeches of: "American Negro Writing," 209; "The Literature of the Negro," 98; "Not My People's War," 91

Wright, Richard, life of: assassination rumors, 226; background and influences, 29; Black-white relations, 71–72, 73–74; in Chicago, 16, 17, 30; childhood cat incident, 66–67; death and funeral, 206, 226, 239; education vs. informal learning, 6, 10, 47–54, 55–56, 58, 59–60, 252n19, 256n29; expatriate experiences, 10, 31, 109–110, 176–78, 198, 221, 227; family background, 64–65; friendships, 213; health decline, 229, 234–35, 240, 243–44; Maggie (aunt), 71, 72–73, 129; marriages and relationships with women, 159–61, 170; and nature, 211, 225, 235; in New York City, 130–36; overview, 1; photos of, 57, 177, 195, 233; reading habits, 112, 225; at Smith Robertson Junior High School, 49, 54, 74; trauma, 29, 45–46; travels, 176–77, 182, 241; violent incidents, 68–69

Wright, Richard, nonfiction writing of: "Biography of a Bolshevik," 119; *Black Power*, 78, 138, 198, 199–200, 201, 241, 242; *The Color Curtain*, 110, 177, 189, 204–5, 242; "Ethnographic Aspects of Chicago's Black Belt," 123; Federal Writers' Project (FWP), 111; "How 'Bigger' Was Born," 34; "I Choose Exile," 225; "I Tried to Be a Communist," 17, 29, 87–88, 207, 212; "Memories of My Grandmother," 17, 18–19, 26, 28, 31, 33, 51–53, 146–47, 167, 255n5; *Pagan Spain*, 161, 175, 177, 188, 240–41; "Personalism," 191; "The Psychological Reactions of Oppressed People," 158; research skills, 119–24, 126–27; "Tradition and Industrialization," 176; travel writing, 177–78, 198–203; *White Man, Listen!*, 85, 177, 187–88, 243. See also "Blueprint for Negro Writing" (Wright); "The Ethics of Living Jim Crow" (Wright); *12 Million Black Voices* (Wright)

Wright, Richard, poetry of: "Ah Feels It in Mah Bones," 103; "Between the World and Me," 263n4; "Child of the Dead and Forgotten Gods," 144; "Everywhere Burning Waters Rise," 144–45; haiku, 225, 234–40; "I Have Seen Black Hands," 98–99, 112; "A Love Red Note," 144; "A Red Slogan," 103; "Rest for the Weary," 144; "Strength," 144; "Transcontinental," 103–4; "Yearning for What Never Was," 13

Wright, Richard, worldview of: on civil rights reform, 217–18; class consciousness, 67–74, 78, 221–22; CPUSA involvement, 85–86, 87–88; and CPUSA withdrawal, 7, 20–21, 28–29, 32, 33, 93–94, 102–3, 154, 189; Marxism, criticism of, 79–80, 213–14; Marxism, early adoption of, 80–83; Marxism, influence of, 148–49, 151–53; Marxist beliefs, clandestine, 214–15; Marxist perspectives, 52, 143, 210–18; Marxist sociological frameworks, 99–106; on outsider status, 52–53, 79, 257n11; philosophical influences, 189; political views and evolution, 95–110; post-CPUSA views, 106–110, 195–96; revolutionary philosophy, 143–149; on US policy, 91; on women's status, 170–75, 254n54; on World War II, 31–32

Wright, Richard, writing of: Chicago years, 112; commodity fetishism and alienation, 154–57; dialectical materialism, 75–76, 149–54; feminist criticism of, 158–61; influences, 117–18; journalistic background, 117; legacy and impact of, 7–9, 245–46; literary criticism of, 4–5; nature imagery, 70–71, 178, 187; prose style, 70–71, 73; and publishing industry, 44, 221; themes, 219; "thick description," 118;

writing ability and aspiration, 47–48;
writing process, 19–20
Wright, Roy, 160

"Yearning for What Never Was" (Wright), 13

Young Communist League (YCL), 81
Young Men's and Women's Christian Associations, 135

Zero magazine, 47
Zhou Enlai, 205